THE MISSING PEACE:
The Search for Nonviolent Alternatives
in United States History

Cover Illustration: Detail from
Benjamin West, *Penn's Treaty with the Indians* (1771-72).
Courtesy of the Pennsylvania Academy of the Fine Arts, Philadelphia.
Gift of Mrs. Sarah Harrison (The Joseph Harrison, Jr. Collection).
Used with permission.

THE MISSING PEACE:
The Search for Nonviolent Alternatives in United States History

James C. Juhnke & Carol M. Hunter

Published by Pandora Press
co-published with
Herald Press
2001

National Library of Canada Cataloguing in Publication Data

Juhnke, James C.
The missing peace: the search for nonviolent alternatives in
United States history

Includes bibliographical references and index.
ISBN 1-894710-13-4

1 Nonviolence — United States — History. I. Hunter, Carol M.,
1948- II. Title.

E179J83 2001   303.6'1'0973   C2001-901976-9

Co-published with Herald Press,
Scottdale, Pennsylvania/Waterloo, Ontario

International Standard Book Number: 1-894710-13-4
Printed in Canada on acid-free paper.

Cover design by Clifford Snyder
Book design by Nathan Stark

10 09 08 07 06 05 04 03   12 11 10 9 8 7

Table of Contents

Acknowledgements   7

Preface
  History and the Myth of Redemptive Violence   9

Chapter 1
  The Original Peacemakers: Native Americans   15

Chapter 2
  The Holiest War on Record: War for Independence   35

Chapter 3
  Republican Peace Experiments: A Usable Past   53

Chapter 4
  Liberty For All: The Antislavery Movement   77

Chapter 5
  The Crossroads of Our Being: The Civil War   103

Chapter 6
  Revolution Derailed: Reconstruction   123

Chapter 7
  Capitalism, the Constitution, and the Common Good:
  Workers in the United States   139

Chapter 8
Gender Matters: Peace Begins at Home   155

Chapter 9
Violent Means Undermine Progress:
    War and Peace 1898-1918   175

Chapter 10
"The Good War": Misremembering World War II   197

Chapter 11
The Civil Rights Movement: Participatory Democracy
    and Nonviolence in Action   215

Chapter 12
The Cold War: Pyrrhic Victory   235

Chapter 13
Nature and the Ecology of Warfare:
    Peace With the Land   255

Epilogue
History and Hope for a Nonviolent Future   269

Notes   277

Index   315

Acknowledgements

This book owes much to a host of mentors, fellow scholars, and our history students who have challenged our thinking and suggested new interpretations. We first met in 1992 and discovered our common interests at a "Nonviolent America" conference, sponsored by the Kansas Institute for Peace and Conflict Resolution (KIPCOR) at Bethel College.[1] Over the years, the professional peace historians in the Peace History Society, the Peace Studies Association, and the Consortium on Peace Research and Education inspired us with their research and vision. At their annual meetings these associations gave us opportunities to present papers for critique and discussion. In this project we accepted historian Patricia Limerick's challenge to "escape specialization and think big."[2] Although our approach was relentlessly revisionist, we necessarily depended upon the great body of professional experts in American history, whose primary research and writing provide a rich reservoir of published historical information.

We are especially indebted to our colleagues and students at Bethel College and Earlham College, both Christian liberal arts colleges with longstanding and vibrant peace traditions. Bethel and Earlham provided

---

[1] The term "America" as a synonym for the United States is problematic. "America" refers to two continents and use of the term to refer to only the United States has become associated with U.S. expansionism and domination. Therefore, although the usage is common, the authors have tried to limit its use by using "United States" as both adjective and noun but "Americans" rather than the cumbersome "people of the United States."

[2] Patricia Limerick, "A How-To Guide for the Academic Going Public," *Perspectives* 37 (December 1999): 20. For all other notes on the text, please see the Notes section p. 277ff.

sabbaticals for sustained research and writing. The librarians at both schools helped us find books. The Center for the Study of Anabaptist and Pietist Groups at Elizabethtown College, Pennsylvania, and the Institute for Mennonite Studies at Associated Mennonite Biblical Seminary in Elkhart, Indiana, provided space and support for research and writing. This book represents one of a number of projects sponsored by the Nonviolent America program of KIPCOR.

Hundreds of students have read one or more of these chapters and given us helpful feedback. Early in the project, Valerie Schrag, research assistant sponsored by the Mennonite Central Committee Voluntary Service Program, mobilized a group of high school and college students to read and critique selected chapters. Although we risk omitting names of scholars who encouraged us with careful reading and suggestions, we wish to mention the following: Jeff Bach, Marc Becker, Michael Birkel, Marya Bower, Perry Bush, Dan Buttry, John W. Chambers, Mary Garman, Rachel Goossen, Jim Harder, Anna Juhnke, William Juhnke, Donald Kraybill, Robert Kreider, Joe McCartin, E. Fletcher McClellan, Steven F. Nolt, David Ortman, Titus Peachey, Howard Richards, Aaron Rittenhouse, Alice Shrock, Barbara Steinson, Daniel W. Stowell, Tom Taylor, William Vance Trollinger, Jr., Lonnie Valentine, J. Denny Weaver, John Howard Yoder, and Kirsten Zerger. C. Arnold Snyder, Clifford Snyder and Nathan Stark of Pandora Press provided excellent services on an accelerated publication schedule. For the title, "The Missing Peace," we thank Rachel Hunter.

Finally, we gratefully acknowledge the love and support of our spouses, Anna Kreider Juhnke and Robert Hunter. With patience, affection and devotion, they have shared our journey of ideas.

James C. Juhnke and Carol M. Hunter

Preface

History and the Myth of Redemptive Violence

The United States is a nation of both peace and war, of public order and disruptive violence. Yet the mystic chords of our national memory seem to have been touched not by the better angels of our nature, but by some fierce demons beyond our control. Every day, on average, more than 6,000 Americans suffer physical injury from violent assault, and more than sixty-five people die from homicide. At its peak in the 1980s, our homicide rate was about fifteen times that of industrial nations such as France, Japan, Germany, and the United Kingdom. American citizens own more than two hundred million guns. More than a decade after the end of the Cold War, the United States has 7,200 nuclear warheads deployed, sufficient to destroy all civilization on planet earth.[1]

A recent NBC special on "America the Violent" placed the dollar cost of violence at over half a trillion dollars including $100 billion in urban decay, $180 billion in lost work and disrupted lives, $85 billion in criminal costs, $65 billion spent in private protection against violence, and $100 billion in medical costs. The subtitle of the series was revealing: "America the Violent: Fed up and Fighting Back." For many, the only way we can conceive of fighting violence is with more violence. The result, not surprisingly, is more violence. We fall victim to mimetic violence, violence mimicking the very violence it is intended to destroy.

People from surprisingly different walks of life are analyzing the problem of violence in American life and coming to broadly similar conclusions. Social scientists, theologians, school teachers and parents are all recognizing the necessity of nonviolent alternatives. But many feel they have no foundation from which to build. They worry that they must fly in the face of "human nature" and years of violent history to take the first steps toward a less violent culture. In one sense this position is absolutely right. A major transformation of culture, from one celebrating violence to one practicing non-violence, requires reaching masses of people and transforming that unconscious sense of who we are and what makes life worth living. Thomas Merton, the beloved Trappist monk, understood the necessity of this when he said, ". . . nonviolent action must establish itself in the minds and memories of modern [people] not only as *conceivable* and *possible*, but as a *desirable alternative* to what [they] now consider the only realistic possibility: namely political technique backed by force."[2]

How can we do this? As authors from two historic peace tradition colleges [Bethel (Mennonite) and Earlham (Quaker)], we would like to suggest that one important place to begin is with the teaching of history. As Howard Zinn points out in *Declarations of Independence*, both Sigmund Freud and Albert Einstein, well-known psychologist and physicist, used history rather than human nature or science as evidence to explain the persistence of war.[3]

Is this a problem with our past—that it really is only carnage and inhumanity—or is this a problem with the way in which history is taught and sold? In 1965 as African Americans struggled with the question of justice and identity in a society that attempted to strip African Americans of any sense of their African heritage and any sense of personal pride and dignity, James Baldwin made this observation:

> For history, as nearly no one seems to know, is not merely something to be read. And it does not refer merely, or even principally to the past. On the contrary, the great force of history comes from the fact that we carry it within us, are unconsciously controlled by it in many ways, and history is literally *present* in all that we do. It could scarcely be otherwise, since it is to history that we owe our frames of reference, our identities, and our aspirations.[4]

Is Baldwin ascribing too much to history? It is worth reflecting on our "frames of reference, our identities, and our aspirations" and what has shaped them. We have created a culture that values greatness, affluence, power, individualism, and freedom. To obtain these goals, we have concurrently created a culture that supports an incredible amount of violence: the systemic violence of poverty, hunger, unemployment, homelessness and racism and the individual violence of guns, drugs, homicide, rape and domestic abuse. Certainly many factors contribute to justifying and perpetuating this culture, and we need to carefully tease apart problematic ends from problematic means. To do so, we need to evaluate the presuppositions that underlie both means and ends. What is the learned history that is shaping us?

A connection between contemporary violence and the history that we have been taught may appear preposterous or ludicrous at first, since few of us (historians included) remember any of the history we were taught. When asked to recall history, we think we are being asked for a trivial pursuit of obscure dates and events. Few people remember these details of history, but we all carry a very vivid history that has been absorbed, rather than processed, and so remains unconscious. Our nation, we all instinctively assume, is a country made by war. In public schools we learn a history of freedom and independence won through war with Britain, land expansion and growth through war with Native Americans and Mexicans, preservation of the Union and freedom for slaves through the Civil War, achievement of world power through naval power projected overseas, and deliverance of the world from Nazi and Communist totalitarianism through war and threatened war. Richard K. Leiphart, a veteran of World War II from Leola, Pennsylvania, in 1995 expressed a common viewpoint in a letter to the editor: "Remember, war is hell and the idea is to kill before you are killed. You can thank God for all those U.S. soldiers who sacrificed themselves for you so you were able to be born into such a great country."[5] Leiphart said he was "more than glad" that the United States dropped the atomic bombs on Hiroshima and Nagasaki. The U.S. is a great and free country, we are to conclude, because Americans have been effectively violent.

The power and prevalence of this historical narrative is demonstrated by a simple exercise that Colman McCarthy, a popular journalist and history teacher, uses to begin his history classes. He asks the students to identify the following ten people: Robert E. Lee, Sojourner Truth, Ulysses S. Grant, A. J. Muste, Napoleon, Adin Ballou, Caesar, John Woolman, Dwight Eisenhower, Dorothy Day. His results are consistent, whether in high school, college or law school. Students know five: the five generals — the five who perpetuate the notion that greatness and freedom are dependent upon the effective use of violence. Why?[6]

Our purpose in this text is to begin the process of emancipating U.S. history from the tyranny of our violent imaginations. These imaginations, stirred by stories of liberty and freedom achieved through violence and war, shape our understanding of who we are, our meaning and purpose as a nation, our paradigms for evaluating contemporary problems and the options we believe are available. The linkage of violence and freedom in U.S. experience has grown into a powerful national myth, marked with appropriate holidays (holy days) like the Fourth of July, Memorial Day, Veterans' Day, and George Washington's birthday. Like all great myths, this one is compounded of truth and falsehood, born of the urgent need to explain and justify human experience. It has roots in an ancient mythic structure, one which theologian Walter Wink argues is embedded in a "domination system" going back to the origins of Western civilization. According to Wink "the distinctive feature of the myth is the victory of order over chaos by means of violence." This pervasive myth, which he argues is the "dominant myth in contemporary America (more influential by far than Judaism or Christianity)," is variously called "the Babylonian creation story, the combat myth, the ideology of zealous nationalism, and the myth of redemptive violence." "It is," Wink claims, "the spirituality of the modern world."[7]

This book is a challenge to the myth of redemptive violence in U.S. history. Our challenge is threefold:

1) to demonstrate that violence in the United States has done more harm than good, often escalating rather than diminishing violence. The violence of even arguably "just wars" has left a legacy of death, destruction and debt which has perpetuated and intensified the violence of poverty, racism, the workplace and the home. Violence has limited freedom.

2) to offer a different lens from which to view history: one of mutuality and interdependence rather than of self-willed triumph. A just and lasting peace is marked by a concern for the welfare of all and a recognition, in Martin Luther King's words, of the "inescapable network of mutuality."[8] For this reason, efforts for peace move toward reconciliation and mutuality, rather than demonizing "the other" as "enemy" and "evil." Peace cannot be separated from justice. Therefore we offer an alternative framing question for our interpretation of history, one that asks how a given event moves people toward reconciliation and justice or away from that goal.

3) to provide hope and encouragement for a less violent future by re-remembering those people and events who worked for nonviolent alternatives, but whose stories are often missing from traditional texts. Often the stories are missing because the alternatives were rejected or

because they were not considered "successful." This approach robs us of the ability to learn from mistakes. Narrating events without discussing alternatives that were tried leaves us with a rather deterministic, inevitable interpretation of history, subverting the notion that personal choice had anything to do with outcomes. We want to rethink the notion of "success" and reclaim the hidden heritage of a "nonviolent America."

Some day it may be possible to write a comprehensive full-length peace-minded U.S. history narrative. For this volume we have had to be more modest in length and more thematically selective. Many important persons, events, and details which are clearly relevant to our theme do not appear on these pages. Nevertheless, we have ranged across the entire scope of U.S. history, from the Native American encounter through the end of the Cold War. The reader will observe in the table of contents that the chapter topics are quite conventional—substantially political with a mix of social history themes. At all points we raise the kind of questions that peacemakers have raised: What are the issues and what are the alternatives? Who was working for peace and justice in this situation? Was this violence/war necessary?

This book is not a history of peace movements in the United States. A number of such histories have already been written.[9] Our intention rather has been to survey the general course of U.S. history from the viewpoint of peace values. We take a broad view of these values, assuming there is much to be learned from different peace traditions, both secular and sacred. We are not arguing for a particular position in the nonviolent spectrum from completely passive nonresistance, such as Tolstoy advocated, to limited violence by the oppressed, like slave resistance. Rather we are presenting a shift in viewpoint from the myth of redemptive violence which acclaims the effectiveness of violence in securing freedom, to the celebration of what makes for a peaceful and just society for all the citizens of the world. In our understanding, peace is both personal and communal; local and universal; spiritual and political. Violence typically subverts both justice and peace. We attempt to demonstrate an alternative reading of history, one that celebrates those people and those structures and systems which offer non-violent models in the struggle for freedom and a more peaceful and just society.

As college teachers of U.S. history, we sense in our students a yearning for grounds of hope for the future of our nation and world. In the nineteenth century a triumphalist version of national history was deliberately taught in U.S. public schools to acculturate immigrants and make loyal citizens of them. The twentieth century added the myths of progress and abundance through free enterprise to this unifying narrative. Until recently that project was substantially successful. Hope was rooted in national unity and greatness. But since the 1970s, critics from many different perspectives have recognized and lamented the shattered unity, each offering different causal analyses and different solutions for the current despair, alienation and fragmentation. Many of the attempts to move away from the myth-making aspects of traditional history have accurately exposed the inconsistent and contradictory uses and abuses of foundational concepts like freedom, equality, equal opportunity and hard work. But they have often done so by concentrating so narrowly on exposing the myths that they have left students cynical, bitter and often skeptical of all history as simply propagandistic constructions of a particular interest group or ego-centered social constructions of reality.

We believe a new historical self-understanding is essential. In our time hope must find its inspiration in a new vision which transcends national boundaries and generates the capacity to resolve conflicts nonviolently both within and among the nations. This is why any new historical narrative must root itself in the mutuality and interdependence of all people. It is a time to tell what Vincent Harding calls the "humanizing lessons" of nonviolent resistance in order to develop ". . . new visions of human unity and new understandings of the paths toward resolving human conflicts . . . ."[10]

A great task of our times is not simply to expose and destroy the old myth of redemptive violence in its U.S. setting, but also to construct a new system of common meaning. We need systems of myth and symbol which support a culture of nonviolence. To this end we offer a new understanding of U.S. history that honors the aspirations and dreams of people who strove diligently and peaceably for a community of common good. This process has generated much fruitful dialogue between us as authors as we have thrashed our way through our own varying interpretations and perceptions. This is a work in process. The issues raised are too multi-layered and sweeping in scope to yield a seamless and consistent reinterpretation. We invite the readers to join us in building a historical foundation for those who share this dream of a more peaceful and just world.

Chapter 1

The Original Peacemakers:
Native Americans

The original Americans, like all human communities, were people of both peace and war. United States history textbooks, however, lift up the warriors, not the peacemakers. The notable Indians in the master narrative of American history are the military heroes—men such as Pontiac, Tecumseh, Geronimo, Crazy Horse, and Sitting Bull. Sherman Alexie, popular Native American novelist and poet, put a cogent question in the mouth of one of his characters: "When are the Indians ever going to have heroes who don't hurt people? Why do all of our heroes have to carry guns?"[1] If the textbooks mention Native American peacemaking traditions at all, they do it in a generalized introduction that lacks notable events and named people. The textbooks' central story itself is a grand drama of white conquest and development. White Americans advance over the continent, overcoming heroic Indian fighters along the way. Indian military resistance may be heroic, but that seems mainly to honor the valor of the white invaders.[2] White Americans build historical monuments for the Indian warriors, not for the peacemakers.

There is a missing peace to the Native American story. The challenge is to recover it, to make it real, and to integrate it eventfully with the broader narrative of American history. Each of the five hundred Native American tribes or nations had its own distinctive peace tradition. The relentless white invasion challenged and subverted that traditional peace heritage. External assault on any community tends to elicit counter-violence. Even so, there are many hidden and inspiring stories of Indians meeting violent threats with peaceable restraint. For an honest and true understanding of Indian-White encounter in North America, we must learn about the Indian peacemakers and peace traditions. And we must confront the question of which Indians contributed most to the survival of Native American culture and identity in the face of their holocaust. Was it the Indian warriors who ensured ongoing life for their people? Or was it their peacemakers and peace prophets?

Origins and Holocaust

The original Americans migrated from Asia to North America in a number of waves between 40,000 and 12,000 B.C. Over thousands of years these East Asian peoples spread throughout north, central and south America. They separated into myriad self-ruling bands and found ways to eat, to survive the elements, to create distribution networks, and to develop socially and politically in every ecological niche of the hemisphere. Before the Europeans arrived, Native Americans developed agriculture, built cities, and oversaw the rise and fall of elaborate civilizations. By 1500 there were more than seven million people north of the Rio Grande, and more than 72 million in the entire hemisphere. The American hemisphere's population was as great as, likely larger than, Europe's.[3]

The encounter with white Europeans after 1492 was devastating for the Native American people, partly because of the military violence of the invaders, but mostly because of the epidemic diseases they brought. Compared to Europe, America had been relatively disease free. But the thousands of years of isolation had an awful consequence. The Native Americans had no natural immunities to Europe's great biological killers—smallpox, measles, influenza, bubonic plague, diphtheria, typhus, cholera, and scarlet fever. The fatal microbes spread rapidly— quickly outrunning the actual European explorers and settlers. The results were almost beyond imagining, especially in Central America, which was more densely populated. In 1494, when Christopher Columbus and the men on his second voyage arrived at the island of Hispaniola (present day Haiti and the Dominican Republic), the Native population was about eight million. By 1496 it was between four and five million; by 1508 less than a hundred thousand; by 1518 less than twenty thousand; and by 1535, "for all practical purposes, the native population was extinct."[4] In Mexico, seventy-five percent of the population died of smallpox within a four-year period.[5] Throughout the hemisphere—South, Central and North America—the pathetic story was repeated. These diseases did not simply come and disappear. They came and spread and killed repeatedly, according to one expert, "at intervals of four years and two and a half months, on the average, from 1520 to 1900." All across the Americas, Europeans moved into lands where native peoples had been devastated and demoralized by epidemic diseases.[6]

Europeans in the seventeenth century thought the raging epidemics were the work of God. Thomas Hariot, a British scientist who observed the unprecedented deaths in the wake of white contact, concluded it was divine punishment for "wicked practices."[7] Governor William Bradford's Plymouth Colony was built on land only recently occupied by Patuxet Indians who were wiped out by smallpox. Bradford wrote in his diary after one epidemic, "For it pleased God to visit these Indians with a great sickness and such a mortality that of a thousand, above nine and a half hundred of them died, and many of them did rot above ground for want of burial."[8] The Puritans saw God's providence in all things, including their own deaths from disease or in warfare with the Indians.

In the more secular twentieth century, observers are more inclined to focus on the question of how the Native American holocaust of disease was linked to human decision and action.[9] There were indeed some cases in which the Whites attempted to foster epidemics—by, for example, distributing infected blankets to Native Americans.[10] It is also true that U.S. government officials in later years failed to take steps to prevent smallpox epidemics among demoralized tribes on their reservations, long after modern vaccination procedures were available.[11] Even so, it should be acknowledged that the epidemic diseases which killed so many Native Americans were, for the most part, beyond human understanding and control.

Added to the biological holocaust is the story which is better known and easier to comprehend in moral terms—the willful European destruction of Native American tribes through organized warfare, unorganized killings, and ecological devastation on the relentlessly expanding frontier. The Whites saw the Reds as "savages" who stood in the way of "civilization." One historian, with an eye on the Balkans, called it a giant "ethnic cleansing."[12] It is probably better to use the word "genocide,"—the deliberate extermination of peoples—and compare it to other world-historical genocides such as the Nazi crusade against the

Jews in Europe and the Khmer Rouge assault on Kampuchean peoples in Cambodia.[13]

For many reasons we must face this double holocaust of disease and war, describing its enormity, and call it by the proper names. One of the most important of these reasons is to appreciate the context in which Native Americans developed strategies for cultural survival. Under unbelievable stresses, they had limited choices. But they survived.

Original Landscapes of Peace

The tribes living along the North Atlantic coast, who first welcomed the invading Europeans, had been there for centuries. They were agriculturalists, who supplemented corn production with hunting and fishing. They had fully rounded cultures of religious ritual, family relationships, and social and political development. They did not have an alphabet or written language, did not know the uses of the wheel or sail, did not tend herds of domesticated animals, and were unaware of the uses of gunpowder and many other such mixed blessings of modern civilization. But they were able to keep peace and to make war in their own ways without the benefit of swords and muskets.

Iroquois

An Iroquois "League of Peace," put in place before Europeans set eyes on North America, was one remarkable Native American experiment to replace violence with nonviolence. The League originated in the Great Lakes region of what is now northern New York between the Hudson and Niagara Rivers. According to Iroquois legend, the League was born not out of a great imperial war or a battle-scarred independence revolution, but out of the genius and vision of a leader-prophet named Deganawidah (The Master of Things), a Huron by birth and Mohawk by adoption.

Deganawidah's time of effective leadership is not known with certainty — perhaps the early 1400s. Tribal tradition invested Deganawidah with magical powers as well as political wisdom. He reportedly came from the north in a miraculously floating stone canoe. It was a time of social decay and violence. The five Iroquois peoples (from east to west: Mohawks, Oneidas, Onondagas, Cayugas and Senecas) were making war upon each other — tribe against tribe and person against person. Rampant violence, including the rise of cannibalism, had forced the people to abandon their agricultural villages and cornfields on the hills and to eke out a more precarious and primitive existence in the lowland forests.

Among these disrupted peoples, Deganawidah came preaching a gospel of peace. The people, he said, should stop killing each other, should accept the rule of law, and should come together in new rituals of unity. There should be a new confederation of self-ruling but cooperating tribes, with broad popular participation in decision making. Deganawidah's core message had three parts, each with two branches:

Righteousness means justice practiced between men and between nations; it means also a desire to see justice prevail.

Health means soundness of mind and body; it also means peace, for that is what comes when minds are sane and bodies cared for.

Power means authority, the authority of law and custom, backed by such force as is necessary to make justice prevail; it means also religion, for justice enforced is the will of the Holder of the Heavens and has his sanction.[14]

To promote his program, Deganawidah visited the elders of the five nations. The League legend tells how he recruited and converted three key persons who had been caught up in the old way of violence. The prophet invested them with positions of authority in the new order. One female chief, Jigonhsasee, who had been giving food and hospitality to warriors, became the "Mother of Nations." Women in the new order were authorized to "possess the titles of chiefship" and to name the new chiefs. Hiawatha, an agonized soul who had descended into cannibalism, became Deganawidah's effective spokesman and messenger. (The prophet himself had a speech impediment.) And the great wizard and evil power, Atotarho, whose hair had been filled with writhing snakes, was made whole and named the "Head Chief of the Five Nations." An early task for the chiefs' council of the new League was disarmament. At Deganawidah's suggestion, they uprooted a great pine tree and threw all of their arms into the hole. Then they "replanted the tree, thus hiding the weapons of war forever from the sight of future generations."[15] The pine tree was a great symbol of unity.

Although the stories of the founding of the Iroquois League were enriched with legend and myth, there is no doubt that Deganawidah was a historical person. He built on past tradition, while inventing new political institutions. He understood that the people needed powerful myths and rituals to overcome their impulses to violence and anarchy, and to generate wider loyalty to the Iroquois League in the face of separate local and tribal interests. The role of myth and ritual in founding national charters is commonplace in the history of civilization. What is distinctive about the Deganawidah Epic, compared to the chartering myths of other nations, is that this one found its unity in remembering the establishment of internal peace, rather than in celebrating triumphal military victory over threatening external enemies (the Greeks over the Persians at the Battle of Marathon; the Roman Constantine over Maxentius at the Battle of Milvian Bridge, the British over the Spanish Armada, the Americans over the British at Yorktown). The Great League of Peace and Power did in fact unify the self-ruling villages of the Five Nations in the century before the Europeans arrived.

A founding myth of peace, of course, does not guarantee the practice of peace in everyday social life and in political relationships. Within the Iroquois League the threats to harmony and order continued—witchcraft, cannibalism, blood feuds and ritual torture. Outsiders, both neighboring Native American tribes and invading Europeans, were more impressed with the effectiveness of Iroquois militant power than with their peace and benevolence. The gap between ideals and achievement, however, is a part of all human communities. Unfortunately, Europeans and white Americans preferred to imagine the Iroquois as a great military empire. They have shown far greater interest in the gory details of violent Iroquois practices of warfare and torture, than in the natives' genuine but limited successes in, to use the words of historian Matthew Dennis, "cultivating a landscape of peace."[16]

At the core of Iroquois culture was a "Condolence ceremony," a complex set of rituals of mourning at the death of loved ones—especially momentous at the death of a chief. The people overcame their grief and their fears that death had assaulted the health and peace of the community. The focus was on the community and the renewal of kinship ties, rather than on the life and achievements of the deceased individual. The grieving people "used the occasion to recite their history, rehearse social and political principles, and renew their commitment to order and reason."[17] The Condolence ceremony was so foundational for Iroquois life that it became the ritual model for diplomatic relations with outside groups. To have good relationships with the French or the

English, for example, the Iroquois would ritually acknowledge their commonness by transforming them into some kind of relatives or kinsmen.

From the Iroquois perspective, prospects for a wider peace embracing many different peoples depended upon successful *adoption* of outsiders — individuals and groups — into the Iroquois League. Outsiders understandably were not all eager to be adopted. The problem was especially acute for outside victims of Iroquois "mourning wars," forcibly captured and adopted to make up for population losses which resulted from diseases or other causes. Native American adoption practices were quite incomprehensible to Europeans. Indeed, the European concept of peace was so radically different from the Iroquois practices, that mutual understanding was virtually impossible. How could Whites understand that adoption rituals, often involving physical pain or torture, might be a functional (or flawed) expression of a Native American effort to establish peace? How could the Iroquois imagine that the wholesale slaughter of their people by Europeans in military engagements was an advance for civilization?

The Great League of Peace and Power preserved unity and harmony among the Five Nations before European contacts. Then the Whites brought epidemic diseases, economic dependence, imperial conflicts, and annexation of the land. For more than a century the Iroquois overcame these threats. They were a decentralized confederacy, not a unified empire as romantic Europeans liked to imagine. But they had the advantage of an inland location, along major trade routes and distant from imperial centers of power. Iroquois agricultural production supplied food when game was overhunted. They kept up their population by absorbing prisoners of war and of raiding parties. By the 1730s they had become a colonized people, but their strong cultural institutions helped secure their distinct cultural identity into the future.[18]

White colonial leaders, notably Benjamin Franklin, were impressed with the political principles of the Iroquois confederacy. The League of Peace and Power became one source of ideas for the United States Constitution, despite the cultural chauvinism and anti-Indian racism of the founders. An Iroquois symbol, the bundle of arrows, appears on the Great Seal of the United States.[19] A less militant symbol for the Great Seal, equally true to the Iroquois charter, would have been the great pine tree under which all those broken arrows and rejected instruments of warfare were buried.

Massasoit, Metacom, and the "Praying Indians"

Indian cultural survival depended upon both resistance and accommodation. What happened between Whites and Indians was not a climactic battle on the frontier line resulting in total triumph on one side and tragic extinction on the other. The unequal cultures intermingled and interpenetrated. In early New England the Wampanoag chief Massasoit, his son Metacom, and the early "praying Indians" made three quite different choices in levels of resistance and accommodation. Chief Massasoit, a so-called "war chief" in fact was more notable for making peace than for making war. In 1621 he visited the new and struggling Plymouth Colony and concluded a treaty of friendship with them— initiating a peace that lasted more than half a century. To be sure, Massasoit's policy did not express a simple benevolent pacifism. He needed the alliance with the Puritans to gain strength for rivalry against other Indian tribes, especially the Narragansetts. In 1637 Massasoit did not interfere when the colonies of Massachusetts and Connecticut made war against the Pequot Indians, burning their villages, slaughtering women and children, and killing the survivors or selling them into slavery. Even so, Massasoit deserves major credit for the generation of peace between 1621 and 1676.

The possibility of that peace depended upon a middle ground of mutual understanding between Puritans and Indians. Massasoit was able to see some compatibility between English colonies and the Indian tribes.[20] The English colonies, like Indian tribes, were loosely-knit alliances that changed over time. The colonists, like the Indians, expected protection and privileges from their king, in exchange for allegiance. Massasoit saw that he could negotiate a tribal accommodation to Puritan ways without necessarily giving up self-rule and self-respect. In his lifetime Massasoit succeeded in maintaining peace on this basis. His son, Metacom (derisively labeled "King Philip" by the English), lacked the father's character and prestige, and faced an ever-increasing tide of White settlement. He was drawn into a disastrous war, "The Second Puritan Conquest" or "King Philip's War."[21]

The Indians in fourteen so-called "praying towns" of New England made a very different accommodation. They were mostly from smaller and more marginal Indian groups, and were at first more vulnerable than members of the larger well-established tribes such as the Narragansett or Wampanoag. They had not made a fully free choice to become Christian, nor did they have full self-rule in their villages. Yet they found margins to create a way of life that mixed their traditional ways with the dominant Puritan culture. They invested Christian religion with traditional Indian meaning by enthusiastically embracing certain external repetitive ritual forms (singing, prayer, instruction) while remaining quite indifferent to Puritan theology.[22] They apparently continued their traditional practice of burying physical objects with the bodies of deceased members—a custom very different from that of the Puritans.[23] They also learned to read and write English, a skill that gave them status and posed a threat to non-literate Indian leaders such as Metacom. Armed with literacy, the "praying Indians" were able to get better representation in colonial courts and to gain greater protection for their lands.

In 1675 a devastating war broke out between the Indians and settlers—known as "King Philip's War." The background to the war included the rising status and power of the formerly marginalized "praying Indians," and the decreasing success of the illiterate Chief Metacom's political strategy of tribal self-rule within the English colonies. The Indians in the "praying towns" suffered grievously during that war—especially those who opted to join the uprising on Metacom's side. After the war only four such towns remained, and the Indians in them formed a dependent class of servants and tenant farmers. Their strategy of selective mastery of the white man's skills, combined with selective maintenance of traditional markers of Native identity, enabled them to survive, and to pass on Native American identity to the next generation. Chief Metacom was killed, drawn and quartered. The Puritans sold his wife and children into slavery.

Lenni Lenape (Delaware)

Another Native American tribe whose peaceable inclinations have been recognized even more widely than those of the Iroquois, is the Lenni Lenape (Delaware), whose name means "the original people." In 1682 or 1683 some Lenape chiefs at their village of Shackemaxon (part of the present-day Kensington section of Philadelphia) met with William Penn and agreed to a Great Treaty of Friendship. That legendary treaty, cited by Voltaire as the only agreement between Europeans and Indians never sworn to and never broken, was later celebrated in famous paintings by Benjamin West and Edward Hicks.

The Lenape were known as mediators and peacemakers already before William Penn arrived. In 1676 a Lenape chief named Rinowehan, with the encouragement and authority of Governor Edmund Andros of New York colony, helped to mediate a threatening conflict between the Iroquois and the Susquehannocks.[24] The Lenape reputation for mediation or peacemaking was associated with a name, "Gantowises" — meaning "women" — which they accepted for themselves. Some scholars, accepting the interpretation of early Moravian missionaries, believe that this name was a badge of honor, originating in its use for Iroquois women of royal lineage who had a highly-honored role as peacemakers. Other historians say that the Iroquois pinned the label of "women" on the Lenape after defeating them in battle.[25] The term "Gantowises" lost status when translated into the English as "women," because the English had no equivalent role of honor for women. The Lenape, of course, were neither the first nor last of peace-minded people to be scorned as effeminate.

The Lenape did not have central authority or a confederation such as the one that strengthened the Iroquois. Some historians have associated this decentralization with weakness and peaceableness. Paul A. W. Wallace, for example, wrote with a tinge of condescension that "[the Delawares] were not a warlike people. They could hardly be, with so little organization and discipline. They had no central 'fire' or national council. The local community was supreme, as though the need of concerted military action was not thought of."[26]

The Lenape have the honor of producing the first and only *written* record of tribal history in North America.[27] Lenape storytellers kept the tribal oral memory alive in the form of epic songs which included the creation of the world, a great flood, extensive migrations, and a succession of leaders. At some point the Lenape story tellers (or one exceptionally creative genius among them) devised a system to assist memory with written symbols or pictographs scratched onto bark or pieces of wood. In its most complete form, the Lenape epic song (Wallam Olum or Red Record) consisted of 183 verses. Some observers have speculated that this writing form may have been a continuous tradition from Asia, because a few of the pictographs correspond to ancient Chinese writing. The Lenape pictograph for "peace" (or friendly, peaceful, pleasant), a small isosceles triangle (^), is much like an archaic Chinese pictograph meaning "union" or "harmony." More cautious and objective scholars doubt the antiquity and historical accuracy of the Red Record.[28] It was most likely influenced to some extent by the encounter with Whites.

One anthropologist has suggested that it took its shape in a time of upheaval in the early 1800s and represented a yearning for "a Golden Age which never was."[29] However there is little doubt that the Red Record reflects traditional Delaware memories and values.

The Lenape Red Record began with creation of the world and ended with the coming of the Europeans: "Friendly people, in great ships; who are they?" Images of war and peace are found throughout. The pictograph for "war" or "destruction," a cross (x), appeared nearly twice as often as the one for peace. Nevertheless, the Red Record is a reminder of the human yearning for peace and an evocation of the roots of peace in past, present and future. One of the uses of peace refers to a period of peaceful living immediately following the creation. Another refers to "an island, the pleasant abode of the dead." Others refer to times of social harmony associated with notable chiefs: "After him, Peaceful One was chief while they went to Snake Land," or "When all were friends, Wolf Man was chief." Other chiefs, less capable or fortunate, were remembered for pain and death: "When White Fledgling was chief, blood flowed again in the north and in the south." In some cases the story-teller justified the tribe's resort to retribution against enemies: "In right-minded indignation, all said, 'Let us despoil! Let us destroy!'" As a whole, however, compared to older traditions of European history which are centered on imperial conquest, the Wallam Olum records a remarkably benign tribal epic.

The pathways of peace in the Delaware Valley both before and after the Whites arrived are worth reflection. Compared to New England and Virginia, where Indian-European relationships were scarred by vicious and devastating warfare, the Delaware Valley was relatively peaceable. From the arrival of the Whites until 1755, colonists and Indians engaged in no major warfare. The Quaker founder of Pennsylvania, William Penn, surely deserves substantial credit for this achievement. Penn was a benevolent pacifist, exceptionally respectful of Native American rights and culture by the standards of his time. He learned the Indian languages and dealt with them honestly and respectfully in clearing title to the land.

Even so, Penn's friendly policies depended on a friendly Native response. In the judgement of historian David Hackett Fischer, "Penn's Indian policy would have been a disastrous failure in Massachusetts or Virginia," where the Natives were more bellicose.[30] Fischer's speculation may not be fully warranted. Trust begets trust. The Powhatans in Virginia responded violently to early British belligerence. In any case, the relatively peaceful development of the Delaware Valley deserves to be honored. The seeds of that landscape of relative peace were planted not only in the pacifist Quaker movement in England, but also in the Native American communities of the Delaware Valley where people of hospitality and peace lived and thrived before the Whites ever arrived.

Prophets and Revitalization

Essential indeed to cultural survival was hope. Native Americans knew how to envision a future of hope in the face of disaster. "Our cultural ways cannot be destroyed," said the tribal elders to their children. "Even when our ways seem to be destroyed or forgotten, in every seventh generation the Great Spirit will reveal them to the people again."[31] Thus it happened repeatedly in the Native American experience. When their situation seemed most hopeless and desperate, when the stress was greatest, prophets would receive new visions for the salvation of the people. The prophets announced that recent disasters came from the people's abandonment of traditional ways and their acceptance of the destructive ways of the Whites, especially the drinking of alcohol. The prophets proposed disciplines and rituals of dancing, praying and making special offerings to revitalize the community. The prophets had varying success in winning converts, and not all tribes produced prophets in equal numbers. Between 1740 and 1890 the Delaware Indians participated in fourteen of these new religious movements.[32]

The Indian prophets had many fantastic dreams, both militant and peaceful. The prophets most interesting to white Americans, the ones most likely to receive attention in U.S. history textbooks, were those whose movements resulted in events of dramatic violence. Thus the Shawnee Prophet, Tenskatawa, and his brother, Tecumseh, are famous for a militant movement of inter-tribal unity and regeneration that they led from 1805 to the War of 1812. But the Whites knew how to deal with a military challenge. At the Battle of Tippecanoe, General William Henry Harrison's troops routed the Indian forces and he became a national hero—eventually president of the United States. Tecumseh sought British military assistance and died in October 1813 as a brigadier general in the British army at the Battle of the Thames, attempting to beat back the U.S. invasion of Canada. As Tecumseh's biographer explained, the

Americans "took pride in his passing, for in conquering the red champion they could assure themselves that they were worthy of his kingdom."[33]

Meanwhile the Seneca "peace prophet," Handsome Lake, offered a radically different vision from that of Tenskatawa, the "war prophet." Beginning in 1799, after wasted years of drunkenness, Handsome Lake had a series of prophetic visions that dealt first with apocalyptic themes of sin and divine punishment. Later visions offered a social gospel of regeneration through temperance and technological change. Handsome Lake met Jesus in his visions, and saw himself as a message-bearer of the truth for Native Americans, in some sense an equivalent to Jesus. His social vision called for strengthened Indian identity and control of life on reservations, combined with white technologies and social-economic roles. Handsome Lake endorsed and strengthened a momentous Iroquois transition: the men shifted from hunting to farming; the women shifted from farming to homemaking.[34]

The male hunting life was traditionally associated with warfare. Handsome Lake, to the relief of white political authorities, refused to join the militant Tenskatawa-Tecumseh movement. During the American-British war, he also resisted United States' efforts to recruit "volunteer" soldiers from the Iroquois tribes. His effort had only limited success. From 1812 to 1814 more than six hundred Iroquois officers and enlisted men signed up for military service. Even though they rejected his anti-war counsel, many of these soldiers honored and respected Handsome Lake as a prophet and religious leader. The prophet died in 1815. Through the next three decades his followers rehearsed his teachings and practiced the rituals he had prescribed. In the 1940s they established the Handsome Lake Church, an institution committed to Native American traditionalism over against the evangelical Christian movement which had won many Iroquois converts. The Handsome Lake Church became an American religious denomination. Handsome Lake's rejection of warfare in the early nineteenth century remains an important testimony to the depth of the American peacemaking heritage.

Cherokee "Civilization"
Strategies for cultural survival were as varied as the different cultures of the tribes themselves. In the early years of the new republic, the Cherokees of the American southeast made a remarkable effort to preserve political self-rule by selectively adapting to western "civilized" ways.[35] They contended vigorously about which parts of the white culture

to adopt. Some Cherokees became Christians and found ways to complement their tribal-national rebirth with the Christian gospel of hope and personal rebirth. A different kind of renewal came in 1821-1822 when Sequoyah, a brilliant man who could not speak or read English, created a Cherokee alphabet so they could read, write, and even publish newspapers in their own language. Both of these new sources of revitalization could divide the people—the first into Christian versus traditional parties, and the second into English speakers and Cherokee speakers.[36] All change came hard. And, as it turned out, no degree of acculturation could guarantee significant self-rule for the Cherokee nation. Under President Andrew Jackson the United States government removed the Cherokees from their homeland to a reservation in "Indian Territory" beyond the Mississippi River. Cherokee suffering and death on their "Trail of Tears" in 1838 is one of the most discreditable events of United States history.

The Cherokees achieved much within the limited choices they faced. They would not have achieved more had they engaged in suicidal warfare as an alternative to removal westward. Their neighbors, the Creeks, fought the invading whites ferociously, but gained no advantage for all their dying and killing. Wilbur Jacobs, writing about earlier Cherokee history in his book, *Dispossessing the American Indian*, said, "The Cherokees and their allies were likewise eager to stop the bloody conflict in which they found themselves engulfed . . . . The Indians, above all, wanted a fair deal in trade and honest clarity in treaty terms and negotiations." Jacobs even suggested that peaceloving Indians may be responsible for peacemaking impulses in the dominant culture: "Is it possible that the American penchant for peace has an anchor chain deep in the historical past that ties us to the Indian?"[37]

Plains Indians, Cheyenne
The encounters of Plains Indians with invading whites before and after the Civil War generated some of the most pervasive and pernicious stereotypes of Native Americans. Thanks to generations of dime novels and thousands of Hollywood movies, Whites reflexively imagine a history of cowboy and Indian shootouts or of befeathered Indians swooping down from the hills to attack white wagon trails moving westward. Again, the image has some truth, but is substantially false. "The preoccupation with Indian depredations," says John D. Unruh, Jr., author of the most authoritative history of the overland trails, "has

resulted in radical distortion of the historical record."[38] To be sure, the Indians did kill many Whites who flooded into and through their lands. But even more impressive were the events of mutual aid. The overlanders depended on Indians for route information, trail guidance, assistance at river and stream crossings, horses and supplies, and the transportation of letters to friends and families back in the East. From 1840 to 1860 inclusive, by Unruh's count, 362 overland emigrants and 462 Indians were killed. Francis Jennings, historian of Indian America, wrote in view of these numbers: "An emigrant was safer from attack on the trek than he would be on the streets of any large modern city."[39]

One plains tribe saddled with a reputation for special ferocity was the Cheyenne, allegedly "the most warlike tribe of the warlike Plains Indians." George Bird Grinnell, author of *The Fighting Cheyennes*, called them "a proud, headstrong, and obstinate people."[40] Grinnell's stereotype helped sell books; it also obscured one of the most distinctive of Native-American peace traditions. The Cheyenne Peace Chiefs, a council of forty-four leaders, were entrusted with the core moral teachings of the tribe. Their legendary founder, Sweet Medicine, appointed the first chiefs and told them: "You chiefs are peacemakers. Though your son might be killed in front of your tepee, you should take a peace pipe and smoke. Then you would be called an honest chief."[41] The same high moral standard of nonviolence is continued in the instructions given to new Peace Chiefs to this day: "If you see your mother, wife, or children being molested or harmed by anyone, you do not go and seek revenge. Take your pipe. Go, sit and smoke and do nothing, for you are now a Cheyenne chief."[42] In the Peace Chief tradition moral power came through the patient acceptance of suffering, rather than through angry revenge.

The Cheyennes' tribal memory locates their origins in the region of present-day southern Minnesota, where they evolved a semi-settled agricultural economy. In the 1700s and 1800s, along with other tribes on the fringes of the Great Plains, the Cheyennes adopted a more nomadic lifestyle as they acquired horses and followed the migration routes of the bison. As the Plains Indian culture developed — counter to the normal shift from nomadism to settled agriculture — the ideals of the Cheyenne Peace Chiefs inevitably came into conflict with the flamboyant militancy of the Cheyenne war societies. (Plains Indian warfare was highly ritualized, consisting of brief and often indecisive conflicts by small parties. The object of much of the fighting was to gain the status of striking a "blow" or *coup* against the enemy, rather than massive killing.)[43] The power of the Cheyenne Peace Chiefs was moral rather than political, and it was weakened when the white invasion strengthened the warriors' case for a violent response. White military officers made no distinctions between Cheyenne dog soldiers and Cheyenne Peace Chiefs. If Cheyenne warriors, violating the counsel of the Peace Chiefs, attacked white settlers or soldiers, the United States army or militia felt quite justified in organizing massacres of the Cheyenne villages where the Peace Chiefs lived with their people.

In 1862 three Cheyenne Peace Chiefs, Black Kettle, White Antelope and Lean Bear, traveled to Washington, D.C. and received peace medals, American flags, and official documents to prove their friendly status to the frontier soldiers. Two years later Lean Bear, with the peace medal on his breast and the documents in hand, was shot and killed as he approached white troops in friendship. Black Kettle intervened to prevent Cheyenne soldiers from fighting back. Two years after that, November 1866, Black Kettle, White Antelope, and other chiefs and their people were camped along Sand Creek in southeastern Colorado territory, under the guarantee of protection by the territorial governor. A volunteer militia led by Colonel J. M. Chivington, an ordained Methodist minister, viciously and without provocation attacked and massacred some 500 men, women and children in this peaceable village. Chief White Antelope refused to fight back or to flee. He stood in front of his lodge with arms folded, and was shot to death while singing his death song, "Nothing lives long, Except the earth and the mountains."   The white soldiers returned to a heroes' welcome in Denver, where they exhibited more than a hundred Indian scalps between the acts of an evening theatrical performance.

Chief Black Kettle somehow survived the Sand Creek massacre. In November 1868, Colonel George Armstrong Custer and his Seventh Cavalry organized a surprise attack on Black Kettle's peaceable village along the Washita River in western Oklahoma Territory. Black Kettle was flying the American flag, and assumed protection under the Treaty of Medicine Lodge which he had signed thirteen months earlier. Black Kettle refused to fight back against Custer and was cut down along with his wife. They remained faithful to the nonviolent Peace Chief ethic: "Do not go and seek revenge. Take your pipe. Go, sit and smoke and do nothing, for you are now a Cheyenne chief."

The West Coast

Native American tribes beyond the Rocky Mountains engaged in almost no warfare among large groups prior to the impact of white invaders.[44] They benefited from an abundance of natural foods for hunting, gathering and fishing. They developed elaborate ceremonies that enabled non-violent resolution of conflict between groups. At the potlatch ritual in the Northwest, prominent individuals gave away their wealth in order to gain honor and privilege. The potlatch was a polar opposite to modern capitalism. The potlatch reduced violent warfare, rather than fostering it through competition to acquire wealth.

Perhaps the most consistent of peaceable Native American tribes was the Sanpoil, a small group of about two-hundred people in the Pacific Northwest. The Sanpoil social order was democratic, not dominated by powerful chiefs. Economically they subsisted on salmon from the Columbia River. Their principled nonresistance left them vulnerable to raids by other tribes, but their long-term social and cultural survival remains a documented fact. Tribal wisdom remembered the response of a chief after one especially vicious raid: "Our children are dead and our property is destroyed. We are sad. But can we bring our children back to life or restore our property by killing other people? It is better not to fight. It can do no good." In 1877 the Sanpoil dreamer-prophet Skolaskin responded to invitations to join the Nez Perces tribe in war against encroaching Americans with the words, "God made the world for us to live on, not to fight or sell." Chief Komotalakia of the Sanpoil told the Whites, "We do not wish to die fighting, but to die in peace . . . . We have been constant and true to the Whites. Long ago our chief set us the example and we have always followed it." One social consequence of Sanpoil nonresistance was an unusually high ratio of men to women in the tribe. Their men did not die in warfare. Sanpoil pacifism did not save them from anguished dislocation and internal conflict when the Whites took their land and forced them into economic dependence on a reservation together with rival tribes. True to their tradition, however, the Sanpoil did not have the blood of enemies on their hands.[45]

Who Guaranteed Cultural Survival?

Who was responsible for Indian cultural survival in the face of the double holocaust of disease and war? How did it happen that Indians, contrary to expectations of Whites who predicted their extinction ("The Last of the Mohicans," etc.) were able to survive as distinct peoples? How can it be that the Indian population today grows rapidly, that Indian creative art and literature inspire the world, and that Indian spirituality attracts modern people who have lost religious roots? Was this an achievement of violent warriors—the textbook heroes? No, it was not. Courageous as they were, the warriors did not save their peoples. They perished in battle after battle across the decades and across the continent. The memories of their sacrifice were not irrelevant to Indian identity, but the real unsung heroes of Native American history were those who resisted nonviolently. Indian ways of living survived because of the patient, persistent, and creative traditionalism of ordinary women and men, and because of the special role of charismatic prophets who set forth new visions for the life of their people. While they worked to sustain traditional values, the prophets as well as the ordinary people accommodated to European culture at some levels. They borrowed selectively from white ways in order to create a viable separate space and identity in American society. Their choices were severely limited, but they were remarkably creative and successful within those limits.

For all Native American peoples, the most significant sustainers of cultural identity were the thousands of women whose lot it was to grieve the death of sons and husbands killed in war, and then to persist in their communities to keep traditional ways alive in the face of repeated disasters. Patiently, silently, and covertly these women sustained their cultures in ways that non-natives could not see or recognize. "My mother taught me everything connected with the tipi," reported one southern Cheyenne woman.[46] Native American women sustained kinship relations, continued native foodways and planting rituals, used ancient herbal medicines and remedies, and practiced seasonal observances and celebrations.[47]

Some Indian women contributed much more than patient domesticity to cultural survival. Among the Pomo tribes of north central California, women "Dreamers" had a role as local religious prophets and healers in a cult known as "Bole Maru" (Dream Dance). The cult began in the 1870's as a nationalistic revitalization movement and continued in the twentieth century under a succession of powerful women Dreamers: Annie Jervis, Essie Parrish, and Mabel McKay. The message and the rituals of the cult changed in each generation according to new challenges and new visions of the leaders. Greg Sarris, a scholar of one-quarter Indian background whose Native American identity was reestablished by McKay, tells of the complexity and vitality of this tradition in his book, *Keeping Slug Woman Alive*. Sarris quotes McKay's prophecy of hope and survival from the "Old Man," her grandmother's grandfather, in the face of the European arrival and assault: "You will find a way, a way to go on even after this white people run over the earth like rabbits."[48]

Reconciliation

In 1968, the white grandsons of Custer's Seventh Cavalry, out of some strange need to rehearse the violence of their grandfathers, planned to replay the Washita massacre on the exact site and November day it had happened a century earlier. Their mock cavalry needed Indians for their play-acting celebration. The Cheyennes, infinitely patient and hospitable, agreed to set up a village for the occasion. They asked only that the re-enactment be historically accurate, and that they be allowed to re-inter the bones of one of the original massacre victims. The bones had been on public display in a small museum in the nearby town of Cheyenne. The Indians saw the centennial as a time for mourning, not for celebration.

The re-enactment went awry. The Cavalry re-enactors charged down on the Cheyenne village prematurely and unexpectedly, brandishing sabers and firing loud blanks from their rifles. The Cheyenne children ran in terror to their parents. Once again the Cheyennes had been betrayed. What could they do with their own anger at the cavalry, headed by Captain Eric Gault, "Commanding Officer, Grand Army of the Republic, Grandsons of the Seventh Cavalry, Reactivated?" At the concluding centennial ceremony, an old Cheyenne peace chief called Gault forward, took the Cheyenne blanket which had been on the bronze coffin of the re-interred victim of 1868, and placed it over Gault's shoulders. It was a gesture of reconciliation, and it broke through the tension and hostility. Lawrence Hart, himself a Peace Chief, reported that the following scene was "hard to describe . . . . People broke down and cried . . . these grandsons of the Seventh and grandsons of Black Kettle. A reconciliation occurred exactly one hundred years after that battle and it was initiated by one of our contemporary Cheyenne chiefs." Gault presented Hart with his prized "Garry Owens" pin, a gift which Hart took as a promise that the Washita massacre would never again be re-enacted.[49]

If the Washita centennial remembrance of 1968 had resulted in bloodshed instead of reconciliation, it would have made national headlines. A goodly number of brutal killings might even have earned the event a mention in ordinary history textbooks. Instead, thanks to the Cheyenne chiefs, peace broke out. Among Whites it became a largely forgotten event among people they preferred to remember as the "fighting Cheyennes." Among the Cheyennes, the event reestablished an ancient and authentic heritage of peace.

Chapter 2

The Holiest War on Record: War for Independence

The War for Independence of 1775-83 is the most sacred event in United States history. Images from that war have stirred the souls of generations of school children: Paul Revere looking up to the Old North Church in Boston for the signal of British attack; John Hancock's bold signature on the Declaration of Independence; George Washington on his knees in prayer at Valley Forge; John Paul Jones on the *Bonhomme Richard* defiantly shouting, "I have just begun to fight!" During the war America's religious leaders interpreted the victories at Saratoga and Yorktown as evidence that God was raising up a new "Chosen People" to fulfill God's purposes on earth, like the ancient Israelites who were God's Chosen People in Old Testament times.[1] Until today, American historians who are otherwise quite secular in approach, freely use mythical language to refer to the "founding fathers," the "pantheon of Revolutionaries," or the "Revolutionary luminaries."[2] Even severe anti-war critics make allowances for this war. In 1842 an outspoken pacifist from Maine called it "The Holiest War on Record."[3]

The American "Whigs" — as the rebels of 1775-83 called themselves — rebelled in the name of high ideals.[4] Thomas Jefferson in the Declaration of Independence eloquently set forth the ideals of human equality, freedom, and government grounded in the will of the people. Commander in Chief George Washington rallied his soldiers, "Freemen, fighting for the blessings of Liberty," against the "base hirelings and mercenaries" on the British side.[5] American idealism, together with a stunning military triumph, set the groundwork for a new national experiment with republican government. The successful defeat of an empire inspired the world. For two centuries victims of imperialist oppression, from Simon Bolivar in Peru to Ho Chi Minh in Vietnam, have supported their own military struggles with quotations from the American Declaration of Independence.

Was This War Necessary?

The very fact that the leaders and events of 1775-83 were raised to mythical status should give us pause. Is it really true that the *violence* of the War for Independence was essential to the *freedom* achieved in the wider social and political transformation known as the American Revolution? What was the relationship of the war to the rise of democracy? Would it have been possible to establish a democratic nation without a war?

It is worth remembering that nations sometimes gain independence without war. In the nineteenth century Canada achieved separation from Great Britain gradually and peaceably. At the end of the twentieth century Blacks in South Africa took over power from an oppressive white minority regime without a major war. Were there also possibilities for peaceable change in the British Empire in the 1760s and 1770s?

The American War for Independence was a civil war. Unlike the African and Asian peoples who fought against European colonial masters in the twentieth century, the Whigs on one side of the Revolution shared a common political and social culture with the Loyalists and British on the other side. Nearly all colonial leaders were Englishmen. They were proud of their membership in the British Empire and nostalgic about their original homes back in the mother country.[6] The English in America had patterned their colonial governments after the British models. Colonial assemblies took their shape after the House of Commons. Colonial governors exercised the power of the King. To be an Englishman was to have claim to a tradition of popular liberty. In their decade of struggle with the British Parliament from the Stamp Act of 1765 until the outbreak of war in 1775, the colonial leaders insisted that they were only claiming the historic rights of Englishmen—including the right to be represented in a body which levied taxes against them.[7] Their claims to liberty were as much a tribute to their own English political tradition as an indictment of tyranny. Politically, the colonists were among the most free of peoples on the face of the earth. They did not need to leave the Empire to extend that freedom or make it secure.

Moreover, thanks to their place in the British Empire, the American colonists were among the most prosperous people on earth in their time. By 1765 there were between 1,750,000 and 2,000,000 people in the colonies, and their economy was undergoing explosive expansion. Benjamin Franklin, who was among the proudest partisans of the Empire, delighted in telling Londoners that the American population and economic productivity would before long far exceed that of the mother country. British North America was a leading center for iron production, shipbuilding, fur trade, agriculture, milling, fishing and meatpacking. In earlier decades, the Spanish Empire had been the envy of all Europe for its access to New World sources of precious metals. But enterprising British settlers and merchants had demonstrated that the route to greater wealth lay in the opportunities of free people to work and to produce. The British Empire was a mercantile system, regulated and protected in an effort to make it as self-sufficient as possible. The regulations were not excessively oppressive nor were they rigidly enforced. Within this system, in the words of one historian, "America waxes rich and strong."[8]

Why then, if the British colonies were in such a favored position, did they revolt against their mother country? It happened because the British, in 1763 after the Seven Years War (French and Indian War), initiated a new program of regulation and taxation of the colonies without taking into account the conditions and interests of the American colonies. The Seven Years War, also called the "Great War for the Empire," had been an unqualified British victory over their French competitors for empire. The war had also saddled the British with debt. They assumed that it was reasonable to keep a standing army in North America and to require the colonies, who had benefited from the defeat and departure of France from North America, to contribute toward the expenses of their defense in the future.

The keepers of the British Empire lacked an adequate vision for the future. They needed to make substantial adjustments in colonial governance—a change in the constitution of empire. Instead they imposed new taxes and controls without opening the way to new governance structures. They did not offer greater voice and representation for the colonies in imperial affairs. The result was a series of escalating crises. The colonies responded with hostility to the new rules and taxes, notably the Stamp Act of 1765, the Townshend Acts of 1767, and the Coercive Acts of 1774.

The war happened also because colonial leaders in America overreacted. They thought they saw a grand design of absolute tyranny in the new imperial legislation, especially after 1774 and the Boston Tea Party when King George III and Parliament decided to punish Boston for their disobedience. In fact, no such grand tyranny existed. The fumbling and inconsistent policies of the king and parliament were improvised and subject to change. Colonial politicians were trapped in an eighteenth-century political theory that predicted centralized tyranny. The theory was set forth in the writings of a group of "Commonwealth Men" who were widely read in the colonies. It was based on historical images of what had happened to ancient Greece and Rome. Political systems go through a predictable life cycle, said these writers. Republics, losing the virtue essential to freedom, become empires. Empires gain wealth and power; they become corrupt and evil. The result is insupportable tyranny that must be overthrown.[9]

This political theory did not serve the colonists well. It led them to see conspiracies and tyrannies where none existed. "The act of revolution was out of proportion to the provocation," wrote historian Neil Lehman. "The revolution was not so much directed against tyranny inflicted, but tyranny anticipated."[10] The anti-imperial ideology empowered inflammatory publicists such as Thomas Paine, a colonial newcomer who never reconciled himself to political authority of any kind, including, later, the new American republic. In an immensely influential pamphlet of 1776, *Common Sense*, Paine dehumanized King George III, "the royal Brute of England," and invited the colonists to hate monarchy and follow their impulses to rebellion.[11] The Declaration of Independence accused the Crown of planning "absolute despotism" — rhetoric that revealed the colonists' ideology more than the facts of the case. When the war forced people to choose sides, some two-thirds of the politically active people in the colonies joined the rebel side. Thousands were neutral or undecided.

Not everyone was hostage to ideology. On both sides of the Atlantic were practical leaders who knew what was needed to avoid a military confrontation between colonies and mother country. The strong voices in the House of Commons favoring reasonable change to accommodate American interests included William Pitt, famous organizer of British victory in the Great War for the Empire, and Edmund Burke, who understood as well as anyone of his generation the relationship of tradition and revolution. Although Pitt and Burke failed to convince King George III toward compromise, the British "March of Folly" which lost the colonies was not inevitable.[12] British historian J. H. Plumb has lamented that "historians have underestimated the extent of British sympathy for America which flourished in the 1760s and early seventies, just as they have overlooked the reasons for its decay once rebellion turned to war."[13] Any adequate understanding of the events of this time — or of any era in history — involves an appreciation of the choices which the people then living believed they had opportunities to make.[14] It is poor history to impose the eventual outcome — a civil war within the Empire — on the persons and events in the decade before the war.

What were the available options? One obvious reform would have been to grant formal representation for the colonies in the British House of Commons. Benjamin Franklin, along with many thoughtful leaders on both sides of the Atlantic, favored such representation, especially in the earlier years of the conflict. Francis Maseres, attorney general of Quebec from 1766 to 1769 wrote a pamphlet in 1770 entitled "Considerations on the Expediency of Admitting Representatives from the American Colonies into the British House of Commons."[15] The Americans did have an informal, if somewhat limited, voice in Parliament. Between 1763 and 1775 five Americans were elected to Parliament in by-elections.[16] More significant were the Americans who officially represented the interest of their colonies in England. In times of crisis these colonial "agents" testified before closed sessions of Parliament. In 1765 Franklin gave four hours of testimony before the House of Commons on the colonial reaction to the Stamp Act. The House also heard from Americans from Massachusetts, New York, and Virginia at that time. A step up from this kind of representation to formal election and membership in Parliament was not unimaginable or impossible. Such a step would have placed the powerful slogan, "No taxation without representation," in an entirely different light. Colonial representatives in Parliament might have helped to moderate the British government's ill-considered and self-defeating measures.

Thomas Hutchinson, conservative lieutenant governor and governor of Massachusetts from 1758 to 1774, opposed constitutional change but suggested a number of proposals to get more imagination, flexibility and common sense into the system. In 1754 Hutchinson had supported Franklin's "Albany Plan" for inter-colonial union, a proposal which, if adopted, would have set a very different course for colonial separation from England. Parliament had the right to tax the colonies, Hutchinson said, but it was foolish and counter-productive to do so. Parliament might understand that fact, and gain other useful information as well, if official royal commissions would visit America and meet with all the colonial Assemblies. Hutchinson believed the failure to communicate on both sides played into the hands of radicals who stirred the people to rebellion.[17]

Joseph Galloway, friend of Benjamin Franklin and leader of the Quaker Party in Pennsylvania, proposed the boldest plan to change the constitution of the empire. Galloway's plan was debated in the fall of 1774 at the meeting of the First Continental Congress. It called for the creation of an American branch of Parliament. In response to the Boston Tea Party, Parliament had passed the Coercive Acts to bring Boston to its knees and isolate it from the other colonies. Galloway hoped to break the impasse. His American Parliament, which he called a "Grand Council," would share powers with the British Parliament over American affairs. The presiding officer would be a "President General" appointed by the king. Colonial assemblies would appoint Grand Council members. Both the Grand Council and Parliament would have the power to introduce bills, and both would have to pass them to become law. Thus Parliament would keep its power to make general laws and the colonies would gain the right to participate in imperial legislation.[18] John Jay of New York supported Galloway. Edward Rutledge of South Carolina said, "I think it is almost a perfect plan."[19] Galloway's plan promised a route to both inter-colonial solidarity and British accommodation.

The Continental Congress debated Galloway's plan for two days and then rejected it by the narrowest of margins, six colonies to five. One of the opposition arguments was that the separate colonies would not be willing to yield authority to an inter-colonial legislature. In this regard, the plan was too radical. Patrick Henry, firebrand from Virginia, warned that the British might bribe such a legislature to do its will. Most of the delegates were less farsighted than Galloway and still hoped to maintain the colonial system without constitutional change. They did not want inter-colonial union and independence. Rather they wanted more autonomy for their colonies within the Empire. They believed that Britain would back down, as she had in the crises over the Stamp Act and Townshend Acts, if faced with unified coercive action in support of

Boston. This strategy, of course, backfired. King George III was offended by the First Continental Congress' belligerence. He became more than ever inclined to settle the matter by force. That Congress had failed, both in its assessment of the situation and in its actions. In May 1775 when the Second Continental Congress met, Galloway did not attend. The Battles of Lexington and Concord had taken place and the war was under way.

The proposals by Franklin, Hutchinson, Galloway and others for reform of the British Empire were not cure-alls. They would not have resolved all the dysfunctions of the imperial relationships. But administrative perfection was hardly necessary. As historian Bernard Bailyn has written, "the 'dysfunctions' that may have existed could have continued to function 'dysfunctionally' for ages untold."[20] The Galloway plan, if it had been accepted and promoted by George III's Prime Minister, Frederick Lord North, as a face-saving compromise, would not have needed to solve all problems indefinitely. Knowing what we do in retrospect about the development of the British Empire in the nineteenth and twentieth centuries, we can see that the Empire's future lay in the direction of a commonwealth system in which the British colonies were subject not to Parliament but to the Crown. Development in that direction would have been stressful and confused. But a scenario of conflict resolution short of all-out war in the 1770s is not only imaginable, it is realistic. If warfare must be a "last resort" to be justified, the War for Independence was not a just war.[21]

Nor is it accurate to assume that certain triggering events inevitably led to war by some kind of ironclad logic. To be sure, the outbreak of violence often has a galvanizing or cathartic effect upon participants, as well as upon the historians, teachers, and students who welcome the focus and drama that wars offer to the classroom. But some wars are avoided even after provocative incidents of violence occur. In February 1775 Lord North offered a belated "Conciliatory Proposal" to avoid war. Colonial patriot leaders in London found North's specific proposals quite unacceptable, but they were prepared to treat this initiative as a prelude to further negotiations.[22] The actual intentions and responses of these patriot leaders in London need to be acknowledged and taken seriously, even if they did not know, as we imaginatively assume we know today, that a wider war at that point was inevitable.

The Alternative of Nonviolent Resistance

From 1765 to 1775 the colonists had carried out a series of successful campaigns to overturn the British proposals for new regulation and taxation. These campaigns had been largely nonviolent. They were aimed at redress of specific grievances and were not guided by modern theories of civil disobedience or activist nonviolence. Nevertheless, the organizers of resistance demonstrated how far it was possible to nullify the effective power of unpopular government by withdrawing popular consent.[23] The Stamp Act of 1765 set the pattern. It was passed in March and set to go into effect by November, which gave the colonies time to organize a coordinated and effective resistance. Colonial assemblies passed protest resolutions. Nine colonies sent delegates to a Stamp Act Congress in New York City. Beginning in Boston, the "Sons of Liberty" organized mass protests against Crown-appointed stamp commissioners to force their resignation. Colonial merchants were intimidated to boycott British goods until Parliament repealed the tax. The campaign kept stamps from being sold. The Act was never enforced and Parliament repealed it in March 1766.

The resistance campaigns of 1765, 1767 and 1774 nullified British legislative power in the colonies. They also gradually created extra-legal political institutions, culminating in the Continental Congress. At regional and local levels, "Committees of Correspondence" began to replace the policy-making and administrative functions of the established government. In October of 1774 the Continental Congress created a "Continental Association" in whose name local resistance groups could act to influence public opinion, recruit leaders, and force policy change.[24] Until the Battles of Lexington and Concord on April 19, 1775, the resistance campaigns had been mostly nonviolent and had resulted in little or no loss of life. Gene Sharp, a strong proponent of nonviolent alternatives to military action, has seen in these developments an instructive precedent for achieving political objectives without destructive warfare. In Sharp's view, the colonists in the spring of 1775 unfortunately decided to create the Continental Army, not realizing the potential transforming power of nonviolent resistance. By resorting to warfare they alienated their supporters in England and engaged in a costly military conflict which they came very near to losing. What they had gained nonviolently, they almost threw away violently.[25]

Some of the most important nonviolent victories in the colonial struggle against British policies are absent from history textbooks. The texts raise to mythical status the Boston Tea Party in December 1773—an event of violence against property rather than persons. One popular college text tells reverently how Samuel Adams and his friends, out to "save the country," dumped the offensive tea into the Boston harbor: "For an hour the only sounds echoing through the crisp, moonlit night were the steady chop of hatchets breaking open wooden chests and the soft splash of tea on the water."[26]

Missing from this textbook, and from the historical memory of nearly all Americans, is the story of the Philadelphia Tea Party that took place at the same time. While Boston turned to violence, the Philadelphians resolved their tea crisis nonviolently. When the tea-bearing British ship *Polly* reached Delaware Bay, the Philadelphians refused its cargo as surely as had the Bostonians. Backed by massive public support, the Quaker merchants persuaded the British captain, Samuel Ayres, to take the tea back to London. They smoothed the way by advancing funds to buy supplies for the journey. John Penn, the proprietary governor of Pennsylvania, treated the situation with benign neglect. Meanwhile Thomas Hutchinson in Boston forced a showdown with Samuel Adams and the anti-British hotheads. If Boston had behaved like Philadelphia, ongoing negotiations with London would have been possible.

Not all historians agree with Gene Sharp that the colonial campaigns against British taxation and regulation were basically nonviolent in nature. Richard Maxwell Brown has seen the 1760s and 1770s as an exceptionally violent period. Mob riots against the Stamp Act and Townshend Acts had roots in "the habitual use of the riot as a purposive weapon of protest and dissent in both Great Britain and America during the preceding two centuries."[27] In Brown's view, the practice of mob violence and vigilantism prepared the way for the War for Independence, and the war itself strengthened the rationale for violent popular action against alleged domestic enemies. In America the people were sovereign and believed that in given cases when the government was unresponsive, they could act on their own with violence against evildoers for the public good.[28]

Other historians have distinguished between the behavior of public mobs before and after the Revolution. Gordon Wood has said that pre-revolutionary America was a class-structured society, and that crowd riots were, for the most part, harmless rituals in which the lower classes released their pent-up frustrations. Rioters in the colonies were not inclined to take human life or to be genuinely destructive. They respected the established social system so much that even their riots "tended to reinforce that structure even as they defied it." In the new republic, however, after the War for Independence, mob violence in America lost its restraint and social control. The paternalism and respect for hierarchy that had characterized mobs in the eighteenth century disappeared. Mob violence became even more frequent and more destructive.[29] The War for Independence made America both more free and more violent.

Crusade and Carnage

The American rebels justified their warfare in both religious and political terms. Politically, they argued that the colonies had a right to defend themselves against systematic British tyranny. British policies to tax the colonies were imposed "slavery," they said. Moreover, because tyranny was associated with British militarism, the American struggle could be seen as opposed to the corrupt European system of warfare among kingly dynasties. It was a war of ordinary citizens against "standing armies" in peacetime, such as King George had inflicted upon the colonies. It was the first of America's wars for peace.[30]

Some Americans viewed the war as a religious crusade. Puritan ministers of New England were especially well equipped to see the war as a holy cause. America was an arena for God to use his newly chosen people to complete his purposes on earth. From the beginnings of the Massachusetts Bay Colony, this new community saw itself as part of God's plan for the regeneration of all humankind. In the religious revival of the 1730s and 1740s known as the "Great Awakening," Jonathan Edwards became convinced that the thousand-year reign of God known as the "millennium" (Revelation 20: 2-7) was at hand and that it would begin in America. During the War for Independence, Puritan preachers used "millennial" thinking to justify the war as the cause of "God's New Israel" against the tyrannical British "antichrist." To join the Continental Army and to support the war in other ways became a holy duty, because the new American nation had inherited the promises of God.[31] Historian Charles Royster has argued that the foundational American character emerged out of these evangelical religious ideas and attitudes combined with the military code of personal courage, responsibility, discipline and benevolence.[32]

For a war to be justifiable, not only must the goals be worthy, but the killing and destruction must not be so extensive that they outweigh the higher objectives. The American War for Independence was a limited war in comparison to the total warfare of the twentieth century, or in comparison to the utter devastation of European religious wars of the seventeenth century (Thirty Years War, 1618-1648). And yet the numbers of people sacrificed are worth noting. Approximately 25,000 people on the American side died in the eight years of war, including those who died in battle, from disease, and as prisoners of war. In addition were the war "casualties"—those who survived but were crippled by injury or disease—estimated at another 25,000[33] Are these numbers significant, considering that the colonial population was around two million? Comparable death and casualty totals in the United States today, the per capita equivalent, would be about two million dead plus two million casualties. What is the impact on a society of losses at this level? What cause in today's world would justify the sacrifice of two million American dead and another two million wounded—especially if alternative means of resolving the conflict were on the table? From a bloodless demographic point of view, the nation could absorb such losses without difficulty—either 25,000 in 1776 or two million today. For the families of those who lost their lives and treasure, the concern is not so easily dismissed.

The memories of the War for Independence, as for all wars, ought to include the actual experiences and feelings of the real people who killed and were killed, rather than just the heroic glosses of the war propagandists or of romantic painters. There was a vast gap between the soaring rhetoric of the commanders, most of whom were from the upper classes, and the reality of the soldiers, most of whom were young (mostly 18 to 23) and from the lower classes.[34] Men in eighteenth-century battles had the special terror of facing massed formations which advanced into devastating fire, followed by hand to hand combat. At the Battle of Bunker Hill the marching British grenadiers took devastating losses as they marched up toward the elevated American defensive enclosure. The Americans ran out of ammunition and retreated, except for some thirty trapped men who "were bayoneted by the British infantry eager to settle scores."[35]

Captain John Henry, son of Patrick Henry, fought at one of the battles of Saratoga. The father's biographer described the aftermath of that battle: "He walked over the battlefield, occasionally pausing to recognize those among 'the fallen' whom he knew. Then he drew his sword from its scabbard and, snapping it into pieces, dashed it on the ground and went 'raving mad.'"[36] He resigned his commission nine months later because of his "ill state of health."[37] Elisha Bostwick, a Connecticut soldier, apparently was able to hold onto his sanity as he described the mutilation of his comrades:

> A cannon ball 'cut down Lt. Youngs platoon which was next to that of mine[;] the ball first took off the head of Smith, a Stout heavy man and dashed it open, then took Taylor across the Bowels, it then Struck Sergeant Garret of our Company on the hip [and] took off the point of the hip bone[.] Smith and Taylor were left on the spot. Sergeant Garret was carried but died the Same day now to think, oh! what a sight that was to see within a distance of six rods those men with their legs and arms and guns and packs all in a heap[.]'[38]

General Washington preached fervently to the troops before every battle of the virtues of honor, fame, and courage that were central to his own identity as an aristocrat. These virtues, the general believed, could also inspire free men from the lower classes. Some soldiers, no doubt, took Washington's rhetoric to heart. But it requires a special act of faith to believe that high morale in the Continental Army ultimately accounted for the American victory. Some 20 to 25 percent of soldiers in the Continental Army deserted; the rate in militia units was even higher. Army morale was sapped by wretched living conditions, inadequate food and clothing, delayed compensation, and a defensive strategy which involved many losses and retreats, year after year in an eight-year war. There were at least fifteen "major mutinies" of soldiers against their officers.[39]

In January 1781, Continental soldiers mutinied, first in Pennsylvania (2,400 men) and then in New Jersey (200 men).[40] They overwhelmed their officers and made demands regarding pay and terms of service. The Pennsylvania group was strong enough to win its case, but General Washington wrote to Congress, "Unless this dangerous spirit can be suppressed by force there is an end to all subordination in the Army, and indeed to the Army itself." At Washington's order, the New Jersey soldiers were overcome, even though they demanded the same settlement regarding payment and terms of service which had been granted to the

Pennsylvania mutineers a few days earlier. Loyal officers designated twelve of the rebels to execute two of their leaders in the mutiny. One eyewitness, Dr. Thacher, described the capital punishment of Sergeant David Gilmore: "He was led a few yards distance and placed on his knees. Six of the executioners, at the signal given by an officer, fired, three aiming at the head and three at the breast, the other six reserving their fire in order to dispatch the victim should the first fire fail. It so happened in this instance. The remaining six then fired, and life was instantly extinguished."[41] During the entire war at least forty men from the Continental Army were executed for various offenses; some estimates run as high as seventy-five.[42] Such extreme measures did not end the problem of desertions, but no one at the time believed that patriotic zeal alone was sufficient to keep the soldiers in the Continental Army at their posts. Their occasional mutinies against Continental military authority paralleled the general American resistance to England.

Victims of War: Native Americans and African Americans

Native Americans had their own viewpoint on the justice of the War for Independence. Part of the freedom that the white revolutionaries sought was the freedom for Europeans to invade and take over Native lands. In 1763 the British government had announced a new policy to prohibit the sale of, and settlement on, lands between the Appalachian Mountains and the Mississippi River. In effect, the Proclamation of 1763 created a vast Indian reservation in the West. Colonial leaders, including George Washington, ignored the British regulation, excusing themselves that it was just a temporary measure "designed to quiet the minds of the Indians." Washington advised his friends to seize opportunities to survey and claim lands in the west before others got to them.[43]

The war brought death, destruction, and dependency—not freedom—to the Native Americans. With a few exceptions (Oneidas, Tuscaroras, and some Mohawks), those tribes who fought in the war joined on the British side. Not only did the British offer an alliance for resistance to the invading Americans, but the British were in a position to be more generous with gifts and weapons than were the poorly organized Americans.

From the Great Lakes to Florida, the War for Independence gave reason and opportunity for Reds and Whites to slaughter each other on the frontier. In 1778 an Indian army of Senecas and Cayugas, led by British officers, attacked and destroyed white frontier towns and farms in New

York and Pennsylvania. In reprisal a colonial army under General John Sullivan swept through settlements of the Iroquois Confederation, "killing men, women, and children, burning villages, destroying fields of corn and other foodstuffs, and cutting down orchards." Marauding Reds and Whites "made a wasteland of the Ohio Valley."[44] In June 1780 Indian troops overwhelmed and burned the Rundle's Station settlement in Kentucky, killing some 200 men, women and children. The Whites could not rest until they had taken an equal number of Indian scalps and more. One of the most discreditable massacres took place in the spring of 1782, after the Battle of Yorktown had virtually ended the war in the east. A group of Pennsylvania militia men, some three hundred strong, came upon the Moravian missionary outpost of Gnadenhutten where ninety peaceful Christian convert Delaware Indians were staying. The Whites executed most of the Delawares—men, women and children.

During the war Americans slaughtered the Indians; after the war Englishmen betrayed them. At the Treaty of Paris, September 3, 1783, the British ceded to the Americans all the western lands to the Mississippi River, without mentioning the Native Americans or any claims or rights that the Indians might have to those lands. Any argument that this was a just war must set aside the Native Americans as a great exception.

Nor did the high revolutionary ideals of freedom pay their promised dividend for most African American slaves. Thomas Jefferson, himself a slave owner, was well aware that the institution of slavery contradicted his principles. In the first draft of the Declaration of Independence Jefferson had blamed King George III for pressing this evil institution on the colonies. But southern colonial leaders would have none of it. They did not intend to get rid of slavery once the king was out of their way. Indeed the War for Independence strengthened, rather than weakened, the institution of slavery in the American South.

There was an Emancipation Proclamation during the war, and it came from the British side. On November 7, 1775, on board the *William* in the harbor at Norfolk, Virginia, the governor of the colony, John Murray, Earl of Dunmore, declared martial law and invited slaves to leave their masters and join the royal forces.[45] Those who made it to British lines would be granted freedom. Dunmore's proclamation, more a military tactic than an act of good will toward Blacks, enraged and terrified white plantation owners with the prospect of a slave insurrection. Some eight hundred black slaves made their way to the British side, and thousands more imagined the prospect of freedom. Most of the emancipated slaves died of disease. In 1778 Jefferson estimated that thirty thousand Virginia slaves had run away, although most had no chance of getting to the British side.[46] When the war was over, the victorious Americans, having won a war for freedom, demanded that the British give their surviving slaves back. The British resettled some of the freed Blacks in Nova Scotia. Many of these later returned to Sierra Leone in Africa.[47]

Lord Dunmore's Proclamation prompted General George Washington to reverse an earlier decision to forbid the recruitment of Blacks for the Continental Army. During the war, the separate states found it increasingly difficult to meet their recruitment quotas, and they passed more liberal laws for black enlistments. About 5,000 Blacks fought in the war for independence, nearly all in predominantly white units. During the war they submitted scores of petitions for their freedom.[48]

For African Americans in the deep South, where the largest numbers were concentrated, and for the next three or four generations until the end of the Civil War, the legacy of the War for Independence was grim indeed. White slave owners ruled the South and they interpreted the Declaration of Independence to protect their rights in human property. The Constitutional Convention of 1787 made the slave system legal and permanent. Slavery was the price of Union. Southerners entrenched slavery and extended it westward, empowered by the acquiescence of northern racist politicians who, however ambivalent they may have been about the slave system, were terrified by visions of sexual race-mixing and racial violence. They let the South develop its "peculiar institution."

Legacies: Home Rule and Rule at Home

Much of the best scholarship on the American Revolution in the past century has addressed the question of the Revolution as a social movement. Conservative or "consensus" historians have seen the Revolution as a war for independence which wrought no major domestic social transformation. The same sort of cautious and well-established people ruled the new nation, say the conservatives, as had ruled the old colonies before political independence. Meanwhile the progressive or "Whig" historians have argued that the Revolution empowered the common people and weakened the grip of the traditional upper class. Gordon Wood's 1992 book, *The Radicalism of the American Revolution*, was a definitive statement from the "Whig" perspective. Its subtitle was,

"How a Revolution Transformed a Monarchical Society into a Democratic One Unlike Any That Had Ever Existed."

The role of violence in the American Revolution deserves as much attention as the rise of democracy. Especially worth challenging is the notion that democracy depended upon violence. Wood's book makes clear that, although the War for Independence accelerated the social transformation that doomed aristocratic power and pretension in America, the fundamental changes toward democracy were well under way before the war. Bernard Bailyn, a "Whig" historian who has illuminated the ideological roots of the revolutionary impulse, has argued that the war was neither inevitable nor necessary to the rise of American democracy: "There had been nothing inevitable in the outbreak of revolution . . . . What was inevitable—what no one could have restrained—was America's emergence into the modern world as a liberal, more or less democratic, and capitalist society. That would have happened in any case."[49]

To think clearly about the American Revolution and the War for Independence, then, it is necessary to understand that the success of the movement toward democracy did not necessarily depend upon triumph in war. Moreover, some of the undesirable dimensions of the new democratic order—the penchant for violence and the disregard of minority rights in the new republic—were in part the legacy of the war.

The paths to political autonomy by the United States and Canada deserve comparison. Church historian Mark Noll has noted that Canada "chose not the way of revolution and independence but of Loyalism and peaceful change." While the United States developed its ideology of divine blessing manifested in military triumph, Canada avoided revolutions and civil wars. Nevertheless, in Noll's view, Canada has a stronger claim to be considered a "Christian nation" than does the United States: "Canada did not tolerate slavery, it has not thrown its weight around in foreign adventures, it has not done quite so poorly with its Native Americans, it has not puffed itself up with messianic pride, it has tolerated much less social violence, . . . it has cared more humanely for the poor and weak members of its society, and its educational structures make some provision for teaching religion."[50] The comparison prompts a question: Would the United States have developed a more humane social and political order if it had not been born in the revolutionary violence of a war for independence?

Legacies: War Begets War

One legacy of successful wars is the encouragement they give for people to resort to violence in the future. The War for Independence taught Americans to reach for the musket to solve problems. American culture also contained powerful strands of anti-military thinking. But agitators for war in the future—in 1799, 1812, 1846, 1860 and beyond—could always make their case in terms of an idealized memory of the War for Independence, and with the presumption that the next war would defend or extend liberty. Even the seceding Confederate States in 1860 were quite convinced they would triumph in their military defense of their rights against outside control. The Confederates were replaying the War for Independence, with the Union instead of Great Britain as the presumed author of tyranny.

Abraham Lincoln was second to none in his respect for the revolutionary generation. More than his contemporaries, however, Lincoln sensed the paradoxes of violence, liberty and political order. In 1838 Lincoln, then a young lawyer in Springfield, Illinois, gave an address to the Young Men's Lyceum in which he observed that the War for Independence had called forth base human passions, as distinguished from sober judgement. The revolutionaries had directed their motives of hatred and revenge "exclusively against the British nation," and had fortunately and paradoxically advanced the noble cause of liberty. But passions of war, extended into times of peace, were dangerous. "Passion has helped us," said Lincoln, "but can do so no more. It will in future be our enemy." In 1838 Lincoln worried that the Revolutionary War legacy was encouraging dangerous internal violence in the country. In 1860, as president-elect, Lincoln would discover that the enemy he identified— the destructive passion of 1776—once again held America by the throat.[51]

Chapter 3

Republican Peace Experiments:
A Usable Past

A Usable Peacemaking Past

Americans are so accustomed to celebrating war heroes that we have forgotten our usable peacemaking past. We have overlooked our peace heroes as well as the peaceable impulses of those in our history who reluctantly endorsed war, or who participated in wars they personally believed to be unjust. We have diligently remembered the wars we won, even when, as in the War of 1812, we had not won them.

In the early decades of the American republic, the country was more fervently committed to the ideal of peace than to the arts of warfare. This peace commitment was not at the fringes of national identity; it was near the core. Quaker pacifism had put a permanent stamp on the character of the middle colonies and states, especially Pennsylvania, which served as host for the nation's capital until it moved from Philadelphia to Washington, D.C. in 1799. A classical republican or "Whig" political ideology, imported from England and Americanized in the Revolution, saw America's mission in terms of peace. If there was no nationwide "peace movement" in the United States before 1828, it was because the national mission seemed to make it unnecessary. The experiment in democratic republicanism was itself a peace movement, an updated and more secular version of the earlier holy experiments in Pennsylvania and New England. While Europe was convulsed by war in the wake of the French Revolution, the United States stood apart in relatively peaceful isolation.

Americans had divided minds about war and peace. The Federalists and Republicans who guided U.S. politics in the early republic deplored warfare and standing armies. Benjamin Franklin said there was no such thing as a good war or a bad peace, but he endorsed the War for Independence. Thomas Jefferson has been called a "half-way pacifist."[1] He wrote that "if nations go to war for every degree of injury there would never be peace on earth," but in 1801 he ordered a naval task force to the Mediterranean for action against four Muslim states of North Africa.[2] The expressed peace ideals of America's early leaders seemed only a slight deterrent to military actions. Therefore we are tempted to write off those ideals as a kind of adolescent innocence or dreamy utopianism which American leaders had to overcome as they faced the hard realities of national development.

Do the almost-forgotten peaceable impulses of American founders deserve their obscurity? Or are they part of a usable past?

Peaceminded Quakers

From the 1680s to the 1750s the Quakers established a peace-minded social order in America, centered in the Delaware Valley and the colonies of Pennsylvania and New Jersey. In 1681 King Charles II made this peaceable "Holy Experiment" possible when he granted a huge tract of land in America to William Penn, a pacifist from a military family. Penn's Quaker-led community became one of the four distinctive English-speaking regional culture areas in the new world—alongside Puritan New England, the Anglican Chesapeake Bay region, and the Presbyterian English-Scotch-Irish frontier. Because the Quakers eventually lost political control of Pennsylvania, their pacifist experiment is often considered a failure.[3] In a broader cultural sense, however, as well as in specific details of community organization and character, the Quaker experiment in social harmony was a remarkable success. It not only shaped the character of a distinctive region, but it made an ongoing contribution toward an American democracy of voluntarism, free enterprise, and freely competing social and religious groups.[4]

The peace ideal turned Quaker Pennsylvania into the cradle of American social and religious variety. In contrast to New England where Puritans attempted to impose religious unity, Penn projected an ideal of harmony and love. In Penn's view, social order did not depend upon everyone believing the same creed (as in New England) or fitting into a single hierarchy (as in Virginia). The Quaker ideal was a revolutionary vision and it was pursued more diligently in Pennsylvania than anywhere else in the new world. Liberty of conscience, rooted in the belief that the light of God was present in every person, was a moral absolute. Pennsylvania had an exceptionally open immigration policy, and welcomed a host of non-Quaker peoples who eventually outnumbered the Quakers.

One result of the jostling of competing religious groups in Pennsylvania was movement toward a uniquely American invention — the concept of a religious "denomination." Different German-speaking groups, for example, included Lutherans, Reformed, Moravians, Mennonites, Dunkers, the Ephrata Society and the Schwenkfelders. These competing Pennsylvania German religious groups began with confident visions of divine truth that excluded outsiders. But they slowly learned mutual toleration as they became more secure in their denominational identity. They gained confidence in relationship to each other and to the Quaker party which led colonial Pennsylvania politics. Meanwhile in Virginia and New England, the established Anglican and Puritan churches persecuted the Baptists long after the cooperative religious system of different groups in Pennsylvania was in place.[5]

Another result of these diverse groups in Pennsylvania, and the ways the dominant Quaker party addressed conflicting interests, was that Pennsylvania made a distinctive contribution toward a stable system of political parties in the new republic. The idea that political parties could define and promote broad public interest, rather than behaving as "factions" which agitated for narrow group interests, was first expressed in Pennsylvania.[6] This new development in political party functioning grew out of experience in the middle colonies, rather than immediately from the teachings of William Penn. But it had immense implications for the long-range peace and stability of American democracy.

The Quakers saw liberty in terms of the Golden Rule: "Do unto others as you would have them do unto you." Their means for keeping local peace reflected their ideals. They created a distinctive set of local public officers known as "peace makers" to deal with non-criminal disputes. Their sheriffs, in a different public office, acted as social referees to handle disputes among different groups. The Quaker criminal codes reduced the number of capital crimes and substituted hard labor for corporal punishment. They led the world in prison reform as well as in limitation of capital punishment.[7]

The flowering of Quaker culture lasted from the 1660s to the 1750s. Then the religious Quakers withdrew from politics in behalf of a more perfectionist inward reform, led by such men as John Woolman, Anthony Benezet, and Israel Pemberton. In the 1790s a group of young, single Quaker women in Philadelphia created new institutions to help the poor—including new schools to educate poor white and black females.[8] The Quakers undertook an assault on the institution of slavery. They purged their church of members who owned slaves. They contributed to the new nation not through political control, but through reform projects and campaigns in behalf of Blacks, women, Native Americans, prisoners, and others. This new stage of Quakerism constituted "a new Holy Experiment" which influenced society at large through private organizations.[9] In 1750 the Quakers were the third-largest denomination in the British colonies. Their numbers then went into a long-term decline in comparison to other religious groups. Nevertheless their moral force as a pacifist conscience to the nation remained a permanent part of the American landscape. Quaker pacifist reformers exercised an influence in the United States far greater than their numbers.

Peaceminded Republicans

Another kind of American peace orientation had roots in European political thought. This political philosophy has been called "classical republicanism," and its promoters were more from Virginia and New England than from the middle colonies. From the scholars of the French Enlightenment, and from the English Whig opponents of monarchy, early American leaders learned to assume that the making of war belonged to kings and their conspiracies with ruling aristocracies. Ordinary people did not make war. Wars rather resulted when reigning monarchs (and in the English case, the king-in-Parliament) established alliances with their national military forces which were run by an elite corps of aristocrats. Royal governments granted offices, titles and money to the aristocratic corps in exchange for loyalty and obedience. This alliance of the monarchy with the military resulted in standing armies which were a perpetual threat to peace, as well as a threat to the basic freedoms of the people. "The liberties of Europe," wrote James Madison in *The Federalist* #41, "have with few exceptions been the price of her military establishments."[10] Mercy Otis Warren, who wrote a history of the American Revolution, agreed: "A standing army is the most ready engine in the hands of despotism to debase the powers of the human mind, and eradicate the manly spirit of freedom."[11] True peace and freedom would not be achieved, the classical republican (or "Whig") political thinkers assumed, without overcoming the corruption of this military-aristocratic-government alliance.[12]

Monarchies justified their standing armies and their alliances of military power with the aristocratic class by saying they were essential to order and stability. How could a republic, without a standing army, guarantee political stability and avoid civil strife? The classical republicans answered by asserting the superior *virtue* of citizens in the new republic. Because the American people were free citizens, and because they generally owned land or property which gave them a stake in society, they would be willing to make the sacrifices essential for the common good. Virtuous citizens would scorn corrupt alliances. They would not seek to turn government connections to private advantage. In case of outside military aggression, they would freely volunteer as members of their local militia. The republican confidence in local militia (though it must be a "well-regulated militia," as they wrote into the Bill of Rights), and their acknowledgment of national self-defense in case of aggression, meant that republicans were not absolute pacifists who refused to participate in defensive wars. They did believe that the people's virtue would make for peace in the American republic.

Thomas Jefferson, the most eloquent of the classical republicans, was a "half-way pacifist."[13] Jefferson believed that democratic virtue grew on farmsteads where free people mingled labor with soil. Slaves and indentured servants who did not own property could not be trusted with the vote or with political responsibility. America's future success would depend on the nation's ability to make property-owners out of as many citizens as possible. The Louisiana Purchase of 1803 was not only a means to guarantee America's national power and greatness by doubling the national domain. It also fit into the Jeffersonian goal to make secure a farm-based social order of republican virtue. As industrious small farmers spread across the new land and put it into production, America would surely become more prosperous, more inclined to peace, and less vulnerable to military-aristocratic complexes such as afflicted Europe.[14]

Classical republican thinking lost its force as the country expanded into a system of interest-based politics and profit-oriented economic development. But it remained one source of a distinctive American political discourse, especially in continuing distrust of intrusive "big government." It is an authentic ancestor of late twentieth-century alarm about the "military-industrial complex" which resulted from World War II and the Cold War. It is part of the background of ongoing concerns to empower people who are without property and jobs.

English Common Law and Violent Self-Defense

Peace on the American frontier, as well as in the established settlements, depended upon the rule of law rather than the arbitrary power of those people who had the most guns or prestige. Peace without law cannot last. To be sure, systems of law can also entrench the ruling classes who use violence to keep the poor and dispossessed classes in their place. United States history is rich with such misuse of law; legalized slavery is only the most obvious example.[15] Nevertheless, the ancient English system of common law as it was implemented in America served to restrain excessive personal violence. English common law helped make livable communities possible.

English common law promoted the settlement of civil disputes in peaceable exchange or in a court of law. In situations of conflict where someone's life was threatened, that person did not have the right to kill in self-defense. As long as a threatened person had an avenue of escape from the scene of conflict, he or she was legally obligated to retreat from violence. English common law established a "duty to retreat" from the attacker or enemy as far as possible. Only when a threatened person had his or her back to the wall, with no means of escape, could he or she use lethal violence in self-defense. If one killed an attacker in self-defense when one could have escaped, one was guilty of murder. The common law "duty to retreat" doctrine assumed that human life and civil order were higher values than human pride and the right to violent self-defense. It helped to limit the number of homicides. Although the doctrine was challenged both legally and in the folkways of some groups of English people, the duty to retreat remained the law; it was retained in the English Criminal Law Act of 1967[16]

The "duty to retreat" doctrine became part of the rule of law in the United States. In numerous court cases it became the basis for conviction of people who killed others in self-defense when they could have avoided violence. As the new republic developed, however, the doctrine was challenged in decisions appealed to state supreme courts. Not until the twentieth century, however, did the U.S. Supreme Court definitively overturn the doctrine. In 1921 Justice Oliver Wendell Holmes wrote a decision in *Brown v. United States* that established the civil right of citizens to stand their ground and kill in self-defense. America's abandonment of the "duty to retreat" doctrine helps explain why America today has the highest homicide rate of modern nations. Nevertheless, the "duty to retreat" doctrine remains a historical fact—an almost-forgotten part of the peace heritage of the United States.

Contrary to common images of the musket-carrying frontiersman, Americans in the colonies and early republic did not live in a gun culture. Probate records listing the possession of people in great detail show that only fourteen per cent of the people owned guns, and half of those guns were not in working order. Even members of militia units lacked guns. At the time of the French and Indian war, only about twenty-five per cent of militia members had firearms. Moreover, the minority who did own guns did not have absolute gun rights. Michael Bellesiles, a historian who researched the origins of the national gun culture, has observed that in the colonies, "No gun ever belonged unqualifiedly to an individual. It could not be seized in a debt case, could not be sold if that sale left a militia member without a firearm, had to be listed in every probate inventory and returned to the state if state-owned, and could be seized whenever needed by the state for alternative purposes. Guns might be privately owned, but they were state-controlled."[17] According to Bellesiles, America's gun culture did not emerge full force prior to the Civil War.

The Popularity of Peace

Most Americans, of course, were neither pacifist Quakers, nor classical republican political philosophers, nor legal experts on "duty to retreat" doctrine. The popular mood in the country shifted wildly between militancy and peaceableness depending on national and international political currents—especially when gratuitous insults by foreign governments offended the young and insecure nation's pride. Unfortunately, American history textbooks tell more about recurrent war hysteria than about the profoundly held yearnings for peace. One moment of powerful self-definition came in December 1799 when George Washington died unexpectedly, less than four years after stepping down as president. From pulpits, civic platforms, and newspaper editorial offices, Americans eulogized their founding military and political leader. The emphasis upon peace in these eulogies can be a big surprise two centuries later. Their national hero, they said consistently, was above all a man of peace.[18] Washington's greatest military achievement was not victory in any battle but rather his decisive action to disband the army after the war. Then as president, while European nations floundered in revolution and war, Washington kept the peace. Said Henry Lee, commander of the army that put down the Whiskey Rebellion in 1794:

Maintaining his (Washington's) pacific system at the expense of no duty, America, faithful to herself, and unstained in her honor, continued to enjoy the delights of peace, while afflicted Europe mourns in every quarter under the accumulated miseries of unexampled war.[19]

Indeed, at that moment President John Adams was struggling to keep the United States out of a war with France.

Benjamin Rush, a physician from Philadelphia, was a prominent spokesman for popular peace concerns in the new republic. In 1789 when President Washington appointed Henry Knox as a permanent Secretary of War, Rush proposed a national Peace Office to oppose the functions of the national War Office. Rush sarcastically recommended that the following inscriptions be placed on the door of the War Office:

1 An office for butchering the human species.
2 A Widow and Orphan making office.
3 A broken bone making office.
4 A Wooden leg making office.
5 An office for creating public and private vices.
6 An office for creating a public debt.
7 An office for creating speculators, stock jobbers, and bankrupts.
8 An office for creating famine.
9 An office for creating pestilential diseases.
10 An office for creating poverty, and the destruction of liberty, and national happiness.[20]

America's popular novelists and writers reflected the contradictory claims of the peace ideal and the violence which was so present in the formation and expansion of the United States. Charles Brockden Brown wrestled with questions of pacifism and heroism in his powerful adventure novels *Wieland* (1798) and *Edgar Huntly* (1799). Brown was a birthright Quaker from Philadelphia. James Fenimore Cooper, whose first novel, *The Spy*, was published in 1821, persistently addressed the issues of violent conflict and the pacific or martial means of resolving it. Herman Melville shared Cooper's concern for conflict resolution, a concern which "lay at the heart of their fiction." Melville's *Moby-Dick* (1851) is full of Quaker pacifist idealism, and can be interpreted as a call to a nation wracked by the crisis over slavery to return to its original peaceable ideals.[21] Scholars of early American literature have chronicled and analyzed in detail the theme or "myth" of violence, especially on the frontier, where writers imagined that white European civilization was being regenerated through its raw encounter with nature and with nature's people—the Indians.[22] But it needs to be recognized that alongside the myth or ideology of civilized racial violence, a quite different ideology of peace and conflict resolution also characterized and energized the American literary imagination.[23]

Teaching materials in public schools also reflected America's peace yearnings and commitments. The widely used *McGuffey's Readers* saw no contradiction between American patriotism and peace idealism; indeed, the themes belonged together. Beginning with the *Eclectic First Reader* in 1836, these books attempted to shape the moral character of young Americans both by celebrating heroic U.S. patriots and by condemning the evils of militarism and warfare. One anti-war McGuffey story told of two brothers who unknowingly killed each other on the battlefield and were buried side by side. Another graphically portrayed the miseries of the battlefield and described warring nations as "mingled in promiscuous massacre and ruin." Some selections criticized the Mexican War of 1846-48, albeit indirectly. The McGuffy peace idealism was explicitly Christian. One lesson stated, "I can look to nothing but the progress of Christian sentiment upon earth to arrest the strong current of its popular and prevailing partiality for war."[24]

Decisions for Peace

The American peace ideal bore fruit in specific cases when leaders chose a costly peace policy even though going to war would have been widely popular. Strong leadership by Presidents John Adams in 1799-1800 and Thomas Jefferson in 1807-08 saved the country from war during their respective administrations. These men were from opposing political parties—Adams a Federalist and Jefferson a Democrat-Republican.

1) John Adams and the "Quasi-War" with France.
On February 18, 1799, President John Adams stunned the young nation, which had prepared itself for war with France, by taking a lonely and unexpected initiative for peace. Naval hostilities were already under way, and an army had been mobilized to meet the crisis. Leaders of the Federalist party, including the key members of President Adams' cabinet, were convinced that war with France would strengthen their party and defend national pride. Yet President Adams, with scandalous disregard of his cabinet, his party, and his own political future, sent to Congress an announcement that he was authorizing new peace talks rather than asking for a declaration of war. The action contributed to Adams' defeat in the election of 1800. Years later Adams wrote, "... I desire no other inscription over my gravestone than: 'Here lies John Adams, who took upon himself the responsibility of the peace with France in the year 1800.'"[25] He was a man of conviction: "Great is the guilt of an unnecessary war."[26]

The context for Adams' peace initiative, and for United States foreign policy generally, was the warfare which convulsed European nations in the wake of the French Revolution—from 1793 to 1815 (with a temporary pause 1801-02). The European wars initially boosted the United States economy as American commerce was able to meet a war-induced demand in Europe for trade goods, both military and non-military. But trade could not be separated from diplomacy. England and France as warring nations each interfered with outside trade to the other, and disputed the United States' claim that "free ships mean free goods." The first U.S. political party system reflected the European wars. Hamilton and the Federalists took the British side, and Jefferson and the Democratic-Republicans favored France.

In 1793 the British closed French ports to neutral shipping and captured several hundred United States vessels in the French West Indies. A war against England was narrowly averted with the acceptance of "Jay's Treaty" with England in 1795. France, angered that the Jay Treaty violated the French-United States post-War-of-Independence agreement, responded with increasing hostility. France mistakenly assumed that the United States was now firmly allied with England. In 1797 and 1798 the French seized more than three hundred American ships. When President Adams sent three diplomats to Paris to negotiate grievances, they found that the French demanded a bribe of $250,000 for the privilege to even talk with Talleyrand, the French Foreign Minister. The incident, known as the "XYZ affair," triggered war hysteria in the U.S. President Adams got caught up in the war spirit and helped lead war preparations and naval reprisals in the West Indies. From 1798 to 1800 the Americans captured more than eighty armed French vessels. In May and June, 1798, Congress voted to create an army of 10,000 men, and to provide for an increase to 50,000 if necessary. Adams nominated George Washington Commander in Chief of the army, and accepted his recommendations for other officers—all Federalists. Alexander Hamilton, Adams' rival within the Federalist Party, was in active command and intoxicated by prospects of military glory. He hoped to take East and West Florida, Louisiana, Mexico, and perhaps even more, from Spain, France's ally.[27]

Although John Adams as a man of principle had never wanted war, he had much to overcome in order to take his lonely and controversial initiatives for peace in 1799-1800. France had undoubtedly and flagrantly insulted America's national pride. Overt hostilities were already under way. The president's political future was on the line. An open break with Hamilton could split the Federalist party and cost Adams' re-election in 1800. There were also less tangible psychological forces at work, as there always are when men engage in the threats and counter-threats that lead to war. Both within himself and from outside taunts, Adams needed to defend his masculinity. In the words of a recent biographer, he "struggled to convince himself that he was not afraid of war and that he possessed the 'manly determination' to lead the country into conflict if no other choice existed."[28] In a letter to Washington explaining his decision, Adams defensively distanced himself from "'the babyish and womanly blubbering' for peace at any price" which might lead Americans to accept a less than honorable treaty with France.[29] As surely as men prove manhood in war, the refusal of warfare puts a burden of apparent female-like weakness upon male decision-makers.

On the other hand, Adams was prompted toward peace. From France came some fresh signals in late 1798 that Foreign Minister Talleyrand would welcome peace talks. One of these signals came via George Logan, an idealistic Quaker doctor from Philadelphia who had undertaken a private peace mission to Paris and returned with official word that France had lifted her embargo and released American prisoners. The Federalist majority in Congress, unpleased with Logan's mission, officially censured the doctor and passed a bill to outlaw such private meddling in matters of diplomacy. Another courier of news about changing French attitudes was Thomas Boylston Adams, the president's son.[30]

President Adams was also concerned about the implications of warfare and militarism for the republic. The appointment of prominent men as high army officers increased the power and wealth of their class. Although Adams believed in government by an aristocracy of merit, he shared the Whig distaste for a standing army—a "many bellied Monster" he once had called it.[31] Now his newly-created American army needed to be fed through the levying of new direct property taxes. Some German-American farmers in counties north of Philadelphia resisted the tax, were thrown into jail in Bethlehem, and then were liberated from prison by an armed mob led by John Fries, a Bucks County auctioneer. The federal Army, with an excessive display of strength, captured Fries and brought him to Philadelphia where he was convicted of treason and sentenced to death.[32] On Adams' desk as he wrestled with the alternatives of a war declaration or a peace initiative was the matter of whether to pardon Fries or to have him hanged. (Fries was eventually pardoned.) If Adams opted for war, how many additional executions of tax resisters would he have to approve before it was over? Hadn't the War for Independence involved popular resistance to taxes levied for the support of a standing army?

Adams does not deserve sole credit for the outbreak of peace between the United States and France in 1799-1800. At one critical moment Washington, whose authority was massive, let Adams know that he would support a peace initiative—the ex-president's last major gift to the nation in the months before his death. Talleyrand, whatever his reputation in other cases, was essential to the process. For the United States the benefits of peace were substantial. Cutbacks in military development made it possible to reduce taxes. Merchants and ship owners, who had opposed war despite the French seizures of American ships, could continue to profit from trade with belligerent Europeans. American friendship with France set a cordial stage for negotiating the Louisiana Purchase in 1803. The nation was spared much expense, much killing, and, as the Jeffersonians were willing to speculate, a possible drift toward Hamiltonian military dictatorship. The course of events, however, seemed to diminish Adams and his divided and declining Federalist Party. President Jefferson, not Adams, got the credit for the reduced taxes and for the Louisiana purchase which the Adams-brokered peace with France had helped to make possible.

2) *Thomas Jefferson and the Embargo as a Substitute for War*

In the summer and fall of 1807 President Thomas Jefferson, like Adams eight years earlier, chose a strategy of peace in the face of a crisis which could just as well have produced a war. This time England was the primary antagonist. By the end of 1805 Napoleon was in control of the European continent and the British Royal Navy had nearly absolute control of the seas. Neither France nor England respected America's neutral shipping rights, and the British used their power not only to confiscate American ships but to abduct American sailors and to force (or "impress") them into the Royal Navy. Some of these men were British deserters—an estimated 20,000 of whom escaped the Royal Navy for opportunities in American merchant shipping. The war in Europe had inflated prices for commercial goods. American merchants could turn a profit even if only one out of three or four of their ships got through the British blockade, but they complained bitterly about interference with the shipping rights of neutrals. The British argued that any United States trade with France helped Napoleon in his imperial ambitions. In June 1807 a U.S.-England war crisis flared when a British naval vessel, the *Leopard*, in quest of British sailors who had mutinied and deserted, fired upon a U.S. frigate, the *Chesapeake*, and killed three persons.[33]

President Jefferson, unlike Adams in 1799-1800, did not have to risk his political future to avoid war. He had the support of his party and was nearing political retirement. After an extended time of frustrated negotiation, Jefferson decided to initiate a total embargo—a prohibition on all exports to all countries from American ports. The embargo lasted for fourteen months, from December 1807 to March 1809, the end of Jefferson's second term. It did succeed in avoiding war. Nevertheless, typical American history textbooks treat the embargo as a near total failure, and the 1812 war of James Madison, Jefferson's successor, as a partial success. The embargo was a "Jeffersonian nightmare," and the war was "The Second War of Independence." Textbooks often quote the "O Grab Me" epithet ("embargo" spelled backwards) which critics used to scorn the embargo, as well as the heroic wartime words of Oliver Hazard Perry on Lake Erie, "We have met the enemy and they are ours." What accounts for this apparent pro-war bias?[34]

One problem is that the textbooks judge Jefferson by unrealistic triumphalist goals rather than by the realistic and more modest achievement of peace. They judge the embargo as less desirable than a U.S. military victory, ignoring the fact that victory would have been both unlikely and very costly. In 1807-08 victory would have meant that warring nations, England and France, would accept U.S. rights of free trade and stop interfering with American vessels. Victory would also have meant that England in particular would end her policy of impressing U.S. seamen into the British navy.

President Jefferson himself in part was responsible for the United States' unrealistic expectations. He overestimated the likely British response to his combination of American threats and idealism. England was at war. Full relief for American grievances would come when the Napoleonic wars were over, and not before. In the meantime, the best the United States could do was to stay out of the European war. Jefferson's embargo achieved that goal. It was an alternative to war. It was not a low-cost means to achieve an equivalent of military victory, nor should it be judged by that standard.

The embargo required great national discipline, especially from the commercial interests. Jefferson soon experienced how difficult it was to generate a patriotic willingness to make sacrifices in a nation engaging not in war, but in a nonviolent substitute for war. Most merchants obeyed the embargo, but the effort produced no heroic martyrs whose honor could be celebrated in a campaign to stir the blood of national unity. Violators of the embargo rules became increasingly bold, though they remained a minority. The press focused upon cases of disobedience to the law and upon signs of growing anger and disunity in the country. President Jefferson, at root a great idealist who had confidence in human goodness, did not find a way to inspire the nation to a high sense of duty and discipline needed for a peaceable moral equivalent for war. Although his half-way pacifism had avoided war, he ended his presidency in frustration. In light of the costs of the war the United States might have fought in 1807-08—the killing of thousands of people, the wasting of fortunes and property, the empowering of nationalistic militarism—the country got a good bargain.

The War of 1812: Unnecessary and Ineffectual

In 1812 President James Madison led the United States into a war with England that was no more necessary or well-advised than war would have been for Jefferson in 1807-08. The maritime issues were substantially unchanged in Madison's administration. The war in Europe continued. The United States had repealed her total embargo, but continued the policy of economic coercion in other forms. In 1810 the American war spirit received a great boost when a group of youthful "War Hawks," mostly from western states, were elected to Congress. The War Hawks, led by Henry Clay of Kentucky, were obsessed with British insults to national honor both at sea and in the west, where they encouraged Indian resistance to the American advance. Like Hamilton in 1799, the War Hawks relished the prospects of expansionism. They wanted Canada, Florida, the fur trade—an end to the British presence in North America. Henry Clay boasted that the rifle-bearing militia marksmen of his own state could by themselves take Canada. President Madison, not equal to the courage of Adams and Jefferson, caved in to the pressures of a belligerent minority.

Madison's request for a declaration of war came just as England was removing one of the major U.S. grievances. In 1811 crops failed throughout England. By the spring of 1812, the British need of U.S. trade became so great that the government repealed the "Orders in Council" which had authorized attacks on American shipping. The repeal was June 16, 1812. Two days later, the United States Senate, unaware of England's changed policy, voted by a margin of nineteen to thirteen to accept President Madison's recommendation for declaration of war against England. The Senate also voted on a declaration of war against France at the same time, which the president had not asked for. That measure went down eighteen to fourteen.

One historian charitably termed the result "America's strangest war."[35] A three-pronged invasion of Canada failed on all fronts; the navy lost more engagements than it won; a British force landed in the Chesapeake Bay area, easily took Washington, and set fire to the Capitol and the White House. In 1812, when the war began, England was fully preoccupied with Napoleon. By 1814 Napoleon had been defeated and England was in a position to press its advantage in North America. As the war went badly, the United States fractured on political and regional lines. New England bitterly opposed the war. In late 1814 the New England Federalist dissidents held a convention in Hartford, Connecticut, to consider constitutional changes. An extremist Federalist minority proposed secession from the union and a separate peace with England. The war ended officially on Christmas Eve of 1814 with the signing of the Treaty of Ghent. The sides merely agreed to stop fighting and to restore the boundaries of 1812. The Americans, fortunate not to have lost territory, got nothing on the issues for which they had fought—impressment, search and seizures, or Indian alliances. Several thousand Americans and Englishmen had killed each other for no good purpose, unless one considers the slaughter of Indians and the taking of their lands a good purpose.

The war had a bloody postscript. On January 8, 1815, two weeks after the treaty was signed, a British assault force outside New Orleans foolishly crossed an open plain to attack well-defended American positions commanded by General Andrew Jackson. The American artillery mowed down the British—2,000 men in a brief time. Although the battle had no effect on the peace treaty, and although rifle-fire had little to do with the outcome, the American people celebrated the Battle of New Orleans as a great triumph of frontier militia marksmanship over professional British military corruption.[36] A new popular song swept the country—"The Hunters of Kentucky"—feeding the illusions that the United States had won the war and that Henry Clay's hardy Kentucky militiamen had gotten the victory. "We can hide our shame for the moment in the smoke of Jackson's victory," one observer later characterized the government's mood, and "brag the country into a belief that it has been a glorious war."[37]

Andrew Jackson and a Culture of Violence

A surge of nationalist fervor and expansionist sentiment followed the War of 1812 The United States economy and population grew at an astonishing rate. A dynamic and optimistic new nationalism expressed itself in many ways: growing popular participation in local and national politics, a host of new reform movements to correct and improve the character of American democracy, a series of Supreme Court decisions by John Marshall's court to uphold rights of property and national commerce, and Noah Webster's advocacy of a new national language. As the nation expanded in the 1820s and 1830s, violence and rioting within the country increased and took new forms.

In response to the War of 1812 and to the new mood of national belligerence, peace-minded people created nearly fifty new voluntary peace societies. In 1828 most of these local and state groups came together in the American Peace Society, led by a retired Maine sea captain, William Ladd. The peace societies were a new form of war resistance, akin to other voluntary reform associations that thrived in those decades, but they failed in their grander goal to create a national culture of peace. It was Andrew Jackson, the hero of New Orleans and president of the United States from 1829 to 1837, who became the dominant symbol of America.

Andrew Jackson believed in the republican ideal of the nation's founders. He aimed to reform and to restore a republic of virtue in the face of alarming signs of political corruption.[38] Unlike John Adams and Thomas Jefferson, however, Jackson was not restrained by enlightened codes of civility or by fears that an American military class might pose special dangers for the character of the republic. Personally, Jackson was an exceptionally impulsive, passionate, and violent man. The violent impulses were reflected in the public policies of the age of "Jacksonian democracy," extending beyond his own administration to the Mexican-American War of 1846-48.

Jackson's personality was not a quirk. It reflected profound cultural forces from three regions that contributed the most to the dark violent side of America's character. The first region was the English-Scotch-Irish borderland of Jackson's ancestors.[39] For six centuries the borderland between England and Scotland had been the scene of unrelenting invasion and counter-invasion. The people of that region evolved a social system for survival in face of protracted violence—a system that placed high value upon personal self-rule, clan loyalty, and the right of self-defense. They were far removed from the English common law "duty to retreat" doctrine. The borderlanders were hostile to outsiders, quick to avenge insults, and suspicious of organized government and of organized religion. They taught their children, especially the boys, to express their wills without restraint. Jackson's American mother taught her son a code of moral behavior which had deep roots in Europe: "Andrew, never tell a lie, nor take what is not your own, nor sue anybody for slander, assault and battery. Always settle them cases yourself."[40]

A massive migration of English-Scotch-Irish borderlanders to the U.S. began in 1717. In America this particular European culture merged with the culture of another region which in many ways suited their style—the western frontier. On the frontier people were removed from many of the legal controls and social pressures of civilization in established settlements to the east. The notion that each individual should carry lethal weapons, rather than keeping weapons safely at a central armory under community control, was distinctive to the frontier.[41] The borderlanders were ruthless fighters against Native Americans, and Andrew Jackson earned a reputation as one of the greatest of Indian-fighters. As president, Jackson presided over the forcible removal of the civilized tribes of the Southeast to designated "Indian Territory"—later Oklahoma.

The Old South as a region was also clearly distinguished by high levels of violence, especially crimes against persons. The murder rate in South Carolina and Kentucky, for example, was far higher than in Massachusetts. Southern violence had to do with social reputation and honor. Southern society was rigidly layered, with African American slaves at the bottom level. Social pressure dictated that white men should resort to violence to preserve white manhood and personal status when their property, self-esteem or families were threatened.[42] Lower-class violence took the form of rough-and-tumble wrestling, eye-gouging, and direct physical maiming. Upper-class men were more likely to defend their honor by resorting to formal duels in cases of unresolvable insults and disputes. In 1806 Andrew Jackson and his enemy, Charles Dickinson, settled their dispute by firing pistols at each other from twenty-four feet. Dickinson took his bullet in the groin and died hours later. Jackson was hit non-fatally in the chest and carried the bullet, along with resulting health problems, for the rest of his life.[43] The event established Jackson not as a murderer but as a man of honor and of iron will. Henry Clay, Speaker of the House of Representatives, believed that dueling was a "pernicious practice" which violated his religious obligations. He voted to outlaw dueling. Nevertheless, in 1826 Clay fought a duel with John Randolph and later gloried in "a state of composure and satisfaction, which I should not have enjoyed, if the occasion had not occurred." Clay and Randolph both survived the duel with enhanced honor and social status.[44]

Although the South and the West were especially violent regions, the problems of violence, including the practice of dueling, were nationwide. The rise of urban immigrant slums set a context for ethnic and religious rioting. From the 1830s to the Civil War there were at least thirty-five major riots in the cities of Baltimore, Philadelphia, New York and Boston. The violence extended to cities in the Midwest and Lower Mississippi Valley as well. Violent mobs directed their hostilities against Blacks, Catholics, abolitionists, factory owners, bankers and others.[45] Urban rioting had been an expression of popular resistance to authority in the colonial era, but the urban riots of "Jacksonian Democracy" were more destructive and less respectful of the people and symbols of power.

Doing Evil to Achieve Good: Florida and Mexico

In 1818 Andrew Jackson, then a general in the U.S. Army, had taken the law into his own hands with an invasion of Spanish Florida. President James Monroe had commissioned Jackson to pursue and punish Indians who were using the Florida border for protection after raids across the border into the U.S.. The president's orders, however, specifically forbade attacks on posts under the Spanish flag. Jackson attacked and defeated the enemy, hanged two Indian chiefs without trial, executed two British citizens who allegedly had helped the Indians, and seized the Spanish posts of St. Marks and Pensacola. Instead of disavowing Jackson's illegal and unauthorized aggression, the U.S. government used the event to intimidate Spain into selling Florida to the U.S. and into agreeing to a boundary for the Louisiana territory which extended to the Pacific Ocean and included Oregon. If Spain had refused to deal, the U.S. would have found an excuse for taking Florida by force. The means were morally discreditable, but Jackson emerged an ever-greater national hero.

In 1846 President James K. Polk, who was nicknamed "Young Hickory" for traits he supposedly shared with "Old Hickory," Andrew Jackson, initiated a war of aggression against Mexico. Polk, like Jackson, was descended from a line of English-Scottish borderers. Critics of Polk's war condemned it as unprovoked aggression, and also because it was designed to extend the institution of slavery into new territories and states. But the anti-war arguments lacked conviction and force in the face of the marvelous fruits of national expansion. The Mexican War added half a million square miles to the United States, including the California harbors of San Diego and San Francisco. The ends appeared to justify the means.

Anti-slavery northerners objected that the war would extend slavery. In 1819 Mexico had gained independence from Spain; in 1829 it formally ended slavery. Slave-owning American settlers who moved into Texas ignored the prohibition against slavery—as well as the Mexican requirement that all settlers convert to Catholicism. In 1835-36 the Texans revolted, defeated the Mexican army at San Jacinto, declared an independent "Lone Star Republic," and sought annexation to the United States. Congress took action to annex Texas in 1845, after the election of Polk to the presidency. Mexico prepared for war. Ulysses S. Grant, who fought in the Mexican War as a lieutenant-colonel, later wrote in his personal memoirs, "The occupation, separation and annexation [of

The Missing Peace

Texas] were, from the inception of the movement to its final consummation, a conspiracy to acquire territory out of which slave states might be formed for the American Union."[46]

Nor did Grant approve of the way Polk moved deliberately to force war upon Mexico. Polk ordered General Zachary Taylor to occupy disputed territory between the Nueces and the Rio Grande rivers in the hope that Mexico would strike a first blow. Then he could claim justification for a full-scale invasion all the way to Mexico City. And so it happened. In Grant's view, the war was both evil and unnecessary. The United States might have acquired all this territory through the process of natural settlement, negotiation, and eventual purchase. Instead the United States fought a war which inflamed passions, divided the country, and led directly to the Civil War, or, as Grant called it, "the Southern rebellion." "Nations, like individuals, are punished for their transgressions," Grant wrote. "We got our punishment in the most sanguinary and expensive war of modern times."[47]

The most famous act of protest against the Mexican War was by Henry David Thoreau of Massachusetts who spent a night in the Concord jail for refusing to pay the poll tax. Thoreau wrote an antiwar and antislavery essay, "On Civil Disobedience," (first titled "Resistance to Civil Government") which made a case for disobedience to unjust laws which violated moral and religious law. Thoreau had been influenced by debates within the abolitionist movement which had led to the creation of the Non-Resistance Society in 1839.[48]

For the thirteen thousand U.S. troops who died in the Mexican War, the war was costly enough in its own terms. Although the U.S. troops won every significant battle, the conditions of army life were wretched. According to official statistics, 6,750 men deserted, from a total of 90,000 regulars and volunteers. General Taylor complained that the Mexicans offered women and 320 acres of land each if they deserted. Some 47% of the regulars in Taylor's initial army of 4,000 men were foreigners.[49] One enterprising deserter to the Mexican side was an Irish Catholic, Captain Thomas Riley. Riley was commissioned a lieutenant in the Mexican army and organized the Battalion of St. Patrick, which fought in the Mexican defense of Monterrey and Buena Vista in the north, and later in the battle of Churubusco on General Winfield Scott's way from Vera Cruz to Mexico City. General Scott defeated them, court-martialed the survivors, and had fifty of them hanged. Today a plaque at the church of San Jacinto in Mexico City is inscribed "In memory of the heroic San Patricio Battalion martyrs who gave their lives for Mexico during the unjust American invasion of 1847."[50]

The standard American history of the Mexican War, a massive two-volume work by Justin H. Smith (1919), did not mention the names of Riley and the Battalion of St. Patrick. In a footnote Smith credited General Scott's restraint in hanging only fifty deserters at Churubusco, as some eighty had been captured and were eligible for execution.[51] Indeed, Smith's concluding paragraphs commend this war of conquest because, among other reasons, "Humanity and moderation—such humanity and moderation as are practicable amid hostilities—gilded our arms." Having conquered all of Mexico, the Americans "gave back much that we took, and paid for the rest more than it was worth to Mexico." The Mexicans, "being what they were," got what they deserved. Smith saw the Mexican War as another event in the march of human progress—the power of redemptive violence: "Forcible acquisitions may indeed be commendable. In that way Rome civilized Europe, England gave peace, order and comparative happiness to India, and our own country came into being; and none of us would undo these results."[52]

Justin Smith was a more thorough historian than Ulysses S. Grant. But Grant's moral warnings about warfare leading to even more destructive warfare have gained force in the twentieth century, with its repeated experience of total war. Some historians report that Americans have not fully shaken off their sense of guilt for the conquest of Mexico. The invasion clearly violated the code of international ethics.[53] Yet the results were gratifying and apparently essential for America's manifest destiny. California's gold, discovered in 1849, enriched the nation. New Mexico's uranium a century later helped build the first atomic bombs. To justify such fruits of conquest one might agree with Ralph Waldo Emerson, who opposed the war but welcomed the annexations because "most of the great results of history are brought about by discreditable means."[54] For Emerson in this case the ends justified the means. Another option is to accept General Grant's invitation to imagine alternative histories less afflicted by violence. Grant imagined that the United States might have taken over the Southwest and California peaceably by a massive settlement of English-speaking peoples over several decades. We might also imagine that a separate nation might have come into existence on the west coast, and that the Republic of Texas, and a Republic of California might have joined with the United States in a confederation less addicted to violence and expansionism than was the American nation in reality. Such a scenario would have violated the ideal of manifest destiny, but the peaceable co-existence of the United States and Canada already contradicted that ideal.

Manifest Destiny and the 49th Parallel

In the nineteenth century, "manifest destiny" was a flexible concept. Expansive nationalists looking at a map of North America could see how geography dictated a unified arena for United States democracy, from east coast to west coast and from the Arctic Circle to the Rio Grande. "To me, sir, " said one congressman during the War of 1812, "it appears that the Author of Nature has marked our limits in the south, by the Gulf of Mexico; and on the north, by the regions of eternal frost."[55] Canada's existence as a separate nation refuted the idea of manifest destiny as a geographical concept. In two wars, the War for Independence and the War of 1812, the United States invasions failed to subdue and absorb Canada. The ideology of manifest destiny would have been quite serviceable to justify another major war for that purpose. And yet it became possible after 1815 for the United States and Canada to accept each other's existence and eventually agree to a common undefended border.[56]

In 1815, immediately after the war, the U.S. and Great Britain began a naval arms race on the Great Lakes, with each side speeded on by rumors of escalation on the other side. The British knew the Americans wanted Canada and feared the United States' ability to build armed vessels more rapidly on the Great Lakes in case of another war.[57] Nevertheless in 1817 the British Minister to Washington, Sir Charles Bagot, and the American acting secretary of state, Richard Rush negotiated a disarmament agreement to limit the number of warships on the Great Lakes. The next year a joint commission agreed to set the boundary to the Rocky Mountains at the 49th parallel. In 1842 the Webster-Ashburton Treaty settled a disputed boundary between Maine and New Brunswick, although critics on both sides considered the agreement a betrayal of vital interests. The Oregon boundary was settled at the 49th parallel, with Vancouver Island going to Canada, despite President James K. Polk's dangerous and unnecessary bluster and saber-rattling.[58] If Polk's style of expansionist hostility had dominated either side in diplomatic relations after 1815, the U.S.-Canadian boundary problems may well have resulted in conflict and war. For the benefit of all, and in contradiction of manifest destiny, two nations in North America found it possible to live at peace.

William Stafford, an American poet of strong peace convictions, celebrated the undefended U.S.-Canada border with verses set over against battlefield memorials. His poem was titled, "At the Un-National Monument along the Canadian Border."

> This is the field where the battle did not happen,
> where the unknown soldier did not die.
> This is the field where grass joined hands,
> where no monument stands,
> and the only heroic thing is the sky.
>
> Birds fly here without any sound,
> unfolding their wings across the open.
> No people killed — or were killed — on this ground
> hallowed by neglect and an air so tame
> that people celebrate it by forgetting its name.[59]

Peace Gains and Losses

The themes of war and peace in United States history are closely related to each other. Idealistic visions of peace were especially prominent in colonial Pennsylvania, in the ideas of classical republicanism, and in early American popular culture. The ideals bore fruit as they were applied in specific cases of diplomacy and conflict resolution. Presidents John Adams and Thomas Jefferson, guided in part by a classical republican philosophy, took effective actions to avoid warfare in 1798-99 and 1806-07. Study of the outbreaks of peace in United States history should accompany the study of war. Neither the achievements of peace nor the outbreaks of war should be considered inevitable.

Peace ideals were more central in the early years of the republic, when the Quaker presence and memory was strongest and before the classical ideal of a republic of virtue gave way to aggressive nationalist expansionism and competitive commercial capitalism. Those who are inclined to put down the peace impulse as irrelevant or misguided have argued that the pacifist inclinations of the early republic were a product of immaturity and innocence. They said that once the United States grew up, she would have to accept certain realities of national and international relations. Even Thomas Jefferson, the half-way pacifist, agreed to the founding of the U.S. Military Academy at West Point, in New York. He gave in to the argument that the United States would need a professional standing army capable of defending its interests and projecting its power across the continent and, eventually, around the world.

The classical ideal of the United States as a republic of special virtue has been subjected to withering critique. The United States in reality turned out to be far less exceptional among nations than the founders anticipated. J. G. A. Pocock, historian of political thought, effectively contrasted the ideals with the realities: "Democratic federalism grew into the greatest empire of patronage and influence the world has known . . . . America may have guaranteed the survival of the forms of corruption it was created to resist."[60] By "patronage" Pocock meant that United States government officials granted jobs and financial awards to friends not on the basis of merit or virtue, but on the basis of self-perpetuating bureaucratic power. It is ironical that the nation founded to oppose a militarist-aristocrat-government complex turned toward an expansionist manifest destiny and eventually created the largest interlocking military-industrial-government complex in the world.

It remains important to acknowledge the gap between ideals and realities. But a responsible view of American history must avoid both cynicism and triumphalism. Peacemakers in United States history were not just dreamers; they were actors. Their achievements, however limited, must be honored and their visions must be revisited for inspiration to meet current and future challenges.

Chapter 4

Liberty for All:
The Antislavery Movement

How could a nation founded on principles of liberty and equality tolerate slavery? Historians have written volumes to answer this dilemma. Winthrop Jordan, Carl Degler and others argued that Europeans, particularly the English, had long racist traditions and so accepted the notion of African inferiority, even subhumanness.[1] Edmund Morgan suggested that American freedom depended upon a system of slavery. To prevent the development of a rebellious underclass of unpropertied "rabble," English colonists invented a system to enslave a group of people who did not know the rights of Englishmen, rather than sharing the abundance of land in the New World.[2]

Thomas Jefferson, perhaps the most articulate spokesperson for human rights of his time, recognized the terrible paradox of slavery in a "free" country. He described it as having the "wolf by the ears; and we can neither hold him, nor safely let him go. Justice is in one scale, and self-preservation in the other."[3] As a slave owner, Jefferson chose to keep his slaves for "self-preservation." Jefferson's decision might have alerted all future antislavery advocates that the struggle against slavery was going to require more than persuading slave owners that slavery was unjust and morally intolerable. In fact, in the early years of the country most people, if they even questioned slavery, accepted it as a necessary evil. While the evils of slavery seem obvious to contemporary readers, it did not seem obvious to the vast majority of white citizens who took its existence for granted and grew up accepting without question the prevalent justifications for the "peculiar institution." Politicians told them slaves were better off in the United States than in "savage" and "heathen"

Africa, although as Barbara Fields points out, those who had actually been to Africa knew these stereotypes were false.[4] Southern supporters of slavery, like George Fitzhugh, even went so far as to suggest that southern slaves were better off than northern factory workers, concluding that the "unrestricted exploitation of so-called free society is more oppressive to the labourer than domestic slavery."[5] Protestant ministers assured their congregations that God ordained slavery, reminding them that the Bible was full of support for slavery, from the example of Abraham, who was a slaveholder, to the command of St. Paul that slaves obey their masters.[6] For many, whose lives seemed untouched by the pain of slavery, it simply was not an issue.

Why did a handful of people begin to oppose slavery? Why did some people come to see this system as morally wrong in a climate where it was generally accepted? This question has portentous consequences for contemporary discussions and it is important to discuss it from both a slave and free perspective.

For slaves, the evils of slavery were daily realities. But to challenge the system of slavery rather than simply accommodate to it often required of slaves (as it does of battered women and children today, and oppressed people everywhere) enough self-respect to recognize the abuse and enough courage to challenge it. Frederick Douglass, one of the best known of the "self-emancipated" slaves observed, "Give [a slave] a bad master, and he aspires to a good master; give him a good master and he wishes to become his own master."[7] A good master treated a slave with a measure of respect. Only a very few records of all those who attempted to escape slavery are known, but those records, many in the form of narratives written by the slaves themselves or written with the aid of a sympathetic friend, tell powerful stories of men and women who came to recognize their own humanness and made the choice to live free or die in the attempt. Separated by miles and laws from much of African culture, surrounded with the rhetoric of liberty, but kept in chains, many children of Africa could say with Martin Prosser, who helped his brother Gabriel organize a slave rebellion in Virginia in 1800, "I can no longer bear what I have borne."[8]

Throughout the colonial period, but with a dramatic crescendo in the early nineteenth century, a few white voices also spoke out against the system of slavery. Who were these people and how did they learn to see clearly enough to stand courageously against what was taken for granted by the majority in their society? It is instructive to follow the painfully slow evolution of thought among the Quakers, the group most associated with anti-slavery activity. Because of its early practice of religious toleration, colonial Rhode Island was home for a number of Quakers. These Quakers commonly were involved in shipping and trade; part of which involved trading in slaves. Elizabeth Buffum Chace, an active antislavery Quaker, quaintly but profoundly observed "that the spirit of early Quakerism came to realize the terrible iniquity of the slave trade . . . ." As a result the Yearly Meeting censured the "importation of Negroes" in 1727. But this action did not touch the issue of slave ownership. Forty-six years later, the Yearly Meeting merely recommended that "Friends, who have slaves in possession, treat them with tenderness . . . ." Not until 1780 did the New England Yearly Meeting abolish slavery among its members.[9] While the Quakers were about fifty years ahead of the rest of the nation, it is important to reflect on the fact that they took fifty-three years to move from an acknowledgment of the problem to elimination of slaveholding among their members. Even then, Quakers in the early nineteenth century did not agree about wider participation in activity to abolish slavery from the nation.

Elizabeth Buffum suffered ostracism and criticism from her closest friends in Quaker meetings when she organized the Female Anti-Slavery Society of Fall River, Rhode Island in 1735. The tension between her antislavery activism and the belief of the meeting became so intense that, as she wrote, "after a long struggle I was compelled, in order to secure my own peace of mind, to resign my membership in the Society [of Friends]."[10] Controversy among Friends eventually led to a split in the Quakers between the Hicksites and Orthodox in 1827-1828 — a split which was repeated later by all the major Protestant denominations including the Methodists, Baptists, and Presbyterians.[11] While both groups maintained antislavery activity, the more evangelical Orthodox tended to favor political means, while the more liberal Hicksites favored direct action. The antislavery Quakers, once convinced of the rightness of their cause, became a major moving force in nonviolent resistance to slavery. This resistance took many forms including forming antislavery societies, participating in the free produce movement, publishing tracts, and aiding fugitives on the underground railroad.

Nonresistance and Antislavery

Quakers, with their historic peace testimony, were but one group to offer nonviolent resistance to slavery. In fact, the antislavery movement makes a fascinating study of the many variations and nuances of peacemaking, including the way in which arguments over these differences derailed some of the movement's effectiveness in the struggle against slavery. Three groups were most visible and consistent in their adherence to nonviolent principles: the Quakers, the Garrisonians and the Tappanites. These three groups had major differences in religious perspective, the nature of nonresistance, the roles of women, and their relationship to the institutional church and the political system.

Quakers believed in "that of God in every[one]" or "the Light within." This made them strong believers in the capacity of all to do good, and the possibility of appealing to the "Light within" as a way of bringing slavemasters to voluntary emancipation of their slaves. The belief in the divine within everyone also made most Quakers careful to make a distinction between condemning slaveholding and condemning slaveholders. Believing "God is no respecter of persons," Quakers were also much more tolerant and encouraging of women in leadership than the vast majority of their contemporaries, and women like Lucretia Mott and Elizabeth Buffum Chace were visible and vocal in their antislavery work. Generally, Quakers valued quiet, simple lives and most of them preferred to oppose slavery by appeals to conscience and by the witness of their honest, hospitable lives.

The Garrisonians were the most radical of the three groups. William Lloyd Garrison (1805-1879) son of a Calvinist mother and a sea-faring father, found his calling in publishing. Garrison composed the constitution of the Non-Resistance Society, formed in 1838, and outlined a program of complete abstention from violence, even in self-defense. Even more controversially, he pronounced that nonresistants should acknowledge only the authority of "divine government," and therefore should not participate in earthly governments. This included a refusal to vote as well as a refusal of military service and a refusal to pay taxes. Calling for immediate abolition of all slavery, Garrison labeled the U.S. Constitution "a covenant with death and an agreement with hell" because it supported slavery. He proposed that northern states should secede (peacefully) from the slaveholding South.[12] While this proposal might have allowed portions of the North to live less tainted by slavery, it is much less clear that it would have had any effect on the system of slavery in the South.

Garrisonian nonresistants spoke out against other forms of violence as well—domestic abuse, drunkenness and capital punishment, as well as slavery. They saw slave ownership, regardless of how one treated slaves, as an act of violence. In his desire to break completely with any complicity in slaveholding, Garrison insisted upon separation from any institutions that in any way upheld slavery, including the church. Few churches had taken a stand against slavery and he encouraged "coming out" of the "slavery-sanctifying" churches. He further alienated many church members by supporting the right of women, like Abbey Foster Kelley, to speak publicly and to be paid as an antislavery lecturer.

In May of 1840 the white antislavery movement split into two parts. Two wealthy merchants, the brothers Arthur and Lewis Tappan, questioned Garrison's radical pacifism, particularly his refusal to participate in the democratic process. Convinced that the Constitution (as well as the Bible) could be read as an antislavery document, they wanted to get involved in changing the government. The Tappans and their followers began to form the Liberty Party, a political party devoted to legally ending all slavery. Inclined to be more favorable towards both the institutions of government and the mainline churches (even though they had taken no stand against slavery), they also were more inclined to accept social norms regarding proper behavior for women. This meant that women would be allowed to attend meetings and organize in female societies, but they would not be permitted to speak to mixed-gender audiences.[13] The Liberty Party drew members from the more Calvinistic Congregationalists and Presbyterians, reflecting a less sanguine view of human nature than the Quakers, and a greater willingness to live with moral ambiguity than the Garrisonians. Always preferring nonviolent means, they nevertheless were open to the idea of "justified violence" under extenuating circumstances. For instance Lewis Tappan refused to use force to defend his own property from anti-abolitionist mobs, but his brother Arthur chose to arm himself. Centered in New York City, this group formed the American and Foreign Anti-Slavery Society and the American Missionary Society.

Colonization

Whites who lived closest to slavery were most likely to be aware of its inherent flaws. Yet it is not commonly recognized or acknowledged that until the 1830s most white antislavery activity occurred in the slaveholding states. Elihu Embree and Benjamin Lundy published some of the earliest antislavery newspapers in the South. The latter's paper, "The Genius of Universal Emancipation" estimated that in 1827 there were 106 antislavery societies in the South as compared with only twenty-four in the North. Several individuals came out with antislavery books, including Joseph Doddridge, an Episcopal minister in western Virginia (1824) and Robert J. Breckinridge of Kentucky, who wrote *Hints on Slavery* in 1830. The former understood the fallacy of the racial defense of slavery, arguing "We debase [slaves] to brutes and then use that debasement as an argument for perpetuating their slavery."[14]

Among southerners opposed to slavery, one of the most popular options was colonization. The American Colonization Society, organized in 1816, was supported by such notables as Henry Clay of Kentucky, and James Madison and James Monroe of Virginia. The society raised money to send slaves back to Liberia (est. 1822) in West Africa as free men and women. The proposition was expensive, funds were short, and soon it became more effective as a means to eliminate a free black population than to eliminate slavery. The racism was transparent. Only one founding member, Rev. Robert Finley, even took the time to discuss the proposal with any black leaders, and unfortunately he died in 1818. Nevertheless, as Carl Degler points out, in the minds of white southerners, colonization was clearly associated with an antislavery position, and a list of its proponents and detractors in general attests to that alignment.[15]

While a few black leaders like Lott Cary, Paul Cuffee and John B. Russwurm supported the colonization idea because it promised black freedom and independence, most African Americans vehemently opposed it. Blacks in Philadelphia held four mass meetings between 1817 and 1819 to protest the colonization society. Attracting upwards of 3000 African Americans to their meetings in the Bethel AME Church, the attenders unanimously denounced the colonization scheme. Their reasons are revealing. For many there was an allegiance to the United States as home and a deep resistance to leaving, in spite of its problems. Others had well-founded suspicions of schemes proposed by Whites, especially when one of the society's justifications for its existence was the unconcealed belief that Blacks were too inferior to make good American citizens. Rev. Jermain Loguen, a self-emancipated slave from Tennessee, mocked the logic that in the United States Blacks were "scum and offscourings of the earth," but if transported to Liberia, they would become "noble Christianizers of heathen Africa." He concluded, "We recognize in it [the Colonization Society] the most intense hatred of the colored race, clad in the garb of pretended philanthropy."[16]

The reason that most united free Blacks against colonization was a sense of solidarity with "their brethren in chains," believing that to accept colonization in Africa would strengthen the slave system by raising the price of slaves and removing the free black population. One of the meeting's resolutions stated "we feel there is more virtue in suffering privations with them [slaves], than fancied advantages for a season."[17]

These differing perceptions regarding the colonization movement are instructive and reflect some basic dissensions in analysis and perspective that were characteristic of the antislavery movement. Whites were acting with a great deal of presumption: presumption that the United States either could not or should not be a racially mixed democracy and presumption that Blacks who knew no home other than the United States would want to "return" to Africa.

Nevertheless, any southerner who spoke out against slavery and remained in the South demonstrated remarkable courage. Apart from the colonization movement, southern motives for opposing slavery were mixed. Some recognized the contradiction with religious tenets of the Golden Rule or of all humans created in the image of God. Samuel Janney, a Quaker from Virginia, objected to slavery because "it degrades men by regarding them as property."[18] Mary Berkeley Minor Blackford of Fredericksburg, Virginia, freed her slaves, assuming they would return to Africa. When they didn't, she hired them as house servants. She also ran a Sunday School for slaves, teaching them to read the Bible, in spite of a Virginia law that fined or imprisoned people for such behavior. Ironically, although the Grand Jury threatened her, Blacks could not serve as witnesses and no White could be found to testify against her, so she was never formally charged. With great prescience, she wrote in her diary:

How the practice of injustice hardens the feelings is perfectly wonderful; what is done under our own eyes would shock us to the last degree were it not for this hardening process. I am convinced that the time will come when we shall look back and wonder how Christians could sanction slavery.[19]

In addition to humanitarian and theological arguments, southerners made economic arguments against slavery. Perhaps the best known is that of Hinton Rowan Helper of North Carolina, who wrote *The Impending Crisis of the South*, first published in 1857. By examining data from the 1850 census (which had been supervised by the southern nationalist James D. B. DeBow and is notoriously inaccurate), Helper showed the economic superiority of the nonslave states over the slave states. In spite of numerous problems, the argument had its impact, eroding yet another basis for justifying slavery.

Gradual Emancipation

The northern states had freed their slaves at the time of the Revolution through a process of gradual emancipation, generally over a period of twenty to thirty years. This system gave slave masters a number of years of service from slaves, but also was intended to give masters responsibility for educating slaves in basic literacy and job skills to enable them to begin life successfully as freedmen and women. While not without problems, gradual emancipation effectively eliminated slavery in the northern states where the slave population was small.

Proposals for gradual emancipation of the rest of the nation's slaves often included colonization. It was hard to imagine a United States of equal black and white citizens. In January, 1824, the Ohio legislature proposed that Congress should set aside a certain sum each year to "repatriate" all persons of African descent, until there were none left in the country, slave or free. Eight northern states endorsed the idea, and Rufus King of New York introduced a bill in the Senate to create the funds for the proposal from the sale of public lands. But it met with such strong opposition from Georgia and South Carolina, foreshadowing much of the sectional conflict to come, that no action was taken. Most of the cost in repatriation schemes was in transportation.

Because southern wealth was primarily in slaves, the issue of compensating masters for their emancipated slaves was especially controversial.[20] Compensation would cost five or six hundred million dollars, a staggering sum. Moral purists argued that masters should not be compensated, since it rewarded them for their compliance with evil.

Nevertheless, some men like Elihu Burrit and John Greenleaf Whittier favored compensated emancipation, financed by the sale of public lands, as the honorable way for the country to disengage itself from complicity with an immoral system. Resources could be found to sustain the system of slavery, why not to eliminate it? With hindsight, it is worth comparing the cost of compensation to the five or six billion dollars spent on the Civil War, not to mention lost lives and a legacy of bitterness, and to ponder whether the war was not a greater compromise with moral purity.[21]

Nat Turner's Rebellion

The threat of danger from an enslaved population was never far from southerners' minds. Although they tried to portray their slaves as happy and contented, slavemasters knew that one of the costs of slavery was living with fear. This fear became vivid reality in August of 1831, when a slave preacher, Nat Turner, led a dramatic rebellion in Virginia. Believing himself to be chosen by God to lead his people out of slavery, Turner set out with his followers and swiftly killed sixty Whites, in a daring march for freedom. Their rebellion triggered hysterical fear and retaliatory violence throughout the South. Many innocent Blacks were killed and the bloody heads of the rebels were impaled on posts as a gruesome reminder to all.[22]

Fear triggered some alternative thinking as well, causing Virginia legislators to suggest proposals to gradually emancipate all Virginia's slaves, as a way of eliminating such violence. The vote to consider emancipation proposals was surprisingly close. The motion would have passed with the votes of twelve more legislators who professed to be antislavery, but were not prepared to discuss abolition.[23] It was a tragic failure of moral courage. Virginians chose to try to make an unworkable system work a little longer. They chose the power "solution" of stronger laws: prohibiting slaves to read, prohibiting slave meetings without a white person present, requiring white men to serve as patrollers, even requiring that white men carry guns to church. Thus, slavery was made more oppressive and Whites lost more freedom, but few Whites made this connection. The interconnectedness of all human freedom was clear to African Americans, however. Frederick Douglass challenged Whites to remember that "No one is truly free when anyone is a slave . . . . The issue is not whether the black man's slavery shall be perpetuated, but whether the freedom of any Americans can be permanent."

Moral Reform

Arguments for moral purity and Christian nonviolence pervaded the abolitionist movement in the 1830s. The religious revivals of the time emphasized both piety and reform. Many abolitionists, both black and white, believed that Jesus had prohibited Christians from violence. Some of them opposed all uses of force, including capital punishment, military service, lawsuits and use of violence in self-defense.

William Whipper, a wealthy black merchant, was a life time advocate of non-resistance. He used his business to aid fugitive slaves, helping them escape to property he owned in Upper Canada. While maintaining that the Holy Scriptures are the "greatest enemy" of war and that "as soon as they become fully understood, and practically adopted, wars and strifes will cease," Whipper argued that a belief in reason alone was sufficient to demonstrate the superiority and necessity of non-resistance. In 1837 he defended the following resolution: "Resolved: That the practice of non-resistance to physical aggression, is not only consistent with reason, but the surest method of obtaining a speedy triumph of the principles of universal peace."[24]

Many black leaders felt that intense efforts to demonstrate exemplary moral behavior would overcome the white belief in black inferiority, resulting in a free society of equals. Samuel E. Cornish, editor of one of the earliest black newspapers, *The Colored American* wrote

> No oppressed Colored American, who wishes to occupy that elevation in society, which God has designed he should occupy, should be intemperate or even touch as a beverage, intoxicating drinks, none should be idle or extravagant, none profane the Sabbath nor neglect the sanctuary of God, but all, all should be up and doing, should work while it is day. We owe it to ourselves and we owe it to the poor slaves, who are our brethren . . . . Let us show that we are worthy to be freemen; it will be the strongest appeal to the judgement and conscience of the slave-holder and his abettors, that can be furnished; and it will be a sure means of our elevation in society, and to the possession of all our rights, as men and citizens.[25]

This early phase of black organized efforts against slavery emphasized a holistic approach to the problem, utilizing a strategy of nonviolent moral reform.[26] Moral reform, as seen in Cornish's quote, was aimed at "elevating" the race and demonstrating that "we are worthy to be freemen," and that Blacks could function as responsible and respected citizens. To this end, many local groups organized schools, lyceums, literary societies, debating clubs, temperance groups, and self-help organizations. Through this self-help ran the hope that a visible demonstration of the humanness and virtuous living of free Blacks would convince the slave-owners to free their slaves.

At the national level a black convention movement, shaped by black ministerial leadership, encouraged the expansion and development of this program of moral reform as a means of both self-improvement and eliminating slavery. These hopes and strategies of the moral-reform movement are expressed in an address by Abraham Shadd, William Hamilton and William Whipper given at the Second Annual Convention for the Improvement of the Free People of Colour held in Philadelphia in June 1832:

> We yet anticipate in the moral strength of this nation, a final redemption from those evils that have been illegitimately entailed on us as a people. We yet expect by due exertions on our part, together with the aid of the benevolent philanthropists of our country, to acquire a moral and intellectual strength, that will unshaft the calumnious darts of our adversaries, and present to the world a general character, that they will feel bound to respect and admire.[27]

This exhortation reveals an underlying assumption that the "evils that have been illegitimately entailed" resulted from differences in behavior and intellect, not physical differences, economics, fear, or any of a host of other possible causes, and that as these differences were overcome through "exertions on our part," the evils would be lifted and racial attitudes would change. This belief in the power of moral reform to eliminate slavery anticipated a moral response from the slaveholders, predicated on the conviction that society could be perfected through the progress of the individual.

Hope that society could be transformed through individual choice was widespread. The fires of the Second Great Awakening sparked massive revivals as Charles Finney, the "father of modern revivalism" preached across upstate New York and Ohio, exhorting people to repent, convert and lead lives of moral purity. The rise of an antislavery movement in the context of a religious revival explains much about the particular strategies, and approaches used. Believers were encouraged to actively work to create a better society, not only to demonstrate the individual's sincere conversion, but as a means of ushering in the millennium, the thousand year peaceful reign of Christ. In their attempts to rid the country of evil, alcohol and slavery were targeted as two of the vilest evidences of sin in the social fabric. As a result, nearly every town touched by revivals began forming temperance societies and antislavery societies. Temperance attracted far more adherents, in part because it was a more socially acceptable cause. Abolitionism was not for the faint hearted; those who spoke against the "peculiar institution" often faced angry mobs, eggings, arson, and ostracism.

The great majority of abolitionists saw slavery as a moral evil, to be ended through what they called "moral suasion." Thus in 1833 the Declaration of Sentiments of the American Anti-Slavery Society called for "the overthrow of prejudice by the power of love—and the abolition of slavery by the spirit of repentance."[28] Members of the American Anti-Slavery Society were committed to using the power of words, rather than physical violence to end slavery, although disagreements later broke out over the extent to which signing the Declaration of Sentiments committed one to being completely nonviolent. The document laid out a wide variety of thoughtful nonviolent means: preaching, lecturing, publishing, political actions, boycotts of slave produce and civil disobedience to any laws that supported slavery. With representatives from eleven states, and signatures from sixty-two men and women, white and black, the Anti-Slavery Declaration heralded a major upheaval in the social order. Yet, for all of its remarkableness as a model of collaborative work and nonviolent sentiments, James McCune Smith pointed out an Achilles heel. "It is a strange omission in the constitution of the antislavery society that no mention is made of social equality either of slaves or free Blacks."

Communitarianism

The spirit of reform led many to seek to create more perfect societies, and a precious few dared to put into practice Smith's call for true social equality. More than sixty utopian communities were started in the 1840s. Two communities are particularly important here, because not only did they practice nonresistance and antislavery, but their communities deliberately included African Americans as equal participants as a way of modeling their belief in the basic equality of all humans. The best known of these is Hopedale, a community formed in 1841 in Milford, Massachusetts, by the Universalist minister, Adin Ballou. Ballou, who served as president of the Non-Resistance Society, wrote *Christian Non-Resistance*, published in 1846, one of the most comprehensive statements of the nonresistance position in the abolitionist period. Ballou made a distinction, not held by all, between non-injurious force and injurious force. Non-injurious force was force used to prevent children, drunks or others incapable of helping themselves from hurting themselves or others.

To some, including Leo Tolstoy (who read *Christian Non-Resistance* in 1890), this was too great a compromise with the idea of force. They saw force or coercion as synonymous with violence and fundamentally destructive to all relationships. Slavery as a coercive relationship was clearly wrong; but the government also exercised coercive powers through taxation and the military, which is why many nonresisters were attracted to anarchy.[29] To live a nonviolent life was to live without coercion. This presented a basic question for the communitarians of how to model noncoercive human relationships.

The Hopedale community owned property (not everyone approved of land ownership), including some thirty houses and a church which also served as a school. The community supported itself through various small businesses including printing, manufacturing clocks, building boxes and making shoes. They experimented with paying everyone an equal wage, with equal division of profits, but settled on giving everyone a basic minimum salary with wage incentives based on production. Although they ran into serious financial problems in 1856, the Hopedale community maintained its nonresistant character throughout the Civil War.

Another nonresistant biracial community was the Northhampton Association in Northhampton, Massachusetts, led by Garrison's brother in law, George Benson, who had been a vice president of the Nonresistance Society. Like Quakers, this community prided itself on being non-creedal and open to all, but there was a general acceptance of antislavery and anti-war and temperance principles among the members. Its main enterprise was a silk thread factory. All members did some manual labor and all were paid equally. Children were taught primarily through physical activities: boys gathered mulberry leaves, girls spread them on the shelves for the silkworms. Geography might be taught by building relief maps outdoors, using mud from a nearby stream. Corporal punishment was strictly forbidden. Garrison was so impressed with their education that he sent his son to boarding school there.

Sojourner Truth, born a slave in New York and named Isabella Baumfree, was the best known African American to participate in the community. At first she was not very impressed with the spartan nature of the community, but she grew in her appreciation for the principles that were being lived out. When she heard the articulate, but despairing Frederick Douglass argue in 1856 that slavery could only end by slave revolt and violent resistance, she rose from her seat and called out, "Frederick, is God dead?"[30] True to her chosen name, Sojourner didn't stay long at Northhampton, but she carried the vision of a vibrant and peaceful interracial community with her.

Another African American, David Ruggles, who had worked for years in New York City aiding fugitives, including Frederick Douglass when he made his escape from Maryland, came to Northhampton to rest. Although only in his thirties, he was destitute and blind—due to the intensity of his work, agitating, educating and even serving time in jail. While there, Ruggles experimented with water cures for the benefit of his health and eventually became enough improved to set up a water cure center of his own.

Like many communities of the 1840s, the Northhampton Association broke up because of insufficient capital after four years of operation. One can raise the question of how much actual pressure these communities brought against the system of slavery, but peaceful interracial communities were a visible (and very controversial) model of a society few Americans believed was possible.

More often northern Whites lacked the courage or imagination to work on an equal basis with African Americans. Quality schools refused Blacks admission, Blacks who did find a way to earn an education could not find work commensurate with their abilities, and while the right to vote was being expanded during the period of "Jacksonian democracy" (1828-1836) to include even unpropertied white males, ninety-three percent of northern Blacks could not vote in 1840. The nation seemed determined to expand slavery, rather than end it, as the unpopular war with Mexico ended in 1848, opening up new markets for slaves in Texas.

Even idealistic African Americans finally had to agree with Peter Paul Simons, a black porter from New York City, who had declared in 1839 the failure of the moral elevation strategy to end slavery and injustice.

While he acknowledged that "no nation of people under the canopy of heaven . . . are given more to good morals and piety than we are," he argued that as attempts at moral elevation had progressed, "it has carried along with it blind submission." He continued "Yes, brothers, our soft manners when particularly addressing those of pale complexions, this very great respect which is particularly shown to them also, moral elevation carries these which are roots of degradation with it . . . . Morality," he argued, "when harassed by prejudice makes a slave of itself."[31] Simons recognized the difficulty of developing a true moral sense in a context which habitually fostered deference rather than equality, docility rather than gentleness, servility rather than kindness, and passivity rather than activism. Therefore he proposed that more attention be given to physical and political elevation than to moral and intellectual elevation.

Direct Action

Indeed, the decade of the 1840s was marked by an increased activism and attention to direct action and politics. Peaceful means were still the means of choice for the greater number of abolitionists. But the focus of direct action differed for Blacks and Whites. For African Americans, northern prejudice and slavery were inseparably linked, so that to fight one was to fight the other. As Peter Simons observed, "northern freedom is nothing but a nickname for northern slavery."[32] The peculiarities of northern practice came as a bit of a shock to fugitives from the South. After spending a harrowing seven years hidden in a crawl space over a storeroom while a slave in North Carolina, Linda Brent finally made her escape to Philadelphia, where she quickly learned that Blacks had the "freedom" to pay full fare on the trains, but were not permitted to ride in the first class cars. She wryly observed, "Colored people were allowed to ride in a filthy box, behind White people, at the South, but there they were not required to pay for the privilege . . . . It made me sad to find how the North aped the customs of slavery."[33]

Blacks organized locally to change these discriminatory practices. A boycott of railway lines in Massachusetts ended successfully when the state outlawed the practice of segregated cars in 1843. African Americans were also successful in ending segregated schooling in Lowell, New Bedford, Salem, Worcester, and Nantucket. These local efforts eventually resulted in the state legislature mandating integrated education throughout the state in 1855.[34]

Another option, popular among Quakers and some Blacks, was to boycott anything produced by slaves. Known at the time as the "free-produce movement," adherents proudly wore linsey-woolsey instead of cotton and sweetened with maple sugar or beet sugar rather than cane sugar. Of course most already abstained from tobacco, another crop produced largely by slave labor. This tactic appealed to the pietism of the time, allowing one to further separate from complicity with the system of slavery. Adherents also believed that they were putting economic pressure on the slavemasters, with the intent of making slavery unprofitable.

But many of the leading abolitionists felt such efforts were futile. Abbey Kelley pointed out that if she must not participate in "any system of fraud or oppression" she would have to boycott all products imported from Ireland and England since the workers were not paid sufficiently. And if she did this she would have to become a recluse, unable to "plead the cause of the poor and needy."[35] William Lloyd Garrison argued that since slavery was not a profitable economic system except for a very few, boycotts based on economic pressure would be ineffective because the "master-passion in the bosom of the slaveholder is not the love of gain, but the possession of absolute power, unlimited sovereignty."[36] Garrison's interpretation explained the intractability of northern racism as well as southern slavery.

The primary means for disseminating ideas in the 1840s was newspapers. Even the smallest towns often had two or three papers and most organizations, however small, regularly published papers. A number of African Americans started papers. In 1837 Samuel Cornish began publishing the *Colored American*, which addressed a broad range of issues, including moral reform, education and antislavery. The best known and longest running of the black-owned papers was Frederick Douglass' *North Star*, later named the *Frederick Douglass Paper*, which published a wide variety of articles and news items weekly for thirteen years. The most consistently inflammatory paper had as its editor the pacifist William Lloyd Garrison who ushered in his first edition of *The Liberator* in 1831 by announcing "I will be as harsh as truth . . . . I will not equivocate and I will be heard."[37] With many black supporters, the paper rolled out antislavery invective until the end of the Civil War. The abolitionist press also printed millions of "tracts," short essays describing the evils of slavery, and saturated the South with them.[38]

Opponents to abolition, however, mounted a campaign that forced the antislavery newspapers and lecturers to defend their own constitutional rights of free speech and a free press. In 1837 a mob in Alton, Illinois, murdered the abolitionist editor Elijah Lovejoy. Lovejoy had been driven out of slaveholding Missouri and hoped to find a more hospitable climate across the river in Illinois. Those who didn't like what he was publishing had already destroyed two expensive printing presses and he was killed trying to protect a third press. Southerners regularly intercepted and burned abolitionist literature coming into their states, and many post offices habitually censored any antislavery material.

Abolitionist conventions were often offensive to the communities where they met, not only for their antislavery ideas, but because Blacks and Whites met together and women were permitted to speak. Meetings of antislavery conventions were broken up, often by prominent citizens and merchants.[39]

Abolitionist attempts to petition Congress to abolish slavery were blocked in 1836 by a "gag" rule, which automatically tabled all antislavery petitions, preventing any debate. This rule was in effect until 1844, when it was repealed through the vigorous efforts of John Quincy Adams. Those who dared to speak out in defense of others' freedom, found themselves having to defend the very freedoms they had assumed were protected by the Constitution, reinforcing the conviction that no one was truly free until all were free.

Increasingly frustrated by the levels of resistance and the apparent ineffectiveness of speeches, preaching, newspapers, tracts and all the other tools of moral suasion, a group of abolitionists began to consider political action, breaking ranks with the Garrisonians. They organized a third party in 1840, the Liberty Party, and began working to elect antislavery candidates to local and national offices. The main platform of the Liberty Party was opposition to slavery everywhere it existed (unlike the later Free Soil Party which only opposed the extension of slavery into the territories, but would leave it untouched in the southern states). Drawing heavily for support from the Tappanites, the Liberty Party ran James Birney for president in 1844. The effect of his candidacy may well have been to swing the close election to the expansionist James Polk, rather than "the Great Compromiser" Henry Clay. Liberty Party support was strongest in New York State, where Birney garnered 15,812 votes, some of which probably would have gone to Henry Clay. Polk claimed New York's thirty-six electoral votes by a margin of just six thousand votes. However neither Polk nor Clay were acceptable candidates to those with antislavery sentiments, Clay having publicly professed, "I prefer the liberty of my own race to that of any other race. The liberty of the descendants of Africa in the United States is incompatible with the safety and liberty of the European descendants."[40]

By 1848, the Liberty Party had decided that it had to expand its platform in order to win more votes. This split the party into a faction led by Salmon Chase and Gameliel Bailey who eventually merged with the Free Soil Party, thus diluting its uncompromising stand on slavery, and a smaller band of radicals who maintained an unequivocal position on the immediate abolition of all slaves and added to their list of reforms women's suffrage, an income tax, prohibition of alcoholic beverages, opposition to land monopolies and opposition to standing armies. The latter resolution argued that there was no justification "whatever for wasting the earnings of [citizens] upon fortifications and standing armies and navies."[41] This remnant group eventually reorganized in 1855 into the Radical Abolitionist Party. The Radical Abolitionists argued that the constitution was an antislavery document and that the federal government was therefore obligated to abolish all slavery. Unlike the vastly more popular and successful Henry Clay, the Radical Abolitionists understood the folly and impossibility of favoring freedom for one group only. Their argument was religiously based in the ideas of the universality and inter-relatedness of human freedom and dignity. They proclaimed, "The moral government of God illustrated in pages of unwritten history forbids us to cherish any expectation of securing our own liberties or the liberties of any portion of the nation to which we belong by any process short of securing the liberties of each and all."[42] But the nation as a whole continued to look for other options in the 1850s.

Fugitive Slave Law and Civil Disobedience

By the 1850s it was clear that attempts by the major political parties to avoid the divisive issue of slavery were failing. In an attempt to forestall a national crisis over slavery, Congress adopted several pieces of legislation in 1850 designed to placate both the North and South. The slave trade was abolished in Washington D.C., and California was admitted as a free state, upsetting the balance of free and slave states in favor of the North. In return, the remaining territory acquired from

Mexico was opened to slavery and a much stricter fugitive slave law was passed. This act jeopardized all fugitives and free Blacks as well as the very fabric of the justice system. An affidavit by the slave-owner was accepted as sufficient proof of ownership; the accused had no right to testify on his or her own behalf and no right to a jury trial. Perhaps the most blatant violation of justice was that judges were paid according to the verdict. They were paid twice as much ($10) for cases in which the accused was returned to slavery as they were for cases in which the accused was set free. Penalties for noncompliance were severe: marshals and deputies refusing to execute warrants were liable to a $1,000 fine (more than a year's salary for most people). Citizens who prevented the arrest of a fugitive or aided in his or her concealment or rescue were also subject to fines of $1,000 and up to six months in prison for each fugitive assisted. A few lawyers voiced some concern about the erosion of constitutional rights, but most followed Daniel Webster, who felt the law was a last ditch effort to preserve the union and as such he was willing to overlook the injustices.

The view of the black community was very different. William Powell, a temperate and peace-loving Garrisonian, asserted that the federal government had declared war on Blacks.[43] This widespread sense of imminent threat led the African American community to respond immediately. They called meetings, and depending on location and experience, people decided whether they wanted to form vigilance committees to protect one another or to simply pack up and leave the country entirely. A number of churches chose the latter option, believing that to stay would leave them with the intolerable choice of fighting or returning to slavery.[44] Others decried the mass exodus, saying:

We repudiate the idea of flight for these reasons; first that we have committed no crime against the law of the land, second resistance to tyrants is obedience to God, and third that liberty which is not worth defending here is not worth enjoying elsewhere.[45]

These words came from a meeting of 350 African Americans in Syracuse, New York, just five days after the law was passed. While the language of resistance was strong, and the potential for violence great, this group actually evolved into a biracial vigilance organization, committed to nonviolent resistance. When a crisis situation arose, and a fugitive slave in Syracuse was arrested under the new law, they were able to execute one of the few successful slave rescues in the nation.[46]

On October 1, 1851 a fugitive slave, William Henry, better known as "Jerry," who had escaped from Missouri eight years before, was arrested under the pretense of a minor offense. The wife of the arresting officer, Commissioner Sabine, aware of the true nature of the arrest, alerted Charles Wheaton, a prominent white citizen who was a member of the Vigilance Committee. After sounding the prearranged signal on church bells, Wheaton, who knew that the sheriff had called out the National Guard and the Washington Artillery, spoke to an influential colonel, Origen Vandenburgh, and convinced him to override the sheriff's request and disband the military units. This action greatly decreased the likelihood of riots breaking out and increased the chances of a successful rescue.

Meanwhile Jerry, in handcuffs, realizing that he had been arrested for being a fugitive, broke from his captors and made a mad dash for freedom. He was caught, but not without a struggle that left him with broken ribs. When he was brought back to the police office, the Rev. Samuel May, a Unitarian pacifist, was able to speak to him and give him whispered assurances that he would be rescued. May then counseled the bi-racial Vigilance Committee, who were finalizing their rescue plans in a doctor's office, to accept violence against themselves, but not to be the perpetrators of injury to others.[47]

As darkness fell, the Vigilance Committee members surrounded the building where Jerry was held, smashed doors and windows to enter, turned off the gas lights, and carried Jerry, who was too injured to walk, to a waiting carriage. The surprised marshals fired a few shots, then fled in confusion, one breaking his arm as he jumped out of a window. Jerry was sped to an African American home where his shackles were removed, then hidden in a home much less likely to be searched, that of a pro-slavery supporter of the fugitive slave law named Caleb Davis. Davis, who had witnessed Jerry's desperate struggle for freedom, had had an instant change of mind regarding obedience to this particular law. The power of visually seeing what had before only been an abstract law, made the fugitive slave law a liability rather than an asset for the South. Jerry was successfully spirited to Canada where he wrote an open letter to the abolitionists of Syracuse thanking them for his freedom.[48]

The fugitive slave law brought several issues into focus for the white abolitionists. The first was obedience to law. A strong and persuasive line of thinking argued that a peaceful society required obedience to laws and that in a country where the people made the laws, the proper recourse was to change the laws rather than violate them. Indeed, seven hundred people signed a petition published in a Syracuse paper, criticizing the Jerry Rescue on the grounds that "if one disagrees with a law, one should use the legal avenues for redress to modify or repeal it, but open resistance is never permissible."[49]

Both those who supported and those who opposed civil disobedience often spoke a shared language, but did not necessarily share the same meanings for that language. For instance both groups claimed to want a peaceful and just society. But supporters of civil disobedience saw a peaceful and just society threatened by a government that could deprive citizens of rights believed to be fundamental, natural and guaranteed to all. Those who opposed civil disobedience believed civilized society was predicated on respect for laws, and that one could not pick and choose which laws one would obey, particularly in a country where one had a part in creating the laws. Both groups tended to use appeals to religion and the Bible, but again, they differed in their interpretations. Those who supported civil disobedience tended to justify their behavior by appealing to some form of belief in a "higher law," arguing that in the face of immediate evil, one could not wait for the slow and precarious process of changing laws. Those who opposed civil disobedience believed that it was their religious as well as civic responsibility to obey the government since Scripture said "Let everyone be subject to the governing authorities."[50]

Supporters tended to quote verses like "love one another as I have loved you" or "do justice, love mercy and walk humbly with your God."[51] There was also a fundamental difference in religious orientation between those whose religious expectations led them to anticipate comfort and prosperity for doing right and those who accepted redemptive suffering as part of the cost of discipleship. The men involved even shared a language of "manhood," but differed over whether the concept obligated them to defend the poor, weak and defenseless or gave them a privileged position of authority.

Thus the fugitive slave law exposed deep cracks in the society. By its very nature, it eliminated the possibility of neutrality on the slavery issue and demonstrated the fragility of social coherence.

Underground Railroad

The symbolic importance of runaways was great, which is partly why the South pushed so vehemently for a stronger fugitive slave law. Runaways undermined the southern argument that slavery was a benevolent institution, and the fugitive slave law that was passed in 1850 showed the extent to which defending injustice required ever greater injustice. In spite of the stiff penalties and great risks, a small but important group of people, moved by compassion, justice, and their own love of liberty, risked that liberty in order to help others.

Throughout the years of slavery, determined and daring souls made desperate attempts to escape. In the years before the war between the states, their numbers increased and a secret, voluntarily organized system of assistance, known as the Underground Railroad, developed to aid fugitives in their flight. Without benefit of telephones and modern communications, elaborate systems had to be worked out to ensure the safety of the "passengers."

Stories of the Underground Railroad have become legendary; sometimes it is hard to separate fact from fiction.[52] Some agents, like Levi Coffin and William Stills, kept meticulous records of those they helped, often as a way of trying to reunite family members with one another.[53] Slaves who told their stories of escape provided another source of information, although most slaves, like Frederick Douglass, refused to reveal many of the details until after the Civil War for fear of jeopardizing others.

The preponderance of the work on the Underground Railroad was done by African Americans and women. Many fugitives had so learned to distrust white people, that they would only seek assistance from other Blacks. Not infrequently Whites in an area would offer financial support, but leave the actual running (and risk) of the "railroad" to African Americans. During the 1850s a number of African Americans worked nearly full-time for the Underground Railroad, earning just enough to get by and utilizing all their resources. They not only helped slaves escape, but helped them get settled, find jobs, and when possible, find relatives. Some fugitives chose to live in one of the northern states; others didn't feel safe until they had crossed the border into Canada, most of them settling in black communities in Ontario. Antislavery newspapers took delight in aiming barbs at the irony of having to flee from a democracy to a monarchy in order to find freedom. Little known African Americans like Stephen Meyer in Albany, John Jones in Elmira, and Jermain Loguen in Syracuse networked with one another, often through their churches, to co-ordinate efforts on behalf of run aways. Their work depended heavily on support from fugitive aid societies, teas, bazaars and benevolence organizations, run by women. There was an international dimension to this support, with help coming from Ladies Aid Societies in Scotland, Ireland and England, as well as from local groups.

Few slaves chose to run away unarmed. J. W. Pennington was one who had been touched by principles of nonviolence to escape from Maryland in 1828 with "not so much as a penknife." He became a Presbyterian pastor and wrote one of the earliest African American histories, *A Textbook of the Origin and History of the Colored People* (1841).[54] The number of escaped slaves who were willing to forgive their masters is more remarkable than the fact that many chose to arm themselves. Sojourner Truth claimed her home was open to the man who had held her as a slave and cheated her. Henry Bibb wrote a conciliatory letter to his former master, forgiving him for whippings and inviting him to his home in Detroit.

One of the most famous "conductors" on the Underground Railroad was Harriet Tubman, called the Moses of her people. While many Blacks kept homes in the North that were always safe havens for runaways, Tubman actually returned to the land of slavery to personally escort more than 200 slaves to freedom. She was well known for always carrying a gun and threatening to shoot any one who might have second thoughts about escape, but in her own words, she "never lost a passenger." One of her most faithful friends was the nonresistant Quaker Thomas Garrett. Garrett lived in the slave state of Delaware, but openly helped anyone who came to him, reputedly nearly three thousand slaves. When threatened by sheriffs with guns, he would shame them saying that only cowards resorted to such means. Taken to court at the age of sixty, he lost all his possessions, including his business property. When it had all been auctioned off the sheriff declared, "I hope you'll never be caught at this again." "Friend," replied Garrett, "I haven't a dollar in the world, but if thee knows a fugitive who needs a breakfast, send him to me."[55]

Garrett's experience with resistance to his work was not unusual. The risks were great for helping fugitives. Carleton Mabee tells of a free black woman who hid two fugitive slave children, only to be caught and sold into slavery herself with her own children, and of a young minister, Charles T. Torrey, who was caught after having helped some two hundred slaves to escape and sentenced to six years of hard labor in prison, where he died.[56] A daring African American in Indiana, Elijah Anderson, was caught helping slaves cross the Ohio River and sentenced to jail in the Kentucky State Penitentiary at Frankfort where he died of "unknown causes."[57]

While most successful fugitives were young single men, the most touching stories are those of women trying to escape with children. The following story is an example of the tenacity and valor of those who risked running away and those people, both black and white, who dared to assist them. A woman known only as "Caroline" escaped from her Kentucky owner, George Ray in 1848 with her four children. She made it safely to Decatur County, Indiana where she found a black settlement near Clarksburg. But safety was elusive; she and her children were captured by Woodson Clark, the man for whom the town had been named.

Members of the black settlement alerted Luther Donnell, a White known to be sympathetic to fugitives. He advised the African Americans to "secure enough assistance to watch Clark's premises so as to prevent the escape of the fugitives" and then began legal prosecution of Clark. Since Caroline and her four children were by now well known, and an easy target, her rescuers divided the family into three groups. Two of Caroline's children were switched with children from the settlement and taken in broad daylight to the home of a Quaker, William Beard. Caroline, disguised as a man, traveled by night with a group of men from the settlement. Her other two children were taken separately by yet another route. Amazingly all were safely reunited in Canada, where Caroline wrote back thanking her assisters. Donnell, however faced charges and was indicted by a grand jury of Decatur County for "aiding and abetting the escape of fugitives from labor." Caroline's former master successfully sued in the United States court at Indianapolis to recover the value of his property. The three thousand dollars was paid by the defendants who in turn were reimbursed by their anti-slavery friends.[58]

The story of the antislavery movement, filled as it is with excitement, courageous and daring heroes and heroines, nevertheless has become one of the foundational stories supporting the myth of redemptive violence. According to this interpretation, the antislavery movement offers a "clear" lesson of history: Nonviolent means to eliminate slavery, whether gradual or immediate emancipation, compensated or uncompensated emancipation, political, legal, moral or religious, all failed. Peter Ripley, who has edited and published the invaluable *Black Abolitionist Papers* speaks for many when he writes "Events of that decade

(1850) proved that slavery was too entrenched to be brought down by peaceful means."[59] This conclusion is shared not just by historians, but by many people discouraged by the negligible response of government and churches to the problem of slavery. To them, only a violent, bloody civil war could end slavery.

Is this the "lesson" of the antislavery movement? Did nonviolence fail? First, we need to correctly identify what failed. There are major failures in this period, but the failure of nonviolent means is not one of them. There was, of course, a failure of the larger society to support the use of nonviolent means to end the conflict between the states. But the failure that is often overlooked is one which repeats itself continually throughout U.S. history. The white abolitionist movement failed to listen sufficiently to African American analysis. Charles Reason, African American teacher and advocate of black rights, spoke plainly when he said, "Abolitionists ought to consider it part of their work to abolish not only chattel slavery, but that other kind of slavery, which for generation after generation, dooms an oppressed people to a condition of dependence and pauperism."[60] White abolitionists tended to fix on a narrow goal of eliminating slavery, rather than a broader goal of creating a society free of racism and injustice. Just like so many of their brothers and sisters in the South, they failed to see the interconnectedness of all human life. The result was a failure to adequately understand the challenges of Reconstruction after the Civil War. This failure to hear and recognize the connection between slavery and racism, was the failure of the larger society to recognize the mutuality of all human activity and condition. This makes the value of those prophetic voices who "treated others as they would want to be treated" all the greater and worthy of our attention.

A final flaw in the argument that "events proved slavery was too entrenched to be brought down by peaceful means" is the assumption that the Civil War ended slavery. A byproduct of the war was the end of legal chattel slavery, a very necessary first step. But it is an illusion to believe that the costly violence of the Civil War ended slavery and its attendant problems; rather one form of institutionalized violence, racial chattel slavery, was replaced with others: peonage, vigilante violence and legalized apartheid. War served to check the abuses of slavery, but the U.S. society continues to wait to muster enough integrity to address the fundamental issue of racial injustice. The clearer lesson of this period seems to be that violence breeds more violence, a reaffirmation of the insight that means and ends must match. We learn that any struggle for justice must be done with an understanding of mutuality and interconnectedness, and that the voices of the most visibly oppressed must be a central part of any accurate and effective analysis and strategic planning.

It certainly is easy to criticize the abolitionists for their many shortcomings. They spent too much time quarreling among themselves over means: whether to participate in politics or remain pure and separate, whether women should be allowed to vote and speak in meetings, the extent to which violence in self-defense or freeing slaves was justified. But their courage and prophetic voices are well worth celebrating. All the many creative forms of nonviolent resistance practiced by the small, but very heterogeneous group forming the antislavery movement are too important a heritage to be dismissed and forgotten. They offer models of insight into recognizing and resisting injustice in a society which accepted the injustice as "normal" and acceptable. The abolitionists provide stirring stories of courage, compassion and character to today's society which suffers from a lack of real heroes and heroines. Their story also reminds us that at every point individual humans make choices, and these choices have long-lasting consequences.

Chapter 5

The Crossroads of Our Being:
The Civil War

The Civil War as Classical Tragedy

"It was the crossroads of our being," said historian Shelby Foote in the opening segment of the 1990 Public Broadcasting Service (PBS) series *The Civil War*, "and it was a hell of a crossroads...."[1] Foote's rich southern accent and his sober sense of tragedy gave a distinctive cast to the immensely popular PBS series. Forty million viewers, more than the entire USA population in 1865, were riveted to their television sets in a ritual of national remembering. Americans cannot let go of the Civil War. Every year publishers put out more books on the momentous and trivial aspects of the war; film makers produce more movies and videos dramatizing war action; and history buffs reenact Civil War encampments and battles. Nor is it a dead past. Saddam Hussein of Iraq had invaded Kuwait several weeks before the PBS series aired. In January 1991, as American forces smashed Iraq in the Persian Gulf War, commander Norman Schwarzkopf kept video cassettes of all eleven episodes of the PBS Civil War series in his bunker in Saudi Arabia.[2]

More than any other event in United States history, the Civil War seems to satisfy the classical definition of tragedy: an awe-inspiring human struggle with fate in which courageous heroes march toward self-knowledge and doom. The Civil War may be compared with that ancient literary crossroads where Oedipus killed his father before becoming king of Thebes. In the hands of great writers such as Sophocles of ancient Greece or Shakespeare of renaissance England, tragedy requires that the fatal flaw lie within the tragic hero. The Civil War meets that requirement, unlike our other wars when the evil enemy could be identified outside of our borders. George III, Adolf Hitler and Saddam Hussein were outsiders. But in 1860 the demons were native to the United States. The institution of slavery had taken deep root in the United States. The thorny legal questions of national union and secession were integral to the American political system. The murderous armies were American—brothers fighting brothers and generals matching wits against former classmates from West Point Military Academy. Thoroughly American, also, were the landscapes on which the armies destroyed each other from Bull Run to Appomattox.

For the South especially, to remember the Civil War has been to embrace a tragedy. Not only did the war destroy forever an old social order based on slavery, but the South's commitment to the high ideal of military honor helped ensure the completeness of the destruction. Robert E. Lee above all symbolized the tragedy by exemplifying the most prized qualities of southern civilization—loyalty, duty, independence, courage, and grace under pressure. The North, though it could not share the grief of an irrevocably lost cause, had its own great tragic figure in Abraham Lincoln, a man deeply anguished over the violence unleashed by his own decisions. Lincoln in turn was cut down by John Wilkes Booth, an actor who played out a final violent act. For all participants in the great conflict, the willingness to make war upon fellow citizens was integral to the tragic meaning of the conflict.

Despite its tragic dimensions, the Civil War cannot meet the classical definition of tragedy if it could have been avoided or if it ultimately resulted in a triumph for human freedom. True tragedy requires both inevitability and defeat. As satisfying as the tragic vision may be in a romantic sense, Americans have an even stronger bias for the promises and possibilities of freedom. We want to believe it is possible to set goals and to achieve them. We do this in two ways as we remember the Civil War. The first and dominant way, the way of the victors from the North, is to find the meaning of the Civil War in what Lincoln called "a new birth of freedom."[3] The war, it is said, preserved the union and freed the slaves. Yes, the costs were most lamentable and, in the narrower sense of the word, "tragic." But the war from the Union's viewpoint was a triumph, or, in the judgement of historian Philip Paludan, who wants to have it both ways, a "triumph through tragedy."[4]

A second and different strand of interpretation, less widely accepted but also running against the grain of classical tragedy, has argued that the war was not necessary or inevitable. If wise people had made timely decisions—to eliminate slavery, to restrain excessive anti-slavery outbursts, to compromise political differences—the Civil War might have been avoided. Historians who have made such arguments, commonly called "revisionists," have emphasized human freedom to choose paths which avoid war.[5]

Options to Avoid War:

1) Let Them Go in Peace

The imagining of alternative courses of action was a very real part of history. On November 2, 1860, on the eve of the presidential election, Horace Greeley, prominent political activist and editor of the influential New York *Daily Herald*, confronted popular fears that the southern states would secede if Abraham Lincoln, the Republican candidate, were elected. Greeley proposed a radical option: "Let Them Go in Peace." If the people of the deep South—and not only a small minority of secessionist hotheads—really wanted to leave the union, the government should not use violence to prevent them from doing so. "War is a hideous necessity at best," Greeley wrote, "— and a civil conflict—a war of estranged and embittered fellow-countrymen—is the most hideous of all wars."[6] Greeley continued to advocate peaceable acceptance of secession in December after South Carolina left the union, and in January as six states of the deep South followed suit. In strong editorials, in personal correspondence, and in a private discussion with president-elect Lincoln (who subscribed to and read the *Daily Herald*), Greeley set forth his arguments for a path to avoid war. In February and March of 1861 the case became stronger as Unionist political forces, who had been on the defensive after Lincoln's election, rallied to defeat the secessionist movement in the upper south states of Virginia, North Carolina, and Tennessee. In the absence of war, the Confederacy would consist only of South Carolina and Georgia plus the Gulf State South (Florida, Alabama, Mississippi, Louisiana and Texas)—a precarious political experiment which some southern Unionists predicted could not survive more than two or three years.[7]

Greeley was both a nationalist and an opponent of slavery. He did not wish to compromise either commitment. The Republican party platform, which he supported, endorsed the "Free Soil" principle: the western territories must be kept free of slavery, although slavery would be allowed where it already existed. Like Lincoln, Greeley was adamantly unwilling to compromise on the question of extending slavery. His willingness to accept secession apparently compromised his nationalism, but he believed that popular support for secession in the South was weak, and that it would be overwhelmingly defeated if put to a popular referendum. In the long run, Greeley believed, the seceding states were too divided and independent-minded to create a successful confederacy. Given enough time to prove their inability to create effective government, and if they were not galvanized to unity by war, they would be ready to come back into the union.[8]

We do not know, of course, what would have happened if Greeley's advice had been taken. Abraham Lincoln was uncompromising on national union, and accepted war rather than secession. When war came it solidified the deep South and brought the upper South into the Confederacy. Greeley has been criticized for overestimating the extent of southern opposition to secession and for imagining that seceded states eventually would want to rejoin the union. The criticism has merit, but it is surely unfair to judge Greeley's position from a point in time after the war had begun and had unified the secessionists. Warfare, including the rigid and hostile national/regional passions it engenders, is what Greeley urgently attempted to avoid. His concerns about the high costs of a civil war make his proposal worth remembering and pondering.

Another possible view, imagined more in retrospect than in 1860, is that the Confederate states might have become a successful nation and entered some form of broader political union with the United States, Canada, and even England. In 1930 Winston Churchill, the statesman and historian who later led England in World War II, wrote an essay which imagined such a wider association of English-speaking nations.[9] In Churchill's elegant scenario the South won the Civil War; Robert E. Lee displaced Jefferson Davis as president of the Confederacy; Lee declared the abolition of slavery; and the Confederacy guaranteed its security though an alliance with England. Eventually in 1905, after decades of trouble, the Confederacy, the United States, Canada, and England joined together in a "Re-United States" which developed such a powerful peacemaking tradition that it was able to intervene and prevent the outbreak of war in Europe in 1914! Churchill wanted to imagine a twentieth century less scarred by total war.

But what about slavery? Is it possible to imagine the end of slavery in North America without the force of civil war and total military defeat of the slave owners? Churchill's notion that Lee could have ended slavery in the Confederacy with a master stroke is hardly believable, in part because Lee was no champion of abolition but also because resistance to such exercise of central government authority was the very basis of the Confederacy. Other scholars have suggested that the Confederacy eventually would have faced a violent slave rebellion. Such a prospect may not have been worse than the actual Civil War after which the South developed new forms of racial domination to keep African Americans as subordinated as they had been under slavery.[10]

A comparison with Russia is instructive. In 1860 more than one-third of the peasant population in Russia were private serfs who had no civil rights and could not legally acquire property. On March 3, 1861, on the eve of the United States' Civil War, Russia undertook a vast reform for peaceable emancipation of the serfs. Serfdom in the Russian Empire, of course, was different from slavery in the United States. Russia was an autocracy. Russian noblemen who owned serfs accepted the authority of Czar Alexander II to abolish serfdom, while southern slave holders cherished personal independence and states rights.[11] Nevertheless, the wider world-historical moral forces which led to the emancipation of serfs in Russia, to peaceful abolition of slavery in the British Empire between 1812 and 1833, and to the success of abolition in Brazil in the 1880s, would surely have worked to isolate and demoralize Confederate slavery. Historian William Pfaff has written, "Had the Confederacy been allowed to go in peace, it seems hardly imaginable that slavery could have survived into the twentieth century. It would have had to be ended by the South itself (the moral cause usefully reinforced by the inevitable mechanization of southern agriculture)."[12]

Whatever the effects of mechanized agriculture upon slavery in the late nineteenth century, slavery was a profitable institution while it lasted. Economic forces alone would not have led to its demise. Robert W. Fogel and Stanley L. Engerman, in a much-disputed book, *Time on the Cross* (1974), argued not only that slavery was a profitable and rational labor system, but also that slave agriculture was thirty-five percent more efficient than family farms in the North and that southern slaves had a standard of living which "compared favorably" to that of "free industrial workers."[13] Professor Fogel offered an anti-pacifist "counterfactual" vision of what would have happened if the Confederate states had been allowed to secede in peace. The Confederacy, he wrote, would have become economically strong; human rights movements around the world would have stalled; and the slave owning Confederates would have built a modern military establishment and used it to conquer the peace-minded Union![14] Fogel's fantasy was as starkly grim as Churchill's was cheerful. Both authors weakened their case by ignoring the Confederate commitment to states' rights and weak central government.

Contrary to both Churchill and Fogel, it is much more likely that the end of slavery in a seceded South would have come through the gradual demoralization of people upon whom the system depended. The trajectory of world history was not on the side of the southern secessionists who argued that slavery was a positive good, a force for civilization, and consistent with the Christian gospel. The moral fervor and ideological rigor of slavery's defenders are undeniable. Alexander Stephens, Vice-President of the Confederacy, was a moderate on the issue of secession. Yet Stephens said in Savannah on March 21, 1861 that the "corner-stone" of the new government rested "upon the great truth, that the negro is not the equal of the white man; that slavery—subordination to the superior race—is his natural and moral condition. This, our new Government, is the first, in the history of the world, based upon this great physical, philosophical and moral truth."[15] The secessionists clearly had the initiative in the deep South in the spring of 1861; a counter-initiative by southern moderate and unionist forces would have come later as the Confederacy learned that the spirit of secessionism undermined its ability to govern effectively. How long would it have been until some sovereign states of the South would have found good cause to secede from the Confederacy? We don't know, thanks to the Civil War.

Professor Fogel praised the decision by abolitionist William Lloyd Garrison to abandon his pacifism and to champion a violent end to slavery. Whether or not Garrison's demand for violence was justified, it should be remembered that President Lincoln and the Union did not go to war to end slavery. Lincoln went to war to save the union. He could not have recruited an army on an anti-slavery basis. Lincoln's first preference was to deal with slavery by containing it within its existing boundaries. That containment, at least within North America, could have been achieved even if Lincoln had accepted Horace Greeley's advice to let the disaffected states of the lower South "go in peace."

2) Compromise

If they had known the grim and costly outcome of the Civil War, the leaders of both South and North likely would have opted for compromise rather than for war. In 1787, less than seventy-five years earlier, American leaders had convened a Constitutional Convention in time of peril. In 1860, although some moderates were calling for a fully representative official convention, this method of adjusting disputes was not even tried. Much depended upon president-elect Lincoln. There were five months between the election in early November, 1860, and the beginning of the war on April 12, 1861 During these months the margins for maneuvering toward compromise gradually narrowed. As president-elect, Abraham Lincoln would have had to act with extraordinary and unprecedented decisiveness to address an unparalleled constitutional crisis. Already before his inauguration on March 4, he would have had to take bold and non-partisan initiatives to transcend Republican party interests on behalf of national unity. That he failed to do so is understandable, for he was not dealing from a position of political strength. Nevertheless, if Lincoln is to be honored as one of the country's greatest war presidents, it must also be acknowledged that he failed disastrously at the prior task of avoiding war.

What might Lincoln have done differently? Instead of isolating himself at Springfield, Illinois, and avoiding comment on the national crisis, as he did after the election, Lincoln might have taken an active leadership role before his inauguration. Immediately after the election, Lincoln needed to assert himself as a moderate national leader, not hostage to the radical wing of the Republican party, and willing to cooperate with moderate unionists in the South. He had been a candidate without support in the South, elected with a minority of popular votes (though with a strong majority in the electoral college), and popularly defined by his famous "house divided" speech from the Senate campaign of 1858 against Stephen Douglas. Lincoln had said, "I believe this government cannot endure, permanently half *slave* and half *free* . . . . It will become *all* one thing or *all* the other." He subsequently had reinterpreted his provocative statement, pointing out that it was a prediction, not a policy, and that "it may have been a foolish one perhaps."[16] The truth was that president-elect Lincoln had no intention and no plan to challenge slavery where it existed. Even though southerners doubted that truth, only about twenty-five percent of them would have favored secession immediately after Lincoln's election.[17] Lincoln could have done much more—with strong public statements and personal correspondence—to convince southern moderates of his intentions, and to empower the southern unionists in their efforts to oppose the secessionist movement. Where great statesmanship was required to control events, Lincoln largely let events control him. David Herbert Donald, distinguished Lincoln biographer, has noted Lincoln's general "reluctance to take the initiative and make bold plans; he preferred to respond to the actions of others."[18]

On December 20, 1860, six weeks after the election, South Carolina seceded from the Union on the assumption that Lincoln and the newly elected Republican Party were committed to abolitionism. Secessionist sentiment in South Carolina was strong and may well have proceeded despite anything Lincoln as president-elect could have said or done. In other states, however, secession was a closer contest. Georgia was especially crucial with a strategic location between Atlantic Coast and Gulf Coast states, with recently developed industrial strength, and with highly respected political leaders. Alexander Stephens, former United States Congressman and later vice-president of the Confederacy, opposed secession and could have done so more effectively with clearer help from Lincoln. Georgia voters in the election of convention delegates to consider secession were almost exactly divided between secessionists and cooperationists.[19] If Georgia had voted to stay in the union, the subsequent votes in Louisiana (January 26) and Texas (February 1) might also have turned out differently. Many southerners who voted for secession did so assuming that this was a step toward reconstituting the national union. Robert Barnwell Rhett, a fire-eating Confederate (later memorialized in the name of "Rhett Butler" in *Gone With the Wind*), was very worried that the southern moderates would jump at the first chance to re-join the Union. He called it "the dread fear of reconstruction."[20] Rhett's fears had a sound basis, but Abraham Lincoln's failure of leadership helped the radical secessionists in the deep South make steady progress toward their goal. On February 4, a month before the new president took office, they met in convention in Montgomery, Alabama, to establish a provisional government and elect officers to the new Confederacy.

The South as a whole, however, was not united on secession; nor was Lincoln's Republican party united on the appropriate response to secession. To save the union without war, Lincoln would have had to forge a political alliance with moderate groups both within his party and within the upper South. Senator William H. Seward, eventually named Secretary of State in Lincoln's cabinet, was the leader of the Republican party moderates. Seward strove mightily to soften Lincoln's position. Seward was alarmed when he read a first draft of Lincoln's inaugural address. Lincoln took a hard-line stance against compromise, promised to reclaim federal property in Confederate hands, and closed with a threat to defend the Union by force if necessary. Seward threatened to refuse to serve on the cabinet if Lincoln did not take a more conciliatory position. Lincoln accepted Seward's advice — for the time being. In March of 1861 the prospects for compromise were still alive.[21]

But long-range success depended on Lincoln's ability to establish himself as a national president, rather than one exclusively dependent on sectional support from a sectional party. To broaden his base Lincoln could have established ties with non-Republican anti-secessionist leaders from the upper South — men such as John A. Gilmer and William W. Holden of North Carolina, John J. Crittenden of Kentucky, Robert Hatton and John Bell of Tennessee, and John Millson of Virginia.[22] Several from this group could have been appointed to top cabinet positions. Such appointments would have severely strained Lincoln's relationship with the strictly orthodox wing of the Republican Party. But a conciliatory policy could have strengthened Unionist control over the upper South and discredited the option of secession throughout the South. In the course of four years in office, if Lincoln had chosen not to arouse a violent crisis with the seceded states, a new configuration of political parties might have emerged. In 1799-1800 President John Adams had made a decision for peace which he rightly suspected would have a devastating effect upon his Federalist Party. To ask Abraham Lincoln in February and March of 1861 to transcend party in a similar way is to call for exceptional statesmanship. But the option did exist.[23]

As the crisis deepened, moderate political leaders offered numerous proposals for the process and substance of compromise. A key issue was the extension of slavery into the western territories, a matter which had been central to negotiations for the Missouri Compromise of 1820 and the Compromise of 1850, which had forestalled violence in their times. John J. Crittenden, a U.S. Senator from Kentucky in the tradition of Henry Clay, proposed to reinstitute and extend the 36° 30′ latitude line (the southern boundary of Missouri) to California. There would be no slavery in territories north of that line, and new states would decide for or against slavery at their time of admission to the union. Crittenden also proposed nonamendable guarantees of slavery where it existed and strict enforcement of the Fugitive Slave Act, among other provisions. A select Senate committee, chaired by Crittenden, discussed the compromise in late December 1860. Popular alarm over the disintegration of the Union was so great that a strong majority of people in the North probably would have voted for the Crittenden Compromise if given an opportunity—at least in the judgement of Horace Greeley, who himself opposed the measure as a compromise with slavery.

President-elect Lincoln sent word from Springfield that he opposed the Crittenden compromise. Lincoln's hard line killed any chance for the proposal. It was, in the words of historian Allan Nevins, "one of the most fateful decisions of Lincoln's career." The non-extension of slavery had been a defining plank in the Republican Party platform. Even though it was not likely that slavery would be successfully introduced in the western territories, Lincoln was not willing to abandon his party's principles before even taking office. He wrote in a private letter that "a crisis must be reached and passed" on the extension of slavery—language ominously reminiscent of King George III's response to the Boston Tea Party.[24]

A statesman seeking to avoid war must seek mediating possibilities among apparently irreconcilable opposing positions. Charles Francis Adams, Republican member of the House of Representatives from Massachusetts, supported his party's plank on non-extension of slavery into the territories. In the face of secession, however, and seeing the need to isolate the radical southern secessionists from the moderate southern unionists, Adams proposed a plan to admit New Mexico immediately as a slave state and thereby technically avoid the question of extension of slavery into the territories. For his proposal Adams had backing from other prominent moderate Republicans, but it did not stand a chance without Lincoln's support. Lincoln had set his face like flint against any modification of the Republican party position on non-extension. Lincoln did not realize as clearly as Adams the seriousness of southern secessionist intentions. Historian Martin B. Duberman, biographer of Charles Francis Adams, summarized the result: "Perhaps superb statesmanship might have bridged the gulf; perhaps a fuller realization of what disunion would entail might have modified the rigidity of attitudes. Neither was forthcoming. For the country which would not, or perhaps could not compromise, there awaited a calamitous issue."[25]

"No More Fuel"

Many distinguished Americans from both North and South welcomed "a little bloodletting," not only to settle a national argument, but also because warfare offered curative and redemptive possibilities. Ralph Waldo Emerson, brilliant essayist and philosopher, praised the coming war: "War is a realist, shatters everything flimsy and shifty, sets aside all false issues . . . . Let it search, let it grind, let it overturn, and . . . when it finds no more fuel, it burns out."[26] The burned out fuel of the Civil War eventually was measured in piles of dead bodies, amputated limbs, grieving families, crushed human spirits, as well as the destruction of material resources — cities, fields, roads, homes, and churches. Emerson's romantic literary image perversely became an apt description of the Federal military strategy of attrition which finally won the war. The war was not settled in one big battle, or in fifteen big battles, but rather by sustained massive killing and destruction until the South, with fewer people and resources, had nothing left with which to fight. Burned out were the 600,000-plus people who died in the war, and some twenty billion dollars in financial costs.[27]

Advances in military technology accounted for much of the killing. Most significant was the "rifling" of the barrels of muskets and of artillery to make shooting much more accurate. A rifled musket barrel had a spiral groove which caused the bullet to spin as it flew toward its target. Increased accuracy strengthened entrenched defenses while it made attacking more difficult. Attacking infantry had to stay behind cover for greater distances and then cross larger battlefields where they were exposed for longer times to effective fire from defending muskets and artillery. An attacking army of massed men could win major battles only by sacrificing huge numbers of men. Major battles fought in traditional ways invariably favored the defense. On the two occasions that Robert E. Lee took his Army of Northern Virginia on offensive campaigns across the Potomac River, he lost battles pivotal to the course of the war. After Lee was stopped at the Battle of Antietam, September 17, 1862, Lincoln issued a preliminary Emancipation Proclamation. In Lee's second invasion northward, the Battle of Gettysburg, July 1-3, 1863 (together with the fall of Vicksburg on the Mississippi River at the same time), turned the tide of the war. "Pickett's Charge" at Gettysburg was a parable of the war—15,000 Confederate men moving across an open plain into a hail of accurate Federal fire from rifled muskets and artillery. After a hideous slaughter, the surviving attackers retreated, reorganized, and prepared for yet more bloody but inconclusive battles—until the South was completely exhausted.

A combination of uncompromising nationalism and military honor contributed to the massive scale of killing. Both Abraham Lincoln and Jefferson Davis were ardent nationalists who turned the survival and success of their nations into absolute values which outweighed any imaginable human sacrifice. Lincoln's commitment to the Union was absolute, not subject to compromise. The appalling loss of life and treasure caused him great anguish, but he never contemplated the possibility that the costs might become so high that he would negotiate a settlement that would dismember the union. The war, in Lincoln's definition, was a domestic insurrection. Secession was not a legal fact and the Confederacy was not a legitimate nation. During the election campaign of 1864, Lincoln foresaw the possibility that General George McClellan, the Democrat party candidate, might be elected on a peace platform and might proceed to an armistice leading to Confederate independence. But on Lincoln's watch there would be no such armistice, whatever the cost.[28]

Jefferson Davis matched Lincoln in unconditional nationalism. In 1864 when two unofficial northern representatives came to his presidential office in Richmond to sound out possibilities for armistice and negotiated peace, Davis said: "The war . . . must go on till the last man of this generation falls in his tracks, . . . *unless you acknowledge our right to self-government*. We are not fighting for slavery. We are fighting for Independence,—and that, or extermination, we *will* have."[29] Davis was consistent to the end. Even after the Confederate armies collapsed, he vainly called his officers to a "new phase" of decentralized guerilla fighting.[30] By that time the Federal army under General William Tecumseh Sherman had unleashed its campaign of terror and destruction upon the civilian population and countryside in Georgia, South Carolina, and North Carolina. The absolute nationalism of political leaders had helped to produce conditions of total war.[31] War became not only a contest between armies fought to the point of annihilation. War also became a contest between peoples in which strategies of terrorism brought civilian populations to the point of total demoralization.

The code of military honor required that men keep charging into battlefields even when they knew they would die, and that generals keep sacrificing their armies even when they knew that the war would be lost. Honor was compounded of both valor and virtue. General Lee could order the most appallingly disastrous actions and yet be acclaimed as a model hero in the southern tradition, so long as he bravely and unselfishly accepted personal responsibility. It was "Lee's finest hour," said Shelby Foote of Lee's dignified behavior in the wake of his misguided order that made Gettysburg into the bloodiest battle of the war.[32] Lee had serious doubts after Gettysburg (July 1863) whether the South could win the war. By early November 1864, after Lincoln's election to a second term destroyed prospects for a more flexible Federal administration, Lee knew for a near certainty that the defeat of his army was inevitable. Yet Lee continued to fight on for five more months, absorbing huge losses among his own men and extending the term of devastation that northern troops were wreaking upon the South elsewhere. Lee's expressed reason for surrendering on April 9, 1865 — to avoid excessive "sacrifice of life" — would have been valid twenty-one months earlier. Lee's persistence in sacrifice for what he knew was a lost cause satisfied the code of honor and won approval in history books and biographies. But the price of honor was high.[33]

Killing and Courage

The ideal of military honor shaped the meaning of that most basic of battle activities — people killing other people. The act of killing, at the heart of war, has long been a strangely taboo subject in the memory of war. Recruitment campaigns call men to "fight and die," rather than to "kill" for the country. Literature about the Civil War is filled with vivid images of heroic suffering and death. But killing as such, the enactment and remembering of that climactic moment when a soldier finds another person in his sights and pulls the trigger to kill him, remains largely undescribed and unexplored.[34] Killing had a special impact in the Civil War, both because rifled weapons made it possible to pick out one's human target with deadly accuracy at longer range, and also because it was a war among Americans and brothers who could not easily deny their common humanity. Stories abounded of soldiers from opposing armies at rest, or in winter quarters, withholding fire and saluting each other.[35] It was not honorable to kill when courage was not at stake, although those who did so were given the vaguely positive label of "sharpshooters."[36]

A great hidden fact, buried under mountains of remembered courage, is that most rifle-carrying infantrymen in the Civil War (and in World Wars I and II) could not bring themselves to kill. Despite their military training, their belief in the war objectives, and their courageous charge into the fields of fire, when the moment came to aim and shoot at a specific person on the other side, they could not bring themselves to do it. They either failed to fire their guns, fired so as to miss the enemy, or busied themselves with non-lethal activity. Such a refusal was to be expected from principled religious pacifists. Christian Good was a nonresistant Mennonite from the Shenandoah Valley who was drafted into the Confederate army, where he refused to fire at the Yankees in battle. When his captain reprimanded him, Good said, "They're people; we don't shoot people."[37] Good was part of an exceptional minority in his ability (and courage) to articulate his conscientious objection. But in his basic refusal to kill, he belonged to a larger majority. Precise numbers cannot be known, but it is likely that non-firers constituted eighty to eighty-five percent of the infantry.[38]

S. L. A. Marshall, a U.S. Army Brigadier General, conducted post-battle interviews with World War II soldiers which became the first authoritative and convincing evidence for the high percentage of non-killers in the ranks.[39] For the Civil War, that evidence is supported by post-battle inventories of discarded weapons. After the Battle of Gettysburg, officials picked up and examined 27,574 discarded muskets. Nearly 90 percent of the muskets were still loaded, and 50 percent of the loaded weapons had been loaded more than once. Six thousand of the multiple-loaded weapons had three to ten rounds in the barrel; one had twenty-three rounds.[40] How can we account for all these unfired and multiple-loaded muskets? It took far less time to fire a weapon than to load it. Obviously, thousands of men at Gettysburg carried loaded weapons and failed to fire them. Moreover, there was no rational advantage for loading a musket more than once. The most reasonable explanation is that soldiers who were not firing at the enemy continued to reload their weapons in order to convince their comrades and superiors (and perhaps themselves) that they were contributing to the battle. Their courage to face death was not in question. Soldiers with muzzle-loading muskets had to stand upright on open battlefields and use gravity to pour the powder and to ram the bullet into the barrel. Thousands of them courageously stayed on the battlefield in support roles that contributed to the killing that they could not themselves directly perform.

How was it possible, if eighty percent or more of the infantry were not shooting to kill, that the Civil War casualties were so extensive? One answer is that a high proportion of deaths came from artillery rather than from individually fired muskets. The firing of cannon was at greater distance and involved close teamwork which spread responsibility for the killing. Another answer is that the minority of infantrymen who shot to kill were exceptionally effective with rifled muskets in battles of long duration and with strong support from the nonfirers. After World War II the U. S. Army reformed its training system and successfully increased the percentage of killers in its ranks.[41]

The Coming of the Lord

Militant Christian religion had a significant role, largely unacknowledged in popular war films and literature, in bringing on the war, intensifying the will to fight, and extending the war's duration.[42] In the years before the war, the major Protestant denominations—Presbyterian, Methodist, Baptist—contributed to sectional tensions and anticipated the breakup of the political order by undergoing hostile separations.[43] When war broke out, northern religious leaders welcomed it as a sign of the coming of the Lord. Christian religion in the North was more diverse than in the South, where rationalism and Unitarianism had not taken hold. But Puritan religious assumptions continued to define the national faith. Julia Ward Howe, a mother of young children who yearned to make a contribution to the war effort, captured the central images in the text for her stirring poem, "Battle Hymn of the Republic":

> Mine eyes have seen the glory of the coming of the Lord,
> He is trampling through the winepress where the grapes of wrath
>   are stored,
> He hath loosed the fateful lightnings of his terrible swift sword,
> His truth is marching on.

I have seen him in the watchfires of a hundred circling camps
They have builded him an altar in the evening dews and damps,
I can read His righteous sentence by the dim and flaring lamps
His day is marching on.[44]

Howe and other Protestants believed that the Lord was coming to America to fight the final battle against evil, as describd in Revelation, the last book of the Bible. In Rev. 19:15, Christ, leading the heavenly armies, has a sharp sword coming from his mouth, and "he will tread the wine press of the fury of the wrath of God the Almighty." This cataclysmic "day of the Lord," foretold by the Hebrew prophets, would precede the "millennium," the thousand-year reign of Christ (Rev. 20:2-7). When Howe saw the "watch- fires of a hundred circling camps" of the Union army, she saw God's presence and the coming fulfillment of God's plan for United States history and for world history. Indeed, the coming Kingdom of God depended upon the triumph of God's Kingdom in America. The United States was a redeemer nation, and the war would reveal its redemptive democratic possibilities. Yankee Protestant ministers proclaimed: "Oh! what a day will that be for our beloved land, when carried through a baptism of fire and blood, struggling through this birth-night of terror and darkness, it shall experience a resurrection to new life, and to a future whose coming glory already gilds the mountain tops . . . . The day of the Lord is at hand!"[45] President Lincoln was not a church member and not greatly interested in Jesus as a religious or historical figure, but he did believe in providence and in America's transcendent mission. Lincoln came to see the war as God's judgement on the nation for the evils of slavery, and the triumph of the Union as the "last best hope of earth" for freedom and democracy.[46] Lincoln's sense of America's world mission, eloquent in a very different way from that of Julia Ward Howe, was nevertheless ribbed with Puritan steel where it counted.

The southern churches were more uniformly evangelical in religious expression and conservative in theological doctrine than the North, and no less convinced that God was on their side. A generation before the war they had developed a biblical rationale for slavery and for the duty to protect it. Southern clerics spoke of the war as a "baptism of blood," more than as the coming "day of the Lord," but their sense of national mission had much in common with that of the North. An Episcopal rector said, "A grand responsibility rests upon our young republic and a mighty work lies before it. Baptized in its infancy in blood, may it receive the baptism of the Holy Ghost, and be consecrated to its high and holy mission among the nations of the earth."[47] Christian conviction combined with the ideal of honor to sustain Confederate morale in a losing cause. After the war the white southerners, having been denied separate political identity, developed a distinctive religious culture—the "Religion of the Lost Cause"—to sustain their regional faith. It became the southern civil religion, nurtured both within and beyond the churches.

At the outset of war, soldiers on both sides marched forth in triumphant self-confidence.[48] As the war dragged on and as soldiers coped with death and defeat on the battlefields, the armies of the Union and the Confederacy became scenes of massive religious revivals. One enthusiastic southerner declared that "the armies had been nearly converted into churches."[49] A northern religious paper said, "Probably no army, in any age, has ever witnessed such outpourings of the Spirit of God as our own armies have experienced."[50] More than 100,000 soldiers on both sides professed conversion—probably a higher total number in the North but a higher proportion of the smaller southern armies. For individual soldiers, religious conversion was a means of reassurance of salvation after death. The revivals broke out in home communities as well as in the armies, and also had a social as well as personal function. They created evangelical communities of common ideals and religious equality. The exact consequences of religious conversion cannot be measured. We do not know whether a converted soldier was more or less likely to engage in actual killing. Religious experience and conviction on both sides worked to steel resolve and to prolong the war in the face of despair. Christian faith helped combatants face death with courage and leaders to remain steadfast in the faith that God was on their side. The year after the war, as more than half a million families mourned their dead, a Baptist minister put a holy gloss on the event: "Righteous wars are means of grace."[51]

Benevolence and Brutality at Home

Wars bring out the best and the worst in people. Among the worst were cynical profiteers who took advantage of human misery to enrich themselves. Most shocking were racist riots in northern cities directed against Blacks and the military draft. On July 12-16, 1863, violent mobs terrorized New York City and killed at least 105 people—the worst riot in United States history. Many of the rioters were exploited Irish Catholic workers who lived in miserable tenements, feared competition from black workers, and exploded in anger against being conscripted into a Yankee Protestant war for black freedom. Rich men were able to buy exemptions from the draft for $300. On both sides there were charges that this was a "rich man's war and a poor man's fight."

The war also called forth great sacrifices of volunteer charity. The New York City Woman's Central Relief Association provided the germ idea for the major charitable establishment, the United States Sanitary Commission. The Sanitary Commission sent medical personnel and supplies and other needed items to the front. The American Red Cross, founded later by Clara Barton, grew out of this Civil War work. Nearly every local community had a Soldiers' Aid Society through which women volunteers raised funds and sewed clothing for the soldiers. Dorothea Dix, the Union superintendent of nurses, became famous for her strong administration of ministries of mercy. The war forced greater independence upon women responsible for running plantations and farms, and also brought large numbers of women into government office work as clerks and copyists for the first time. After the war, the opportunities which had opened briefly soon shut again firmly.

The Civil War, more than any event of the nineteenth century, turned America into a gun culture. The war armed an entire generation, taught them to kill, and let them take their weapons home after the fighting. According to historian Michael Bellesiles, "The war had introduced the majority of American males to the use of firearms; peace brought those weapons into their homes."[52] The mass marketing of guns, and the mystical identification of guns with individual and national freedom, was in large part a product of the Civil War.

War Memories: From Disillusion to Celebration

With the passing of time, Civil War veterans allowed their memories of horror to fade. They celebrated the glory. Oliver Wendell Holmes' passage from disillusionment to celebration was particularly significant. In 1861 Holmes had gone directly from Harvard University into the war, and served three years with the Twentieth Massachusetts Infantry, a group that had five-eighths of its men killed or wounded. Three times Holmes was seriously wounded, recovered, and returned to the war. He left the army as a Lieutenant-Colonel before the war was over, wearied by the "wear & tear (body & mind) of regimental duty," and disgruntled with his father who implied that duty and honor required more.[53] Two and three decades later, however, Holmes delivered Memorial Day addresses that idealized the influence of war upon those who experienced it: "Through our great good fortune, in our youth our hearts were touched with fire."[54] War, and violent sports for those who lacked the challenge of war, taught men to lead. In 1884 at the Harvard University Commencement Holmes said, "If once in a while in our rough riding a neck is broken, I regard it, not as a waste, but as a price well paid for the breeding of a race fit for headship and command." The meaning of the Civil War, for Holmes, flowed not from the emancipation of slaves, but from the courage and strenuousness it fostered among the fighters. "War, when you are at it, is horrible and dull. It is only when time has passed that you see that its message was divine."[55]

Holmes' view of the war's meaning had an impact on national policy. In 1903 he was on the Massachusetts Supreme Court when President Theodore Roosevelt appointed him a member of the United States Supreme Court. Holmes became famous as a champion of civil liberties, but he also wrote decisions which legitimated the denial of the vote to African Americans in southern states.[56] Holmes' romanticized memories of his own coming of age through violence in the Civil War also affected his crafting of the Supreme Court decision of 1921 in *Brown v. United States*, which struck down the "duty to retreat" doctrine inherited from British Common Law. The legal "duty to retreat" prohibited persons from harming others in self-defense as long as it was possible to escape from the scene of violence. Holmes asserted the right of a person under attack to "stand his ground" and defend himself, even if it involved killing the assailant. It was, for Holmes, a matter of human nature: "A man is not born to run away." The law "must consider human nature and make some allowances for the fighting instinct at critical moments."[57] The American legal right of self-defense was established, in part, as a result of Holmes' personal experience in the Civil War.

Tragedy and Beyond

The death of Abraham Lincoln brought the Civil War drama to a tragic completion. Shelby Foote explained the "enormous dramatic grip" of the war in terms of theatrical climax: "Even when everything slackens off and we're about to have this pitiful little ending where the war peters out, damned if John Wilkes Booth doesn't shoot Abraham Lincoln. God Almighty is a great dramatist."[58] After the tragic drama was concluded, spectators stood in awe and amazement at the spectacle of nobility meeting doom, and of heroism in the face of perplexing fate.

The tragic view, however powerful as literary image, contradicts alternative views that find triumph and progress in the outcome of the Civil War. Even the South, where tragedy comes more naturally, eventually saw the war as triumph. Yes, the South formally had failed to preserve slavery and a separate nationality. But former Confederates insisted that the war had not been about slavery at all. In the immediate post-war years Radical Republicans from the North attempted to impose a new social and political order on the South. Southern leaders defeated that attempt. In 1877, after the Hayes-Tilden election, northerners and southerners agreed on a political compromise that ended Reconstruction. As long as the South did not re-institute formal slavery, it could do what it pleased. The victims of this arrangement, sacrificed on the altar of sectional compromise, were the African Americans. White southerners had achieved the substance of what they wanted: states rights, white supremacy, and honor. The great question for interpreting the Civil War, for which there can be no definitive answer, is whether Blacks might have gained more in rights and human welfare, at less cost and on a quicker timetable, if the Civil War had not been fought.[59]

The North had a more obvious case for claiming the Civil War as triumph, even if the catastrophe fell short of ushering in the "Day of the Lord" or the thousand-year reign of Christ on earth. Lincoln's Emancipation Proclamation, and memories of the fallen president's nationalistic idealism, served to endow the war with high moral purpose, even as the North acquiesced to southern terrorism, lynching, and denial of civil rights to African Americans. Not until a century after the Civil War were southern blacks able to launch a new Reconstruction to gain basic freedoms that supposedly justified the war of 1860-1865 Meanwhile the American mainstream, both North and South, remembered the war as a time of redemption, and expected future wars also to contribute mightily to freedom and democracy.

Chapter 6

Revolution Derailed: Reconstruction

Bedazzled by the apparent moral achievements of the Civil War, most Americans find it hard to understand how profoundly corrupting that war was for post-war relationships between the races and between regions. Our popular images from the war are glorious: Lincoln's towering leadership, the Emancipation Proclamation, the slaves' joyous welcome of their day of liberation, Grant's generosity and Lee's dignity at Appomattox. In contrast, we remember the post-war era of Reconstruction as mean and despicable. While the triumphant war saved the union and freed the slaves, the failed Reconstruction corrupted the politicians and betrayed the freedmen. Caught in this contrast, we forget that the violence of the war was the primary author of the post-war debacle.

The vast gulf in our popular historical imaginations between splendid Civil War and tawdry Reconstruction flows in part from the belief that warfare is redemptive. We assume that warfare is not only awesome and exciting but also a source of freedom. "With the Union's triumph," wrote historian Eric Foner, "freedom truly defined the nation's existence."[1] Now the nation could cling to a moral certainty: *The Civil War freed the slaves.* With that foundation stone in place, Americans could set aside the post-war betrayal of black rights as a rather embarrassing footnote to the triumphant main story. For example, the final episode of Ken Burns' 1990 TV documentary on the Civil War skimmed over Reconstruction and flashed forward fifty years to the 1913 reunions of Union and Confederate veterans embracing each other at Gettysburg. Once again the failures of Reconstruction, which so contradicted the promise of the war, faded into the shadows of proud celebrations of the Civil War.[2]

What antidote could be potent enough to cure our disconnected images of Civil War and Reconstruction? One curative mission is to shift perspective from white policy makers to the African Americans on their journey from slavery to emancipation to renewed forms of enslavement. The black surge toward freedom in the Reconstruction era was a great tribute to the human spirit—marked by a desire to reunite with families, develop economic independence and learn to read, rather than take revenge. Another important task is to understand the intimate connection between the destructive violence of the Civil War and the continuing violence of its aftermath. Fortunately, in recent years the works of historians such as Eric Foner, Leon Litwack, and Vincent Harding have offered a healthier and more complete account of the Reconstruction era. Their information and insights challenge the reigning popular White triumphalist narrative of national history by suggesting that white dominion in the South was not undermined, but reformed and made more lasting and durable, by the violence of the Civil War and Reconstruction.[3]

The response of William Lloyd Garrison to the abolition of slavery foreshadowed the general American inclination to seize upon the end of formal slavery as a reform sufficient unto itself. Garrison had gone from scapegoat to hero. His radical abolitionism, once unpopular, had become national policy. By the war's end, Garrison thought his work was finished. He viewed the Emancipation Proclamation (January 1, 1863), the election of Lincoln to a second term (November 1964), and Congress' passage of the Thirteenth Amendment abolishing slavery (January 31, 1865), as the fulfillment of his dream. In 1864 Garrison attempted without success to disband the American Anti-slavery Society. At the end of 1865 he stopped publishing his abolitionist newspaper, *The Liberator*. What further reform was necessary? Slavery was sin, but now the nation had been redeemed.[4]

Black Community Revitalization

On the conventional political-historical time line, the era of Reconstruction begins in 1865 at the end of the war and ends with the election of Rutherford B. Hayes and the compromise of 1876. In fact the liberation of slaves became an issue early in the war, and the betrayal of that liberation took place in much of the South already before 1876.

It has taken a long time for most historians to understand to what extent the slaves were co-authors of their own liberation.[5] Soon after the war began, black slaves in parts of Virginia emancipated themselves. In 1862 slaves in the lower Mississippi Valley and along the Atlantic coast took initiatives to oppose their masters, to walk away from the old plantations, and to begin lives of greater independence. Some stayed on, or left temporarily and returned to abandoned plantations and began to work the land as their own. Some volunteered for the Union army as regular soldiers and as paid workers. The movement toward freedom took a thousand forms and it grew to a climax in 1865 in the months after the war ended. Blacks withdrew from churches where they had been forced to sit in balconies and denied leadership, and molded their own congregations into instruments for freedom. They started new schools, often with teachers barely more literate than their students. They created a host of mutual benefit and benevolence societies. They used national holidays to publicly celebrate and confirm their new independence. They organized regional conventions to state their demands and outline common programs.

In the language of black preachers who gave spiritual meaning to this freedom movement, it was the day of Exodus of God's people from the bondage of Egypt into the promised land of freedom. In the eyes of modern social science, the awakening was a "revitalization movement." The spiritual and scientific views support each other. The black rising toward freedom was a profound spiritual renewal of a very broad social and cultural system. A revitalization movement, in the words of historian Edward Magdol, is "a deliberate, organized, conscious effort by members of a society to construct a more satisfying culture."[6] Such movements can take various forms. An example we have seen in chapter one was that of Native American tribes, beaten down and demoralized, who rekindled their own communal life with fresh spiritual vision and social disciplines.[7] The black revitalization of the 1860s took its own forms.

The military played a paradoxical role in the black revitalization. Men who joined the Union army found it an agency of both liberation and death. But hopes that military service would insure the rights of citizenship were soon dashed. Some 186,000 black men served in the army during the war, a third of whom were eventually listed as dead and missing. Far more died of disease than in combat. The disease rate was three times as great for Blacks as for Whites. Some Blacks on islands off the South Carolina coast, living on plantations abandoned by their

former white masters, realized that *freedom* for them lay in possession
and cultivation of the land, rather than in allowing themselves to be
conscripted into the regimentation of army life. At times when Union
conscription-raiding parties were in the area, these black freedom-seekers
left their homes at night to avoid the bondage of military service. "They
have made a camp somewhere and mean never to be caught," said one
report.[8]

And yet many Blacks, both former slaves and freemen, gained prestige
and leadership skills in the army which enabled them to take roles later
in the Reconstruction governments. The most famous black regiment
was the 54th of Massachusetts, which in July 1863 made a heroic but
failed assault on Fort Wagner, a Confederate stronghold at the entrance
to Charleston harbor. Blacks took great pride in this event which proved
their manly valor and their worthiness for citizenship. White supporters
of black rights seized upon the Fort Wagner assault as a great symbol of
black potential—both during the war and in subsequent historical
memory. In 1935 the black historian, W. E. B. DuBois, in a path-breaking
history of Reconstruction, exposed the perverted values of a white society
which ignored the achievements of black people until they joined in
officially sanctioned murder. Whites overlooked the most brilliant black
achievements until, wrote DuBois, "The slave killed white men; and
behold, he was a man!"[9] In 1989 a popular Hollywood film on the Fort
Wagner assault, *Glory*, indoctrinated a new generation of Americans into
the imagination that the highest moment of black liberation was a violent
one. Contrary to popular images, as far as Reconstruction was concerned,
the main achievements were constructive and nonviolent. Blacks
distinguished themselves more for restraint than for violent retaliation
against their slave masters.[10]

The experience of liberation was deeply personal. It was felt most
profoundly the first time one dared to refuse a white person's order to
work, or that first moment one self-consciously addressed white
superiors as equals, rather than averting one's eyes and stepping aside.
"What you doin', nigger?" asked Eliza Mixon's master in Alabama.
Testing her new status the young black girl shot back, "I ain't no nigger.
I'se a Negro and I'm Miss Liza Mixon."[11] The planter's amazement and
anger were surely more than matched by Eliza's sense of liberation—
remembered decades later when she recounted the story. Freed slave
women hoped to carve out new identities as managers of households
rather than as field hands, sharing in field work as a matter of choice.

The sturdy black refusal of white orders and of rules of deference was especially impressive given the threat of violent white reprisals.

The freedpeople set forth some of their strongest demands and aspirations in connection with statewide conventions to promote their cause. In September 1865 a committee of blacks in Wilmington, North Carolina, called a state convention with these words:

> These are the times foretold by the Prophets, "When a Nation shall be born in a day," the good time coming. Four millions of chattels, branded mercantile commodity, shake off the bands, drop the chains, and rise up in the dignity of men. The time has arrived when we can strike one blow to secure those rights of Freemen that have been so long withheld from us.[12]

The Wilmington document claimed equal civil rights for Blacks, including suffrage, and urged blacks to create labor associations and land associations to protect wage contracts and to purchase land.

Benjamin Montgomery, a freed slave from the plantations of the brothers Joseph and Jefferson Davis, presided over the most remarkable experiment of black independence in the Reconstruction era. The large Davis plantations were located at Davis Bend, eighteen miles south of Vicksburg in a huge horseshoe bend on the Mississippi River. Already before the war, Montgomery had run a plantation store and handled cotton transactions for the Davis brothers. Jefferson Davis, chosen president of the Confederacy, left the plantation in 1861 His brother, Joseph, had to flee the following year because of the war. Joseph had been an enlightened reformer who put his slaves in charge of their own discipline and government. After Joseph's departure, Benjamin Montgomery guided the operation. In 1865 the black laborers at Davis Bend raised nearly 2,000 bales of cotton and earned a profit of $160,000. Eric Foner has called Benjamin Montgomery "an embodiment of nascent black capitalism."[13] Montgomery's story must be seen as part of the wider black chapter of cultural revitalization—an especially ironic chapter in view of Jefferson Davis' leadership of the Confederacy and commitment to chattel slavery.[14]

The Promise of Land Reform

Land reform was the most important goal in the great black revitalization movement. Only if the former slaves could gain ownership and control of the lands on which they had labored for generations could their drive toward freedom develop an economic and social base necessary for long range success. A black man in Charleston, with little formal education but much experiential wisdom, told Whitelaw Reid, a northern journalist, "Gib us our own land and we take care ourselves. But widout land, de ole massas can hire us or starve us, as dey please."[15] "Forty acres and a mule" became the rallying cry for land reformers. Land should be theirs, wrote black historian Vincent Harding, "not only by the threefold claim of cultivation, loyalty, and warfare, but as part of the all-consuming justice of God."[16]

Northern whites, including those who believed the purpose of the war was to free the slaves, did not comprehend the connection between land and freedom. Or if they understood it, they lacked the intention and will to grant that kind of freedom to African Americans. Once again, just as in the antebellum period, white reformers failed to listen seriously to the very people they purported to be helping. One magnificent opportunity for land reform was in the South Carolina Sea Islands, where all southern white inhabitants, including the fiery secessionist planter Robert Barnwell Rhett, left after November 1861 Ten thousand slaves stayed. They were eager to possess and cultivate the land on their own. Cotton production was associated with an oppressive market system, African Americans preferred to grow edible staples like corn and potatoes. But northern reformers found it in their own interest to revive the plantation cotton economy and to attempt to make it work with free black workers. A mixed group of northern entrepreneurs, Treasury officials, and army officers acquired much of the land for themselves at tax auctions. For them, "free labor" meant Blacks working for wages on white-owned land. For the former slaves, "free labor" meant ownership of the land and self-sustaining production independent of the market. A host of idealistic romantic reformers (or "Gideonites" as they were called) also came to the Sea Islands during the war—forerunners of twentieth century Peace Corps volunteers. They undertook noble work for the education and welfare of freedmen. But the future was not in the Gideonites' hands, for only a minority of freedmen were able to become self supporting. The Sea Island "rehearsal for reconstruction" was not a total failure, but the performance fell far short of the hopes of Civil War reformers.[17]

Davis Bend and the Carolina Sea Islands were wartime experiments not typical of the plantation south in general. More common was

Louisiana, where Union General Benjamin F. Butler instituted a new system of labor, partly free but substantially coerced, on the old plantations. On the estates of landowners loyal to the Union, Butler required Blacks to work for a fixed schedule of wages plus benefits. Abandoned estates he did not propose to divide up among Blacks, but to lease to northern investors. That policy came to rule elsewhere. The Union's "free labor" vision was for emancipated slaves to remain on the plantations as white-controlled wage-earning laborers.

The months after the end of the war, the summer and fall of 1865, were crucial for the possibility for a more just order in the South. Northern journalist Whitelaw Reid saw May and June as a pliable moment. The South was, Reid wrote, ". . . like clay. The Washington potters could mold it to their liking."[18] Reid thought the South would have accepted almost any conditions imposed by the Union. His observation may have been overly optimistic. In any case the leaders of the victorious Union did not have a comprehensive plan for reconstruction of the defeated and demoralized South. Abraham Lincoln had shown no interest in a program for confiscation and redistribution of land. At best he may have supported a limited suffrage for Blacks — allowing the vote only for those who were literate. But Lincoln died on April 15, six days after Lee's surrender at Appomattox. The inept new president, former slave-owner Andrew Johnson, inaugurated reconstruction policies which were disastrous for civil rights and the nation as a whole.

Alternative policies were proposed and at hand. In 1862 Congress had passed a Confiscation Act authorizing takeover of Confederates' property, a measure which President Lincoln had neglected to implement during the war. In January 1865 General William Tecumseh Sherman had issued Special Field Order No. 15 to address the plight of Blacks who were following his army. Sherman set aside for black settlement a large coastal area south of Charleston, thirty miles inland, with forty acres and the loan of army mules for each family. By June "some 40,000 freedmen had been settled on 400,000 acres of 'Sherman land.'" Sherman's field order was not a comprehensive reform plan for the entire defeated Confederacy, but it could have been confirmed and then used as a precedent and model for land reform elsewhere. The Freedmen's Bureau, officially named the Bureau of Refugees, Freedmen, and Abandoned Lands," had been authorized to divide abandoned plantations into forty-acre plots for settlement and eventual sale to freedmen and loyal refugees. In addition to this land, the federal government still controlled millions of acres of land from the Louisiana Purchase and war with Mexico, 94 million acres of which would be given to railroad corporations and even more sold or given to homesteaders. For good reasons, Blacks in the South expected land reform. Their hope for land of their own was a pivotal part of the revitalization movement.

The U.S. Congress did not meet after the war ended in April 1865 until January 1866. In that long interval President Andrew Johnson took administrative action to restore the Confederate states to the Union on terms favorable to former slave owners. This was the first, or "Presidential," Reconstruction. The old southern states held conventions, adopted new constitutions, and convened legislatures that moved quickly to reestablish white control over black labor. Their repressive measures, the notorious Black Codes, included requirements for African Americans to sign annual contracts and punishments for those who quit before the contract term expired. Some codes were "apprenticeship laws" that granted to employers the labor of black "orphans" who were separated from, or allegedly not adequately cared for, by their parents. These laws took cynical advantage of freed people's poverty and of the separation of families under slavery. Under President Johnson's Reconstruction, most of the freed people who had settled on abandoned or confiscated property were evicted. Land was restored to the Whites.

The Black Codes created a white backlash in the North. When the Thirty-ninth Congress finally met in 1866, the Republican majority denied seats in Congress to southern Whites elected by the new governments. After a long struggle with the president, and after gaining a veto-proof majority in the elections of November 1866, Congress overturned Presidential Reconstruction. The Republicans reimposed military rule and forced southern state governments to be reconstituted from ground zero. Central to the second, or "Congressional," Reconstruction were the Civil Rights Act of 1866, the Fourteenth Amendment (birthright citizenship for all) ratified in 1868, and the Fifteenth Amendment (voting rights) ratified in 1870. Although Congressional Reconstruction disfranchised the Confederate leaders and gave Blacks the right to vote, the so-called radicals were not unified on land reform. They focused more on ways to guarantee the future dominance of the Republican party.

The delay of radical Reconstruction helped ensure its eventual failure. President Johnson's Reconstruction, temporary though it was, reinvigorated the demoralized Confederates. After their experience in reestablishing government on their own terms, and after instituting new means short of slavery for white control of Blacks, southern Whites had a new understanding of postwar possibilities. Their backs stiffened. And they turned to violent means of resistance that the recent war itself had fostered and sanctified.

Violence and Reconstruction

The South had been an exceptionally violent region already before the Civil War. The roots of that violence were manifold—immigrant origins from regions of high violence in the British isles, the relative anarchy of the frontier, a hierarchical social system with oppressed slaves at the bottom, and more.[19] But postwar violence had a more immediate origin in the experience of war itself. As a leading historian of American violence, Richard Maxwell Brown, has put it, "The latter part of the 19th century was one of the most violent periods of American history . . . . The major part of this violence is traceable to the Civil War."[20] The violence of the Reconstruction era flowed directly from experiences of men whose inclinations to violence were enhanced by participation in war.[21]

The war generated violence by giving men weapons, by training them to kill, and by throwing them into the most bloody sequence of military battles of American history. Tens of thousands of the weapons manufactured in the war remained in the hands of former soldiers after the war, and Whites had higher quality weapons than Blacks. Wartime foraging practices taught ordinary soldiers to prey on the private property of local people and undermined respect for law. Less well known than the famous battles, but no less important for post-war civil upheavals, was an internal civil war within the Confederacy.[22] Southerners had fought against each other with astonishing violence during the war, and that violence extended and proliferated in many ways after the war. Southern unionists and secessionist guerillas had clashed with special violence in the hills and mountains of Appalachia and the Ozarks. Class conflicts between non-slave owning small farmers and the landowning aristocrats had flared when the Confederacy's military fortunes failed and the desperate government resorted to military conscription.

The immediate aftermath of the war was an especially violent time. Confederate soldiers returning home from their collapsed armies, desperate and hungry, attacked and plundered stores of the defeated Confederate government. Already in January of 1865 a Georgia newspaper reported that half of the state's northern counties "had been turned into a wasteland by outlaw bands of soldiers and deserters."[23] This violence of the spring and summer of 1865 provided the context for Presidential Reconstruction. Behind the Black Codes was not only an inheritance of racism and slavery from the past; the first Reconstruction governments were attempts to restore order in the face of anarchic violence. As humiliated victims of war themselves, the former Confederate leaders directed their anger against their former slaves.

The Ku Klux Klan was a product of the Civil War as surely as of inherited racism and a tradition of violence. The Klan came into its own as a counterrevolutionary terrorist organization in response to Congressional Reconstruction of 1867-68. The Klan had been founded in 1866 in Tennessee by a Confederate general, Nathan Bedford Forrest, who was notorious even among the military for having his troops kill African American soldiers at Fort Pillow, Tennessee after the fort had surrendered. The Klan, whose original organization was based on army units, spread into all the southern states as an extralegal military force whose goal was "to destroy the Republican party's infrastructure, undermine the Reconstruction state, reestablish control of the black labor force, and restore racial subordination in every aspect of Southern life."[24] The Klan targeted black leaders for intimidation and murder. Seven black members of the 1867-68 constitutional conventions were murdered, and dozens more suffered attacks on physical body and personal property.

In the presidential election of 1868, Blacks in Camilla, Georgia held an election parade. A gang of armed Whites, led by the local sheriff, fired on the parade and chased after its fleeing members. They killed and wounded more than a score of Blacks. In the same election, white gangs in New Orleans broke up Republican political meetings and invaded the plantations. They killed "as many as 200 blacks."[25] Only rarely did Blacks respond with violent retaliation. When they did so, they suffered an awful vengeance. In the election of 1872, black veterans and militia officers took over the county seat of Colfax in Louisiana. After three weeks of control, they were overcome and slaughtered. Fifty men who had surrendered and laid down their arms were massacred.[26]

Klan membership crossed class lines. Respectable citizens, planters and professionals, controlled the organization and generally chose the targets for violence. Most of the Klan members were ordinary farmers and laborers. They wore white hoods in part to remain anonymous, but they knew they could destroy black property and murder black people without fear of legal consequences. For the most part, law abiding southern Whites were silent in the face of Klan violence. That silence continued in the post-Reconstruction era and into the twentieth century, when white mobs in the South lynched hundreds of black men for real and imagined crossings of the color line. Like the Klan violence itself, the inability of public officials to enforce law and order against vigilantism was in part a legacy of the Civil War. Southern Whites had suffered much, and were striking back, exchanging violence for violence.

The historical evaluation of Republican governments in the South under radical Reconstruction has been bitterly contested — "the dark and bloody ground of Reconstruction historiography."[27] The radical governments labored under formidable disadvantages, not least of which was the violent hostility of most white southerners to the radical Republican coalition of Blacks, white northerners (carpetbaggers), and white southerners (scalawags). The radical political coalition itself was beset with internal conflict. They disagreed among each other over issues of social equality (such as laws against intermarriage of Blacks and Whites) and of subsidies to railroads and public works. They had to provide programs of public education and social welfare in a region that lacked a tradition of activist government. A series of bad harvest years, an economic recession in 1865, and a more severe depression in the 1870s, brought on financial distress which prompted many northern investors to cut their losses and return home. With each passing year, social and political reformers in the North gradually lost their commitment to the rights and welfare of former slaves in the South.

The North's withdrawal of military forces from the South in 1877, however, should not be seen as the primary cause of the failure of Reconstruction to provide for equal rights. Reconstruction violently imposed upon the South from the outside North was not viable in the long run. The prospect for a more humane social and economic order in the South depended more foundationally upon the relative power and the relationships of three groups in the South. One group was the Old Planter Aristocracy, the white leaders of the Confederacy. Another group was the "Other South," the small white farmers plus those white leaders who had been members of the old Whig party and had led Unionist forces before the war. The third group was the black freedpeople.

For the Republican Party in the South to sustain a political movement in the long run, the "Other South" Whites (plus "carpetbaggers" who intended to stay) and the Blacks had to work together in a coalition based upon common economic interests. That coalition depended upon an adequate social and economic base. But the abandonment of land reform early in the Reconstruction era kept black small farmers from emerging as a viable social force. Instead they were reduced to impoverished sharecroppers, unable effectively to assert their common economic and political interest with their natural allies. Instead, the old planter aristocracy eventually won over to their side those of the "Other South" by resorting to a new politics of race. The white South, led by the Democrat party, achieved what they called "Redemption" by appealing to the racial fears of Whites and to the Lost Cause of the Confederacy.

Violence helped bring "Redemption." But the character of southern white violence changed after 1873. The Ku Klux Klan of 1866 to 1871 had been local and covert—an uncoordinated response of rage to military defeat and to Congressional Reconstruction. In 1871 Congress passed a Ku Klux Klan Act that extended the national government's authority to intervene in the states in behalf of constitutional rights. The government took strong legal and military action against the Klan, especially in South Carolina. After 1873, in most southern states, the Klan was a lesser force in the political achievement of "Redemption" than the new violence that was well organized, carried out in public, endorsed by high Democrat party officials, and directed against Republican Reconstruction institutions such as courthouses, jails and militia units. This Democrat Party violence was more widespread and eventually more effective than the earlier Ku Klux Klan violence. The political campaigns that ended Reconstruction and put the exclusively white Democrat party into control of southern states were, in the words of historian Michael Perman, "with little doubt, the ugliest in American history."[28]

Truth and Reconciliation

Formal slavery in the United States came to an end under the worst possible circumstances. The result was a transformed system of labor relations in the South. Black laborers became sharecroppers, living in dispersed homesteads rather than in concentrated slave quarters. The days of plantation gang labor were no more. But in the end, the bruised southern white upper class, denied the leading role in national politics they once enjoyed, found new ways to dominate, exploit and terrorize their own former slaves. The plantation oligarchy's bitter memories and resentments from the war, supported by a majority of northerners who wanted to put the war behind them, guaranteed that their new means of racial dominion would be as violent and vengeful as the old system of slavery. In a sense, it was even more deeply embedded in the nation's psyche, because it was buried from the nation's conscience by the self-congratulatory rhetoric of eliminating slavery. The prophetic voices of freed people proclaiming that true liberation for *all* people necessitated both eliminating slavery *and* eliminating racism had been ignored. Even more than before the war, African Americans, many of them direct descendents of former masters, became the objects of vented white rage. In despising "the other," one ended up in profound ways despising oneself. Unfortunately the new system of racial segregation and control emerged strong and durable enough to last for another whole century.

Would an alternative model for reconciliation after the Civil War have been possible? The question is unanswerable, but nevertheless worth reflection. Several directions for an answer have already been suggested: restorative justice for the slaves; careful listening to the former slaves; a willingness to act in the best interests of all, not just one group; an understanding of the linkages between slavery and racism; a more rehabilitative context for the confederates; compassionate rather than vengeful leadership. But in suggesting this are we asking humanity to have a greater generosity of spirit than is possible?

In the 1990s the country of South Africa took dramatic steps to overcome its own system of racial domination. In previous decades, politicians and social scientists had invariably predicted that South African apartheid would not be ended without a destructive race war. For decades the white majority had imposed a rigid caste system through forced migrations, assassinations, torture and disappearances. While no formal war was ever declared, no black home was untouched by violence. When the system finally gave way in the early 1990s, the country faced similar questions to those faced by the United States in 1865. How does one transform a hierarchical, racialized ideology into an inclusive and just democracy? How does one heal years of abuse?

The new regime, led by Nelson Mandela, created a "Truth and Reconciliation Commission" to establish a foundation of honesty and justice on which to build a new coalition government. The South African

Truth and Reconciliation Commission, headed by Anglican priest Bishop Tutu, had three parts: a forum for victims to investigate human rights violations, a reparations and rehabilitation commission to take steps necessary to bring restorative justice, and an amnesty commission to which perpetrators could appeal for "earned" amnesty.

The work of the commission was broadcast on national television, so that everyone knew what was going on. Many Whites watching were horrified to see the extent of violence from which they had been sheltered. While the work of the commission has been controversial and the reparations have been slow in coming because of the enormous economic problems facing South Africa, the Truth and Reconciliation Commission remains a bold model of courage, honesty and justice for other countries trying to move beyond tyrannical pasts to more peaceful futures.[29]

In addition to the commission, the country approved the most progressive constitution in the world. Its bill of rights includes not only freedom of religion, expression, and assembly, but children's rights, fair labor practices, a healthy environment, education, housing and health care. The constitution also explicitly prohibits discrimination on the basis of race, gender, sexual orientation, age, disabilities, language and a host of other enumerated categories. By law at least thirty percent of parliamentarians must be women. In 1994 the government announced a land reform program "to redistribute thirty percent of the land from white to black ownership within two years." The goal was not fully met, but it was not forgotten.[30] Thus South Africa is rising to the challenge with a systemic reconstruction that occurred primarily through negotiation rather than warfare.

Mandela's South Africa and Andrew Johnson's United States were vastly different from each other. Perhaps the most notable difference is that the oppressed group in South Africa was a numerical majority (nearly 80%) so that power sharing in the government became mandatory if a new coalition government was to have any viability. Unfortunately this overwhelming majority have been so impoverished that South Africa lacks adequate resouces to meet their needs or fulfill the promises that have been made. Yet the willingness of key leaders to talk, and the openness to honesty, change and forgiveness embodied in the Truth and Reconciliation Commission have most strikingly set South African reconstruction apart from that in the United States.

Both countries continue to face the legacies of violence. There are no short cuts to overcoming years of entrenched and habitual violence. In South Africa, crime is soaring and there have been more than 10,000 reported political murders since 1994. Homes are barricaded, and many people continue to live in fear. These problems are exacerbated by rates of unemployment from forty to eighty percent and by the AIDS epidemic which has already infected as many as one in four people.

But the good news is that cycles of violence can be broken. For all of its shortcomings, the Truth and Reconciliation Commission has offered the world a glimmer of light—an opening through the dark abyss of violence. This opening rests on the three branches of the commission:

1) *Truth telling* (listening seriously to the stories of the oppressed)

2) *Restorative justice* (mobilizing the resources necessary for reparations and rehabilitation of the victims of injustice) and

3) *Forgiveness and mercy* (recognizing that oppressors often see themselves as trapped and in need of an alternative way of living and recognizing that eventually victims need to let go of their bitterness by forgiving).

Part of the insight of the South African Truth and Reconciliation Commission is that it acknowledged that all three of these aspects must be present in order for true reconciliation to happen. It was not designed as "victor's justice," where only the losers are put on trial. Mercy for perpetrators without justice for victims would only perpetuate the old system. Justice for victims without mercy for perpetrators would not open possibilities for reconciliation. And no form of transformation is possible without first knowing the truth about one's own society. It is never too late for a country to begin implementing truth, justice and mercy. Reconstruction in the best sense of the word is still a possibility for both South Africa and the United States.

Chapter 7

Capitalism, the Constitution, and the Common Good: Workers in the United States

Between the Civil War and the First World War an industrial revolution in America unleashed prodigious economic growth, while creating a crisis situation for workers. The resulting industrial warfare challenged the promise of American democracy as profoundly as it was tested in the Civil War. Workers and employers became adversaries in a conflict without clear rules. The workers struggled to maintain a sense of human dignity and worth in the increasingly commodified world of material production. The employers moved to maximize production and profit with a minimum of cost.

To guide their adventure into industrial change and conflict, Americans tested new interpretations of their founding principles: freedom, opportunity, equality and democracy.[1] In the American colonies, New England Puritans defined freedom as the power to know and do the will of God. In Virginia freedom meant the ability to control one's self and to exercise benevolent control over others in a hierarchical social order. The American Revolution and new influences from the Enlightenment broke down regional differences and gave rise to new understandings of freedom. James Madison, the principal author of the Constitution, warned in *Federalist Paper* #10 that factionalism arising from "the various and unequal distribution of property" could endanger the new nation.

In the early republic Americans identified freedom with political democracy and broadly equal economic opportunities and conditions. Free labor, whose ideal was the small farmer, was defined as work done by independent people who owned their means of production. Thomas Jefferson believed that the future of freedom in the United States depended upon its remaining a nation of small farmers. With the Louisiana Purchase of 1803, Jefferson believed, the country had acquired sufficient land to guarantee, for the indefinite future, an American social order of freedom, rooted in the character of small landowners who controlled the means of their own production.

Capitalist industrial development in the late nineteenth century created substantial wealth, but it was not evenly distributed. Material rewards disproportionately went to risk takers and investors, rather than producers and workers. Both workers and employers continued to claim the language of freedom, opportunity and democracy, but with differing interpretations. To employers, freedom meant the ability to create wealth unhindered by regulations. To workers, freedom meant sufficient return for a reasonable day's work to be free from want, poverty and chronic exhaustion. The language of equality increasingly became limited to a minimal political equality although workers reminded the nation of the inherent instability in too great a disparity between the richest and the poorest.

During the depressions of the 1870s and 1890s wages were cut while rents and consumer prices remained the same or increased. Workers responded with protests and strikes. When government troops or Pinkerton agents were brought in to end work stoppages, violence erupted. A looming class struggle seemed to threaten the very basis of democracy.

From Self-Employment to Wage Slavery

Aggrieved industrial workers charged that the new system turned them into slaves. Industrial slavery, they said, was akin to the racial slave system. To achieve justice they faced a new civil war, this time with labor pitted against capital. In the twenty years from 1880 to 1900 more than 23,000 strikes broke out involving six million workers. The era saw "some of the most violent struggles between labor and employers in the history of capitalism," according to historian Eric Foner.[2]

Were industrial workers slaves? Southern defenders of slavery George Fitzhugh and John Calhoun loved to contrast the benevolent patriarchy of slavery with the cruelty of the northern "wage slavery." Arguing that masters looked after their slaves in infancy and old age, unlike the system of "free competition," Fitzhugh concluded that "The older system of slavery and dependence proves itself superior to the defects inherent in the newer system of liberty and equality."[3] However, the captains of industry, who employed the workers and controlled their terms of employment, believed the charge of wage slavery was false. Their workers, they said, were free. Employers and employees both had liberty of contract. If workers did not want their jobs, they could leave. Moreover, the industrial revolution brought unprecedented prosperity and economic opportunity to the country. Immigrants flooded to America from Europe, and to the cities from the countryside, to take the factory jobs. So how could it be true that this was a new system of slavery?

Working conditions in the new factories were often dehumanizing. Mill towns and factory towns crowded people together. Much turn-of the-century work was hard, dirty and dangerous. Coal miners worked in cramped, dark mine shafts, breathing deadly coal dust. Steel workers faced backbreaking labor filling skips with ore and fuel, and unbearable heat from blast furnaces. Meat-packers became enured to animal squeals, blood and nauseating stench. Hours were long: for most mill workers, twelve hours a day for six or seven days a week was common. Children as young as ten worked alongside adults for a fraction of the wages, particularly in textile mills and in the mines, where their smaller size was considered an asset. The law forbade workers even to talk with each other about their work environment. It is no wonder that labor began to look for ways to redress these conditions. The inhumane conditions were due to primitive technology, as well as the uncaring greed of factory and mine owners.

The Civil War transformed not only the southern economic system of slavery, but also the northern economic system of small worker-owned farms and businesses. The war accelerated the country's movement into a global market system based on the rise of heavy industry, of corporations, and of the railway network. Industrial organization had far-reaching social and economic consequences. Traditional notions of time, work and family changed. Clock time superseded agrarian time, which had been based on the cycles of nature. Working for one's self with the freedom to set hours and conditions was replaced by working for someone else who set the hours and conditions. Master and apprentice relationships were replaced by boss and laborer relationships. In 1880, eighty percent of people were self-employed. By 1920, eighty percent of the people worked for someone else. These changes were very disturbing at the time, although they now are accepted as natural.

Before the industrial revolution, any citizen who aspired to personal freedom might take a job as a wage-earner, but only as a temporary step toward eventual property ownership and greater independence. As early as 1809, journeymen house carpenters began a strike declaration with the words of the Declaration of Independence: "Among the unalienable rights of man are life, liberty and the pursuit of happiness . . . . By the social compact, every class in society ought to be entitled to benefit in proportion to its usefulness." The freedom gained by independence from England was not only political, it was also economic. It implied the freedom and independence which comes from knowing hard work and useful labor will reap fair and secure economic benefits. This is what was meant by the "social compact." Well before Karl Marx produced his short revolutionary manifesto critiquing capitalism, American workers were calling for an end to what they called "wage slavery."

Labor historians Paul Buhle and Alan Dawley have observed, "For those reared in the tradition of the independent artisan, working for wages seemed a form of slavery for it entailed a loss of personal autonomy and a sense of control over one's own destiny."[4] Anyone caught *permanently* in a wage-earning position, lacking property and security for old age, was not a free person. Life on the financial edge did not allow enough savings to facilitate a physical move or re-training. With wages just above subsistence levels, these workers were stuck. Then the industrial factory system created a whole class of wage-earners who not only lacked property, but who also worked for subsistence wages in desperately poor working conditions and faced unemployment in times of economic depression. By the definitions of "freedom" in their times, workers in the nineteenth century, especially those laid off in depressions of the 1870s or 1890s had some claim to identify themselves as unfree.

Inequality and Welfare

From colonial times onward there had been rich people and poor people in America. Inequalities of wealth were especially visible in the cities, where enterprising people gained wealth through commerce and financial investments. Before the industrial revolution, however, the United States remained predominantly a rural society of agricultural producers. In the 1870s and 1880s, the rise of a fabulously wealthy new class of industrialists upset the old balance. Wealth became concentrated in the hands of a few, symbolized by the great fortunes and conspicuous consumption of the "new rich" families who built lavish mansions, aped the fashions of high English society, and sought to marry their children into titled European families. In 1890, ten percent of the population held seventy-three percent of the national wealth. Industrialists such as Andrew Carnegie and John D. Rockefeller considered their wealth to be "earned." Whether it was flaunted in "conspicuous consumption" or used for philanthropic purposes, the concentrated wealth did little to ease the material needs of those living in drafty, crumbling tenements with too little to eat.

Most American history textbooks today acknowledge the plight of the poor people at the bottom of the economic system in the late nineteenth century — the victims of child labor, of unhealthy and unsafe working environment, of the absence of insurance protection against unemployment and old age. The United States government seemed reluctant to take on this new responsibility as part of its constitutional mandate "to promote the general welfare." In fact the country lagged decades behind European countries in enacting programs of social insurance for the unemployed, indigent and elderly. Germany initiated workmen's compensation in 1884 and old-age pensions in 1889, a welfare system more extensive than the United States would realize until the New Deal of the 1930s.

The United States, however, did have a substantial late-nineteenth-century welfare program that is not as well known. In the years after the Civil War, the government put into place a program of benefits for war veterans that constituted the country's first national welfare-state system.[5] Union veterans were among the most highly honored of U.S. citizens. They and their defenders turned this reputation into economic coinage. In the 1890s, more than forty percent of the federal budget went to Union veterans and their survivors. By the 1910s, almost one in five persons over age sixty-five received government pensions. The social welfare program, massively biased against poor Whites and Blacks in the South, was often more generous to its recipients than were the social welfare programs of European nations.

The veteran's benefit program was an ironic testament to the power of militaristic patriotism in the United States. In a country that in principle opposed federal government social welfare payments for victims of poverty and unemployment, there was lavish social welfare generosity for families of those who had been willing to engage in the violence of war, ostensibly to "preserve the union." Many who received this aid were truly needy. In general, however, it was a warped welfare system, oriented not to workers and the elderly, but a foreshadowing of massive government payments for military volunteers and veterans in the twentieth century. It was a subtle but profound skewing of the country toward militaristic, not domestic solutions to unemployment and poverty. In short the government rewarded (and continues to reward) participation in state-sanctioned violence while neglecting the preventable violence of industrialization.

Attempts to Humanize the Wage System: Cooperative Visions of Workers

As American politics emerged into a two party system of Federalists and Democrats, workingmen began to form their own parties, claiming that the major parties were "instruments of the oppressing class." In 1828 the first Workingman's Party was formed in Philadelphia, the founding city of American liberty. Soon the party spread to every state and had its own political candidates. It proposed to abolish child labor and shorten the working day, but more broadly to bring justice to the poor and oppressed, from the abolition of slavery to peace with the Indians. Among their far-seeing reforms were universal suffrage, free public education, and free trade. They proposed to abolish monopolies, capital punishment, imprisonment for debt, and the prevailing militia system. Although the Workingman's Party elected few of their own candidates, the "labor vote" prompted the major parties to include at least watered-down versions of workers' programs into party platforms. The party strengthened the sense of power in united action of working people, and gave momentum to later movements.

One of the earliest and strongest movements to challenge the rise of industrial capitalism called for cooperation, not competition, between labor and management. In 1869 Philadelphia garment workers started the group known as the Most Holy Order of the Knights of Labor, under the leadership of Uriah Stephens. This group envisioned a "Cooperative Commonwealth" where management and labor would work together for the cooperative good of all. They did not accept as members the "social parasites" who did no real work—bankers, investors, stock brokers and lawyers. But all working people, male or female, skilled or unskilled, black or white, were invited to join. In 1886, sixty thousand Blacks, including laundresses and domestics, were members. In the Cooperative Commonwealth, government would be restored to the common people, and poverty would be eliminated — a dream that is echoed in contemporary movements for participatory democracy. The Knights of Labor motto showed their belief in the interconnectedness of all human life — "An injury to one is an injury to all."

By 1879 the Knights of Labor were nationally organized. Local assemblies were composed of all workers in a given area — not stratified by job or skill or place of employment. They elected a president, called a Grand Master Workman. During the Knights' most active years, this Grand Master Workman was an Irish Catholic, Terrence V. Powderly. Their greatest success was in 1885, with a national strike against wage cuts ordered by the infamous railroad tycoon Jay Gould. That success brought membership to over 750,000 or ten percent of all non-agricultural workers.[6] But Gould retaliated by provoking another strike, one for which he was better prepared. Refusing arbitration, Gould hired Pinkerton agents to intimidate strikers and keep the trains running.

A second blow came to the Knights the same year when they were implicated in the Haymarket affair. Another labor organization, the Federation of Organized Trades and Labor Unions of the United States and Canada, set May 1 (traditional Labor Day) 1886 as the deadline for an eight-hour day in all trades. Powderly, who had reservations about strikes, did not support the call for strikes if the demand was not met, but some assemblies of the Knights did. On May 3, one striker was killed at the International Harvester plant in Chicago. A group of anarchists called for an open and peaceful meeting the following day to protest the killing. A drizzly rain was falling and the crowd was dispersing when police arrived. A bomb was thrown — to this day no one knows by whom. One policeman was killed and several injured. In the subsequent trials, eight anarchist leaders were sentenced to death, despite a lack of evidence. Four were hanged, two reprieved, and one committed suicide in prison. One of the eight, Albert Parsons, carried a membership card in the Knights of Labor. The association with anarchism, as well as internal problems of organization and strong anti-immigration stands, particularly in the West, led to the decline of the Knights. Labor organization in the country took a more conservative turn.

The American Federation of Labor (AFL), a combination of national craft unions, replaced the Knights of Labor as the leading labor organization. A founder and the leading spirit until his death in 1924, Samuel Gompers was an English immigrant who worked in a cigar factory. The work was tedious and so the workers had someone read to them while they prepared and hand-rolled tobacco leaves into cigars. Much of this reading was intellectual, generating discussions about politics and economics, Marxism and Darwinism. But Gompers set aside the utopian ideals that characterized the Knights of Labor. The AFL concentrated on pragmatic, achievable goals such as higher wages and shorter hours. With effectiveness as a goal, the AFL organized primarily skilled white males, the group most able to negotiate for better hours and working conditions. By the turn of the century, AFL membership exceeded half a million, and it grew to four million by 1920.

Some workers became more convinced that their relation with management would be antagonistic, rather than cooperative. Immigrants from England, Germany, and Eastern Europe had experience with European industrialization and now faced the challenge of organizing in factories and mines where it was not unusual for the work force of different nationalities to speak twenty or thirty different languages. In 1905 some socialist labor leaders organized the Industrial Workers of the World (IWW). Their goal was to create "One Big Union" of all races, ethnicities, skilled and unskilled workers to unite, as the name suggested, all the workers of the world. They recognized that an emerging global marketplace was affecting the relationship of labor and capital. English money built U.S. railroads; U.S. meat and wheat supplied Europe.[7] The IWW reflected the social diversity of American laborers. They organized into language sub-groups and printed publicity in various languages. Unlike the Knights of Labor, the IWW was deeply rooted in class consciousness. Opposed to initiating violence, members of the IWW were frequently targeted for arrest.

One of the most persistent labor activists was a diminutive, grandmotherly woman, dressed in long old-fashioned dresses, who stirred up workers with her fiery words spoken with a lilting Irish brogue. Mary Harris Jones (1837-1930), affectionately known as "Mother Jones," lost her four children and husband in a yellow fever epidemic in 1867. During the remaining sixty years of her life, Mother Jones' activities on behalf of labor kept her at the center of action: with the Knights of Labor, the railroad strike of 1877, the founding convention of the IWW in 1905, the Colorado miners in 1914, and the steel workers at Homestead in

1919. One of her greatest concerns was child labor. She frequently took jobs in mills so that she could collect evidence of child labor and conditions. More than a quarter of a million children under the age of fifteen worked full time at the turn of the century. In the summer of 1903, Mother Jones joined 75,000 striking textile workers in Kensington, Pennsylvania. Ten thousand of these strikers were children, joining the demand for shorter hours and better wages. She noted in her autobiography that "Every day little children came into Union Headquarters, some with their hands off, some with the thumb missing, some with their fingers off at the knuckle. They were stooped little things, round shouldered and skinny."[8] She decided to lead a group of striking children on a march from the textile mills to the vacation home of President Theodore Roosevelt at Oyster Bay, New York, calling on him to "hear the wail of the children who never have a chance to go to school, but work ten to eleven hours a day in the textile mills." The President was not in a listening mood and refused to see them. But the issue gained public exposure.

Attempts to Humanize Commercial Agriculture: Farmers and the Populist Movement

Agriculture also changed dramatically in the late nineteenth century, moving from small relatively self-sufficient farms, to larger enterprises that produced one or two crops for the commercial market. Depressed conditions led farmers, as surely as workers, to imagine and work for a more just social order. In the late nineteenth century farmers, who suffered from high interest rates, arbitrary railroad rates, fixed currency, and low prices for their produce, became politicized. The difficult reality for farmers was that they were producing more and earning less. The situation was even more desperate for farmers who didn't own their own land but worked for others on "shares." This system was particularly widespread in the South, where the sharecroppers were freed slaves and poor whites working on cotton plantations. Sharecroppers were furnished agricultural supplies and basic food and clothing by a "furnishing merchant," who kept records of every transaction. Interest charged on these supplies could run as high as 50%-200%.[9] When harvest time came, the farmer and merchant weighed the crop and "settled" the books. Inevitably the farmer's crop was not sufficient to pay for the supplies and interest and so the "crop lien" system developed, whereby

whereby the farmer would mortgage next year's crop in order to survive the winter. Many of the farmers were illiterate, and merchants did not give them options to pay cash or buy elsewhere. Although cotton production exhausted the soil, "the Man" (as the furnishing merchant was called) required that debtors continue to plant cotton, rather than rotate with other crops.

In September 1877 a group of farmers in southeast Texas met to discuss their problems and organize a "grand social and political palace where liberty may dwell and justice be safely domiciled."[10] Although this group only lasted for three years, the idea spread to surrounding areas and a "Farmers Alliance" formed. Like the emerging industrial labor movement, their first plan of action involved self-help, cooperation and education. S. O. Daws, a sharecropper from Mississippi, became the first of many articulate traveling lecturers, educating farmers about the ways of the economic system and exhorting them to act cooperatively to meet their needs. An Irish-born lawyer, Mary Elizabeth Lease, was one of the most effective lecturers. She attacked the eastern moneyed interests (as far east as London bankers), and told Kansas farmers in 1890 that "Wall Street owns the country. It is no longer a government of the people, by the people, and for the people, but a government of Wall Street, by Wall Street and for Wall Street . . . . Money rules, and our Vice-President is a London banker. Our laws are the output of a system which clothes rascals in robes and honesty in rags."[11]

Farmers formed cooperatives to buy and sell their produce in order to receive fairer prices. The tactic proved successful, but met with deep opposition from local merchants and manufacturers. Even though farmers could use their land or crop as collateral, banks refused to lend them money to build silos to house their grain. So they turned to political channels, hoping to influence the government sufficiently to help finance their plans. The result was the formation of the Populist or People's Party. Their platform, made public in Omaha, Nebraska in February 1892, declared, "The fruits of toil of millions are boldly stolen to build up colossal fortunes for a few, unprecedented in the history of mankind; and the possessors of these in turn, despise the Republic and endanger liberty." The Populist party platform also included free coinage of silver (to increase the amount of money in circulation), a graduated income tax, (to redistribute wealth for the common good), government ownership of railroads and telegraph lines (to insure fairer rates), direct election of

Senators (to increase democracy and hopefully prevent a Senate of millionaires), the initiative and referendum (to give citizens more participation in law-making and decision-making), a shorter working day, and immigration restriction (to prevent downward pressure on wages).

Thus the Populists stood in the tradition of the earlier Workingmen's Party. They looked at ways to make the economic and political systems more democratic. The democratizing efforts bore fruit, as most of their platform eventually became law. However, the Populist party lost its edge as it was absorbed by the Democratic Party in the election of 1896. In addition, strategic differences split the movement, the racial climate made alliances between black and white farmers difficult, and general economic prosperity undermined the impetus to reform. Many of the basic problems of farmers remained unaddressed. By the late twentieth century, family farms had all but disappeared. Each year more food is produced on farms owned by absentee corporate owners and imported from other countries.

Looking for Answers: Middle Class Reformers

Another voice raised to challenge the excesses and abuses of industrialization came from Christians who believed the gospel message should be applied in the workplace. Loosely organized around the teachings of Baptist Walter Rauschenbush and Congregationalist Washington Gladden, the movement tended to appeal to intellectuals and the middle class.[12] A number of adherents were of the "employing class" so despised by the IWW. One little-known but notable example is Samuel M. Jones, who grew wealthy as the owner of a factory which produced his improved "sucker rods," utilized by the booming petroleum industry to pump oil from wells.

Jones was born in Wales in 1846 and emigrated to the United States with his family three years later. At fourteen, he left the family farm in New York, becoming one of the few genuine "rags to riches" stories of the era. Like Andrew Carnegie, he became wealthy from the oil industry. However, Jones was appalled by Carnegie's book, *The Gospel of Wealth*, which defended the accumulation of wealth by those who best knew how to use and judiciously share it. In the margins of Carnegie's book, Jones wrote, "Oh, horrors" and "This is the highest pitch of absurdity."[13] Influenced by the social gospel, Jones set about to apply the Golden Rule ("Do to others as you would have them do to you." Matthew 7:12) to his factory in Toledo, Ohio and later to city government when he became mayor of Toledo in 1897. Stressing "brotherhood, equality and municipal socialism" (by which he meant city-owned utilities), he also advocated kindergartens (because it is cheaper to educate than build prisons), an eight-hour day for all municipal employees, and a program to aid transients.

Jones frequently wrote letters to his friend Nelson O. Nelson, who had similar ideals. In 1890 Nelson established what he hoped would become a model factory community just north of St. Louis. Named after a French profit-sharing pioneer, Leclaire community was Nelson's dream that business could become "an educational institution that would stand for something nobler and better than the miserly miserable idea of profit making." Workers had shorter hours, higher wages, paid vacations and insurance programs—all innovative ideas. According to Nelson, "we made the factories within and without as commodious, healthy, and attractive as we knew how, for men and boys spend most of their lives in and about them." The community included inexpensive housing, a cooperative store and a club house where notable reformers came to speak. But of greatest consequence and significance, Nelson believed in profit sharing with his workers, and refused to accept more than 6% return on yearly profits.[14]

While men, as business leaders, could make choices about how their factories were run, middle-class women reformers generally had to use other means to address the inequalities created by late nineteenth-century urbanization and industrialization. These women, young, college-educated, idealistic and middle class, chose to settle in deprived neighborhoods, creating community centers and settlement houses. Their work was practical and "hands on." Jane Addams and Ellen Starr built Hull House in Chicago, offering child care for working mothers, job training, and a health clinic, as well as cultural events like lectures, music, art studios and a Little Theater movement. Lillian Wald's Henry House Settlement in New York City offered similar services, including English-language classes for immigrants.

These women realized that they were able to help only a very few of the thousands of slum dwellers. Therefore they agitated for housing laws, juvenile courts, workmen's compensation laws and legislation against child labor. In 1912 Wald helped establish the federal Children's Bureau. Addams recognized the linkages between oppressive working conditions and war and helped found the Womens International League for Peace and Freedom. In 1931 she won the Nobel Peace Prize.

Eugene Debs and The Socialist Movement

Perhaps no figure of the early twentieth century is a clearer symbol of the national protest against the social revolution wrought by industrial capital than Eugene Debs. Born in Terre Haute, Indiana in 1855, Debs was the son of immigrants from Colmar, Alsace. As a fervent believer in democracy, he chose to become involved with the struggle of laborers. In 1894, he was the leader of the American Railway Union, an attempt at industrial unionism. When George Pullman cut wages and jobs, but kept rents at the same rate in his "model" town, the union led a nationwide strike. By not handling Pullman cars, the union effectively stopped rail transportation. The government fought back by attaching mail cars to each train, so that it would be a federal violation not to deliver mail. The U.S. attorney-general Olney swore in 3400 special deputies to keep the trains running. Debs was arrested for violating a federal injunction which claimed that the strike violated the Sherman Anti-Trust Act by restraining interstate commerce. He was sentenced to six months in jail. He used the jail time to read widely, including much socialist literature. Nick Salvatore, in his biography of Debs, portrays him as someone who refused to allow technological innovation to undermine American democratic traditions and who created native roots for American socialism.[15]

During World War I, the government passed a strict sedition act, under which many were arrested for speaking against the unpopular "European War." Debs was among those arrested for speaking against the war. He wrote, "I have no country to fight for; my country is the earth; I am a citizen of the world." In the address for which he was arrested, given in Canton, Ohio on June 15, 1918 to a crowd of over 1,000, he spoke of creating an industrial democracy where workers controlled their own jobs and labor and could be "free men instead of slaves." Socialists, he concluded, have a "duty to build the new nation and the free republic ... to proclaim the emancipation of the working class and the brotherhood of all mankind." At his sentencing, he denied that he advocated violence in any form: "While there is a lower class, I am in it; while there is a criminal element, I am of it; while there is a soul in prison, I am not free."[16] From jail in 1920, he ran for president of the U.S. on the Socialist Party ticket and garnered 919,799 votes—more than in any of his three other campaigns for president.

Federal Response

Corporate interests enlisted the help of the courts to defend their control over working people and the workplace. The Fourteenth Amendment to the Constitution, ratified in 1868, was written to guarantee equality before the law for Blacks—as well as for all citizens. In the post-war era, the courts abandoned black rights, but extended to corporations the legal protections for "liberty of contract" under the Fourteenth Amendment. Corporations, like individual workers, said the courts, were "persons." Standard Oil, U.S. Steel, and any corporate giant was entitled to protection against any state that would, in the Amendment's language, "deprive any *person* of life, liberty, or property, without due process of law." The law established the myth of the labor contract as an agreement between two equivalent persons, and stood against the rights of laborers to organize and get better contracts. Populist leader Ignatius Donnelly ridiculed the notion that corporations were persons. Would the Supreme Court now rule that "corporations have the right to marry and rear children?"[17] The court's interpretation of the Fourteenth Amendment was one of the most blatant instances in U.S. history of government's ability to twist the language of liberty into benefits for the wealthy corporations and to the disadvantage of the poor.

With few exceptions the government intervened in labor disputes on the side of the business owners and not the side of labor. State and federal troops were sent to end the strike in the Carnegie-owned steel mills in Homestead, Pennsylvania.[18] In 1877 federal injunctions stopped a national railroad strike without addressing the grievances that prompted the strike. Again in 1894, the Pullman strike was effectively halted by adding mail cars to every train, for it was a federal crime to interfere with the movement of the mails. In the Ludlow mine strike of 1914, troops moved in with Gatling guns and burned to death thirteen women and children who were living in tents. Baldwin Felts, owner of coal mines in West Virginia, hired troops to fire on the strikers' tent colony in Matewan. During the depression of 1894, when veterans marched on Washington to get their "bonuses" from the Civil War, the army destroyed their encampment. For the most part the government acted as an agent of corporate interests, rather than as a disinterested proponent of the general public welfare.

By the turn of the century, even business owners and the government began to recognize a need to "rationalize" the apparent rough edges of capitalism. The major political parties presented two political/economic options, much less radical than the IWW or Debs's Socialism. Theodore Roosevelt's program was tagged the "New Nationalism" and Woodrow Wilson's the "New Freedom." The former argued that big government was necessary to control and regulate big business, while the latter argued that the government's role should be to preserve "free" competition by breaking up monopolies, but otherwise leaving businesses alone. Both obviously required an increasingly active federal government.

The Progressive Movement of the early twentieth century attempted to respond to the profound changes brought by the industrial revolution. Presidents Theodore Roosevelt and Woodrow Wilson and other reformers suceeded in passing the Food and Drug Act, direct election of senators, workmen's compensation and graduated income tax. Most historians acknowledge with Robert Wiebe that the Progressive Movement was fundamentally a "search for order" amidst rapid change, although they differ as to whether the desired outcome was liberal change or a return to the status quo. American capitalism was to be reformed, not transformed. In 1917, when the United States entered World War I, socialist and radical reformers were pushed to the far fringes of American political life. The Socialist party opposed the war and was outlawed by the government. When an anti-capitalist Communist order emerged out of the postwar chaos in Russia, an overwhelming anti-communist popular reaction in the United States guaranteed that radical critics of American capitalism would be permanently marginalized.

Ongoing Patterns

Several patterns emerge from this brief survey of labor and economic history until World War I. One of the most significant is the persistent warnings by those in power, as well as those seen as powerless, that too great an inequality in the distribution of wealth contributes to violence and instability in a society. These warnings often went unheeded in the past. They were again relevant in the latter part of the twentieth century. From the mid-1970s onward, the gap between rich and poor widened once again. By the late 1990s, the average income of families in the top twenty percent of the income distribution was more than ten times as large as the poorest 20 percent of families.[19] In 1999 the average chief executive officer (CEO) in the United States made 475 times the income of the average worker. The gap between the boss and the rank and file was widening. In 2000 the average CEO of the 365 largest companies earned $13.1 million dollars. Total CEO pay increased 6.3% from 1999, while salaried-worker pay went up 4.3%.[20] The capitalist system has changed in many ways since the 1890s, and the reasons for the growing inequalities in the late twentieth century were not the same as those of the late nineteenth century.[21] Nevertheless, it is clear that inequality is the natural outcome of capitalism. The United States, with the freest economy of industrialized nations, has the greatest economic inequality.

A second pattern is the consistent desire of workers to have some control over their work and working conditions. Industrial workers, like all people, yearn for the wholeness which comes from a meaningful relationship to the material products of one's labor and to the community of fellow producers. Companies which ignore the human desire for integration and connectedness exact a high toll from their workers, and contribute to a dangerous alienation in the wider national community. Those companies that attend to such needs can reap the benefits of better worker morale, attendance, and productivity.

A third observation is the interplay between the two fundamental values of freedom and equality. The late nineteenth century was a critical turning point. By earlier definitions, freedom in the United States depended upon a strong majority of citizens who owned productive property and participated in the democratic political order. Freedom was linked to a measure of economic equality. By the new definitions of those who rationalized labor-management relations in the emerging industrial order, freedom was linked more to the marketplace than to production. As long as autonomous individuals entered into labor contracts freely, the system, it was said, fostered freedom. As the leadership of the labor movement shifted from the utopian Knights of Labor to the conservative American Federation of Labor, the American dream of freedom based on ownership of productive property faded. Power and decision making in the American capitalist economy was clearly to be more in the hands of big business and big government than in the hands of the people.

Chapter 8

Gender Matters:
Peace Begins at Home

A Revolution for Whom?

In the warm spring of 1776, fifty-six outspoken and idealistic men forged a new experiment in liberty and self-government. Boldly proclaiming to the world that "all men are created equal" and "have certain inalienable rights," they signed a document that became a prototype for liberation movements around the world. Abigail Adams, the perceptive wife of one of these men, carefully followed the proceedings from her home in Massachusetts and voiced deep concern that this revolution would be a revolution for only men if the delegates failed to "remember the ladies." In a remarkable exchange of letters, Abigail wrote to her husband John on March 31, 1776:

> . . . in the new Code of Laws which I suppose it will be necessary for you to make I desire you would Remember the Ladies, and be more generous and favourable to them than your ancestors. Do not put such unlimited power in the hands of the Husbands. Remember all Men would be tyrants if they could. If particuliar [sic] care and attention is not paid to the Ladies we are determined to foment a Rebellion, and will not hold ourselves bound by any Laws in which we have no voice, or Representation."[1]

John's reply was quick and dismissive. On April 14, 1776 he wrote "As to your extraordinary Code of Laws, I cannot but laugh . . . . Depend upon it, We know better than to repeal our Masculine systems."[2]

We know from the long and detailed letters that John deeply loved and respected his wife. She was his anchor throughout his life. We also know that John Adams had an unusually keen sense of fair play, perhaps indicated most vividly in his courageous defense of British soldiers accused of murder in the Boston massacre of 1770. Then why was he rigidly unable to recognize the obvious injustice in expecting women to submit to a system in which they had no voice?

Social Constructions of Gender

An adequate definition and understanding of the concept of "gender" can help us understand the dilemmas faced by the Adamses, as well as shed light on contemporary issues relating gender and violence. There are obvious biological differences between the male and female sexes. The term "gender," however, refers to socially constructed differences between males and females. Psychologists and anthropologists have shown that every culture assigns meanings to sexual (biological) differences. These meanings differ among cultures and even among classes within the same ethnic group.

Significantly, these meanings change through time. The Adams' generation was strongly influenced both by belief in natural law and by an understanding of Christianity that decreed men's dominance over women. John Adams, acknowledging his male privileges, was apparently unable or unwilling to consider the possibility of different relationships. Abigail Adams, however, recognized that the prevailing constructions of gender put all the political, social and economic power in the hands of men. She wanted change. The fundamental problem, she understood, was not in assigning meaning to sexual differences, but in permitting difference to result in unequal power. Two hundred years of effort since Abigail's call for power-sharing have tempered the extremes of male dominance, but contemporary gender constructions still predispose men to be tough, strong, aggressive and in control, while women are expected to be accepting, docile and agreeable.

Gender Issues and Violence

The unequal power relationship between the sexes identified by Abigail Adams shapes the public as well as private spheres so pervasively that many consider it a natural consequence of our genes and our hormones. Research, however, shows that this is not true. In her extensive study on sexual inequality, anthropologist Peggy Sanday concludes that "male dominance is a response to pressures that are most likely to have been present relatively late in human history."[3] Riane Eisler argues similarly that the current power imbalance between the sexes is not "natural" but rather a characteristic of warrior societies. Men are valued over women because of their generally superior strength, since it is "the power to take rather than give life that is the ultimate power to establish and enforce domination."[4] Eisler observes that from Sparta to Hitler's Germany, from Khomeini's Iran to the Japanese Samurai, warrior societies share certain commonalities: "male dominance . . . hierarchic and authoritarian social structure and a high degree of social violence, particularly warfare."[5] Men in warrior societies frequently justify violence as protection of possessions, including "their" women and children.[6] Cultural and belief systems evolve to support the mythology of these societies, including divine blessing by a generally male god upon "holy wars," jihads, or crusades. A study of 156 different societies has shown that rape is most prevalent where men have exclusive roles in important decision making and the culture encourages men to be tough, aggressive and competitive. The United States offers men images of toughness and competitiveness, tempered by other images of the sensitive male, loving father and supportive husband; it ranks near the middle of rape-prone societies.[7]

This chapter suggests that how we think about gender matters: that some formulations of gender tend toward greater peace and justice, while others, too often, lead to violence and injustice. Currently the issue of domestic abuse is a vivid litmus test for understanding how gender constructions may hinder the creation of a more peaceful and just society. "It is exactly in the family," wrote Thelma Goodrich, "that women's oppression and men's power are enacted most plainly and personally."[8]

The statistics are shocking. In the 1990s, family violence killed as many U.S. women every *five* years as the total number of Americans who died in the *thirteen* years of U.S. troop involvement in the Vietnam War. [9] Every nine seconds in the U.S., some woman's husband or boyfriend beats her; two to four million women are abused each year. Estimates vary because much abuse is not reported. This abuse is not simply a momentary loss of temper, but the establishment of control and fear in a relationship through violence and intimidation. The violence is not just slapping or punching—it produces serious injury. From puberty to menopause (ages 15-44), the *leading cause* of trauma requiring medical attention for women is domestic violence, exceeding car accidents and falls. The American Medical Association estimates that thiry-five percent of women who visit medical emergency rooms are there for injuries related to ongoing partner abuse.[10] More than half of all women experience some form of violence from their spouse during marriage, and 25% of all couples experience repetitive abuse.[11] Thirty percent of murdered women are killed by a husband, lover or estranged spouse, approximately three women a day, according to the FBI's *Crime in the U.S.*[12] The *leading cause* of death for pregnant women in the United States is homicide. Medical conditions can be managed and disease can be controlled, but violence against pregnant women is simply ignored.[13] Contrary to popular belief, domestic violence does not occur just in poor urban areas. In fact, in more than 25% of middle class divorces, repeated violence was an issue.[14]

The economic cost of abuse is staggering. The Colorado Domestic Violence Coalition estimates that medical expenses alone from domestic violence totals at least 3 to 5 billion dollars. Businesses forfeit another 100 million dollars in lost wages, sick leave, absenteeism and non-productivity.[15] Why is such violence an unacknowledged part of the contemporary U.S.?

Traditionally the causes of domestic abuse are understood to be the abuser's personal characteristics and life experiences, like stress, unemployment, poverty, substance abuse, past child abuse, and depression. Yet amelioration of life problems has not been shown to effectively stop domestic abuse in a relationship. Other suggested explanations for abuse are biological causes, such as abnormally high levels of testosterone, glycerides, or steroids. Research is inconclusive but leans towards finding no sharply differing biochemical levels in abusers.

Professionals working with both perpetrators and survivors of domestic abuse theorize that people use violence to maintain power and control over others. The use of violence is a choice that is reinforced every time it works, and abusers seldom pay a price for that choice. Thus, the observations of therapists and psychologists dovetail with the research of anthropologists and historians indicating that societies that have a high tolerance for violence (warrior societies) value power and control while devaluing what is perceived to be "feminine." "Not by accident," observes author Andrea Dworkin, "is the United States a nightmare of violence against women. Men in power make choices for violence."[16] Whether the underlying emotion is frustration, jealousy, anxiety, or low self-esteem, battering men use violence to get or regain the power and control they assume is theirs based on a social construction of gender woven into the fabric of society. In this case, the gender construction tells men they should be in charge and narrows their range of options for dealing with emotions, predisposing them toward the use of "manly" violence. A psychologist, Dr. Christine Courtois, sums this up when she reports that young women who are raped are victims of "an endemic societal manifestation of the power imbalance between the sexes" where "men are conditioned into roles of power and domination ... and females ... are conditioned to be passive and dependent."[17]

Myriad forces support and perpetuate this conditioning of men and women. Media, advertising, schools, home environments, politicians, public policy makers, and religion all weigh in with modifications of the basic theme, creating interesting individual nuances. Yet Courtois' general observation continues to be true: that there is a "power imbalance between the sexes" that traps both men and women in a limited range of behaviors. Men feel pressured to "prove their manhood" by being powerful and in control, and unleash their anger and fears of the feminine on women, who are acculturated to accept. Women carry scars of brutality on their bodies and the pain of internalized self-hatred and shame in their souls, too often refusing to resist injustice. How and why do we continue to find ourselves held hostage to constructions of gender that are detrimental to all?

Historical Constructions of Gender

Historians identify three general phases of gender relationships, corresponding roughly to the centuries of U.S. colonial and national history. These phases—agrarian patriarchy, separate spheres and companionate marriage—overlap each other and all have been modified by subculture norms. All three persist in some forms today.

The first period, approximately 1630 to 1830, was characterized by agrarian patriarchy. Church and natural law influenced thoughts on gender. The general interpretation of the Biblical story of human origins asserted that man was created first and woman was the "second sex" and the weaker sex because Eve was the first to succumb to temptation. Because of this, women were considered incapable of independent reason, and were expected to be under the guidance and protection of a father or husband (or some responsible male) for the duration of their lives. This expanded into a cultural system that valued "a stable social hierarchy ruled by "natural" male leaders ... not only as family practice, but as political doctrine that placed masters over servants, older ahead of younger, and wealthier above poorer."[18] Such a system could embrace slavery as part of a stable system rather than an inherently destabilizing injustice. The order of hierarchy was reflected in punishment patterns: men could punish wives, wives could punish children (but not their husbands), and children in some cases could punish slaves (but not their mothers or fathers). Under English common law, married women were "civilly dead" and virtually unrepresented politically. Only men had the right to vote, to sign contracts; married women had few or no property rights; in cases of legal divorce men generally received custody of the children. If women were educated, it was only basic literacy to enable them to read the Bible; only men could attend college and learn "scholarly" languages like Greek and Latin. Since most families survived economically on farms or running small businesses, women contributed as workers, but men generally managed the finances and property. Sons inherited the bulk of the family wealth; daughters might be mentioned in wills, but property inheritance was a male privilege.

Men and women had separate cultural worlds, and both men and women developed deep camaraderie among same-sex groups. The contrast with today is most noticeable for men. It was not considered at all unusual for a man like Alexander Hamilton to sign letters to his friend John Laurens with "I love you" or to find that Frederick Douglass used more terms of endearment for his fellow escapee Henry Harris than in his extensive writings to his wife of forty-four years. Expressions of love between men were an accepted part of "refined sentiment."

It was within this system of agrarian patriarchy that Abigail Adams encouraged revolutionary thought to be expanded to include women. She was not alone in her thoughts, although it took almost sixty years for the first organized women's movement to be formed in the United States. But alternatives were visible, perhaps most clearly in a group of religious dissidents from England, known as the Society of Friends, or Quakers. The early Quakers, reacting to the hierarchical culture of the Anglican English, attempted to create a more egalitarian society, challenging male dominance and its accompanying forms of hierarchy, including slavery. With a radically different interpretation of the creation story, founder George Fox observed in 1653 "For man and woman were helpmeets, in the image of God and in Righteousness and holiness, in the dominion before they fell; but after the Fall, in the transgression, the man was to rule over his wife. But in the restoration by Christ into the image of God and His righteousness and holiness again, in that they are helpmeets, man and woman, as they were before the Fall."[19] Or as theologian Rosemary Ruether points out, ". . . unlike other Christians, [Quakers] did not believe God had created a mandate for social subordination 'in the beginning.' They saw the subordination of class and gender as sinful usurpation, the wrongful fruit of the fall, already overcome for those who are 'in Christ.'" [20]

Emphasizing the fundamental equality of all humans before God, (believing there is "that of God in everyone"), Quakers from their inception encouraged both men and women to use their gifts, to speak as they were led by the Holy Spirit within, to be equally educated, to be ministers and leaders, and to act with autonomy. In contrast to the prevailing notions of women as passive and domestic, Quaker women were encouraged to engage publicly, to speak openly, and to travel from meeting to meeting. As a result, it is not surprising that Quaker women like Lucretia Mott and Susan B. Anthony were disproportionately represented in the social movements which undermined slavery and female subjugation in the nineteenth century.[21] The Quakers deliberately chose a different starting premise and came to very different conclusions about the "proper" roles for men and women. Their theological premise, which challenged the violence inherent in unjust gender roles, challenged violence in all forms, including "redemptive violence," resulting in the well-respected "peace testimony" of the Quakers.

While the Quaker model emphasizes human equality, another alternative model of gender relationship was present during the early period, but generally ignored because of prevailing prejudices. Under the Great Peace of Deganawidah that established the *Hodonensaunee* (Iroquois Confederacy), five (later six) warring nations were brought together. The Iroquois, although by no means pacifists, have maintained a commitment to peaceful relations among member tribes of the league which has endured for more than four hundred years. Within the group, each sex had particular roles, but overall power was balanced in the community. Women did the agricultural and child-care work; men did the hunting and framing work for the longhouses. But political power was balanced: only women could vote; only men could hold certain leadership positions. Thus, if enough women were displeased with the performance of a man as leader, they replaced him. Similarly, economic power was balanced. Women controlled the food they produced, and there were instances of women ending unwanted conflicts by withholding food from the men. The great binding law, *Gayanashagowa*, outlined these relationships, including hereditary rights for women.[22] The Iroquois thus offered a model of gender relationships based on separate gender roles, but with a harmonious balance of power between the sexes.

The second period of gender constructions corresponds roughly with the nineteenth century, 1830-1919. The major changes in this period coincide with the rise of industrialization and commercialism. Notions of agrarian patriarchy persisted on the plantations of the South, but expanded ideas of democracy and the movement of work outside the home helped foster a new gender system based on "separate spheres." The male sphere was understood to be the public world of business and politics; the female sphere was the private world of home and church. The early part of this period was affected by the religious revivals known as the Second Great Awakening, which encouraged active participation, personal responsibility, social reform and a greater emphasis on piety, self-restraint, discipline and frugality. Men were viewed as the more passionate sex, and the goal of the good woman was to help man control his passions for his own sake and for the good society. Sexual advice writers believed that excess sexual energy robbed man of his stamina for work and suggested hard work as the best cure. Women, by contrast, were seen as passive, and the cure for ailing women was often absolute enforced rest. Increasingly mothers, rather than fathers, were expected to supervise the education and discipline of their children. Whipping became less common as a punishment.

Slaves lacked rights to marry, yet were not totally unaffected by prevailing notions of gender. This was seen most dramatically following emancipation when the ideal to which most freed people aspired was a male bread winner and a woman free to stay at home and raise the children. The disruption of the family system under slavery created one of the most effective arguments against slavery. Harriet Beecher Stowe, in her best selling book *Uncle Tom's Cabin* (1852) appealed to women with touching scenes of mother love, powerfully making the argument that even under the idealized conditions of the "benevolent" Christian Shelby family, slaves were property and children could be sold away from their mothers. As the slave mother, Eliza, braves whips and dogs and ice floes to save her child, the message is clear (however problematically)—that slaves are not property, but human beings, with the same passions and love as white mothers.

The connections between the condition of slaves and white women intersected in important ways in the antebellum period creating a few significant alliances in the common struggle for freedom. In 1848, in Seneca Falls, New York, some three hundred women and forty men, including the self-emancipated Frederick Douglass, created the first organized movement in the U.S. to advance a serious critique of male privilege. The convention, called by Elizabeth Cady Stanton, Lucretia Mott, Martha Wright and Mary Ann McClintock, adopted a "Declaration of Sentiments" patterned after the U.S. Declaration of Independence, which listed women's grievances against men: requiring obedience to laws they had no part in making, forbidding married women to own property or to keep their wages, taxing the property of single women, unjust divorce laws, excluding women from "profitable employments" and from colleges. The Declaration concluded: "In view of the unjust laws above mentioned, and because women do feel themselves aggrieved, oppressed, and fraudulently deprived of their most sacred rights, we insist that they have immediate admission to all the rights and privileges which belong to them as citizens of the United States."[23]

The hope was for "immediate admission." But the reality took decades. The Civil War drained the energy and attention of the quarreling nation, and Reconstruction fractured both the unity within the women's movement and the alliance with African Americans. The 14th amendment for the first time introduced the word "male' into the constitution, conveying that citizenship is a male privilege and thus dashed women's hopes for the right to vote under the 15th amendment, which simply says "the right of citizens of the United States to vote shall not be denied or abridged . . . on account of race, color or previous condition of servitude."

Unrest and change characterized the period between the Civil War and World War I. Huge waves of immigrants from Eastern and Southern Europe threatened ideas of "Americanism." Rapid industrialization was marked by unprecedented profits for some and poverty for others. Labor's challenge to the wage system involved more than seven million workers in strikes, often violently suppressed. Rapid settlement of the western frontier created boom towns and fierce Indian wars. The country's expansion reached to the far ends of the globe as Hawaii, then Guam, Puerto Rico and the Philippines became U.S. territories. Women entered college in increasing numbers, and (in part because of the huge loss of men in the Civil War), developed single, professional lives.

Cutting through each of these changes were issues of race, which was being redefined as immigration changed the ethnic mix of the nation. The country shuddered through a painful rebirth process, in which African Americans struggled for the long-denied dignity of citizenship while at the same time entry into"whiteness" became even more firmly equated with privilege, civilization and power. Science supposedly proved the superiority of Caucasians, and much discussion was given to whether immigrant groups like Irish, Italians and Jews might be considered "white."[24]

Also intersecting and shaped by each of these issues was the changing "process of manhood." The rising white middle class saw immigrants, laborers, African Americans and educated women as threats to their "manhood." This only makes sense if one understands "manhood" operating as historian Gail Bederman indicates— as a linkage between "anatomy, identity and particular arrangements of authority and power." Her provocative study examines the ways in which threats to the idea that "people with male bodies naturally possessed both a man's identity and a man's right to wield power" led to a "process of remaking manhood." The result emphasized "masculinity" (physical power, aggressiveness, sexuality) rather than the older concept of "manliness" (emphasizing honor, character and self-mastery).

To demonstrate their virility and insure their access to power, men joined fraternal organizations, organized the Boy Scouts and the YMCAs, and began body-building and hunting for sport. If they were Christian, they advocated "muscular Christianity" and joined the Men and Religion Forward Movement. But these avenues to masculinity were limited to white males in order to perpetuate myths of white male superiority. The two largest and most unmistakable public domains of male physicality— sports and the military—were not completely opened to African Americans until the second half of the twentieth century. Bederman rightly observes, "Male dominance and white supremacy have a strong historical connection."[25]

One of the most visible manifestations of this concern for the development of powerful manhood is the rise of aggressive sports, particularly prize fighting and college football. As Michael Welch points out in an article examining violence against women by football players, "organized sports emerged as an arena for men to define and express a type of masculinity based largely on physicality and domination of one's opponent," including "the sanctioned use of aggression/force/violence." He goes on to explain, "In America, sports continue to be the strongest reference point for promulgating the most sacred values of a male-dominated, success-oriented, status-seeking society."[26]

Much of the complexity of gender roles today, including the devaluing of the feminine, may well be seen most dramatically in the sports arena. Masculine success is defined in opposition to femininity. It is not accidental that words like "sissy" and "pussy-foot" were coined in the 1890s to demean men by comparing them unfavorably to women. What is perhaps more astonishing is the persistence of these epithets today. The most stinging indictment against a young athlete is "You throw like a girl." As Michael Messner, former athlete and sports psychologist points out, it is not the actual "throwing like a girl" that is the motivator/threat. It is the fear of being called a sissy, of being a girl.[27] Sports manager and sociologist Todd Crosset concurs. "One important reason the world of men's athletics is hyper-masculine and hostile towards women is that [women] are constantly degraded and demeaned through comparisons which men and coaches encourage. On one team I swam for, if you couldn't finish practice you did another workout in the diving pool. We called it the woman pit."[28] Thus, the threat to white manhood in the late nineteenth century shifted ideas about masculinity towards an increasingly physical, aggressive and anti-female spectrum.

In addition to team sports, another manifestation of separate spheres for males was the popularity of saloons and of lodges like the Odd Fellows, Moose, Eagles, and Knights of Columbus. In 1901 five and a half million men belonged to lodges, about five times the number of union members. Even more popular were saloons. Jon Kingsdale reports that many urban working-class districts had at least one saloon for every fifty adult males. He argues that saloons "played three significant roles in a growing urban industrial environment: it was a neighborhood center, an all-male establishment and a transmitter of working-class and immigrant cultures." Alcohol proved to be a "stimulus to self-expression and fellowship," qualities that were severely limited by the contemporary ideals of "strenuous manhood."

However, as beer consumption increased from 27 gallons at mid-century to 2953 gallons per year in 1911-1915, concerns grew over the negative effects of alcohol and alcoholism.[29] Women, raised with the idea that they were the more moral sex and therefore the guardians of social decency, responded with a massive and effective temperance movement. Supported by evangelical revivalism, and fueled by the experiences of alcohol-related domestic violence and poverty, the temperance movement challenged the saloons. For twenty years, from 1879 to 1899, Frances Willard, a charismatic educator and organizer, served as president of the largest organization, the Women's Christian Temperance Union (WCTU) with more than 150,000 members. Under Willard's leadership, women crusaded for a "maternal commonwealth" which would import domestic moral values into the political arena.

Thus, for very different reasons from those that prompted the women at Seneca Falls, Willard became a supporter of women's right to vote, supporting what she called a "Home Protection Ballot." The earlier argument had been based on gender equality and rights; the latter argument was based on gender difference and altruism. Rallying women with calls to Christian duty to their homes and churches, Willard exhorted, "As God led us into this work by way of the saloon, He will lead us out by way of the ballot. We have never prayed more earnestly over the one than we will over the other. One was the Wilderness, the other is the Promised Land."[30] After decades of organizing and agitating, both of these objectives were achieved with the passage of the Prohibition amendment (18th) to the U.S. Constitution in 1919 and the passage of the Suffrage Amendment in 1920.

The passage of both amendments, but particularly the amendment granting women the right to vote, generated so much controversy because it challenged constructions of gender, beliefs about sex roles and social organization. As historian Nancy Woloch points out, "Opponents of suffrage consistently asserted that the sexes had different functions, that each occupied a separate sphere and that any perversion of this social division would have dire consequences." She quotes an Oregon senator as representative of the fears inherent in letting women vote who asserted in 1866 that "with the vote, women would oppose men, turn society 'into a state of war, and make every home a hell on earth.'" Fifty years later, a Congressman opposed suffrage with much the same argument, suggesting that giving the vote to women would "disrupt the family, which is the unit of society, and when you disrupt the family, you destroy the home, which is the foundation of the Republic."[31] To these fears were added other notions, reflecting cultural beliefs about what it meant to be a woman. Anti-suffragists argued that women were "by nature" physically, mentally and emotionally incapable of voting—that their gentle natures and lack of rationality rendered them unfit to make such decisions.

Jane Addams, social worker, peace advocate and founder of Hull House in Chicago, turned the argument around. She contended that "city housekeeping has failed recently because women, the traditional housekeepers, have not been consulted as to its activities." Men, noted Addams, were as indifferent to civic management as they were to housekeeping details.[32] Her strategy was to accept the era's construction of womanhood as primarily housekeepers (and men as ignorant about such matters), but use it to justify the necessity for women to become involved in public housekeeping, as well as private.

Arguments like this for expanded roles for women in the public sphere exposed some profound tensions between individualism and community values. A prolific writer and contemporary of Jane Addams, Charlotte Perkins Gilman, saw clearly the economic and social risks in the tendency of commercialism to isolate family units. Gilman believed that "maternal instinct" was a biological trait that, if allowed full expression in society, rather than being confined to "motherhood" and the individual home, would eliminate poverty, homelessness, and the prevalent problems of urbanization. "Civilization and Christianity," she argued, " teach us to care for the child. Motherhood stops at 'my child.'" [33] In an intriguing sequel to *Herland* (Gilman's utopia of women), called *With Her in Ourland*, Gilman observes the world through the eyes of a Herlander, someone who has never seen war or poverty or slums. Her male companion begins to see the gendered nature of war (not a part of "human nature" as he tries to argue, but one carried out by males) and the resulting skewing of history to preoccupation with "who fought who—and when" rather than using history as a way of exploring the "inception, development, success or failure of the disease . . . ."[34] Thus, Gilman gives her readers a useful insight into the interconnectedness of gender with social practice and the telling of history.

So far in this brief survey of the nineteenth century, we have encountered three different patterns in understanding the relationship between men and women. These are clearly summarized by Carol Tavris in *Mismeasure of Woman*. Gilman and Addams believed women to be *superior* to men (ethically), Stanton and Anthony believed women should be *equal* to men (politically and economically) and the sports world sees women as *opposites* of men (weak, deficient). Tavris' own position is that the problem with all three of these positions is they still measure women using men as the norm. Her goal is to "examine the consequences for us all, male and female, when only some few of us set the standards of normalcy and universality." She argues that there is "nothing essential — that is universal and unvarying — in the natures of women and men." Therefore, she believes each individual should be free to develop a spectrum of characteristics. However she reminds us "[t]he mismeasure of woman persists because it reflects and serves society's prejudices."[35]

The twentieth century brought major changes in thinking on gender, yet, indeed, the old patterns persist in somewhat altered forms. In the post World War I world, men, disillusioned with a definition of manhood that sent them to the terror and typhoid-ridden trenches of Europe turned to romance, cabarets and speakeasies. "Companionate marriage," an idea which had been around since the Revolution (couples should marry for romantic love and be companions to one another) gained ascendance with a few new twists. The Progressive Era valued the wisdom of experts, and young professions like psychology and sociology became the new authorities on families and what was called "sex-role identity." The prosperity of the twenties coincided with a definition of a good husband as a good provider. This wreaked havoc with men's psyches during the Depression, when high rates of unemployment caused many men to feel deficient in their manhood, setting off a chain reaction of quarrels, alcoholism and abuse.

World War II demonstrated how quickly the power of the government could manipulate notions of gender in the interests of national defense. The government actively recruited women to "man " the weapons factories and ship-building yards, assuring them that such work would not affect their "femininity." Propaganda films compared household skills with industrial tasks: for example comparing operating a drill press with operating a juice extractor in her kitchen.[36] Studies were found confirming that children develop greater social skills and independence when they are put in day care, so women could confidently leave their children. After the war, when returning veterans increased the domestic labor supply, the message changed. Women's magazines, posters, films and other media urged women to find fulfillment in motherhood and domesticity. Studies now showed that children of mothers who worked outside the home were more likely to become juvenile delinquents.

World War II redistributed income and benefits to the men who fought it. The GI bill of rights subsidized college education and home purchases for more than 75 million veterans. More than $145 billion dollars were transferred to veterans. But in a common U.S. pattern, the rate of black unemployment remained two to three times that for Whites and wages averaged about fifty to sixty percent that of Whites. Nevertheless, there is much evidence that the overall pattern of the fifties was one of prosperity for unprecedented numbers, and the desire of returning GI's to settle down and have a home contributed to the well-known baby boom. But success had its price, as William Whyte's *The Organization Man* (1956) showed. In order to rise in the corporation, men too frequently neglected their wives and children, and the ideals of a companionate marriage. This created tension for both men and women. For men, competition replaced camaraderie. Corporate work required no physical strength, although college sports were still the unacknowledged training ground for managerial skills, and corporate board talk was filled with sports metaphors. The post-war era was marked by a nostalgic love affair with a mythological working-class manliness, and the popularity of westerns and sports heroes.

The popularity of both westerns and sports heroes was greatly facilitated by the rise of television. In 1946, there were only 17,000 sets in the United States; by 1957 there were forty million sets in use—almost one for each family.[37] Jane Tompkins, an English professor at Duke University, has analyzed gender relationships in popular western novels, TV shows and movies. She observes:

> For both male and female heroes, gender patrols the borders of expression, keeping men and women from protesting their lot by threatening them with the label of deviance. Women cannot express their rages because to do so marks them as unfeminine. Men cannot register their pain because to do so marks them as unmanly. The gender system works to enforce codes of behavior that are, in their different ways, excruciating . . . . With an irony so

deep it evokes pity, the Western struggles and strains to cast out everything feminine, but in doing so only embeds itself more firmly in the gender system . . . . Striving to be the opposite of women, the male heroes restrict themselves to a pitiably narrow range of activities. They can't read or dance or look at pictures; they can't play. They can't rest. They can't look at the flowers . . . . They can't daydream or fantasize or play the fool. They can't make mistakes.

Tompkins concludes:

Silence, the will to dominate, and unacknowledged suffering aren't a good recipe for happiness or companionability. The model of heroism Westerns provide may help men to make a killing in the stock market, but it doesn't provide much assistance when they go home for dinner at night."[38]

Thus the ideal of companionate marriage existed in tension with the ideal of the "Marlboro Man," the tough, self-controlled cowboy of the western range. There were tensions as well for the women who conscientiously tried to live out the cultural prescription for women's happiness based on staying at home and raising a family. After decades of depressions and war, having a husband, children and a home in the newly developed suburbs was all that many women desired. But one college educated suburban housewife who supposedly "had it all" dared ask the question "is this all?" Calling it the "problem with no name," Betty Friedan's book, *The Feminine Mystique* (1963) found a wide audience of women who resonated with her exposé of this gendered "American dream." She wondered why in 1958 women were only thirty-five percent of college students as opposed to forty-seven percent in the 1920s and why sixty percent of those women dropped out to get married, particularly when U.S. scientists reacting to Cold War fears of Soviet superiority noted that the greatest source of unused brain power was women. She wondered why the promise of "true feminine fulfillment" left so many women feeling quietly desperate and sure that there must be something wrong with them.[39] In a rather unlikely coalition of older professional women, full-time homemakers and college activists, a full-fledged women's movement developed in the 1970s challenging cultural prescriptions of the feminine.

Just when women were beginning to examine gender dynamics, male politicians were enmeshing the country in its second longest undeclared war[40] (second only to the century long undeclared wars against the Native Americans). Certainly no war has generated more controversial passion about its purposes, goals, execution and meanings than the war in Vietnam. Centered in cold-war tensions, the U.S. involvement in Vietnam has generally been interpreted as a war to prevent the spread of communism. But numerous insiders who have begun to analyze exactly what was going on, have found that masculine notions of "toughness" and "winner" among political leaders may have had as much to do with U.S. involvement as anti-communism.

Mark Fasteau, who worked for Senator Mike Mansfield in 1963, and was given the assignment to try to articulate the rationale for U.S. involvement in Vietnam, concluded after much research (including a careful reading of the entire Pentagon Papers) that "Vietnam was not another Munich [referring to the unsuccessful agreements to "appease" Hitler in 1939] and there was no empirical or solid theoretical support for the 'domino theory' [the idea that if Vietnam became communist, all the neighboring countries would follow like dominos]." Instead he suggests that that policy was chosen "for other, not fully conscious, motivations." Those motivations have to do with expressed desires to "avoid the humiliation of defeat" and to demonstrate masculine "toughness," even when it flies in the face of logical "masculine" rationality. "For our Presidents and policymakers," writes Fasteau, "being tough, or at least looking tough, has been a primary goal in and of itself."[41] Much political rhetoric substantiates this; perhaps most telling is Richard Barnett's observation that one can be a "hawk," have one's advice rejected, and still maintain credibility in Washington, while unsuccessful advocacy of a "dovish" position is permanently discrediting. "What," asks Fausteau, "created the climate in which the "soft" position is riskier than the "hard" position? It grows out of the fear of the powerful individual members of the bureaucracy that they themselves will appear "soft."[42] And why are men afraid of being considered "soft?" "Soft" isn't masculine; it's feminine.

Fear of breaking with cultural prescriptions for gender brings us full circle to the opening discussion of domestic violence as a litmus test within the U.S. The poet and novelist Alice Walker reflects: "For the earth to know health and happiness, this violence against women must stop . . . . Out of a woman's security—which always means free agency in society, sexual and spiritual autonomy, as well as the well-being of her children and the sanctity of her home—comes ultimate security for the world."[43]

Numerous organizations have worked diligently at the state and national level for new laws to protect women against domestic violence.[44] The resistance to such laws is instructive. In September of 1994 the United States Congress passed a Violence Against Women Act which allowed victims of gender-motivated violence to sue their attackers for damages in federal court. Supporters of the law argued that violence against women affected their civil rights, that women could not get justice in the biased state courts, and that Congress had authority to act on the basis of its constitutional power to regulate interstate commerce.[45] In May of 2000 a narrow conservative majority (5-4) on the United States Supreme Court struck down parts of the 1994 law, in the *Brzonkala v. Morrison* case. In that case a woman university student was allegedly raped by two football players and the victim did not receive justice from the university or the state courts. The court ruled that "gender motivated" crimes were not covered under the interstate commerce clause. In this case, desire to curb federal power overcame desire to curb a national endemic of violence against women.[46] Another recent court case placed a man's right to own a gun above a woman's right to protection. In 1999 Judge Sam R. Cummings of Federal District Court in Lubbock, Texas, dismissed gun-possession charges against a doctor who used a handgun in violation of a restraining order taken out by his wife. The judge ruled the doctor's right to own a gun had been violated."[47] These cases show that something is at work in the culture which still, in spite of countervailing rhetoric, devalues the feminine and tolerates violence.

Transforming the Culture: Creating a Just Society

A great deal has changed since Abigail Adams warned her husband, "Do not put such unlimited power in the hands of Husbands." And yet the disparity remains, and its ongoing result is violence by those taught to be aggressive against those taught to be passive. The antidote is clear: move to eliminate the imbalances between the sexes in education, economics, politics, the legal system, religious institutions, wherever one sex is able to control outcomes or choices for another. The call to address imbalances in power must also come with a call to embrace diversity, because equality of inherent value, status and power in no way eliminates the wide range of differences between and within the sexes. Ultimately we need to transform society from one in which "difference equals power" to one in which "difference equals diversity," where difference enriches and balances societies but is not equated in any way with systemic inferiority or superiority.

Fundamentally altering gender constructions in order to create a more peaceful and just society is a difficult enterprise. Not only is there culturally embedded resistance to change, but when change occurs, it is often perceived as threatening. In the nineteenth century, rather than greeting emancipation for slaves and education for women as steps toward justice, some men turned to an aggressive, physical definition of manhood to retain control. In such situations, increased violence does not represent as much a breakdown of the social order as an attempt to maintain a particular, gendered social order. But as Alice Walker reminded us, all security/peace is interrelated. Global security is premised on a world in which men and women work in a relationship of valued partnership, rather than control and fear. Men who recognize this interconnectedness, that their well-being is connected to the well-being of every other living being on the planet, will more likely be able to act counter-culturally and share power in the interests of a more peaceful society for all. Journalist Gordon Mott in an essay explaining why he gave up some "male privilege" observes, "My worries about losing my self-worth or masculinity are offset by feeling courageous." [49] Courage, of course, can be viewed as a "masculine" trait, but it is also one that is available to all as a character trait separate from the problematic linkage of male identity and male power. It will take courage and perseverance and conviction to create more equitable constructions of gender—the courage of women to find and use their voices and the courage of men to let go of the struggle to maintain male control and privilege, and work for justice for all.

Chapter 9

Violent Means Undermine Progress:
War and Peace 1898-1918

In 1899 William "Buffalo Bill" Cody redesigned the climactic scene of his spectacular American history show, "Wild West." For sixteen seasons, the climax of the show had been "Custer's Last Fight," with Cody himself coming on stage after the massacre at the Little Big Horn to set things right. Back in 1876, on the plains frontier in the aftermath of Custer's defeat, Cody had killed and scalped a young Cheyenne warrior named Yellow Hand. The American press acclaimed Cody for taking "The First Scalp for Custer." Now, twenty-three years later, the drama of U.S. triumphant expansionism had moved forward with the U.S. military triumph in the Spanish-American War (1898). For the revised and updated version of his show, Cody chose to re-enact the "Battle of San Juan Hill" and the victory over Spain in Cuba. Cody had a special claim to that event as well. Theodore Roosevelt, former assistant secretary of the navy who had organized the "Rough Riders," had gotten the very name for his flamboyant cavalry unit from Cody's "Wild West" show.[1]

Cody took his "Wild West" to Europe and promoted it as a force for "universal peace." His point apparently was that when Americans made war, and when they celebrated the stirring battles of their past, they were moving the world toward peace. Twentieth-century history, as it turned out, did not confirm this theatrical link between peace and violence. Violence instead produced more violence. The Spanish-American War (1898) produced a far bloodier Philippine-American War (1899-1902). World War I (1914-18), a war to end wars, set the stage for World War II (1941-45), after which came the Cold War arms race between the United States and the Soviet Union. No historical task is more urgent than to think clearly about why this escalation of violence took place in a twentieth century which began with such profound self-confidence about the prospects for peace and progress.[2]

Cuba

The Spanish-American War provided a jump-start for militant American nationalism. In ten weeks of fighting after declaring war against Spain in April 1898, the United States won a stunning military triumph. Two one-sided naval battles—at Manila Bay in the Philippines and outside Santiago Harbor in Cuba—determined the outcome. The new modern United States navy, not Roosevelt's Rough Riders, decided the issue. "It wasn't much of a war," Roosevelt admitted later, "but it was the best war we had."[3] John Hay, in line to be McKinley's secretary of state, called it a "splendid little war."[4]

The Cubans and the Filipinos, supposedly liberated from evil Spanish rule, were not at all clear that the United States had met their desires for freedom and justice. They did not want to trade Spanish colonial rule for United States colonial rule. From 1868 to 1878 the Cubans had fought a futile ten year civil war for independence, with the United States staying out of the conflict. In 1895 Cuban rebels launched another revolution, this one in part fostered by economic stress when the United States reimposed high tariffs on sugar. To suppress the 1890s rebellion, the Spanish authorities, led by General Valeriano "Butcher" Weyler, herded Cuban civilians into miserable concentration camps where they died in huge numbers. The "yellow press" in the U.S., a new force of competitive journalism named after a cartoon character named "The Yellow Kid," fed readers a rich and graphic diet of propaganda about Spanish atrocities. U.S. citizens believed that military intervention in Cuba was a justified war of liberation in behalf of an oppressed people. It seemed to be a fight for freedom in the tradition of the American War for Independence.

A basic moral test for military interventions such as that of 1898 is whether the outside nation respects the expressed wishes and the self-rule of the people being helped. Wars of intervention do not serve justice if they do not respect purposes and institutions of the local people.[5] The Cuban rebels in 1898 wanted three things from the United States: official recognition as the legitimate government, military supplies, and a blockade of Spanish ships. The rebels did not want or need U.S. troops on their island. They preferred to win their own victory. What they received was American troops on their soil, the defeat of the Spanish, and U.S. military occupation. U.S. domination of Cuba then was expressed through the "Platt Amendment" to the Cuban constitution (1901), limiting Cuba's power to make treaties and contract debts, asserting the United States' right to intervene with troops to restore order when necessary, and providing for the lease of coaling or naval stations (Guantanamo) to the U.S. The U.S. did not annex Cuba. It tried to prove its anti-colonial good intentions by organizing new programs for public health, education, and agriculture for the Cubans. But the United States' basic disrespect for Cuban self-rule, implicit in the unwanted invasion of 1898 and continued in subsequent economic and political domination of Cuba, poisoned relationships between the two countries throughout the twentieth century.

The Philippines

In the Philippines the aftermath of Spanish defeat was even more disturbing. The United States took the Philippines as an overseas colony, and the Filipinos responded with a three-year military campaign for independence from their new masters. Emilio Aguinaldo, a representative of the nationalistic Filipino middle class which had developed under Spanish rule, was the military leader of the resistance movement. President William McKinley decided to crush Aguinaldo and his patriots. The resulting conflict, lasting from February 1899 to July 1902, was a brutal war directed first against the organized Filipino army, then against dispersed guerrilla units, and eventually against entire regions of resisting populations. The Americans created a concentration camp system which was as devastating as "Butcher" Weyler's camps had been in Cuba. Some 11,000 Filipino civilians died of malnutrition and disease in the concentration camps—not counting those weakened ones who died in a subsequent cholera epidemic in 1902.[6] At the war's end the U.S. forces officially claimed to have killed some 20,000 native soldiers. The total of civilian casualties may have been about 200,000. About ninety percent of the water buffalo in the country, essential for cultivating rice, the staple food of the people, perished in the war.[7]

News of some of the atrocities perpetrated by United States forces did make its way into the press back home. Criticism came to focus on a U.S. marine major, Littleton Waller Tazewell Waller, who was court-martialed for ordering the execution of eleven Filipino prisoners—part of a scorched earth campaign to destroy villages in retaliation for atrocities by Filipino patriots. Waller was acquitted. He claimed to be carrying out the orders of Brigadier General Jacob W. Smith to turn the area into "a howling wilderness." Smith's instructions said, "I want no prisoners. I wish you to kill and burn; the more you kill and burn the better you will please me. I want all persons killed who are capable of bearing arms in actual hostilities against the United States." Smith, thereafter dubbed "Howling Wilderness Smith," was "admonished" and forced to retire, but he remained popular among the soldiers.[8] General Fred Funston, who captured Aguinaldo in a daring and spectacular raid, became the American military hero. Theodore Roosevelt blamed the war upon pacifist critics, "the prattlers who sit at home in peace," who spoke out for Philippine independence and thereby "deliberately invited a savage people to plunge into a war fraught with sure disaster for them."[9]

The contradictions of Americans fighting for freedom by destroying the Philippine national struggle for independence were especially obvious in the case of African American soldiers. An officer of the 25th regiment, a black unit, reportedly had responded to a question about their purpose upon arrival in Manila: "Well, I don't know, but I rather reckon we're sent over here to take up the White Man's burden!" White American soldiers routinely referred to the Filipinos as "niggers." One black soldier who made headlines in the *New York Times* was David Fagen, who had fought earlier in Cuba. Fagen deserted his American unit and became an officer with the Filipino forces under General José Alejandrino. On at least eight occasions he fought against his former comrades. Stories circulated that he had made a bold appearance at a brothel in Manila in dashing Spanish dress. The U.S. army offered $600 for his capture "dead or alive," and eventually a native hunter showed up with a partially decomposed head which he claimed was Fagen's. The evidence was not convincing. Fagen may have lived out the rest of his life among the Negrito tribe. Most of the American black soldiers, in this war as in others, fulfilled military service in the hope of earning a place of respect in American society.[10]

Americans reconciled their brutally-acquired empire with the American ideal of freedom by cultivating an image of the dark-skinned people overseas as uncivilized savage peoples—child-like and incapable of self-rule. Modern social science came to their aid. The reigning doctrines of Social Darwinism held that Anglo-Saxon peoples and their institutions were the product of long evolution—the survival of the fittest in the struggle for life. In the Philippines the inferior people lost out; the war had only accelerated a natural process. U.S. anthropologists, such as W. J. McGee of the Bureau of American Ethnology, taught that "human culture is becoming unified, not only through diffusion but through the extinction of the lower grades as their representatives rise into higher grades."[11] American International Expositions or World's Fairs in major cities (Philadelphia, Chicago, Atlanta, Nashville, St. Louis, etc.) provided opportunities for social scientists to create exhibits to depict the nonwhite world as savage and inferior. The St. Louis "Louisiana Purchase" Exposition in 1903 set aside forty-seven acres to put nearly twelve-hundred Filipinos on display in ethnological villages organized in spheres of higher and lower Filipino "types." Among the designated lower type Negritos was a man dubbed "Missing Link." The Filipino reservation at the St. Louis fair included no one from the Filipino middle class that Aguinaldo represented. To acknowledge the existence of educated, well-dressed, Christian Filipinos would have contradicted the high-minded American mission for the Philippines. The popular display of half-naked Filipinos was designed to highlight the contrast between the simplicity of primitive barbarians over against the wonderful exhibitions of advanced industrial civilization in the main part of the St. Louis fair. The American international expositions both reflected and strengthened the deep racism which underlay the justification for world power imperialism.

United States history books in the twentieth century did not tell a balanced and truthful story about the Philippine-American War of 1899-1902. Although the war's cost in American lives and treasure—to say nothing of the devastation wreaked upon the unfortunate Filipinos—was far greater than that of the Spanish-American War, the Philippine-American war was largely forgotten. Meanwhile the slogan "Remember the Maine and to Hell with Spain" endured in national memory. Typical history textbooks often mentioned something about the 1899-1902 war in passing, but gave major attention to the war against Spain. The chapter on those events usually ended on a triumphant nationalistic note and bypassed the costs and compromises of U.S. imperialism. For example, "In a little more than a century the United States had grown from thirteen states stretched along a thin Atlantic coastline into a world power that reached from the Caribbean to the Pacific . . . . The nation now dominated its own hemisphere, dealt with European powers on more equal terms, and was a major power in Asia."[12]

Progressive Era

From the Spanish-American War through World War I the dominant American spirit was one of confident, reform-minded, nationalistic zeal.[13] In the Progressive Era, a complex of overlapping reform movements responded to the challenges of industrialization, urbanization, immigration and growing social and cultural diversity. Reformers addressed the problems of corrupt political machines, monopolistic trusts, urban decay, child labor, prostitution, alcoholism and a host of other evils. Progressive idealism was rooted in evangelical Protestantism, in the new "Social Gospel" (that Christian faith should address social problems), and in the newly professionalized disciplines of the social and natural sciences. Reformers often began their campaigns with strategies of persuasion, education, or intervention by volunteer agencies, but they eventually moved on to demands that government agencies use their coercive powers to address the problems. Efforts to encourage urban immigrants toward healthful recreation led to political pressures upon city government to build public parks. Campaigns to discourage people from selling and drinking alcohol turned toward state and national laws and constitutional amendments for Prohibition.

A new generation of university-educated leaders brought fresh energy as well as organizational expertise to tasks of social and political reconstruction. Prominent among reform leaders were women: Ida Tarbell, journalist who exposed the business practices of Standard Oil; Florence Kelley, advocate of laws to limit work hours for women; Carrie Chapman Catt, agitator for women's suffrage. Progressive reformers struggled to overcome a "steel chain of ideas" — the older philosophies of Social Darwinist individualism and *laissez-faire* capitalism which stood in the way of organized public action for change. The reigning philosophy which guided the new generation was known as "pragmatism," articulated persuasively by John Dewey, professor at the University of Chicago and at Columbia University. Dewey's public philosophy was one of social reconstruction toward democracy based upon creative and intelligent action.

A re-invigorated peace movement had a prominent place in Progressive reform. After many decades on the margins of American life, limited to small bodies of Quakers, New England reformers, and other religious pacifists, the peace reform movement was vaulted to political popularity and social respectability. A national debate about imperialism set the stage. Opponents of America's new colonialist policy, most of whom had not been connected to peace groups, organized a new "Anti-Imperialist League." The League had its initial base in New England, included strong women reformers, and at its peak claimed to have 30,000 members. Mark Twain, American writer and humorist, served as vice-president of the Anti-Imperialist League for many years. In 1901 Twain wrote a parody of the "Battle Hymn of the Republic," satirizing the base motives of United States imperialism:

> Mine eyes have seen the orgy of the launching of the Sword;
> He is searching out the hoardings where the stranger's wealth is
>   stored;
> He hath loosed his fateful lightnings, and with woe and death has
>   scored;
> His lust is marching on . . . . [14]

In the presidential campaign of 1900, the Democratic party and its candidate, William Jennings Bryan, denounced imperialism as a contradiction of the American commitment to democratic ideals. Roosevelt called the anti-imperialists "simply un-hung traitors." William McKinley, running for re-election won a decisive victory — 292 to 155 electoral votes. In the campaign, domestic economic issues came to overshadow imperialism as a central issue. Even so, McKinley's victory tended to confirm that the American people were comfortable with their nation's new role as a world power. Bryan occupied the high moral ground of American idealism, but McKinley and Roosevelt tapped more powerful springs of nationalistic pride.[15]

The failed challenge to imperialism was quickly displaced by earnest efforts to put America's new world power to the ends of world peace. Older peace groups such as the American Peace Society grew rapidly, dozens of new peace organizations sprang up (sixty-three peace-oriented societies in 1912, by one count), and many prominent public officials enlisted in the cause. Andrew Carnegie, retired steel industrialist and philanthropist, opened his deep pockets for peace society expenses, for new peace buildings in Washington and the Hague and, in 1910, for a ten million dollar Carnegie Endowment for International Peace. A series of national "Peace Congresses" attracted the rich and powerful. Attending one such congress in 1907 were "ten mayors, nineteen members of Congress, four supreme court justices, two presidential candidates, thirty labor leaders, forty bishops, sixty newspaper editors, and twenty-seven millionaires."[16] Political leaders who had been officers of peace groups rose to high government positions—notably Secretaries of State Elihu Root (1905-1909), William Jennings Bryan (1913-1915), and Robert Lansing (1915-1920). In 1899 and 1907 government diplomats and representatives from many nations met at International Congresses at the Hague, Netherlands, and took highly publicized, though limited, steps toward a world court of arbitration.

Some of the greatest minds in America reflected on war and peace. In 1910 Henry James, philosopher of pragmatism, published an insightful essay on the psychology of peacemaking, "The Moral Equivalent of War." James argued that peacemakers should not ignore or deny human impulses to violence, but rather credit their power and find productive ways to channel them. Murderous warfare and loving service are not contradictions, wrote James, but rather expressions of a universal impulse to heroic self-sacrifice. Opponents of war would only succeed in their programs if they offered alternative dramatic human activities which constituted an effective moral equivalent for war. James' essay ranks with Henry David Thoreau's 1846 essay on civil disobedience as a creative and significant statement on nonviolence.[17]

James was influenced by Jane Addams, pioneer of the social work movement and persistent pacifist, who wrote in *Newer Ideals of Peace* (1907), that "those emotions which stir the spirit to deeds of self-surrender and to high enthusiasm," hitherto associated with war, must be mobilized for a "new internationalism."[18] Addams was one of the few middle-class peace reformers who had the ability to communicate with common working-class people. Her social work experiments, beginning at Hull House in Chicago, called young volunteers to leave their comfortable neighborhoods and move into communities of poor immigrants. Addams envisioned idealistic social work on a grand scale as a means of achieving world peace. The United States was a microcosm of a multicultural world. If the depressed multi-cultural immigrant communities in U.S. cities could move toward justice and unity, so might a fractured world cooperate and beat its swords into plowshares.[19] Addams' assumption that the United States experience held the key to world peace was typical of peace reformers in this era, whatever their favored reform.

The ideas of Henry James and Jane Addams, if translated into national-policy social programs, would have required unprecedented government social engineering, as well as personal commitment and hard work for those involved. But the peace movement was inhibited both by its own fashionability and by the excessive social optimism which it shared with progressive reformers generally. "No reform," in the judgement of peace historian Merle Curti, "demanded less sacrifice on the part of America's middle class."[20] The momentum of militant nationalistic idealism made it much easier for the United States to drift toward war in 1917 (in the name of "preparedness") than to provide a peaceable moral equivalent for war.

Proposals for third-party arbitration as a means of settling international disputes received substantial attention in these years. The United States had resorted to arbitration a number of times in the nineteenth century to settle boundary disputes and property claims. In 1872 an international arbitration board awarded fifteen million dollars to the United States from Britain for Civil War damages caused by the *Alabama*, a raider the British had built for the Confederacy. In the administrations of Theodore Roosevelt and William Howard Taft, attempts to submit issues to international arbitration ran into opposition in the U.S. Senate, where worries about compromising sovereignty or national honor were more severe. Only disputes of minor importance could be arbitrated. When William Jennings Bryan became President Woodrow Wilson's Secretary of State in 1913, he championed the idea of a "cooling off period" for the management of international disputes. The Brooklyn *Eagle* labeled Bryan's plan a diplomatic adaptation of the maxim, "When angry, count fifty; when very angry, count a hundred."[21]

In 1913-14 Bryan got thirty nations to agree to bilateral conciliation treaties which required them to submit unresolvable disputes either to third-party arbitration or to an international commission of inquiry for a year-long investigation. Bryan believed that disputes could be settled by diplomacy if generally accepted procedures were in place to overcome crises of war hysteria. Bryan's critics, scornful of his populist idealism and his alleged lack of sophistication in diplomatic affairs, argued that nations would use the extra time to build up military forces which would make eventual war more certain and more devastating. The war which broke out in Europe in August, 1914, eclipsed Bryan's treaties, but the precedent of those treaties did influence peace-keeping efforts in the post-war era.[22]

Anti-Imperialist Imperialism

In 1899 and 1900 John Hay, U.S. Secretary of State, established an "Open Door" policy which defined the United States' interests in China. The policy intended to ensure that European imperialist powers with spheres of interest in China would not exclude the United States from the China market. An "Open Door" in China, as well as elsewhere, would allow powerful United States commercial and financial interests full access to foreign economic opportunities. As a slogan the "Open Door Policy" did not seem self-serving; indeed it had an aura of anti-imperialism. The policy seemed to call for respect of the independence of China and other nations threatened by European colonialism. In fact the policy expressed a new form of imperialism. America had become a giant of industrial productivity and was able to dominate foreign countries economically without needing to establish formal political control. The United States did not need a political empire, such as its annexation of the Philippines seemed to suggest. It controlled what it needed through the Open Door, an idea which, for all its high-sounding idealism, represented a form of economic imperialism.[23]

United States' economic power at home and abroad after the late nineteenth century was exercised and influenced by large corporate bodies representing business, government and labor. These large, complex organizations were interested in cooperative voluntary association, in maximizing production, and in social stability. From the corporate point of view, the Progressive era from 1900 to 1918 was marked more by a "search for order" rather than by fundamental social reform in response to the stresses of industrialization and urbanization. Corporate managers often made basic inter-corporate policy arrangements at a private level, rather than through government. They had a bias for order, not for revolution. This meant that the U.S. role in the world was not to empower revolutions for human rights in the tradition of 1776 (as the U.S. imagined it was doing in Cuba), but rather to keep a lid on class warfare and social revolution both at home and overseas. America's repeated interventions in Latin American countries need to be seen in this light. The "corporatist" dimensions of the brief

Spanish-American war were barely recognizable at the time, but they came to flower in the First World War.[24]

Non-Militarist Militarism

The paradox of a developing United States imperialism masked as "Open Door" anti-imperialism had a counterpart in the way growing American militarism was masked by the thriving peace movement. When President Woodrow Wilson led the United States into war in 1917, it was not primarily because American society had been militarized or that the military mind governed decision makers. It was rather that Wilson and the Progressives imagined that war might be guided and controlled as a means for idealistic peacemaking.

Comparing itself to Europe, the United States seemed not deeply afflicted by militarism. Military professionals in the United States were conservative men from the middle class, not involved in politics and not eager for war—unlike the politically-connected military officials in Germany and other European countries.[25] The United States did build a modern navy, but did not keep up with the pace of the accelerating naval race between Germany and England from 1905 to 1914. The American people, while subject to occasional unpredictable fits of fanaticism, were more inclined to business and commercial values than to a general popular militarism. Even so, expenditures for the army and the navy quadrupled between 1875 and 1910; both army and navy became much larger and better organized.[26]

Alfred Thayer Mahan and Theodore Roosevelt, men of vastly different temperament and style, exercised great influence on United States militarization. Mahan was an introverted, conservative, sophisticated naval officer and historian. In 1890 he wrote *The Influence of Sea Power Upon History*, one of the most influential American-written books of all time. Mahan argued that the United States' rise to greatness among the nations of the world would depend upon a powerful modern navy with overseas coaling stations to guarantee that foreign markets would be open for the products of United States industry. Mahan got his modern navy, although not as rapidly or as large as he wanted. Among his most important disciples was the brash, aggressive, and outgoing Theodore Roosevelt. In 1902 Roosevelt wrote *The Strenuous Life* , a tract in praise of the masculine virtues—"those virile qualities necessary to win in the stern strife of actual life." Roosevelt heaped scorn on the pacifists and anti-imperialists who "shrink from seeing the nation undertake its new duties; shrink from seeing us build a navy and an army adequate to our needs; shrink from seeing us do our share of the world's work, by bringing order out of chaos in the great, fair tropic islands from which the valor of our soldiers and sailors has driven the Spanish flag."[27] No one denied that Roosevelt practiced what he preached. In 1898 as assistant secretary of the navy he saw to it that Admiral Dewey's Asiatic fleet was poised to pounce on the Spanish fleet at Manila Bay in the Philippines.

The combination of military and political forces which Mahan and Roosevelt represented illustrates the seductive power and appeal of nationalist militarism—even in apparently non-militaristic societies. In January 1898, before the war with Spain began, most U.S. businessmen would not have voted for war, and most Americans did not want a colony in Asia. But war generates its own momentum, both in its triumphs and in the death of heroes whose sacrifice must be honored. Thousands of Americans were like Marshall Murdock, newspaper editor in Wichita, Kansas, who initially opposed U.S. involvement, but got swept up into the tide of nationalistic enthusiasm which military victory generated. On May 1, 1898 Murdock wrote, "This war is not going to wake up this nation to its best." By July 22 he editorialized, "The hand of God is seen in this conflict."[28]

In the Progressive Era, the coincidence of emerging United States military power with a popular peace movement tended to blur the boundaries between the forces of militarism and the forces of peace. In 1905 President Theodore Roosevelt won the Nobel Peace Prize for his role in mediating an end to a war between Russia and Japan. When Roosevelt pushed for more modern battleships, peace groups were hesitant to oppose him for fear of losing popular support. The American Peace and Arbitration League supported both a bigger navy and more effective arbitration procedures.[29]

Neutrality vs. War

The war which broke out in Europe in August 1914 confronted the United States with questions of neutrality and involvement as surely as had the Napoleonic Wars of the early nineteenth century. Once again, as in 1807 and 1812, American claims of neutral shipping rights were critical in determining the decision for war and against whom it would be waged. But the context of American international relationships had been transformed by growing U.S. economic and military power, and by changes in military and naval technology. In 1812 the United States had been on the fringes of the system of European world powers. In 1917-18 the United States was able to supply the munitions, financial support, and fighting men to make the difference so England and France could win a total victory over Germany.

From a strictly realistic viewpoint of national interest and security, the United States did not need to join the European war.[30] No one knows, of course, how the war in Europe would have turned out if the United States had not entered. What if Germany had won the war? Germany had swallowed more of Europe than it could have digested. In Eastern Europe, Germany would have been preoccupied for decades attempting to pacify the regions it had taken in the Treaty of Brest-Litovsk, which included the Ukraine. Germany could harly have wrested control of the seas from England. Even if it had, the American economy would not necessarily have suffered more with German world power than it had suffered for decades under English dominance. If Wilson had chosen to hunker down, withdraw U.S. ships from the seas, and wait out the European war, realistic great-power statesmen would have called him shrewd and practical for preserving the United States' resources and manpower and for sustaining a formidable world power unscarred by European wars.[31]

This, however, was not an administration of cautious realists. President Wilson, after initially calling Americans to be neutral in thought as well as in deed, adopted a moralistic view of neutral shipping rights that condemned German submarine warfare while virtually accepting British denial of U.S. shipping to Germany. Bryan, Secretary of State, was as much of a progressive moralist as Wilson. But Bryan put his moral energies to the pursuit of neutrality and peace, while Wilson drifted toward war. Bryan argued against allowing U.S. bankers and financiers to loan money to war-fighting European governments, because pressure to protect those loans might eventually draw the United States into the war. He wanted to prohibit American citizens from boarding ships destined for war zones, lest the sinking of those ships produce a crisis and a war which would sacrifice thousands more lives. When both England and Germany interfered with U.S. shipping, Bryan demanded that the United States protest with equal vigor to both countries.

After a German submarine sank the British passenger liner, the *Lusitania*, on May 7, 1915, Wilson decided to threaten Germany with war if the submarine attacks continued. Seeing clearly that Wilson's policy set a course toward war if Germany resumed submarine warfare in the future, Bryan resigned his position as Secretary of State. Wilson's threats against Germany succeeded in the short run, and helped win his re-election in 1916. But Bryan's assessment turned out to be accurate in the long run. Wilson's policy painted the United States into a corner that required him to declare war (or make an embarrassing policy retreat) in the spring of 1917 when Germany resumed unrestricted submarine warfare, gambling that it could win the war in Europe before the United States could arrive with significant military aid. The United States went to war in behalf of a questionable doctrine of neutral rights—and because Wilson became convinced that he could do more for a future international order if the United States participated fully at the post-war peace settlement.

Bryan was the odd man out. His many critics, both in 1916-17 and in later scholarly assessments, said he was ignorant and naive about foreign relations. The State Department had long been dominated by wealthy, socially respectable, politically-conservative easterners who were offended by Bryan's mid-western informality, his amateurish administrative style, and his radical condemnation of unholy alliances among the eastern "Money Trust," the imperialists, and the militarists.[32] Whatever his limitations in other matters, Bryan was right on target with the large issue of neutrality. His policies represented the road not taken, a road which could well have kept the United States out of the First World War.

Progressive Reform and War

America's war took shape in the context of the Progressive Movement.[33] Wilson's eloquent war message to Congress, April 2, 1917, cast the conflict in terms that extended the Progressive movement's democratic reform spirit onto the world stage. It was a war of freedom and democracy, he said, against imperial German autocracy. The goal was global and idealistic—"a universal dominion of right by such a concert of free peoples as shall bring peace and safety to all nations and make the world itself at last free." It was a war to make the world safe for democracy. To that end the United States was ready to "spend the whole force of the nation" in willing sacrifice.[34] The people of the United States responded with an enthusiastic militant crusade which lifted the optimistic reform-minded spirit of the Progressive era to new heights. The Great War, while it lasted, represented the "flowering of Progressivism."[35]

The crisis of war mobilization was a godsend for progressive experts and their agendas for social organization and control. As barriers against big government programs melted away, suddenly the progressive professionals had work to do. The government organized a host of agencies to manage the economy and the domestic social order—from home to school to workplace to the playground. Progressive city planners seized opportunities to plan and build dozens of military training camps along lines of community organization they had wished for their cities. Progressive crusaders against alcoholism and prostitution focused on keeping the fighting men clean. The prohibition campaign got a special bonus from the fact that many prominent breweries carried German names, and wartime propaganda discredited all things German. Experts in the fields of labor-management relations, urban housing, and social insurance received fresh attention. The drive for national efficiency offered possibilities for economic and social engineering which suited the interests and gifts of professionals who represented the Progressive Movement.

Randolph Bourne, a brilliant critic of the war and of the progressive technical experts who embraced it, observed that there was a "peculiar congeniality between the war and these men. It is as if the war and they had been waiting for each other."[36] Bourne overstated his indictment and left out women progressives from his analysis.[37] Nevertheless Bourne saw clearly, as had few others in his time, that the marriage of progressive peace idealism and the making of total war was doomed to failure. In Bourne's elegant rhetoric the war was a "gay debauch of hatred and fear and swagger that must mount and mount, until the heady and virulent poison of war shall have created its own anti-toxin of ruin and disillusionment."[38]

Bourne had been an intellectual disciple of John Dewey, but he turned against his mentor when Dewey announced his support for the war as an opportunity to apply creative intelligence to social problems. The war, Bourne argued, could not be intelligently guided toward a constructive conclusion. "The American intellectuals" wrote Bourne, "in their preoccupation with reality, seem to have forgotten that the real enemy is War rather than imperial Germany."[39] Dewey and his war-supporting followers were eager to be relevant to the war situation, so they joined the bandwagon and sacrificed the values of social justice, cooperation and understanding which had been central to their pragmatist public philosophy. They allowed "war technique" to overwhelm democratic values. As for the promised control of events which supporters of the war might have gained, Bourne used a violent image: "It is difficult to see how the child on the back of a mad elephant is to be any more effective in stopping the beast than is the child who tries to stop him from the ground."[40] Dewey answered Bourne in a series of articles in the *New Republic* magazine, but Dewey's effort to reconcile pragmatism and war was unconvincing, especially read in retrospect. Each passing week of wartime experience, with its escalating hatred and intolerance, vindicated Bourne's indictment. After the war Dewey shifted his thinking to a kind of "corporate pacifism," a change which Bourne had prompted.[41]

War Out of Control

John Dewey had hoped for a controlled and intelligent war—"no hip-hurrah, no illusions of glory and grandeur, . . . no hatred, no desire for revenge."[42] Under President Wilson's leadership, however, the war became a holy crusade which unleashed nationalistic patriotic excesses that mimicked the autocratic militarism of the German enemy. The victims of popular democratic intolerance were German-Americans, socialists, conscientious objectors, and opponents of war policies.[43] For such people, notably those who were attacked by patriotic mobs, tried and convicted in district court or military courts martial, or subjected to social ostracism and humiliation, the war became a reign of terror.

Intolerance bubbled up from the grass roots in local communities, where citizens were eager to prove their patriotism and "do their bit" to support the boys overseas. It also came from the top down from the government offices occupied by liberal believers in human rights. Newton D. Baker, Secretary of War, was a civilian progressive reformer who initially posed as a protector of the rights of religious conscientious objectors to war. During the war, when peace church leaders informed him that their conscripted young men in military camps were illegally subjected to physical abuse and were being court-martialed and sentenced to twenty-five-year prison terms, Baker lamely responded that he was doing all for them that public opinion would allow.[44] There were 504 court martials of conscientious objectors by June 1919, only one of which ended in acquittal. Baker was trapped by a national spirit beyond his control, but which he, as an architect of the military conscription system, had helped to create. In the same trap were progressives such as the peace-minded Quaker-background governor of Kansas, Arthur Capper. When super-patriotic mobs in McPherson and Harvey counties tarred and feathered Mennonite farmers who conscientiously refused to buy war bonds, Capper failed to investigate or speak against the mobs' actions. He did write an intimidating letter to the Mennonite Joseph Schrag of Burrton, Kansas, "not in my official capacity but as a friend," to get Schrag into line.[45] All over the United States, progressive reformers found themselves cooperating with a kind of democratic repression which was as effective as that of the Prussian autocracy.

Protestant churches and religious leaders added the blessing of civil religion to the war effort.[46] From their pulpits and in the press, clergymen acclaimed the purifying results of war activities, assisted in military recruitment and in Liberty Bond campaigns, and justified hatred of the German enemy. Billy Sunday, a popular and flamboyant evangelist, denounced the evil "Huns" with graphic gutter language. Sunday's response fit his own character, but the excesses of sophisticated progressive religious leaders such as Lyman Abbott, editor of *The Outlook*, revealed a less expected, darker side of the American spirit. On the question of Christian forgiveness, Abbott wrote,

> But I cannot pray for the Predatory Potsdam Gang, "Father forgive them for they know not what they do," because that is not true . . . . I do not hate the Predatory Potsdam Gang because it is my enemy . . . . I hate it because it is a robber, a murderer, a destroyer of homes, a pillager of churches, a violator of women. I do well to hate it.[47]

The most zealous and effective heads of government agencies given the task of generating popular support and unity for the war were George Creel (Committee on Public Information), Thomas W. Gregory (Attorney General), and Albert Sidney Burleson (Postmaster General).[48] As the war progressed, each department became more willing to sacrifice democratic ideals and civil liberties in behalf of national unity—in generating war propaganda, in prosecuting accused war critics in court, and in suppressing anti-war and German-language publications. The U.S. Congress empowered the crackdown with an Espionage Act of June 1917 and a Sedition Act of May 1918, providing for heavy fines and jail sentences for anyone who interfered with the draft, obstructed government bond sales, or said anything disloyal about the government or war effort. One measure of the success of the domestic war crusade was the ability of the government to finance the war in large measure through a series of "liberty loan" drives. All across the country volunteer local committees pressured their fellow citizens to offer their money for the war—sometimes displaying public "slacker boards" with the names of those who did not pay their quota. These highly publicized campaigns "capitalized the profound impulse called patriotism" according to William Gibbs McAdoo, Secretary of the Treasury.[49] The price of patriotic unity was the erosion of personal liberty, an ironic consequence of a war for democracy.

The government created a wartime mass army with a modern conscription system that transformed the U.S. military tradition. The new "Selective Service System," like the war bond campaigns, called forth the energies of local communities. Draft boards throughout the country, staffed by local volunteers, registered more than 24 million men between ages eighteen and forty-five. Of these, more than 4.8 million men entered military service, and 112,432 died. Congress adopted mass conscription only after vigorous debate. James Beauchamp "Champ" Clark of Missouri, Speaker of the House, spoke for "the old volunteer system which has gained us victory in all our wars." But proponents of conscription argued effectively that it was the only equitable way to share the sacrifices of military service. In broader perspective, mass conscription was a triumph of efficient corporate organization which typified the Progressive era.[50]

The greatest U.S. hero of World War I, however, was not an organization man. Alvin C. York, a semi-literate red-haired young man from the hills of Tennessee, symbolized in his individuality the national transformation from peaceful isolation to savage war making. When his draft call came, York applied for exemption as a conscientious objector to war. He belonged to the Church of Christ in Christian Union, a small "perfectionist" church that tried to follow literally the teachings of Jesus. After the Selective Service System twice turned down his exemption, York wrestled with the issue and experienced a new spiritual conversion which convinced him that God wanted him to fight and would protect him. On the morning of October 8, 1918 at the Argonne forest, York led a small patrol of U.S. riflemen on a dangerous flanking movement behind a set of German machine gun emplacements. With incredible courage and marksmanship, York almost singlehandedly with a rifle and pistol killed twenty-five Germans, captured 132, and put thirty-five machine guns out of action. Americans turned York into a military celebrity, a log-cabin hero who had triumphed over the industrial machine. The York legend served American morale in World War II when Gary Cooper starred in the Hollywood movie, *Sergeant York*. Back in Tennessee, York took the view that his war effort had been true to Scripture: "Blessed is the peacemaker." But York's doubts about the killing remained. As a bedridden old man he twice asked his son, a minister, "how God would view what he had done at the Argonne."[51]

The American soldiers arrived at the front late in the war and missed the sustained horror of repeated defensive battles on the trench-lined front for which World War I is famous. Their letters and diaries struck an enthusiastic and adventuresome tone, rich with archaic phrases such as appeared in Sir Walter Scott's nineteenth century romantic novels about medieval knighthood— "feats of valor," "the cause," "gallantry." A U.S. truck driver in the American Expeditionary Force wrote that "war's great caldron of heroism, praise, glory, poetry, music, brains, energy, flashes and grows, rustles and roars, fills the heavens with its mighty being . . . . Oh! War as nothing else brings you back to the adventurous times of old."[52] During the war itself, the thousands of families who grieved the losses of their sons in war could fervently believe in the justice and glory of the cause for which they had sacrificed their lives— even the tens of thousands who had died in training camps, most of them victims of the world-wide influenza epidemic of 1918. The terrors of combat remained hidden from the American people. Not long after war's end, however, a great disillusionment set in.

During the war, Jane Addams and the few other internationalist pacifists who continued to oppose the war after American involvement, were isolated and scorned. However, Addams' courageous wartime critique remained eloquent, prophetic, and psychologically insightful. The war would not achieve its professed goals of justice, she said, because "a finely tempered sense of justice, which alone is of any service in modern civilization, cannot be secured in the storm and stress of war.

This is not only because war inevitably arouses the more primitive antagonisms, but because the spirit of fighting burns away all of those impulses, certainly towards the enemy, which fosters the will to justice."[53] The fate of the punitive peace settlement at Versailles after World War I, and the Cold War militarization after World War II, proved the wisdom of Addams' warning. One instrument for Addams' leadership of the women's peace movement was the Women's International League for Peace and Freedom (WILPF), organized in 1919 and growing out of an International Women's Congress at the Hague of 1914.

Victory and Disillusion

On January 22, 1917, before the U.S. entered the war, President Wilson addressed Congress with a speech titled "Peace Without Victory." A future of peace and justice, he said, would require a league of nations, a new international organization endowed with the authority and power to guarantee agreements among nations. Lasting peace would be a peace among equals, not among victors and vanquished. A peace of victory with total defeat on one side would be, "accepted in humiliation, under duress, at an intolerable sacrifice, and would leave a sting, a resentment, a bitter memory upon which terms of peace would rest, not permanently, but only as upon quicksand."[54] Wilson offered full United States support for a league of nations in behalf of global peace.

The coming years proved the truth of Wilson's early judgement about the price of total victory in war. In January 1918 he outlined his famous "Fourteen Points" for the peace settlement—from number one, "Open covenants openly arrived at," to number fourteen, the League of Nations. But Wilson's proposals were designed for something other than total war. If that war had been, in the words of Prussian military theorist Karl von Clausewitz "nothing but the continuation of policy with other means," a rational and enlightened settlement might have been negotiated.[55] But total war transformed national policies, rather than continuing them. Nations which claimed to be willing to negotiate for stated objectives in fact refused to stop fighting, and eventual winners imposed settlements guided by vengeance rather than by pre-war policies. The deaths of tens of thousands of young men raised the stakes of national honor to levels unknown in peacetime.

Wilson's plans were shredded, first by the vindictive European statesmen at the Versailles Peace Conference, and then at home by partisan congressional leaders who were jealous of their own power and of national sovereignty. The United States refused to ratify the treaty and to join the League of Nations. Wilson hurt his own cause by rigidly refusing to compromise. He ended his presidency as a tragically broken and defeated man.

The most fundamental source of Wilson's failure, however, did not arise from his own political mistakes or from his idealistic internationalism. The war itself caused the failure—a total war fought to total victory. Wilson failed because he chose to join in using means which contradicted his ends. Overseas, the course of the war and of the peace settlement was fully beyond his control. As he had sensed, the peace of total victory on one side and total defeat on the other side only set the stage for another war. Germany, utterly humiliated by its military defeat and by the false charge that it alone had caused the war, was ripe for revenge. Russia was overtaken by the Communist revolution, an event hastened by its defeat in war. The victorious European powers all gave self-interested priority to development of their own national security states. History books commonly blame post-war failures on the misguided Treaty of Versailles. The charge has merit, but it is not reasonable to expect such a treaty to overcome the effects of the war. The stage was set for World War II not simply by the Treaty of Versailles, but more fundamentally by World War I itself.

At home also, Wilson was undone more by the war than by his idealistic internationalism. He chose the wrong means to work domestically for a League of Nations. International cooperation such as Wilson envisioned requires nations to yield up some elements of sovereignty to global institutions for peace and justice. For such a bold progressive internationalist vision Wilson's natural political allies in the United States were the progressive liberals, the peace movement internationalists, and the socialists. In his first term as president, Wilson had had remarkable success with these forces in passing domestic legislative reforms—freer trade, graduated income tax, the Federal Reserve System, the Clayton Anti-Trust Act, and more. These legislative achievements and his re-election in 1916 demonstrated the strength of the progressive-liberal coalition. But when Wilson chose the means of total war to pursue his liberal international program, he alienated the liberal left, whose support was so essential. The zealous war campaigns, the progressive violations of liberal democratic ideals, and the exhaustion of liberal idealism in the war for democracy, helped to demoralize and to split the progressive coalition.[56] Wilson failed because he linked his ideals to total war.

When the United States entered World War I, John Dewey noted that "the American people is profoundly pacifist and yet highly impatient of the present activities of many professed or professional pacifists."[57] Profoundly pacifist, indeed, were the Americans, but also profoundly violent. Like a bloody thread running through the course of national history, violence appeared on the frontier, in race relations, and, during the twentieth century, in world power expansionism. The United States was a unique combination of pacifism and militarism, apparent opposites which at times drew support and legitimation from each other. In their own ways, Dewey and Wilson in 1917-18 made the mistake which had been foreshadowed by William F. Cody and the "Wild West" show. They linked American violence to the ideal of universal peace.

A distinguished body of "realist" critics have blamed Wilsonian idealism for the failure of policy in World War I. George F. Kennan, a realist historian and diplomat of the Cold War era, wrote that a democracy at war reminded him of a huge prehistoric monster with "a brain the size of a pin." The beast is slow to action, but once disturbed "he lays about him with such blind determination that he not only destroys his adversary but largely wrecks his native habitat."[58] Kennan's alternative in retrospect would have been for the U.S. to build up its military forces earlier, to threaten the warring powers into backing off soon after the war began, and finally, if necessary, to fight to save England but without the crusading mentality of total war. Kennan's prescription contained an assumption, remarkable for a "realist," that wars already under way can be tamed. Kennan's scenario surely would have been preferable to what actually happened. Nevertheless the questions which pacifist critics of war, such as Jane Addams and Randolph Bourne, posed to their war-crusading progressive friends in 1917-18 still press for answers: Is it possible to overcome arms races with more arms? Is it possible to drive out war with more war?

Chapter 10

"The Good War":
Misremembering World War II

In 1984 Studs Terkel, a Chicago newsman who has an extraordinary gift for drawing the drama of history out of the stories of ordinary people, put a popular label on the Second World War. The war was, wrote Terkel with quotation marks to suggest irony, "The Good War." Terkel's oral history book won a Pulitzer Prize and afforded a generation of World War II scholars and buffs the opportunity to reflect on what conditions or results might render that war—or any war anywhere—authentically "good." On the face of it, World War II was not a likely candidate for moral approval. That war killed more people, created more refugees, destroyed more cities, and disrupted more social and political systems than any war in human history. Among its legacies were the Soviet Union's control of almost half of Europe, a dangerous military-industrial complex in the United States and the permanent threat of thermonuclear holocaust. So what was good about it?[1]

When Americans spoke nostalgically of World War II, they were doing more than filtering out painful memories—the humiliation of Pearl Harbor, the funeral services for their sons, or the herding of Japanese-American citizens into concentration camps. Yes, memory was selective. But even more, the "Good War" image stood in contrast to America's bad war in Vietnam and subsequent erosion of national purpose and direction. In World War II a unified nation had fought with honor against an evil enemy and had won an unconditional victory. In subsequent wars (Korea, Vietnam, Persian Gulf) the country fought limited battles for ambiguous objectives while national unity and commitment deteriorated. The triumphs of World War II seemed luminous in contrast.

A Time of Unity and Triumph

American clarity of purpose in World War II was a gift from the Japanese military. Their surprise attack on Pearl Harbor on December 7, 1941 shocked the American people with the worst battle losses in the nation's history—over 2400 Americans dead, 1100 wounded, eight battleships sunk, and 162 army and navy planes destroyed. It was a "sneak" attack. The "Japs," as Americans (except for Japanese-Americans) called them, didn't have the decency to declare war. American rage and fascination over the event lived into the twenty-first century. On Memorial Day weekend, May 26-28, 2001, the war-epic Disney film, *Pearl Harbor*, recorded $75.1 million in ticket sales, the best opening ever for a three-hour film.[2]

Four days after Pearl Harbor, on December 11, 1941, Adolf Hitler of Nazi Germany announced his declaration of war against the United States. That declaration also clarified the situation. Ever since Hitler's rise to power and march toward an expanded Third Reich, Americans had been confused and divided about how to respond to Nazism. At the end of 1941, with a two-front war against both Japan and Germany, the United States experienced the catharsis of a clear military challenge and commitment. President Roosevelt had agreed in advance with Prime Minister Churchill that the United States would give priority to Europe rather than to the Pacific. But nothing came close to rivaling the impact of Pearl Harbor in galvanizing the American people for war.

American unity in World War II had to do with political ideals. The United States fought for freedom and democracy against dictatorship and imperialist aggression. To be sure, the image of the war as anti-imperialist was not perfectly clear. The United States was allied with England and France, both of whom presided over world empires that they did not propose to dismantle. The United States' support for the French effort to hold onto her colonies in Indochina after the war later led to disaster in Vietnam. In Eastern Europe the United States' ally was the Soviet Union, an empire headed by the Communist dictator, Joseph Stalin. Despite the character of her allies, Americans convincingly defined the war as a defense of democracy against militant imperialism. The theme of opposing ideologies in deadly conflict loomed large in the series of wartime propaganda films, *Why We Fight*, created by Frank Capra, one of America's greatest film makers.[3] Capra's films gloried in American ethnic pluralism, popular participation in government, and love of freedom. They dramatically portrayed the Axis powers' march of military aggression: Japan into Manchuria (1931), China (1937), and Indochina (1940); Italy into Ethiopia (1935); Germany into Austria (1938), Czechoslovakia (1939) and Poland (1939). Americans fought against aggressive enemies of democracy and freedom.

If the U.S. part in World War II needed any additional moral justification, information from the Nazi death camps for Jews later confirmed the case. Hitler's Holocaust against the Jews in central Europe became the most convincing image of evil in the history of western civilization. Photographs of American soldiers liberating the surviving inmates at Dachau and Buchenwald convinced Americans that ending the Holocaust had been one of their war aims. In fact, the United States had not gone to war to rescue the Jews. Neither the government, the press, nor the leading Christian denominations had taken interest in, or responsibility for, the plight of the European Jews.[4] Capra's "Why We Fight" films had not mentioned Hitler's persecution of Jews. Liberation of the concentration camps was an unintended benefit of the war. No one in the United States (except the Jews) rallied to the cry of "Remember Auschwitz." Everyone wanted revenge for Pearl Harbor.

The war united all kinds of Americans—rich and poor, business and labor, urban and rural, and far left to far right. Even the American Communists joined the war crusade. The peace movement, immensely popular in the 1920s and 1930s, dwindled to a small core almost overnight. This was a momentous shift. Americans had been disillusioned and divided over the roots and effects of World War I. A Senate investigating committee led by Gerald Nye of North Dakota had revealed the huge profits that giant firms such as Du Pont had made during World War I, and had charged that American banking and munitions interest had led the country into that misguided war. The Great Depression of the 1930s had discredited the business interests, while a powerful impulse to isolationism had influenced American foreign policy.

Pearl Harbor virtually eliminated public polarization on foreign policy. During World War II more than fifteen million men and women served in the armed forces. Fewer than 50,000 of draft-age men (a fraction of one percent—.03%) registered as conscientious objectors. Public opinion was so unified, the press and the movie industry were so willing to censor themselves, that governmental coercion or repression of dissenters was hardly necessary. Hollywood caved in to official advice and control with barely a whimper.[5]

Popular democratic censorship may be preferable to official government censorship. The phenomenon, however, is almost unimaginable from the viewpoint of a vigilantly independent press a half-century later. One sensational wartime story that was kept out of the press and off the airwaves had to do with Japanese balloon bombs, about 300 of which reached North America during the war. One bomb killed six people and others started fires—more than enough fodder for a free press to boost circulation with sensational reporting. But the government Office of Censorship asked newspaper editors and radio broadcasters to suppress the stories. The media complied, and the total absence of news about the bombs contributed to a Japanese decision to abandon their balloon bomb project. The contrast of this effective voluntary censorship with the role of the U.S. press in publicizing the worst atrocities of the Vietnam War could not be more stark.[6]

World War II revived the United States economy. Alone among modern industrial nations, the U.S. was spared the devastation of invasion and bombing of cities and industries. The challenge of turning U.S. farms and factories into full production brought full employment and an end to the economic depression. Federal spending ballooned from 9 billion dollars in 1940 to 98 billion in 1944, while excess-profits taxes on businesses and high taxes on the very wealthy helped ensure that economic benefits were shared by the less affluent. African Americans, women, and the poor gained more rapidly than the upper classes. The wartime economic boom led people to assume a cause and effect relationship between warfare and general prosperity. Even if some consumer items were scarce and subject to rationing during the war, it was a time when people accumulated wealth. The pent-up demand for consumer goods helped ensure that general prosperity would continue into the postwar era.

Above all was the fact of victory. In Europe and Asia, and throughout the world, American forces triumphed. The 400,000 U.S. deaths in World War II, almost all military personnel, were agonizing for families affected, but the triumphant national cause made their grief meaningful and bearable. In the Vietnam war 50,000 Americans died, one-eighth of the World War II total, but the Vietnam deaths caused far more national anguish. The heroic dead of World War II had not died in vain. By the end of the war, the United States had reached a pinnacle of world power. The closing paragraphs of historian William L. O'Neill's history of the war, fifty years after the event, said that the triumph was moral as well as military:

> All one can say in the end is that the war was, and remains, well worth the effort and the heartbreak . . . . By passing this greatest of all modern tests America also won the right to become a better nation . . . . More so than now, Americans accepted responsibility for their acts and did not uphold personal gratification as the be all and end all of life. They believed in doing their duty, at home and at the front . . . . The people overcame their enemies, surmounting as well the difficulties presented by allies, a chaotic and divided government, among other faults, to gain what Roosevelt had promised would be 'the inevitable triumph.' 'Sweet land of liberty,' the children sang, and so it was, and so it would remain—thanks to a great generation.[7]

The Costs of Good War Memories

The reasons Americans remember World War II as a "Good War" are understandable. The costs of these positive memories are more difficult to embrace. If Americans believed that the cataclysm of total war was redemptive for democracy, what did it mean for the future of democracy and warfare in the United States and for the future role of the United States among the nations of the world?

Whatever its positive side-effects in the United States or elsewhere, World War II was an overwhelmingly disastrous event for human civilization. The statistics of human deaths are mind-boggling. The label "Holocaust," written with a capital "H," is usually reserved for the Nazi mass murder of Jews, but the war itself was a holocaust ten times over. Over the globe, some sixty million people died in the war, most of them civilians.[8] American deaths, nearly all military personnel, were less than one percent of the total. The Soviet Union suffered by far the most, with some twenty-five million deaths. China lost approximately fifteen million; Poland lost nearly six million (the highest percentage of total population); Germany lost over four million; Japan over two million; Yugoslavia between 1.5 and 2 million; and the United Kingdom about four hundred thousand. These victims were mostly civilians. The proportion of civilian to total deaths caused by war rose from five percent in World War I to sixty-six percent in World War II.[9]

The behavior of armies, notably the treatment of prisoners of war and the massacre of civilians, reached levels of barbarism not previously recorded. The war produced millions of refugees and displaced peoples. Germans and Poles in Eastern Europe were uprooted and forced westward. Jews fled to Palestine and created a new state of Israel, displacing Arabs and turning the Holy Land into a tinderbox of ethnic and religious conflict. Some seven million Japanese who had spread through the far east were forced to relocate. In China, where the Japanese invasion superseded the death-struggle between Communists and Nationalists, millions of people were dislocated. The war also devastated the material cultures of Europe and Asia—destroying not only factories, bridges, dams and human dwellings, but much of the finest art and architecture of centuries. The cities of Western Europe, Germany and Japan were laid waste.

The costs of World War II included financial resources used for the engines of death and destruction rather than for the upbuilding enterprises of cultural creation, education and human welfare. The European nations and Japan exhausted their financial resources and created huge debts. The community of modern industrial nations lost opportunities to address problems of economic development in underdeveloped regions of Asia and Africa. In the postwar era, the United States poured financial resources into the reconstruction of Europe, which had become a fertile breeding ground for totalitarian Communism. The war was followed by huge financial expenditures for another arms race. A world beset by problems of poverty diverted its resources into war machines.

This war changed the nature of the American state. Some wartime economic changes confirmed and extended the welfare state programs that had begun in Roosevelt's New Deal, such as the Social Security system, the guarantee of collective bargaining rights for labor, and the use of deficit spending for economic stimulation. But government programs also moved the country in the direction of a permanent warfare state. The war produced an exceptionally large defense sector, an alliance of business and military interests, a politically weak labor movement, reliance upon income tax, and resistance to using Social Security for income redistribution.[10] The war led to a post-war peacetime militarization which contradicted basic American ideals.

Democracy and Human Rights in Wartime

Positive memories of World War II obscured the fact that democracy and modern warfare are not fully compatible, and at some points are in direct contradiction.[11] Government power must be centralized in wartime; power flows to the administrative core. Military command structures must be hierarchical and authoritarian rather than democratic. Freedom of speech must be suspended in behalf of national unity. People must be coerced into military service; citizens must be taxed to pay for it.[12]

Coercive conscription of young men for military service was the most massive government interference with American lives, a form of government intrusion which had been controversial until World War I. Before 1917 many people in the United States believed military conscription contradicted American ideals. After World War I Americans accepted the draft as a normal part of democratic war-making. The Selective Service Law of World War II, administered at the local level by 6,442 draft boards, provided opportunities for religious objectors to war to perform alternative service in a program known as Civilian Public Service (CPS). Although their work in conservation camps, mental hospitals, and other activities was "in the national interest," the conscientious objectors received no pay for their labor, and their refusal to fight was held up to popular scorn.[13] Those who refused to register for the draft, notably the Jehovah's Witnesses, or who refused to work in CPS camps, were put in prison. Some critics indicted CPS as a program of "slave labor," but there was general agreement that the alternative service system worked better than in World War I, when conscientious objectors had been drafted into the army.

A more blatant and shocking denial of liberty was directed against the Japanese Americans. In the months after the Japanese attack on Pearl Harbor, the United States government detained 112,000 Japanese Americans from west-coast states and shipped them to ten concentration camps in barren "sand and cactus sites" in the interior. These people, two thirds of whom were American citizens, were not charged with any crimes and had no chance for legal defense. The government justified the evacuation on grounds of "military necessity," even though they had not proven a single case of Japanese-American espionage or sabotage. The army gave the victims only a few weeks or days to prepare for removal and to dispose of their properties. Many sold out to opportunistic European Americans for a small fraction of the real value of their property. The evacuation was overwhelmingly popular throughout the country. Walter Lippman, influential liberal journalist, visited California and wrote that the coast should be treated as a war zone: "nobody's constitutional rights included the right to business on a battlefield."[14] Earl Warren, the attorney general of California who later became governor of the state and chief justice of the United States Supreme Court, warned that the very lack of reported sabotage could be part of a plot, "a studied effort not to have any until zero hour arrives." By "zero hour" Warren meant a "repetition of Pearl Harbor" in California.[15] President Roosevelt and members of his cabinet urged the military to evacuate the Japanese Americans in Hawaii as well, but the policy was not carried out. It was not practical because the Japanese constituted a third of Hawaii's population and the bulk of its skilled labor force.[16] The concentration camps, although ringed with barbed wire and supervised by military guards, were more like Indian reservations than like the Nazi camps for Jews. The children were able to attend schools where, as one young internee named Peter Ota remembered, "One of our basic subjects was American history. They talked about freedom all the time."[17] Ota was one of the more than 1200 internees who volunteered for combat in the war. About two-thirds of them were accepted for service.[18]

A long tradition of anti-Asian racism lay at the root of the incarceration of innocent Japanese-Americans. The United States was also at war with Germany and Italy, but Americans were able to see German-Americans and Italian-Americans as individuals rather than presuming their collective guilt. Chauncey Tramutolo, a San Francisco Attorney, remarked how absurd it would be to evacuate as enemy aliens the non-citizen Dimaggio parents, whose sons (Joe, Dominic, and Vincent) were popular major league baseball players.[19] The stories of American soldiers in the European and Pacific theaters of war confirmed the deeply rooted difference in racial stereotyping. White American Marines generated a far greater racial hatred of their Japanese enemies. E. B. (Sledgehammer) Sledge, a Marine who fought on Peleliu and Okinawa while his brother was with the infantry in Europe, reported a "brutish, primitive hatred" for the Japanese, "just a natural feeling that developed elementally." When the German soldiers surrendered, "they were guys just like us." When Japanese soldiers surrendered, American Marines preferred to shoot them. "I've seen guys shoot Japanese wounded when it really was not necessary and knock gold teeth out of their mouths . . . . The way you extracted gold teeth was by putting the tip of the blade on the tooth of the dead Japanese—I've seen guys do it to wounded ones—and hit the hilt of the knife to knock the tooth loose. How could American boys do this? If you're reduced to savagery by a situation, anything's possible . . . . It was so savage. We *were* savages."[20]

The trauma of combat upon battlefield survivors was itself a great cost of the war. Only a fraction of soldiers shared Sledge's experience. Most of the infantrymen in the front lines could not bring themselves to aim and shoot to kill enemy soldiers.[21] The vast majority of military personnel were removed from the dehumanizing chaos and devastation of battle, and instead involved in the vast organized and regimented system designed to support and supply the fighters at the fronts. The great difference between battlefield chaos and rear-line organization is one of the striking paradoxes of war.[22] The overwhelming testimony of veterans of actual battle was that they were sustained not by patriotic ideals but by comradeship with fellow soldiers and by the struggle to survive. The gloss of patriotic glory—the making of battle films and the erecting of heroic statues and monuments—was produced by people who had not been through the trauma of actual battle.

Strategic Bombing

During World War II the United States, for the first time in its history, adopted a strategy of intentional mass killing of enemy civilians. The policy violated traditional standards of justice in war as well as the stated ideals of U.S. leaders. At the outset of the war in Europe, President Roosevelt invoked the "conscience of humanity" in an appeal to the nations at war that their "armed forces shall in no event, and under no circumstances, undertake the bombardment from the air of civilian populations or of unfortified cities."[23] Roosevelt's effort to set limits to the conduct of war honored the "principle of discrimination" between combatants and noncombatants which was an essential part of Christian and classical moral thinking about warfare. Without moral limits, warfare becomes murderous criminal activity.[24] Americans were rightly outraged by the Japanese inhumane treatment of prisoners of war—a repeated violation of conventional moral limits on warfare.

Initially the British and the Germans exercised mutual restraint in selecting targets for aerial warfare, but both nations gradually moved beyond daytime "precision bombing" of military targets to the nighttime terror bombing of urban areas—each nation charging the other with being responsible for the descent into barbarism.[25] The German "Blitz" of London began September 7, 1940 and continued until mid-May 1941, when the German Air Force turned toward the invasion of the Soviet Union. The "Blitz" killed more than 45,000 Londoners and destroyed or seriously damaged more than 35 million homes. In the spring of 1942 the British Bomber Command undertook massive incendiary (fire-bomb) attacks on German cities to assault "the morale of the enemy civil population and in particular, of the industrial workers." The Americans, who were at first committed to daylight precision bombing, in 1944 gradually shifted to accept inadvertent damage to civilians while attacking military targets. Eventually they went further and engaged together with the British in the incendiary bombing of civilian centers. The raids reduced fifty German cities to rubble and ashes. The psychological effects on civilian morale, however, were disappointing. The bombings did not defeat Germany.[26]

The fire raids produced new knowledge about the physical effects of mass incendiary bombing—first observed in July 1943 in the attack on Hamburg, a city with many closely packed wooden buildings. The superheated air above a city with numerous raging fires created a massive suction of hurricane-force winds which intensified the heat and expanded the firestorm area. Most of the victims died from suffocation or carbon monoxide poisoning, but those caught in the greatest heat became human torches. In the Hamburg raid an estimated 45,000 civilians died. It was primarily a British operation.

The most inhumane and devastating firebombing of civilian targets in Europe was the combined British and U.S. attack (February 1945) on Dresden, a non-military, non-industrial cultural center which was filled with refugees. American bombers were the third of three waves of attack over a thirteen hour period. The American attack included 316 bombers with 500 tons of high explosive and 300 tons of incendiary bombs. Some of the explosive bombs had "delayed-action fuses designed to explode while rescue workers and firefighters were at work. Accompanying the U.S. bombers were fighter planes that used machine guns to strafe masses of survivors trying to leave the burning city." Estimates of the number of deaths in Dresden, nearly all of them civilians, ranged between 70,000 and 135,000.[27]

Before the war with Japan started, the United States rushed bombers and supplies of incendiary bombs to the Philippines for possible use in firebombing Japanese cities.[28] That bombing was delayed both because Japan took the Philippines and the United States lacked a bombing base in striking distance of Japanese home islands, and also because the European theater of war was first priority. General Haywood Hansell, commander of U. S. air forces in the Pacific, was committed to "precision bombing" and was reluctant to launch an area incendiary bombing program. In early January 1945, General Curtis LeMay replaced Hansell and helped turn the last year of the war into a fiery hell for hundreds of thousands of Japanese civilians. On the night of March 9-10, 1945, 334 U.S. B-29 bombers dropped 2,000 tons of bombs on a twelve-square mile target of flammable wooden buildings in Tokyo, creating a fire storm that reached 1,800 degrees Fahrenheit in its center. Some people who jumped into canals to save themselves were boiled to death. The total death toll approached 100,000. Later that spring and summer fifty-eight Japanese cities were destroyed by firebombing. The bombers began to run out of targets—except for Kyoto, which was exempted as a historically significant cultural center, and Hiroshima and Nagasaki, which were being reserved for the new atomic bombs.[29]

The mass slaughter of defenseless civilians in bombing raids is hard to justify.[30] Those who justified the firebombing of Japanese cities as a payback for Pearl Harbor were demanding an astonishing vengeance. In the Tokyo firebombing alone, Americans killed more than thirty Japanese *civilians* for every one American *military* death at Pearl Harbor. As other cities were attacked, the ratio escalated. By the end of the war, Americans had killed more Japanese civilians than military personnel. Part of the rationale was that Japanese military production had been widely dispersed into non-industrial urban areas. Modern total war reduced the distinction between combatants and noncombatants.[31] Nevertheless, the strategic bombing of civilians was such a dramatic case of intentional, massive, and indiscriminate action against people who were basically innocent that some historians have compared it to the Nazi killing of innocent Jews.[32] An important difference was that the Nazis killed Jews for ideological, not strategic, purposes. Anti-Semitic genocide continued after a territory surrendered to the Nazis.[33]

Hiroshima and Nagasaki

On August 6 and 9, 1945, the Americans dropped the first atomic bombs on the cities of Hiroshima and Nagasaki, with an estimated combined death total of 200,000 people—overwhelmingly civilians. On August 10, Japan announced that it would accept the terms of unconditional surrender which had been set forth in the Potsdam Declaration of July 26. The American people rejoiced, convinced that the atomic bombs had avoided an even costlier invasion of the Japanese home islands. And yet in the postwar era the atomic bombings became a focus of intense controversy. The atomic bombs had not only violated the conventional rules of war which prohibited the killing of civilians, but evidence emerged that they had been dropped on a defeated enemy which was on the verge of surrender. Moreover, the use of nuclear weapons inaugurated a new era of military technology which rapidly escalated to threaten human civilization in general.[34]

Were the atomic bombs dropped on Hiroshima and Nagasaki necessary to end the war? In retrospect it is clear that United States officials could have pursued alternative policies toward the goal of Japanese surrender. One option would have been to give up the demand for unconditional surrender and to clearly tell the Japanese that they could keep their emperor after the war. Another option would have been to wait until the Soviet Union had declared war against Japan and begun its invasion of Manchuria. A third possibility would have been to invite the Japanese to a demonstration explosion. These options might have been combined. The first and second together would almost certainly have resulted in Japanese surrender. It would have saved the most lives by ending the war without either an invasion or use of atomic bombs.[35]

By July 1945 Japan had been utterly defeated and was seeking ways to surrender. Its leaders, however, refused to contact the United States directly. Instead they attempted without success to enlist the support of the Soviet Union to gain terms other than unconditional surrender. Above all, they wished to keep their emperor, without whom they could not imagine the survival of the Japanese nation. Official Japanese telegrams from Tokyo to Moscow made clear that the Emperor Hirohito had intervened in the political process to end the war and that the main obstacle was that "England and the United States insist upon unconditional surrender." The Americans had broken the Japanese communication code and knew the content of the cables. On July 18, the second day of the Potsdam conference, President Truman entered a handwritten note in his journal referring to a "telegram from Jap Emperor asking for peace."[36] Instead of setting aside the unconditional surrender demand, and making clear that they in fact would not insist upon removing the emperor, the Americans insisted upon including unconditional surrender language in the first official Potsdam Proclamation of July 26. They altered the language slightly to say the Japanese *armed forces* should surrender unconditionally. On July 27 Prime Minister Suzuki responded with a public statement that was translated to mean Japan would ignore [*"mokusatsu,"* meaning "to withhold comment"] the Potsdam Proclamation. Suzuki's intention, as he later interpreted it, was to avoid criticism of the Potsdam Proclamation, to withhold comment and leave a margin for further discussion. The Americans took it for a rejection, and the path toward the fiery nuclear conclusion of the war was set.

The failed communications of July 1945 are a testimony to the demonic momentum of militarism on both sides of the conflict. Both sides tinkered with oblique language signals rather than saying directly what needed to be said to end the war. The leaders of both sides adhered to a public hard line in order to maintain military morale—the Japanese for an honorable and suicidal defense of the homeland, and the Americans for a drive toward total victory. Prime Minister Suzuki, eager to make peace, could not persuade the die-hard militarists in the Japanese cabinet without some clear face-saving device such as modification of unconditional surrender terms. President Truman and his advisors, also eager to end the war, feared that abandoning the unconditional surrender formula would damage military morale and fail to keep faith with those who had sacrificed their lives in the war. The United States had long since abandoned its reservations about mass killing of enemy civilians. Some historians argue that by 1945 mass bombing had become so routine that American leaders, decent men in the grip of bureaucratic evil, "were not seeking to avoid the use of the A-bomb . . . . Thus, they easily rejected or never considered most of the so-called alternatives to the bomb."[37]

The post-war trials of Axis leaders expanded the definition of war crimes to include the crime of plotting and waging aggressive war. At the International Military Tribunal at Nuremberg, eighteen German leaders were convicted and eleven of them executed. The tribunal disallowed their defense that they were following orders of Adolf Hitler, who committed suicide at the war's end and could not be tried.[38] In Tokyo the International Military Tribunal faced a different situation. Emperor Hirohito, the embodiment of the nation, had survived the war and could well have been held responsible for Japanese military aggression. The convenient fiction that the emperor was uninvolved in politics was partly true, but Hirohito in fact had had a real role both in beginning the war and in ending it. However, the emperor was protected because his ongoing presence was believed to be essential in establishing a peaceable post-war order in Japan. The Tokyo trials sentenced twenty-five Japanese leaders to death or imprisonment for conspiring to wage war and for wartime atrocities. In addition 920 Japanese were executed, and some 3,000 imprisoned, on conventional war crimes charges. British and American officials who had authorized mass bombing of civilians were on the winning side and were not brought to trial.[39]

In both postwar Japan and the United States, ordinary citizens did not take responsibility for the war and its excesses. Oral interviewers Haruko Taya Cook and Theodore F. Cook, after extensive conversations in Japan (1988 ff.) akin to those of Studs Terkel in the United States, concluded that "war responsibility is not clearly established in the minds of many Japanese today, no matter how certain the rest of the world may be about it."[40] Interviews with teenagers in 1962 had shown that most of them believed the war "was unavoidable."[41] One prominent Japanese historian, Ienaga Saburo, documented his country's military aggression and wartime atrocities, but the Japanese Education Ministry refused to approve his textbook for use in high schools. Ienaga believed the war with the United States was not inevitable, and that the war's roots were in Japan's invasion of China. His text was too critical of the Japanese military and government to meet the standards of Japan's official remembrance of the war. Ienaga brought a lawsuit against the state to challenge the constitutionality of the process for textbook revision and approval, but his protest was "a one-man crusade . . . (which) did not kindle widespread debate or reassessment."[42] In the 1990s the Japanese government wrestled with fresh demands for apologies and reparations, especially for wartime abduction and exploitation of Korean "comfort women."[43] A *Washington Post* textbook survey in 1994 indicated that coverage and criticism of Japan's actions in World War II was increasing.[44]

Public school textbooks in the United States are no more likely to condemn U.S. strategic bombing of civilians during the war than

Japanese textbooks are to condemn the attack on Pearl Harbor or the Bataan death march. Americans are conflicted on the issue. Professional scholars have been predominantly revisionist—to the point of claiming a scholarly "consensus" that use of the atomic bombs was unnecessary. But public opinion and popular writings on the war have not accepted the scholars' conclusions.[45]

A firestorm of popular protest erupted in 1994-5 when the Air and Space Museum of the Smithsonian Institution planned a memorial exhibit of the Hiroshima bombing around a display of the B-29 Superfortress *Enola Gay*, which delivered the first bomb.[46] The Air Force Association and veterans groups protested that the exhibit portrayed the Japanese as victims and under-emphasized Japan's wartime aggression and the probable costs of an invasion of the Japanese home islands. After several failed attempts to satisfy critics with revisions to the exhibit, the Air and Space Museum canceled its plans and prepared a smaller exhibit which supported the traditional patriotic interpretation. A sixteen minute film accompanying the scaled down exhibit included Chaplain William Downey's prayer before the *Enola Gay* took off: "We shall go forward, trusting in Thee, knowing that we are in Thy care now and forever. In the name of Jesus Christ, Amen." Also recorded was the opinion of Navigator "Dutch" Van Kirk that "the use of the, uh, this weapon did shorten the war and save lives overall, both Allied lives and Japanese lives."[47] Even if more than 200,000 Japanese died in the atomic blast and from subsequent effects of radiation, most Americans remained more than ready to "Thank God for the Bomb."[48]

Nevertheless, Wasn't the War Necessary?

It is possible, of course, to concede that U.S. wartime excesses were deplorable, even inexcusable, but at the same time to believe that it was necessary to enter the war to overcome the totalitarian militarism of Germany and Japan. Granted that it was not a "Good War," wasn't it essential for the future of democracy that the United States make sure the totalitarian militarists did not win? Wasn't the Allied victory essential for U.S. long-range security?

American isolationists and pacifists had tentative and fragmentary answers to these questions, but their approaches were quite different from each other.[49] The isolationists zealously protected American sovereignty and her right to unilateral action in foreign affairs. Leaders in the "America First" movement promoted military power and expressed right-wing hostility toward foreign nations.[50] Historian Melvin Small, in his book *Was War Necessary?*, later summarized a positive case for a kind of regional isolationism. The United States, under the Monroe Doctrine, was dominant and secure in its own hemisphere. Japan wanted an equivalent of the Monroe Doctrine for its own region, and it was not essential for United States security to go to war to stop her. China's vast spaces and huge resisting populations would have limited Japanese ambition and exhausted its resources, without assistance from the outside. By the same principle, Germany and the Soviet Union could have settled their own contest for dominant regional influence in Eastern Europe without American interference. However that struggle was settled, it would not have likely resulted in either Hitler or Stalin making a bid for *world* political domination. In the long run, Germany would have exhausted herself attempting to establish control of Russia (just as Japan in China); or Stalin would have faced natural regional checks to Soviet power in Western Europe. In Professor Small's view, the moral stature of Hitler and Stalin was not relevant to the world of regional power politics. The United States would have been able to retreat to regional hemispheric isolation, protected by its great natural moats— the Atlantic and Pacific Oceans.[51]

When Roosevelt, in response to Japan's aggression, cut off trade and froze Japanese assets in the United States, Japan was forced either to abandon its plan for regional leadership or to go to war. War was not necessary, from the isolationist viewpoint. It could have been avoided either by the U.S. backing off its insistence upon exercising great-power authority in Asia, or by Japan backing off of its plans for regional hegemony. Japan needed outside sources of oil for its regional plans, and had only a two year supply at the time she attacked. Japan made its misguided and disastrous decision to attempt to destroy American naval power in the Pacific by attacking Pearl Harbor. But if the United States had accepted Japanese movement toward an equivalent of the Monroe Doctrine for her region, Japan's attack on Pearl Harbor would not have occurred.

The leading U.S. pacifists rejected the isolationist emphasis on American sovereignty. A. J. Muste of the Fellowship of Reconciliation and Dorothy Day of the Catholic Worker Movement combined a more radical rejection of war with calls for international consciousness. In

December 1939, after Hitler's attack on Poland, Muste called for world-wide free trade, drastic arms reductions begun by the United States on its own, and movement toward federal world government begun by the formation of a United States of Europe. For all nations, Muste argued, the greatest enemy was the method of war which had demonstrated its bankruptcy in World War I and which marked a course to "certain mass suicide." For self-defense a nation should invest its resources in means of "non-violent non-co-operation" such as were pioneered by Mohandas K. Gandhi in India's struggle for political independence and economic justice against British imperialism.[52] Day, like Muste, grounded her argument for nonviolent resistance in religious conviction, but she was less concerned to appear politically practical. Day wrote in June 1940, "We are urging what is a seeming impossibility—a training in the use of nonviolent means of opposing injustice, servitude and a deprivation of the means of holding fast to the faith. It is again the folly of the cross."[53] Milton S. Mayer, a pacifist newspaperman, magazine writer, and former member of the University of Chicago faculty, was more blunt and irreverent: "I do not want Hitler to rule the world, and if he wins this war he will. The trouble is that if we win it he will rule the world anyway." War, said Mayer, would produce more autocracy and militarism in its train, as war had done in the past.[54]

American pacifists in 1941 did not have a well-developed practical nonviolent alternative to the United States' response to German and Japanese aggression. Incessantly they faced the question, "What would you do about Hitler?" Some argued that an alliance with Stalin to defeat Hitler was hardly preferable to an alliance with Hitler to defeat Stalin. One anti-interventionist who saw Stalin as the greater enemy, called the Soviet Union "the bloodiest sponsor of mass murder in the pages of history."[55] In any case, pacifists viewed Naziism itself as the product of a war system. The unprecedented horrors of World War II made warfare itself a questionable means of overcoming evils of any kind. Persons who resisted Naziism nonviolently may have provided more relevant models for twenty-first century conflict than those in World War II who wielded the technological instruments of death.

Throughout the twentieth century, governments invested billions of dollars in the means of warfare, but relatively little in the means of alternatives to war. The question of how to replace war with nonviolent means of conflict resolution was made even more urgent by advances in

military technology in World War II and the Cold War. In a world of
nuclear weapons the next total war would not be a "Good War" for any
of the nations involved. The witness of Muste, Day, Mayer and their
fellow pacifists, small minority though they were, pointed in the direction
that nations must move in the future, if modern civilization is to survive.

Chapter 11

The Civil Rights Movement: Participatory Democracy and Nonviolence in Action

For a period of about ten years, from the late 1950s through the early 1960s, the United States witnessed a sustained movement of nonviolence for social justice: boycotts, sit-ins, pray-ins, marches, and freedom rides. The popular name "civil rights movement" emphasizes the achievement of political and economic rights for black people, but, as Malcolm X cogently argued, these are basic and mutually-linked human rights for all people. According to Vincent Harding, "the freedom struggle of African American citizens has always been a gift of life and truth to the whole society .... The nation could never be whole—released from its 'disease' of saying one thing about freedom, justice and liberty and doing another—until African Americans were whole, internally and externally."[1]

A successful struggle for human rights generally redistributes power from the few to the many, and thus it is fundamentally pro-democracy. Nonviolent action to uphold human rights is effective, as its practitioners affirm, because the "powerless" already have the potential for power. An unjust system cannot remain in power if the majority of people withdraw their support or cooperation. The civil rights movement brought fundamental social change by nonviolent direct action in disobedience to unjust laws and customs. Thus the movement became a model for other pro-democracy movements around the world—in South Africa, China, Poland, East Germany and the Philippines.

Historical accounts of the civil rights movement often set the beginning date at 1954, when the Supreme Court outlawed school segregation in the case of *Brown vs. Topeka Board of Education*. But the origins of the movement lay deep within America's long history of racial oppression and in the rising demands of African Americans for justice. In the 1896 *Plessy vs. Ferguson* decision, a case involving a man one-eighth African American, the Supreme Court had mandated "separate but equal" facilities. But Blacks had received nothing "equal." Their housing, education, job opportunities, income, life expectancy, and health care were all dramatically inferior. Blacks were victims of lynching (1,100 lynchings between 1900 and 1917) and an epidemic of race riots before and after World War I. The fight against Hitler's Germany in World War II brought global attention to the way in which the belief in racial superiority and racial purity could threaten the safety of the entire world. In its subsequent ideological war with the Soviet Union, the United States realized that it was vulnerable on the issue of race. How could one proclaim democracy to be a superior form of government when more than a tenth of the population remained separated, uneducated, in poverty and systematically denied the right to vote? Apart from the desegregation of the Armed Forces under President Truman, the U.S. government showed little response. But masses of African Americans, smoldering from years of injustice, were ready to ignite the fires to make America live up to its promises and ideals.

Ordinary People

The civil rights movement was first and foremost a mass movement of ordinary people. In this, it was profoundly democratic. The movement was made up of masses of common folk who were united in their desire to change the daily humiliation of living with signs dividing the world into "colored" and "white." People were tired of being denied jobs that paid well, service in restaurants, restrooms when they traveled, dignity on public transportation, access to decent schools and libraries. City by city, African Americans in increasing numbers began to say "no" to the system of segregation which relegated them to second-class status and was enforced by tradition, law and terror. In retrospect it is tempting to idealize the courage, fortitude, faith and persistence of those who stood up to taunts, insults, physical abuse and very real threats of death. Did they have resources beyond the reach of ordinary mortals? Ernest Green, who projected an amazing sense of composure and good humor throughout his year-long ordeal as the lone senior among the nine young people who integrated Little Rock High School in 1957, later reflected:

> One thing that I think is very important is this: while the nine of us may have been preselected, there really are nine, ten, thirty, forty, fifty kids in every community that could have done that. It

wasn't that nine people fell out of the sky in Little Rock. We were all ordinary kids. You really do have the ability to do a lot more than either you've been told or you've been led to believe by your surroundings. If given the opportunity, you'd be surprised at how much you can do, how much you can achieve.[2]

A certain mythology has grown up celebrating the spontaneity of much of the movement. While an element of improvisation was always present, major acts of resistance did not just spring up unplanned. A good example is the year-long boycott of city buses in Montgomery, Alabama. The Women's Political Council (WPC) in Montgomery had been actively presenting grievances to the city commission since 1949. Jo Anne Robinson, a professor at historically-black Alabama State College and Mary Fair Burks utilized the WPC to organize black residents in every part of the city in preparation for a bus boycott. So when Rosa Parks gave her history-making refusal to move to the back of the bus and was arrested December 1, 1955, the black population was ready. Parks herself was not just a tired seamstress, as some legends tell, but had received training in nonviolence at the Highlander Folk School in Tennessee. She was an active member of the NAACP—until it was banned in Alabama as a "foreign corporation."[3] To deal with the specifics of the situation raised by Parks' arrest, a new organization was formed. This new organization, the Montgomery Improvement Association, elected a young minister, new to the area, as its president. Martin Luther King, the new president, rose to prominence as an articulate national spokesperson as a result, but it is important to remember that the movement was already underway. It would not have succeeded except for the persistent cooperation of thousands of ordinary people in the black community, many dependent upon public transportation for their jobs, who had planned and enacted a boycott of city buses in Montgomery for over a year.[4]

Empowering People

Many of the "ordinary people" were young high-school and college-age students looking for direct and immediate ways to become involved in change. The sit-in phase of the movement started Monday afternoon, February 1, 1960, when four seventeen-year-old freshmen at North Carolina A&T in Greensboro, North Carolina decided to buy a few school items at a Woolworth Store and then sit down at a Whites-only lunch counter to buy a cup of coffee. The students were not part of any formal organization. They wanted to protest the system which allowed them to spend money in a store but not to sit and eat at its lunch counter. Reactions to their bold actions were varied. A black dishwasher soundly chided them as "troublemakers." A few white women patted them on the back saying, "I think it's a good thing you're doing." A lone policeman who walked in paced behind them "with his club in his hand, just sort of knocking it in his hand and just looking mean and red and a little bit upset."[5] But it was clear that the four had challenged the status quo and this was not about to go unnoticed. Support came from all over the area, as sit-ins spread to other stores that refused to serve Blacks. Franklin McCain, one of the original four, remembers "at the height of the sit-in movement in Greensboro, we must have had at least, oh, ten or fifteen thousand people downtown who wanted to sit-in . . . ."[6] It quickly became a widespread mass movement, modeling some of the best of participatory democracy.

In just three short months sit-ins occurred at more than sixty sites. Ella Baker, a dynamic middle-aged woman who had years of experience organizing for social change, brought together students from fifty-eight different southern communities to coordinate their activities. The granddaughter of a slave, Ella Baker had spent the New Deal years working for the Works Progress Association (WPA) on consumer education, starting consumers' cooperatives and then working for several years as a field secretary for the NAACP. She had a well-developed sense of human equality and a belief in participatory democracy. It is not surprising that the organization that emerged from this meeting of students, the Student Nonviolent Coordinating Committee (SNCC pronounced "snick") reflected values of group leadership and empowering people through direct action.

Ella Baker saw leaders as facilitators and warned of the dangers involved in depending on a single strong leader. "In government service and political life I have always felt it was a disability for oppressed peoples to depend so largely upon a leader, because unfortunately in our culture, the charismatic leader usually becomes a leader because he has found a spot in the public limelight. It usually means he has been touted through the public media, which means that the media made him and the media may undo him."[7] Baker warned against equating the movement with any one leader.

A story from Orangeburg, South Carolina vividly demonstrates the idea of group leadership. Students from two black colleges marched downtown to sing "America" and offer a public prayer for equal rights. Almost immediately they were stopped by the police chief and the fire department. The firemen, holding their hoses ready to blast torrents of water, confronted the students, who were holding only Bibles and hymn books. When the police chief asked who the leader was, twelve hundred students shouted, "I am the leader." When he announced he would arrest the leader, twelve hundred students stepped forward. The police turned on the water cannons and the high-pressure water tore the students' clothing and bruised their bodies. The students moved forward singing, "The Battle Hymn of the Republic," even as the police pounded them with tear gas. So many of the students were arrested that a parking lot was converted into a temporary stockade. At least forty were treated for injuries and exposure in the near-freezing drizzle of rain.[8] Similar scenes were enacted hundreds of times throughout the South, as people claimed the rights of democratic citizenship by acting on them.

Democracy in Action

One of the most daring attempts to make democracy real occurred during the summer of 1964. Robert Moses, a math and philosophy student, Dave Dennis of the Congress of Racial Equality (CORE), and a number of others had been working in Mississippi, the "closed society" that few dared challenge. Working for little more than room and board, these young people were committed to the twin goals of developing indigenous leadership and breaking apartheid in Mississippi by registering people to vote. After two tedious, dangerous and underfunded years, the young SNCC workers did not have much to show for their efforts. Rural Blacks were not always eager to publicly challenge the status quo by going to a courthouse miles from home to attempt (usually unsuccessfully) to register to vote. They had good reason to be cautious. Those who did try to register, like Fannie Lou Hamer, immediately lost their jobs. Others, like Herbert Lee, father of a large family, were summarily killed. Lee's assassin was not a low-life hoodlum, but Mississippi State Representative E. H. Hurst. Attempts to get the Justice Department to file a suit against Hurst failed, reinforcing a pattern of state-sanctioned violence and little federal support for justice in Mississippi. In August of 1963, while thousands marched on Washington and heard Martin

Luther King's famous "I have a dream" speech, Robert Moses held an all-night vigil outside the Justice Department holding a picket sign reading "When there is no justice, what is the state but a robber band enlarged?"[9]

Moses returned to the Mississippi Delta to consider a proposal to bring northern white students to the South during the summer of 1964. The proposal met with immediate resistance from the SNCC workers in Mississippi. While SNCC had always had a few white workers, this proposal was upsetting for a number of reasons. Black SNCC workers had worked long and hard to earn the trust of local residents, a trust that might easily be eroded. SNCC had a long-standing commitment to developing indigenous leadership; Whites had a long history of dominating leadership positions. A reason for bringing Whites into Mississippi stemmed from media racism, which gave more publicity to events involving Whites. In addition, the justice system was more likely to protect white students, particularly ones with well-connected parents. Such disparities between Whites and Blacks were a recipe for resentment, misunderstanding and anger.

Hundreds of white college students responded. The students accepted for the program were idealistic, self-supporting, and had parental permission if under twenty-one years of age. Bob Moses' training sessions were direct and honest. He told the students "The way some people characterize this project is that it is an attempt to get some people killed so the federal government will move into Mississippi. And the way some of us feel about it is that in our country we have some real evil, and the attempt to do something about it involves enormous effort and therefore tremendous risks . . . ."[10] These words had power in the wake of news of the brutal deaths of three civil-rights workers in Neshoba County, Mississippi: James Chaney, a black civil-rights worker from Mississippi and two white workers, Andrew Goodman, a summer project volunteer, and Michael Schwerner, a social worker and the head of the CORE office in Meridian. When their bodies were found buried in a dam, it was evident that the two white men had been shot and that Chaney had been beaten so severely that nearly every bone in his body was broken. Still, when Moses assured those who might be afraid that they could leave with no disgrace, no one left.

A key tenet of participatory democracy is that everyone is prepared and active: Democracy is not a spectator sport. Everyone who participated in nonviolent demonstrations was expected to have been to training sessions. These training sessions gave information on the details of the demonstrations, what to expect and how to prepare. The sessions generally included role plays and simulations of being called abusive names, being threatened and being beaten. People who didn't feel they could remain nonviolent in the face of such abuse were assigned other supportive work such as making phone calls, stuffing envelopes, running errands.

The goals of Freedom Summer were fundamental to a pro-democracy movement: freedom schools, voter registration, and the creation of an alternative, parallel party. Because Blacks were excluded from the political parties, they created the Mississippi Freedom Democratic Party. The Freedom Schools were often taught outdoors for lack of facilities. Many churches were burned for agreeing to let the schools meet in them. The schools were designed to help compensate for the meager education of most rural Blacks who had worked in the fields from the time they were small. Barely literate, they had never been taught basic rights of citizenship or how to read a newspaper. Many could not do enough math to know when they were being cheated at stores. The student workers themselves received crash courses in African American history to equip them to teach a part of history that had been denied to the entire nation. In a training address to students Bob Moses made clear that understanding the interconnectedness of all human life lay at the heart of the struggle for civil rights. "Don't come to Mississippi this summer to save the Mississippi Negro" he told them. "Only come if you understand, really understand, that his freedom and yours are one .... "[11]

Thus, the movement boldly challenged the country to live up to its ideals of freedom, democracy and equality. The democracy espoused could not be reduced to merely voting, but was envisioned as empowered citizens building and maintaining the system and society in which they wanted to live.

Nonviolence as Means

The civil rights movement was not centrally organized. At no time could a single organization speak for "the movement." Organizations were formed and reformed; alliances were created and broken; discussions about strategy and tactics led to bitter disagreements. Detractors charged that the disorganized movement proved that nonviolence was limited and ineffective as a means of change. A brief look at four key organizations which utilized methods of nonviolence can help to evaluate the movement's diversity and achievements. NAACP and CORE were older, northern-based organizations. SCLC and SNCC were southern-based organizations—the former predominantly ministers and the latter predominantly students.

In the 1950s the National Association for the Advancement of Colored People (NAACP) was the largest and best-known organization working for black civil rights. An interracial organization based in New York City, the NAACP used the legal system to bring about change. Charles Hamilton Houston, Thurgood Marshall, and Constance Baker Motley were among the better-known lawyers who worked for the NAACP Legal Defense Fund. They tried case after case, slowly building up a record of cases against racial discrimination in all of its various forms. Their legal victories included the elimination of the all-white primary, the invalidation of the "grandfather clause" (which claimed one could only vote if one's grandfather had), and admission of Blacks to white universities.[12] Many prominent civil rights workers spent time as field secretaries for the NAACP, and most were members or attended meetings. Its painstakingly slow and scrupulous legal work was so threatening to the South that Louisiana and Texas obtained injunctions against it. South Carolina made it illegal for teachers to join, and Alabama outlawed the organization entirely.[13]

Partly in response to this attack on the NAACP, local organizations like the Alabama Christian Movement for Human Rights in Birmingham, and the Montgomery Improvement Association in Montgomery began to develop. In the cities, black ministers took primary leadership. They were visible and accepted leaders, readily in touch with masses of people, received salaries from the black community, and had church buildings available for meetings. Ministers were less vulnerable to losing their jobs. In 1957, recognizing the benefits of sharing experiences, discussing common goals, and engaging common problems, they formed an umbrella organization, the Southern Christian Leadership Conference (SCLC). Within the SCLC, Rev. Dr. Martin Luther King was most influential in communicating principled nonviolence in ways that captured the imagination of ordinary people by building on ideas familiar to them. He developed a love ethic and made it practical. Yet his academic background and knowledge also caused scholars and Christians to rethink the life of Jesus in terms of a model of nonviolence. In a speech given in 1961 King outlined what he saw as the underlying philosophy of the nonviolent movement.

• Ends and means must cohere. If one wants peaceful ends, one must use peaceful means.

• Follow a consistent principle of non-injury. This has an external aspect of avoiding physical violence (don't hit back; don't curse back) but also an internal aspect of avoiding internal violence of the spirit.

• One seeks to defeat the unjust system, rather than individuals who are caught in that system.

• Suffering can be a most creative and powerful social force. "The nonviolent say that suffering becomes a powerful social force when you willingly accept that violence on yourself, so that self-suffering stands at the center of the nonviolent movement and the individuals involved are able to suffer in a creative manner, feeling that unearned suffering is redemptive, and that suffering may serve to transform the social situation."

• There is something within human nature that can respond to goodness. King held to "dualism within human nature," but insisted that "man is not totally depraved . . . the image of God is never gone."

• Non-cooperation with evil is a moral obligation.[14]

From King's philosophy emerged two major strategies. One was to help people understand that all systems are dependent upon the support and compliance of people for their existence. By withdrawing enough popular support (non-cooperation with evil), the system will fall. To be effective, this strategy required large numbers of participants. Boycotts, sit-ins, and freedom rides were all ways of not complying with the system. The second strategy was to expose the evil by creating public situations in which the violence of the system showed itself. This strategy required the courage and commitment of a soldier willing to suffer and die. It had the advantage that it could be used by small (or large) groups to embarrass and shame majority opinion into action. The story of the movement in Birmingham, Alabama demonstrates the use of both of these strategies.

Rev. Fred Shuttlesworth, "a wiry, energetic and indomitable man," in 1956 had organized the Alabama Christian Movement for Human Rights (ACMHR). Meeting weekly in churches, the organization developed a large mass base. Like many other similar organizations throughout the South, their initial approach was to work through the courts to change segregation policies. One of their first suits involved access to city parks. All citizens paid taxes to support the public parks and recreational facilities, but only Whites were allowed to use them. The court ruled in favor of opening the parks to all, but city officials responded by shutting down the parks, so no one could use them. Time and time again, Whites in the civil-rights era refused to give in, preferring hardship and deprivation for themselves, rather than relenting on the issue of segregation.

Following the lead of the student sit-ins in North Carolina, students at Miles College, a black college in Birmingham, began sit-ins at local stores. The ACMHR joined them, targeting those stores that refused to hire black clerks with a "don't buy where you can't work" campaign, a non-cooperation strategy. Blacks were about forty percent of the city population, and the boycott successfully mobilized enough support to be felt by the businesses. A number of businesses soon recognized that harmonious race relationships were in the best interest of making a profit. They took down their colored/white signs on restrooms and water fountains rather than risk losing a substantial portion of their business. However, they had not reckoned with the politicians and their deeply-entrenched investment in maintaining segregation. City building inspectors threatened to close these stores for alleged infractions of the building and safety codes. White customers canceled charge accounts and the merchants backed down.

Shuttlesworth was identified as a "troublemaker." Both his home and his church were bombed. A bomb was thrown into his bedroom, exploding the mattress and springs, but miraculously he was spared. White leaders warned him to get out of town and even many of his black friends felt he should flee for his life. But as he surveyed the damage, Shuttlesworth defied those who hoped he would be intimidated by announcing that God had protected his life through this and "I'm going to stay and help Him work this thing out."[15] Later, Shuttlesworth articulated his insight for others, declaring "You have to be prepared to die before you can begin to live."[16]

In 1963 the ACMHR invited King and the SCLC to Birmingham to organize a campaign based on the second strategy—that of exposing evil. The project, called Project C (for Confrontation) included well-advertised and carefully-planned demonstrations. Other civil rights organizations, the media and the press were all informed of the plans. One of the goals was to create enough of a disturbance so that the federal government would have to take action (as it had by bringing federal troops to Little Rock in 1957). After several days of quiet marching and arrests, police commissioner Bull Connor's patience had run out. He met unarmed demonstrators with dogs and clubs. King reported, "The newspapers of May 4 [1963] carried pictures of prostrate women, and policemen bending over them with raised clubs; of children marching up to the bared fangs of police dogs; of the terrible force of pressure hoses sweeping bodies into the streets."[17] As these pictures were flashed across national and international television and newspapers, the federal government was forced to take a stand. The impact of such demonstrations and the political ability of the Texan president Lyndon Johnson led to the 1964 Civil Rights Act. That act outlawed discrimination on the basis of race or sex.

The Student Nonviolent Co-ordinating Committee began with ties to SCLC and initially agreed with them about the principles of nonviolence. The SNCC statement of purpose was strongly influenced by James Lawson, a ministerial student who was expelled from Vanderbilt University for his civil rights activism:

> We affirm the philosophical or religious ideal of nonviolence as the foundation of our purpose, the pre-supposition of our faith and the manner of our action. Nonviolence as it grows from Judaic-Christian traditions seeks a social order of justice permeated by love. Integration of human endeavor represents the first step toward such a society.[18]

However, SNCC challenged the ministers of SCLC in both the process and the implementation of these ideals. With a younger and more impatient membership, and working in untouched areas like rural Mississippi, SNCC favored empowering people as a means of transforming society. This meant that they relied most heavily on the strategy of withdrawing support from the segregation system. They embraced many forms of direct action, including sit-ins, freedom schools, and voter registration. In addition, its process of decision-making reflected decentralized group leadership, rather than the hierarchal leadership that ministers were comfortable with. As SNCC became more organized, however, it constantly felt the tension between wanting to maintain "the people" as decision makers and the need for making efficient, clear choices.

SNCC often worked with an older organization, the Congress of Racial Equality (CORE), that was also committed to interracial nonviolent direct action. Organized in 1942, CORE emerged from a task force on racial reconciliation within the Fellowship of Reconciliation, a peace organization with broad social and international interests. CORE members, a majority of whom were white, had an intellectual orientation. They discussed at length the philosophic basis of nonviolence. They questioned the use of the law, and how reformers could change hearts rather than coerce compliance to different behavior. CORE members were familiar with Gandhi's nonviolent movement in India. They talked about the potential problems of a mass nonviolent movement in the U.S. where Blacks were a minority and where the culture was Christian rather than Hindu. To a much greater extent than in the other organizations, their focus was on demonstrating the value of nonviolence as a means in transforming social problems. For them nonviolence became both the goal and the means, in contrast to members of SNCC, who saw liberation and empowerment as the ends.[19]

At one point, King was asked to merge SCLC with CORE, but he refused because CORE was a secular organization where commitment to pacifism was the unifying factor. SCLC was a religiously based organization.[20] Nevertheless, CORE members like Bayard Rustin and James Farmer often discussed issues with King. The most visible action of CORE in the movement was the Freedom Rides, designed to test the federal law prohibiting discrimination on interstate public transportation. Small interracial groups boarded Greyhound and Trailways buses, beginning in Washington, D.C. They found that the "colored" and "white" signs had been removed in the bus stations of Virginia and they encountered no problems until they crossed into Alabama. In Anniston, Alabama, their bus was fire bombed and the riders were beaten with sticks and had rocks thrown at them as they tried to get off. One sixty-year-old man went into cardiac arrest. When the riders were taken to the hospital, no one would treat them. The hospital demanded that they leave, but this seemed impossible because an angry crowd surrounded the building. Fortunately for the riders, a caravan of fifteen cars, led by Rev. Fred Shuttlesworth of Birmingham, showed up to rescue them. As Hank Thomas, one of the Freedom Riders recalled "every one of those cars had a shotgun in it. And Fred Shuttlesworth had got on the radio and said—you know Fred, he's very dramatic—'I'm going to get my people . . . I'm a nonviolent man, but I'm going to get my people.'"[21]

The issue of armed self-defense highlighted one of the many differences in approach among those committed to nonviolence. CORE and SCLC members were always unarmed during demonstrations and actions. Some like King and Lawson were committed to principled nonviolence as a way of life. Others like Shuttlesworth were committed to nonviolence as a tactic, but reserved the right of self-defense. For hundreds of participants in demonstrations, nonviolence was a useful and pragmatic tactic. Ernest Green pointed out the logic of nonviolence in his situation as one of nine black high school students daily surrounded by hundreds of potentially hostile Whites—police and parents, as well as the other students at Little Rock's Central High.[22] The white South had always held the upper hand in terms of guns and arms. To respond in kind would have been disastrous. Furthermore, the unarmed presence of demonstrators revealed the violence inherent in maintaining white supremacy. When dogs and fire hoses were turned on praying people in Birmingham, it was clear to even casual observers who the aggressors were. Or as King wrote in his "Letter from a Birmingham Jail," "we who engage in nonviolent direct action are not the creators of tension. We merely bring to the surface the hidden tension that is already alive."[23]

Transformed Opponents

Nonviolence also had the potential to touch the humanity of the opposition. During one of the many marches of the 1963 Birmingham movement, a stunning but not well-known example occurred. Several hundred people gathered at the New Pilgrim Baptist Church to march to Memorial Park, near the city police department and jail. The police building and jail were visible symbols of years of racial injustice and of white determination to keep such injustice in place. The group marched forward in orderly lines of two, as they had been taught. Down the road, they could see their way blocked by firemen with fire hoses capable of tearing bark off trees, and by policemen with German Shepherds trained to attack, lunging on their leashes. Rev. Charles Billups, leader of the group, told them to drop to their knees and pray. Eugene "Bull" Connor, the hot-tempered Police Commissioner, ordered the marchers to turn back. Rev. Billups, with calm dignity, refused. Connor barked orders to turn the hoses on. Rev. Billups looked at the wall of white rage and quietly but firmly said, "Turn on your water, turn loose your dogs, we will stand here till we die."[24] The firemen hesitated. Connor yelled and gave the order a second time. Still, the firemen hesitated. Then, as Myrna Carter, one of the young marchers, tells it, Connor

> started using profanity, cursing [the police and firemen], shaking the hose and shaking them. 'Turn the hose on! Turn it on!' But those people just stood there. They would not turn the hoses on that Sunday. Then the whole group started singing black spirituals. It was just something in the air.[25]

King referred to this incident as "one of the most fantastic events of the Birmingham story . . . Connor's men, as though hypnotized, fell back, their hoses sagging uselessly in their hands, while several hundred Negroes marched past them without further interference . . . ."[26] This story reminds us that nonviolent action transforms not only the participants, but can also transform those who are acting on the side of oppression.

Nonviolent mass action also had its heart-rending defeats, especially in the "closed society" of the delta states—Mississippi, Arkansas and Louisiana. Mississippi set up a "Sovereignty Commission" to maintain the "sovereignty" of the state against all outsiders. James Farmer, head of CORE during the sixties, recalled a terrifying day in 1963 in Plaquemine, Louisiana when police chased the last reporter out of town, shocking him with an electric cattle prod until he fled. The day before, troopers, mounted on horseback and armed with billy clubs and cattle prods, had trampled many peacefully marching children. Now, truly isolated from the outside world, outraged black parents and ministers organized a march to protest police brutality. Once again the troopers "mounted their horses and assembled their weapons as if the crowd of unarmed men and women before them were an opposing army. They then charged into the mass . . . flailing with billy clubs and stabbing with cattle prods".[27] The marchers fled back to a church, "bleeding, hysterical, faint" with the troopers in hot pursuit. "They dismounted and broke into the church, yelling and hurling tear gas canisters, one after the other, poisoning the air." The gas masks protected the troopers as the people "screaming with pain and terror" tried to escape through the back door and into a parsonage. The troopers destroyed everything in the church and began attacking the parsonage, sending "tear gas canisters smashing through the windows." James Farmer tried to phone for outside help, but the operators refused to put through long-distance calls from the black community. The troopers particularly wanted to lynch Farmer. But the black people, many of whom had just met him, were determined to protect him. With daring subterfuge they smuggled him past the road blocks and out of town in a hearse.[28] One cannot understand the subsequent militancy and alienation emerging in the late 1960s without understanding this sustained systemic violence.

Activism, Resistance and Apathy

In understanding our past, particularly as it affects present race relations, it is important to understand all the players—activists, resisters, and apathetic observers. A popular freedom song asked the question, "Which side are you on?" Race, class, geographical origins or religious affiliations were not predictors of "which side" a given person would choose. Some Whites, including a few brave southerners, sided with the protestors. Some Blacks, including teachers and clergy, opposed the movement as too risky, or inappropriate, or more potentially damaging than liberating. Religious language gave a powerful underpinning to the arguments for justice and freedom and profound inspiration through the sustaining use of spiritual songs. Yet supporters of segregation also used religious language, and religious institutions upheld them. Anne Moody, a young black woman in Mississippi wrote tellingly of small groups of well-dressed, polite African Americans visiting white churches on Sunday to worship and being unceremoniously informed that they could not worship at a "white" church.[29]

Sometimes it may seem that during the sixties everyone was lined up on one side or the other of a picket line. In actuality, the great majority of Americans saw a bit of what was going on if they turned on the evening news, but went about their own daily lives hoping that things would work themselves out. These people, too, were history makers, by virtue of their lack of involvement. No one articulated their significance more clearly than Martin Luther King in his famous "Letter from a Birmingham Jail" written during the eventful year of 1963. The letter was addressed to the clergy in Birmingham, who had written a collective public letter urging patience and obedience to the "principles of law and order."[30] In his celebrated letter, King wrote: "I have almost reached the regrettable conclusion that the Negro's great stumbling block in his stride toward freedom is not the White Citizen's Counciler or the Ku Klux Klanner, but the white moderate, who is more devoted to 'order' than to justice; who prefers a negative peace which is the absence of tension to a positive peace which is the presence of justice."[31] Those "hoping things would just work out" in effect supported the status quo, the "negative peace."

Segregationist Resistance

The White Citizens Council that King referred to in his letter was formed in the wake of the 1954 Supreme Court school desegregation decision. Robert Patterson, secretary of the founding chapter in Indianola, Mississippi recalled feeling that "if the Supreme Court and federal government did force integration, that it would completely destroy our school system, and it would create an environment for our children that was just utterly unacceptable." He went on to pointedly observe, "I had the same reaction then as these people in Boston and Detroit and other cities of the North are having when they're talking about busing their children."[32] The Citizens Council had 85,000 members in Mississippi and 60,000 in Alabama by 1956. Members included some of the most influential businessmen and politicians.

Segregationist orators such as Governors Ross Barnet of Mississippi, Orville Faubus of Arkansas, and George Wallace of Alabama, predictably appealed to southern white audiences with proud themes of the Confederacy. But their rhetoric was meant to resonate with northern whites as well. Wallace's 1963 inaugural address announced:

> Today I have stood where Jefferson Davis stood and took an oath to my people. It is very appropriate then that from this Cradle of the Confederacy, this very heart of the great Anglo-Saxon Southland, that today we sound the drum for freedom . . . . In the name of the greatest people that ever trod this earth, I draw the line in the dust and toss the gauntlet before the feet of tyranny, and I say: segregation now, segregation tomorrow, segregation forever![33]

Many in both South and North cherished the illusion of being an "Anglo-Saxon" country despite centuries of immigration from elsewhere — and despite the fact that in some counties of Wallace's Alabama, Blacks outnumbered Whites. The segregationist appeal for "freedom" really meant the freedom cherished by many people throughout the nation to live the myth of white superiority and the myth that black and white lives were not really interconnected.

When George Wallace, with presidential ambitions, made a speaking tour of the North, he successfully played on the further theme of keeping big government out of local and personal affairs. When Robert Kennedy asked, "You think it would be so horrifying to have a Negro attend the University of Alabama, Governor?" the governor replied, " Well, I think it's horrifying for the federal courts and the central government to rewrite all the laws and force upon the people that which they don't want."[34] His response foreshadowed the right-wing political rallying cry in the 1980's and 1990's: Get big federal government off our backs.

The independence of African nations in the 1960's and the growing power of Asia raised a fear in some Americans that in international affairs the Whites were losing power to a Communist-inspired "Afro-Asian" majority. In his inaugural address, George Wallace lumped together this fear with the fear of racially-mixed marriage ("amalgamation"). With a flourish of religion and patriotism he offered to fight the "racist" liberals:

> The international racism of the liberals seeks to persecute the international white minority to the whim of the international colored so that we are footballed about according to the favor of the Afro-Asian block . . . . We warn any group who would follow the false doctrines of communistic amalgamation that we will not surrender our system of government, our freedom of race and religion that was won at a hard price; and if it requires a hard price to retain it, we are able—and quite willing—to pay it.[35]

Segregationists commonly accused supporters of racial equality of being allied with communism. Robert Paterson justified the need for a Citizens Council to maintain segregation, vowing, "We will defeat this Communist disease that is being thrust upon us."[36] Even Lyndon Johnson, who helped assure the passage of the Civil Rights Act and the Voting Rights Act during his presidency, assumed that outside communist agitators had played a major role in the race riots of 1968 in both southern and northern cities. He was dismayed when the rather conservative "Kerner Commission," which he had assigned to investigate the causes of the violence, emphatically concluded that "White racism is essentially responsible for the explosive mixture which has been accumulating in our cities."[37]

The six hundred page Kerner Commission report detailed the racism they found:

1. pervasive discrimination and segregation in employment, education and housing 2. black in-migration and white exodus which have produced massive and growing concentrations of impoverished Negroes in our major cities 3. black ghettoes where segregation and poverty converge on the young to destroy opportunity and enforce failure. Crime, drug addiction, dependency on welfare and bitterness and resentment against society in general and white society in particular are the result.[38]

Today the Kerner Commission report reads like a prophecy of what would happen if their detailed and reasonable suggestions for dealing with systemic racism were not followed. Unfortunately they were not, and American society still suffers from the injustices of virulent racism, not only against African Americans but against Native Americans and the growing population of Hispanic Americans.

Legacies of Nonviolence

In a conversation with an elderly black man, a young white student asked the question, "But did the Civil Rights movement do anything? Racism is everywhere. Has anything changed?" Looking the young questioner directly in the eye, he replied, "We're not afraid anymore." The measure of this transformation can best be appreciated by those who have lived through it. The Civil Rights Act (1964) and the Voting Rights Acts (1965) were significant legislative gains that clearly broke the U.S. apartheid system. Our history teaches us that these gains can be dismantled and reversed (indeed, attempts are being made even as this is written). Yet while they stand they give minorities and women clear standards of fairness to appeal to. With the increased democratization of voting rights has come a significant increase in black office-holders, from local to federal levels. To give just one example, the number of elected officials in the South went from seventy-eight black office-holders in 1965 to 3147 in 1982.[39] A growing number of African Americans have entered professions. Significant legal and political gains were made.

Furthermore, nonviolence as a method gained respect as an effective (although difficult) technique, one which was utilized by activists in other areas including Vietnam protests, women's rights, the United Farm

Workers, the nuclear disarmament movement, the abortion movement and the environmental movement. Beyond the borders of the United States, the nonviolence philosophy of the civil rights movement influenced and shaped nonviolent pro-democracy movements in Czechoslovakia, South Africa, China, East Germany, and the Philippines.

Unfinished Business

Racism should be seen not only as a "system," but as a disease. The disease has been present in this country since its inception. Everyone is infected. Therefore we must recognize our common humanity, the unity of the human race in spite of all of its diversity, while making a serious analysis of the extent and nature of the affliction. This is a promising route for healing the racism that Nathan Rutstein names as "the most powerful and persistent obstacle to the attainment of a just and peaceful society."[40] Why wasn't a major movement with committed sacrificial workers able to end America's most virulent disease? One answer commonly given is that cries for economic justice were ignored. White segregationists in the 1960s had an arsenal of arguments playing on many hopes and fears. They linked integration to a loss of "white" jobs and increase in crime. William Julius Wilson found that young black men in their twenties were four times more likely to be involved in crime. But when education and employment were held constant, there was no significant difference between white and black crime rates, suggesting that education and jobs form the most effective crime-reduction program. In other words if one wants to fight crime, one of the best ways would be to ensure that everyone has decent, well-paying jobs.[41]

Another partial answer lies in understanding that racism takes other forms than the blatant segregation of the South. Malcolm X, growing up in Michigan, Boston and New York, had to deal with the covert racism of the North. Part of the difficulty of dealing with covert racism is that all sides are capable of using reasonable language. In the 1960s "constitutional government"and "freedom of choice" were rallying cries for segregation. Constitutional government meant states rights with no interference from the federal government on matters such as enforcement of federal civil rights laws and desegregation laws. Freedom of choice meant the freedom to choose not to hire Blacks, or sit next to Blacks in public spaces. Today we still hear what some call "code language." Appeals to "color-blindness" and "judging everyone individually" sound instinctively fair and very much like the dreams of the 1960s protestors. But the appeals can provide a cover for ignoring and allowing to continue patterns of racial discrimination. "Freedom" language continues to be used in ways to undermine justice —freedom to hire and fire at will; freedom to sell to whom one will; freedom to use derogatory or inflammatory language.

The civil rights movement brought out some of the finest characteristics of a generation of young people. But many carry scars, deep psychological wounds, from the brutality they witnessed and continue to witness. Perhaps the greatest and most hopeful gift of nonviolence for the permanent elimination of racism in this country has been an increased recognition of what King called the "inescapable network of mutuality."[42] Because all human life is intertwined and interdependent, unjust systems, like racism, negatively impact *all* humans. Therefore nonviolence seeks to defeat unjust systems rather than the individuals who are caught in that system. A nonviolent approach to the problem is built on honesty and dialogue rather than fear and blame. As Pam McAllister observed,

> nonviolence has a "capacity for encompassing a complexity necessarily denied by violent strategies . . . violent tactics and strategies rely on polarization and dualistic thinking and require us to divide ourselves into the good and the bad . . . . "[43]

A thorough study of the nonviolent, pro-democracy movement of our own country can foster hope, grounded in a sober reality, for the possibility of a society built on the principles of freedom, equality and justice.

Chapter 12

The Cold War:
Pyrrhic Victory

Unwinnable Wars

In 1951, in the face of failures by world powers to create a stable peace out of the wreckage of World War II, George F. Kennan admonished the American people to stop thinking that they had won the war.[1] Instead of democratic peace, the war had produced a hostile polarization of two great powers—the United States and the Soviet Union. This was not victory, but a volatile stalemate. Americans who expected the full fruits of total victory, said Kennan, had failed to understand the war. It was one case of a wider phenomenon, the "failure to appreciate the limitations of war in general—any war—as a vehicle for the achievement of the objectives of the democratic state."[2]

Kennan was one author of the United States postwar policy of "containment." At the end of the Cold War, however, Kennan disavowed the militarized way in which "containment" had been carried out. His original concern, he said, had been the danger of "the *political* expansion of Stalinist Communism," with an eye on the prospects of local Communist movements in Germany and Japan. By 1949 U.S. government leaders were identifying the Soviet Union mainly as a *military* threat which might unleash World War III in the near future. In Kennan's view this was a false image of Stalin and the Soviet Union, and it led the United States into an expensive Cold War arms race and into misguided military actions in Korea and Vietnam. A post-war political struggle between the United States and the Soviet Union had been inevitable. The runaway arms race and global militarization were not. [3]

Why the Great Fear?

The Cold War arms race and militarization were products of fear, both in the Soviet Union and the United States. The Russians were paranoid about the prospects for another military invasion from Western Europe, following the examples of Napoleon, Wilhelm II, and Adolf Hitler. The Soviet Union had absorbed by far the highest losses in the war against Naziism, and now demanded that their sacrifices be recognized in postwar negotiations. They also feared encirclement by American military bases and the possibility of a preemptive U.S. nuclear strike.

On the American side, the great fear revolved around three clusters of concern: One was the menace of Russian communism, a challenge both to liberal democracy and to free market capitalism. Another was the threat of nuclear war, which made the United States militarily vulnerable at home as never before. The third was the prospect of losing out in the so-called "Third World," the non-industrialized developing nations outside of the power centers of North America and Europe. The most acute moments of Cold War hysteria came in 1949-51 (Russia gets the bomb; communists win China), in 1957-62 (Russia launches Sputnik; Berlin crises; Cuban missile crisis), and in 1975-81 (communists win Vietnam; hostage crisis in Tehran). Frightened Americans imagined that communist influences within their government were to blame for the insecurity. Anti-communist campaigns drove many faithful and competent government officials from office. The need to combat communism led to bloated military budgets and to a military alliance system around the world.[4]

How dangerous *was* the Soviet Union to the "free world"? Official documents from the Soviet archives, released to historians for the first time after 1991, generally vindicated Kennan's view of Stalin and the Soviet system. Traditionally, Russia had had a fervent sense of its own destiny to lead the world in a kind of universal salvation. To that sense of messianic mission, Marxist ideology added the call for workers of the world to unite under the communist banner. Stalin expected the capitalist world to self-destruct from its own contradictions.[5] Although he insisted upon Russian control of Eastern Europe, he did not intend for Russia to invade Western Europe militarily. Nor did the Soviet Union seriously consider such an invasion at any point throughout the Cold War. Stalin's original intention in 1945-47 was to proceed in a competitive partnership with the West. The sequence of events after the end of the war drove Stalin toward a more belligerent stance. He interpreted the United States' use of atomic bombs on Japan as designed to intimidate the Soviet Union in diplomatic negotiations. He saw behind the Marshall Plan for West European economic reconstruction a U.S. plan to revive German military-industrial potential and direct it against the Soviet Union. He believed the American air bases in Turkey and Western Europe, with bombers capable of delivering atomic weapons over the heart of Russia, were designed for a third world war.

Stalin's paranoia was overblown. But his fears also responded to real conditions. President Harry Truman and his hard-line Secretary of State, James F. Byrnes, did indeed attempt to exercise the power of "atomic diplomacy." The United States did help to rearm West Germany and eventually bring it into the NATO military alliance. Official United States policy persistently refused to accept a legitimate Soviet sphere of influence in Eastern Europe. Truman behaved as though Stalin was another Hitler, poised to launch aggressive war at the first opportunity. The "Truman Doctrine" promised to aid any government anywhere in the world which was threatened by communism.

American fears were also excessive. The postwar demobilization came nowhere near to reducing military personnel and expenditures to prewar peacetime levels. In 1947-49 the number of military personnel on active duty stood at about one and a half million, five times higher than the level of the mid-1930s.[6] At the same time defense spending (excluding debt service, veterans' programs, and aid to the allies) took one-third of the federal budget and five percent of the gross national product, compared to fifteen percent of the federal budget and 15 percent of the GNP before the war.[7] In 1948 President Truman, assisted by a communist coup in Czechoslovakia, manufactured a "war scare" which helped to rescue a failing aircraft industry, to sustain a military buildup, and to ensure passage of the Marshall Plan to aid economic reconstruction of Western Europe.[8]

The temporary 1948 hysteria faded quickly in the absence of evidence for a Russian mobilization and invasion of Western Europe. But the mood of fear took on its own sustained momentum in 1949, a memorable "Year of Shocks."[9] In that year Russia exploded its first atomic bomb; the communists under Mao Zedong won their civil war for control of China; and Alger Hiss, a former State department official, was tried twice for spying against the United States on behalf of the Soviet Union. He was formally convicted of perjury. Frightened Americans doubted that Russian and Chinese communists could have made these gains on their own; they must have had help from communist sympathizers in high places in the United States. The country, as never before, seemed vulnerable to attack from both external and internal enemies.

In early 1950 President Truman directed top government officials to draft a comprehensive statement of strategy for U.S. foreign policy in the face of the growing communist threat. The policy statement, which came to be known as NSC (National Security Council) 68, was a monument to fear. It recommended a massive militarization. NSC 68 warned that "the integrity and vitality of our system is in greater jeopardy than ever before in our history . . . . The risks we face are of a new order of magnitude."[10] To meet this great threat without all-out war, it would be necessary to engage in a massive development of "free-world" military capabilities. The United States would take responsibility for, and capacity to, turn back the communists wherever they attacked. The United States would become the world police force to combat the international communist conspiracy which was at the root of social and political change in the world. The NSC 68 program would be a dramatic reversal of the already stalled postwar demobilization. It would also cost a great deal of money—so much so that Truman kept the NSC 68 document under wraps as a political liability. It would take another international crisis to make Americans willing to foot the military bill.

The crisis needed to implement NSC 68 came in Korea, a country which, like Germany, had been divided into two parts by the failure of a peace settlement after World War II. When Soviet and American troops withdrew from Korea, the divided country descended into civil war, with both sides aiming at reunification. On June 25, 1950, North Korean troops invaded South Korea. President Truman, convinced that the invasion was part of a world-wide communist plan of aggression, threw in United States troops to drive the North Koreans back and to threaten the China-Korea border. Truman got the United Nations to sponsor the action officially, with inadvertent help from the Soviet Union, which was boycotting the Security Council. The Americans invaded North Korea—an attempt at "liberation" which moved beyond "containment" of communism. That invasion failed when Chinese troops entered the war and pushed the Americans back south to the original line which divided the country. General Douglas MacArthur proposed to carry the war into China, claiming that "there is no substitute for victory." The reigning model for "victory" was World War II. But President Truman realized that if the United States bombed Chinese cities to rubble, as was done in Germany and Japan in World War II, the damage to human values and to long-range political stability in China and all of Asia would have been incalculable. When MacArthur publicly challenged Truman's policy, the president fired him for insubordination. The Korean war ended with that nation devastated and still divided. A total of 33,629 Americans had died there.

Truman used the Korean crisis to engineer a major escalation of America's military might—an enactment of the NSC 68 recommendations and an extension of the Truman Doctrine to Asia. This was the key moment in America's "rise to globalism." Truman got emergency powers for war mobilization; re-establishment of the selective service military draft; a $50 billion defense budget; six army divisions in Europe; a doubling of air groups to ninety-five; new strategic bases in Morocco, Libya, Spain and Saudi Arabia; a doubling of the army to 3.5 million; stepped-up aid to the French in Indochina; a firm commitment to Chiang Kai Shek and the Nationalist Chinese in Taiwan. Truman's breath-taking militarization made the world immeasurably more dangerous and required major costs of the American people. Even so, in the words of historian Stephen Ambrose, "so successfully had he scared the hell out of the American people, the only critics to receive any attention in the mass media were those who thought Truman had not gone far enough in standing up to the communists."[11]

Was the Great Fear Inevitable?

Would it have been possible to avoid the anti-communist hysteria which resulted in substituting massive militarization for political containment? One turning point had been the death of President Roosevelt on April 12, 1945, and his replacement by Harry Truman, a politician uninformed and inexperienced in international affairs. Historian Daniel Yergin wrote of "Roosevelt's grand design for postwar international relations."[12] Roosevelt viewed the Soviet Union as a great power seeking its own interests, rather than as a revolutionary state in the grip of Marxist ideology and bent upon leading a worldwide communist revolution. Stalin was not a Hitler. The basis for postwar policy might have been what Yergin called the "Yalta Axioms," the basic assumptions of the wartime discussions and agreements at a port on the Crimean Sea in

1945. It remains an open question whether Roosevelt could have helped Americans to accept the idea of a Soviet sphere of influence in Eastern Europe, and to ease the transition from wartime alliance to postwar political competition with the Soviet Union. There was still truth in Roosevelt's statement from 1932 that the greatest thing to fear was fear itself.

An earlier turning point, momentous in retrospect, had been Roosevelt's failure in 1944 to insist upon keeping Henry A. Wallace on the ticket as his vice-president for another term. Instead, Roosevelt allowed conservative Democrats of the anti-civil rights South and the urban machines to dump Wallace for Truman. Two scholars recently suggested that if Wallace, instead of Truman, had become president in April 1945, he "might have spared the world some forty years of cold war."[13] Wallace had been Secretary of Agriculture under Roosevelt for eight years, and vice-president from 1941-45. In 1945 Roosevelt named him Secretary of Commerce, in consolation for the lost vice presidency. Except for the president, Wallace was "the chief personification of the New Deal," a watchdog so that the war policies would not undermine New Deal progress.[14] He was not comfortable with Roosevelt's statement that "Dr. New Deal" must make way for "Dr. Win the War."

The reform principles of the New Deal, he said, would prohibit excess war profits for big corporate interests. Conservatives hated Wallace's progressive stands on civil rights and women's issues, such as equal pay for equal work. Wallace also had a progressive vision for a new world order that called not only for cooperation among the great powers, but also for the economic development of the non-industrialized nations. Opponents, with more than a tinge of racism, derided his program as "A quart of milk for every Hottentot." Wallace foresaw the post-war economic boom, built on war savings and pent-up demand for consumer goods, which would provide full employment. It was within the reach of western democracies to provide expanding production and full employment, he said, if they would avoid the isolationist and protectionist mistakes of the 1920s.[15]

Wallace lost his position as vice-president in 1944 in part because a coalition of southern Democrats and urban machine politicians convinced Roosevelt that Wallace's progressive peace idealism would cost the party votes in the upcoming election. If Wallace rather than Truman had taken the presidency in April 1945, different policies would have been adopted.

His Secretary of State would have been someone more like George F. Kennan than Truman's hard-line appointee, James F. Byrnes. Wallace, himself a scientist, may well have listened to atomic scientist Leo Szilard and others who warned against using the atomic bomb on Japan. He would not have used atomic weapons superiority to bully the Soviet Union. He would have worked harder toward an international agency to control nuclear energy information. Although he was a Wilsonian idealist who believed in the self-determination of peoples, he probably would have accepted the Soviet regional sphere of influence in Eastern Europe. In fact, Truman later fired him from his post as Secretary of Commerce for suggesting this possibility in a speech in Madison Square Garden on September 12, 1946.

Such an unfolding of alternative policies is speculative. But it illustrates that there were policy alternatives in 1945 which were at least as realistic as the romantic faith in military power which came to dominate American diplomacy. To be sure, the Soviet Union would not have soon turned into a congenial and friendly nation, nor would Stalin have likely backed off from his desperate race to get atomic weapons. Given the outcome of World War II, some kind of Cold War polarization was probably inevitable. War as a rule empowers the ways of warriors. But the climate of competition between the Soviet Union and the United States after 1945 did not need to descend into such costly and fear-ridden militarization.[16] As it happened, instead of Wallace's derided liberal "milk for Hottentots" internationalism, militant U.S. Cold Warriors accepted, and eventually adopted, "an internationalism based on guns for Hottentots."[17]

The Communist Monolith and the "Third World"

The Cold War had three fronts, each of which exacted frightful costs.[18] The first front was in Central and Eastern Europe, and it reached a militarized stalemate along the "Iron Curtain" line that divided East and West. Another front was the race for nuclear weapons and delivery systems, which reached its own stalemate of mutual terror. Neither the Soviet Union nor the United States dared attack each other, for fear of mutual destruction, yet both continued to spend billions of dollars for bombs and delivery systems in order to gain an elusive psychological advantage. The third front was rivalry for influence in the non-industrialized "Third World," where old European colonial empires were falling apart and new governments were struggling to modernize.

In the third-front struggle both sides claimed certain advantages. Communist leaders held to their traditional doctrine that imperialism was the "last stage of capitalism." The Soviet Union, they hoped, could be both the ally and the model for revolutionary development in backward nations. The United States claimed to be anti-imperialist (even while propping up the French colonial regime in Indochina), and benefited from extended economic growth and vitality among free-market nations. From the mid-1960s onward, the rivalry between the United States and the Soviet Union in the Third World was the most dynamic front of the Cold War. In Latin America, Asia, the Middle East, and Africa the Cold War superpowers fought for dominance, often making small civil wars far more devastating. Eventually both sides made disastrous commitments on this front—the United States in Vietnam and the Soviet Union in Afghanistan—which weakened their own internal social and political systems.

In the wake of the 1949 Communist victory in the Chinese civil war, and a treaty between China and the Soviet Union in February 1950, United States policy makers adopted an oversimplified and alarmist version of a unified world communism directed from Moscow. This view of communism as a monolith failed to take account of the power of nationalism to undermine any centrally directed world revolution. In 1948 the Yugoslavian communist government under Josip Broz Tito had successfully established its independence from Soviet political control. Tito was a potential model for other national communist movements in both Eastern Europe and Asia. The Soviet-Chinese alliance itself was fragile and threatened by contradictory national interests on their common border. But United States policy could not orient itself to the possibility of a nationalistic breakup of communist unity. An anti-communist hysteria, climaxing in Senator Joseph McCarthy's witch hunt for alleged traitors (1950-54), held American politicians hostage. Accused civil servants and politicians could survive only if they could demonstrate that they were not "soft on communism." McCarthy's campaign had long-range foreign policy consequences. It discredited and drove from office the core of Asian policy experts who understood the true dynamics of the Chinese civil war and of the interplay of nationalist and revolutionary movements in Asia.

The United States' war in Vietnam resulted directly from American failure to identify with the forces of nationalism in Asia. Instead, the U.S. adopted a rigid anti-communist policy that ignored local conditions. Rather than opposing imperialism in Vietnam, the U.S. accommodated the imperialist interests of France. Once American prestige and honor were staked upon the success of an anti-communist government in South Vietnam, succeeding administrations (Kennedy, Johnson, Nixon) lacked the courage to withdraw, even when unstable South Vietnamese governments repeatedly failed.[19] Each U.S. president escalated the conflict in his own way, with Johnson in 1964 making the crucial decision to commit substantial land forces. Supporters of American intervention argued that communist North Vietnam was a repressive system with aggressive military intentions. That assessment may have been largely correct, but it failed to anticipate the double calamity of prolonged warfare *and* communist victory. The U.S. commitment foundered on the contradictions of a continuing western imperialist legacy, combined with a failed assessment of the forces of nationalism and communism in East Asia.

Vietnam was one of the United States' most unnecessary wars. If America's foreign policy need was to oppose Chinese communism, the best way would have been to accept Ho Chi Minh's national reunification of Vietnam. For many centuries China and Vietnam had been enemies. Not only was Ho a potential Tito, but he sent early signals that he would welcome an opening to the United States. U.S. officials, blinded by their image of the communist monolith and of countries falling to communism like dominoes, assumed that Ho was a puppet of Russia and/or China. Both China and the Soviet Union found that military and financial aid to embattled Vietnam was a convenient and low-cost way to drain U.S. resources and morale without endangering their own homelands. In 1975, as soon as Vietnam achieved national unity, armed clashes broke out at disputed points on the China-Vietnam border. Four years later Chinese armies invaded Vietnam.[20] Fifty-five thousand Americans had died in Vietnam to fight against an international communist system that would have broken apart sooner if the United States had not intervened. The failed war had polarized the American people, eroded confidence in the ability of government to govern effectively, and diverted billions of dollars which could have been used at home and abroad for education, transportation, social welfare and other constructive purposes.

The role of the Central Intelligence Agency (CIA) in Vietnam and elsewhere in the Third World was especially notable. The CIA was created in 1947 to administer foreign espionage operations. Espionage is necessarily secretive. Even at its best it is in tension with the ideal of democratic openness. Leaders of the CIA took advantage of the Cold

War atmosphere of crisis and fear to greatly increase the agency's budget and operations, and to extend its operations beyond intelligence to the administration of overseas policy. The CIA also undertook surveillance within the United States. Two CIA operations in the Eisenhower administration were short-term successes which brought great prestige to the agency but in the long run greatly damaged the U.S. image and interests. In 1953 CIA agents, armed with money and military equipment, helped overthrow a revolutionary government in Iran which had threatened to nationalize the Anglo-Iranian Oil Company. The action helped restore the Shah of Iran to his throne and to guarantee the flow of Iranian oil and oil profits to the west. But the action also engendered hatred of the United States. A virulently anti-American regime took over Iran when the Shah's government fell twenty-six years later.

In 1954 the CIA engineered a coup to overthrow a constitutional government in Guatemala, led by Colonel Jacobo Arbenz Guzman. Guatemala had confiscated lands belonging to the monopolistic United Fruit Company. As in Iran, the long-term consequence was political instability and intense hostility against the United States. Third World nations, with urgent needs for economic and social development, watched as the United States used anti-democratic methods to support anti-democratic regimes in the name of freedom and democracy. The CIA became a potent symbol in Soviet anti-American propaganda.

Throughout the Cold War, Third World countries suffered at the hands of both the Soviet Union and the United States. The great world powers proved most ready to give *military* aid to factions in developing nations. The processes of modern political and economic development, conflict-laden in any case, were distorted and militarized by outside aid. For those unfortunate nations which became battlegrounds for hot civil wars, with outside Cold War superpowers pouring in military aid, the African proverb applied: "When the elephants fight, the grass suffers."[21]

The Dynamics and Costs of Militarization

Through the Cold War, American society became more profoundly militarized than ever before. The force of militarization intersected with other issues of race, class, and gender to transform American society.[22] President Eisenhower was one of the first prominent national figures to see the problem of militarization as a whole and to identify it as one which threatened the essential character of American democracy. In eight which threatened the essential character of American democracy. In eight years as president Eisenhower presided over a tripling of the U.S. nuclear weapons stockpile and a vast expansion of U.S. global military treaty commitments.[23] By the end he seemed wistful about the consequences of his policies. In his farewell address of January 1961, Eisenhower called Americans to "guard against the acquisition of unwarranted influence, whether sought or unsought, by the military-industrial complex. The potential for the disastrous rise of misplaced power exists and will persist." Others expanded Eisenhower's analysis under such labels as the "National Security State" or the "Warfare State."[24]

Eisenhower's warnings were in the tradition of concerns in the early American republic about the evils of "standing armies" and the alliance between high-born military officers and government leaders. In an urban-industrial age the problem was militarization of the economy. Major industrial corporations depended upon military contracts for profits. Retired military officers took high positions in these corporations and used their network of political-military connections to lobby for high military budgets and assure that they would be awarded the contracts. The military establishment dispersed their projects widely to key states across the country to gain support of powerful members of Congress. Politicians used the threat of communism to justify the big military budgets, but the system generated its internal momentum quite apart from external military threats.

Cold War militarization involved more than the power relationships in American political and economic life. The language and symbols of war came to pervade the American imagination. Americans increasingly did their thinking, dreaming, talking and planning in anxiety-ridden military metaphors. To get support for domestic programs of development and reform, politicians tied them to national security, such as the "Interstate Defense Highway System" and the "National Defense Education Act." Reformers advocated new civil rights laws as essential to win the propaganda war against the communists in competition for the hearts and minds of dark-skinned people in the Third World. Federal funds for basic scientific research became available as that research was deemed important for national security. Americans gradually drifted away from the humane inclination to think about and plan for projects of national development and progress in terms of their positive virtues.

Atomic bomb imagery cast an especially long shadow over American consciousness and memory.[25] The mushroom cloud became the universal symbol of atomic destruction. American popular culture—movies, cartoons, novels, and advertising—exhibited a nervous fascination with nuclear war. Magazines published outlines of U.S. cities with concentric circles of the zones of total, intermediate, and moderate destruction in case they were hit with atomic bombs. Two generations of young people grew to maturity with reasonable fears that their lives, along with modern civilization, could perish in atomic holocaust. Psychologists speculated on the effects of such anxieties for growing popular alienation from politics and for the rise of an American culture of self-absorption and hedonism—the "Culture of Narcissim." Civic officials and urban professionals attempted to ease the fear with civil defense programs and bomb shelter projects that only vaguely covered the underlying fear. "When blooms the crocus, buoyed with hope," wrote one cynic, "we view it through a periscope." Until the late 1980s, polls showed that about half of all Americans expected to die in nuclear war, yet few had real interest in civil defense. The bomb produced a kind of "psychic numbing."[26]

In June 1947 the editors of the *Bulletin of Atomic Scientists* created the "Doomsday Clock" and set it at seven and a half minutes to midnight.[27] Ticking toward nuclear holocaust, the clock quickly became a potent symbol of East-West tensions in the postwar world. Fourteen times from 1947 to 1991, the *Bulletin* editors moved the minute hand of the clock backward or forward depending upon the prospects for general nuclear war. In 1953, after a popular uprising in East Berlin and saber rattling in both Moscow and Washington D.C., the editors set the clock at two minutes to midnight. At the end of the Cold War in 1991, the *Bulletin* editors moved the clock back to seventeen minutes to midnight, but in 1998 the clock ticked forward to nine minutes to midnight as India and Pakistan threatened each other with nuclear weapons testing. The United States and other great powers were failing to significantly reduce their huge nuclear arsenals or to forestall proliferation of nuclear weapons development in new countries. The Doomsday Clock, an "icon of the Nuclear Age," continued to symbolize a lasting legacy of the Cold War— the deadly momentum of nuclear weapons technology .[28]

Doomsday Clock, an "icon of the Nuclear Age," continued to symbolize a lasting legacy of the Cold War—the deadly momentum of nuclear weapons technology .[28]

Peace Movement Ideals and Activism

Traditional American pacifists in the early Cold War era continued to advocate nonmilitary cooperation toward a world of justice and peace. Pacifists challenged the assumptions of Kennan's containment policy. Kennan claimed to be a "realist," and insisted that peace could be achieved only by a balance of power among autonomous nations. Peace movement leaders in different ways argued that peace was nurtured not by power balances but by cooperative transnational networks of trade, communication, transportation, technology and monetary institutions. Peace movement internationalists worked for the strengthening of the United Nations. Radical pacifists emphasized the moral and community bases of peace and justice. After 1950, as containment was militarized and the arms race escalated, pacifists seemed further than ever on the fringes of political dialogue. Then the obsession with internal security and the McCarthy campaign against alleged communists smeared the peace advocates with the taint of communism. Many left-liberal people caved in to popular pressures. Even Henry Wallace, victimized for his refusal to disavow political support from communists or communist-front organizations, eventually abandoned his earlier views of the Soviet Union and joined the Cold War majority view. The consistent pacifists, already seen as unpatriotic in World War II, were cast into the role of subversives in the Cold War.[29]

Professional scientists became the most potent new force in the post-war peace movement.[30] Atomic scientists who served on the Manhattan Project to develop the atomic bomb were the best informed about the destructive potential of nuclear power and the impossibility of the United States maintaining an exclusive nuclear monopoly. The scientists used both practical and moral arguments. A "Franck Committee Report" from atomic scientists of June 1945 argued that in a future nuclear exchange the United States, with its urban-industrial concentrations, would be more vulnerable than countries with dispersed populations and resources.[31] Science, by its very nature, transcended national borders. Scientists believed in the values of their own discipline—the scientific

Szilard and others in 1945 organized the Federation of Atomic Scientists to warn the public of the danger of atomic weapons and to promote international control. They achieved a limited victory when Congress created the Atomic Energy Commission, which helped secure atomic energy development from secretive military domination. But the scientists' plans for international controls of nuclear development fell victim to early Cold War hostilities. The United States was unwilling to sacrifice its nuclear weapons lead; the Soviet Union refused to accept a system of inspection necessary for control.

Despite opposition by some scientists, the U.S. government moved forward to mobilize scientific and technological expertise to build a hydrogen (or thermonuclear) bomb and to race ahead with other science-supported military projects. The Cold War fostered a new era of "big science." The government became the primary source of funding for great projects that involved large groups of scientists working in huge laboratory complexes. Prominent scientists, such as chemistry Nobel Prize winner Linus Pauling, who continued public opposition to the nuclear arms race, were subject to investigations and harassment by the Federal Bureau of Investigation and the House Un-American Activities Committee. Pauling had never been a communist and had no incriminating evidence on his record. Nevertheless, government agencies denied his passport applications for overseas travel, rejected his grant applications for research, and pressured officials at the California Institute of Technology to fire him. In 1963 Pauling was awarded the Nobel Peace Prize, but his career illustrated the personal and social burdens of peace activism in the Cold War.[32]

"Go preach disarmament in Russia," said Pauling's opponents. "The communists are responsible for the arms race." In 1961-62, during one of the most tense and volatile moments in the Cold War, a group of peace activists responded with the longest peace march in history. They walked from San Francisco across the United States and Europe to Moscow, 5767 miles in 307 days. Along the way they spoke out for unilateral disarmament and personal responsibility for nonviolent resistance to military programs. In Washington, D.C. the peace marchers met with President John Kennedy's advisor, Arthur M. Schlesinger, Jr., who scorned their efforts and predicted that no communist country would allow them in: "Those are closed, totalitarian societies." In fact, the marchers were denied entry into France but allowed to walk, to pass out leaflets, and speak to people in Poland and in Russia. On both sides who scorned their efforts and predicted that no communist country would allow them in: "Those are closed, totalitarian societies." In fact, the marchers were denied entry into France but allowed to walk, to pass out leaflets, and speak to people in Poland and in Russia. On both sides of the Iron Curtain, people said that the other side was to blame and must take the first steps to disarmament. Each side was closed in its own way. The Walk to Moscow was one of countless creative and dramatic efforts by the many-faceted peace movement.[33]

Peace activists operated through a large number of organizations which differed widely about their central issue concerns, patterns of organization, and strategies for witness and action. Some were liberal internationalists while others, such as the marchers to Moscow, focused on the nuclear arms race. Some peace groups were centrally organized while others were antiauthoritarian. Some worked through conventional politics while others preferred radical direct-action.[34] Three points at which many of these groups were able to form working coalitions and to relate effectively to larger public movements for public policy change were the nuclear test ban campaign of 1955-63, the popular movement against the Vietnam War (1965-73), and the nuclear freeze campaign of 1979-83.

The women's peace movement in the 1970s and 1980s paralleled and interacted with the feminist movement. On November 1, 1961, two years before Betty Friedan's *Feminine Mystique*, about fifty thousand women in more than sixty cities staged a one-day strike against atmospheric testing of nuclear weapons by the United States and the Soviet Union. The women were concerned about radiation contamination from above-ground tests and about the threat of an all-out nuclear holocaust. The leaders of the new protest were impatient with more established peace organizations such as WILPF, which seemed to be mired down in traditional bureaucracy and immobilized by anti-Communist red-baiting. They called the new movement Women Strike for Peace (WSP). In December 1962, one year after the dramatic women's strike, the House Un-American Activities Committee (HUAC) summoned the WSP leaders to official public hearings designed to discredit the movement as inspired or affiliated with communism. The women decided to challenge the committee with a show of solidarity, self-confidence, and good humor. The first witness, Blanche Posner, a retired schoolteacher from New York, lectured the committee as though they were errant school children:

strontium 90 and iodine 131 . . . . They feared for the health and life of their children . . . . If you gentlemen have children or grandchildren you should be grateful to the Women Strike for Peace.[35]

The strategy succeeded, won strong media support, and weakened the HUAC. The WSP developed overseas ties with a women's International Strike for Peace, and was an important influence toward the Test-Ban Treaty of 1963.[36]

On the surface, the work of peace advocates took shape as prophetic opposition to government policy. Before the 1980s, the peace movement experienced only minor success in influencing national policies of militarization and war-making, although popular agitation against the war in Vietnam did limit the choices available to Presidents Johnson and Nixon at key points.[37] But the peace movement's impact was profound in more long-range and cumulative ways which received less publicity. People working in non-governmental organizations built up hundreds of programs for international exchanges. Peace advocates influenced the way public school textbooks treated foreign countries and warfare. Peace scholars generated a new international discipline of peace studies with new ideas and techniques for conflict management and resolution. The peace witness of earlier generations of conscientious objectors to military service, mostly from the three "historic peace churches" (Quakers, Mennonites, Church of the Brethren), had established a precedent for official recognition which was extended during the Vietnam War to those who refused war on other-than-religious grounds.

In the 1980s, with the global nuclear stockpile at over 60,000 warheads, a popular "Nuclear Freeze" campaign led to the first major nuclear disarmament agreement of the Cold War. The freeze movement burst forth in the United States in response to President Reagan's belligerent Cold War rhetoric and military buildup. In Western Europe a resurgent anti-nuclear agitation raised alarms over the placement of new missiles in the Soviet Union (SS-20s) and in Western Europe (Cruise and Pershing missiles). In November 1983, in an attempt to outflank the peace movement, the Reagan administration announced a "zero option" negotiating position. That position called for both sides to reduce their intermediate-range missiles to zero. American officials assumed that the Soviet Union would reject "zero option" because the Soviet Union had a movement, the Reagan administration announced a "zero option" negotiating position. That position called for both sides to reduce their intermediate-range missiles to zero. American officials assumed that the Soviet Union would reject "zero option" because the Soviet Union had a substantial lead in intermediate missile deployment. When the Soviet Union unexpectedly accepted "zero option," the United States was drawn into an agreement which it had proposed in order to deflect the rising peace movement—rather than as a serious option. The INF (intermediate nuclear force) treaty of 1987 eliminated intermediate range nuclear missiles in Europe. In this case a popular peace movement significantly contributed toward nuclear disarmament.[38]

The Cold War Ends

In the spring of 1985 Mikhail Gorbachev took over as chairman of the communist party in the Soviet Union and initiated thorough reforms of the Soviet political and economic system.[39] To move the Soviet Union decisively in the direction of an economic free market and political democracy, Gorbachev needed to end the arms race and to divert excessive military spending to the process of economic reorganization. He also needed cooperation from the United States in order to counter the influence of hardline militarists in his own government. In 1986, Gorbachev brought a path-breaking proposal for a mutual fifty percent cut of all nuclear weapons in five years to a summit meeting in Reykjavik, Iceland, between Soviet and U.S. heads of state. Gorbachev's proposal required the U.S. to abandon its Strategic Defense Initiative (SDI or "Star Wars") program—an immensely expensive anti-missile system that many top American scientists believed could not work. President Ronald Reagan, despite his interest in cutting nuclear weaponry, refused to give up the SDI. The potential breakthrough at Reykjavik was aborted.[40]

Over the next few years, Gorbachev seized the initiative in arms-reduction proposals and negotiations. In the 1987 Intermediate Nuclear Force Treaty, the superpowers for the first time agreed to dismantle weapons carrying nuclear warheads. However, the slowness of the U.S. response, and the U.S. insistence upon unequal agreements that required the Soviet Union to give up disproportional numbers of nuclear weapons, tended to undermine Gorbachev's political position at home. The reform efforts foundered and, in August 1991, the Soviet hardliners attempted

Although Gorbachev, Reagan, and other national leaders played significant roles in the end of the Cold War, the surprising events of 1989-91 rested upon longer-term underlying trends. One of these trends was the separation of economic power from military power as sources of national greatness. The United States and the Soviet Union, like all great powers since 1500, had achieved status by combining military and economic strength. After 1950, however, Germany and Japan became superpowers, and states like Singapore, South Korea, and Taiwan achieved world significance, primarily by developing economic capacity and by relative freedom from military burdens. The great superpowers found themselves burdened with giant weapons they dared not use and with military budgets that drained resources needed for economic development.[41]

Some people believe that the demise of the Soviet Union was due to the leadership of President Reagan and his hard-line advisors in the years from 1981 to 1985. In his first term, Reagan adopted a rhetorical posture of aggressive hostility against the Soviet "Evil Empire" and a major escalation of military expenditures.[42] The Reagan administration did indeed spend a lot of money for the arms race. Between 1979 and 1985, the military budget increased from $130 billion to almost $300 billion. During Reagan's eight years as president, the military was allocated two trillion dollars. Reagan supported the MX missile (whose ten warheads each had the firepower of thirty-five Hiroshima bombs) and the B-1 bomber, both programs which had been cut under President Carter. Reagan also reinstated the production of chemical weapons, and announced the SDI, a missile-defense program estimated to cost a trillion dollars. In an era of absurd overkill capacity, these lavish military expenditures had little actual effect on the relative military strength of the United States and the Soviet Union.[43] The U.S. advantage in missile warheads did not increase.[44]

Reagan's contribution to the end of the Cold War was not the military buildup of his first term but rather his changed view of the Soviet Union in his second term. With his strong right-wing anti-communist credentials, Reagan was able to convince the American people that the Soviet Union, under Gorbachev's leadership, was no longer an "evil empire." Reagan and Gorbachev both became nuclear abolitionists. Their disarmament breakthrough came when Gorbachev realized that Reagan's SDI missile defense idea was not technologically feasible and therefore

Soviet Union, under Gorbachev's leadership, was no longer an "evil empire." Reagan and Gorbachev both became nuclear abolitionists. Their disarmament breakthrough came when Gorbachev realized that Reagan's SDI missile defense idea was not technologically feasible and therefore did not represent a threat to the Soviet Union. The hidden heroes of this disarmament drama were the international scientists, especially the dissident Russian physicist Andrei Sakharov, who got Gorbachev's ear and convinced him to move forward toward disarmament and to let the United States go ahead and waste its money on the phantom SDI. The transnational movement of peace-minded scientists was able to exercise exceptional influence upon Soviet nuclear defense policies when Gorbachev, who was committed to reform, listened to the scientists rather than to his hard-line military advisors.[45]

The "Reagan victory" thesis will continue to be popular among right wing militarists, but it suffers from its limiting assumption that great world events must have their primary origin in the United States. It also ignores the Soviet historical inclination to respond to external military pressure with new repression and military escalation.[46] The end of the Cold War was triggered not by an American military buildup, but by the economic failings of the Soviet Union, by the reforms of Mikhail Gorbachev, and by the timely witness of international scientists who wanted to protect the world from nuclear holocaust.

The Cold War as a Pyrrhic Victory

In 279 B.C. Pyrrhus, the King of Epirus, counted the excessive cost of his victory over the Romans at the battle of Asculum: "One more such victory and I am lost." The Cold War can remind us of Pyrrhus. Victories of this sort are not affordable. The Reagan arms race built up a U.S. mountain of national debt—double the combined debt of all his thirty-nine predecessors. For the coming generation, the U.S. government would struggle to overcome the Reagan debt, and his assumption that the arms establishment was exempt from general attacks on the evils of spending for "big government." The Cold War legacy included radioactive pollution, both in Russia and the United States, that would cost billions of dollars to clean up. In April 2000 the U.S. Energy Department estimated that it would cost between $168 billion and $212 billion to clean up environmental damage at 113 nuclear weapons sites.[47] It would take decades to recover from the Cold War.

died; and that war helped to destabilize Cambodia and led to its
holocaust, which took the lives of six to eight million more people. The
so-called "proxy wars" contributed to the long-range underdevelopment
of the countries where they were fought. Wherever the contending
superpowers had chosen to make a show of supporting their clients, the
costs of excessive firepower were high—Angola, Somalia, Ethiopia,
Nicaragua, El Salvador, and others.[48]

The Cold War was born of fear. The fear produced a massive wastage
of human resources—twenty-one trillion U.S. dollars into non-
productive military expenditures by one account.[49] The great fear of 1945-
1991 also forced a shrinkage of the human spirit, a loss of faith in high
ideals and the ability of people and their institutions to achieve them.
The American experience in the Cold War, in the words of one historian,
was a matter of "Losing Our Souls." Edward Pessen, shortly before his
death in 1992, wrote that United States Cold War policy "was so
grievously flawed that the United States may never fully recover from
its effects upon our values, our freedoms, our politics, our security, the
conditions of our material life, the quality of our productive plant, and
the very air we breathe."[50] If Americans were to recover from the Cold
War they would have to recognize what George Kennan in 1947 had
asked them to recognize of World War II. U.S. victory in the Cold War
was an illusion. The future depended upon finding new non-military
paths to peace and justice, a rediscovered appreciation of "the limitations
of war in general—any war—as a vehicle for the achievement of the
objectives of the democratic state."[51]

Chapter 13

Nature and the Ecology of Warfare: Peace with the Land

The choice for peace or war, nonviolence or violence, is not limited to interactions with other human beings. This choice is equally momentous in our relationships with other living things and with the land, water, and air which sustain us and make life possible. Over the decades of the American past, speculators, entrepreneurs, politicians, and many ordinary people made decisions with lasting consequences that reflected a militaristic and commodity relationship with the land. These decisions were not inevitable. Nor were they always the only choices available. On this point, too, United States history has a missing peace to be rediscovered and reclaimed. A long-term, sustainable, non-exploitive relationship with the environment is indispensable in laying a foundation of peace.

The two great ideals—peace with the earth and peace among people—are part of the same package. When people make war, or when they prepare for war in the name of deterrence, nature suffers. Improvements in military technology have multiplied the environmental damage. Between 1945 and 1990, the great nuclear powers detonated more than 1,800 nuclear warheads at more than thirty-five locations around the globe.[1] By the late twentieth century, nuclear weapons were in place which, if actually used, would make the earth permanently uninhabitable for humans. And yet many Americans have kept their concerns for peace and for the natural environment in separate compartments. Theodore Roosevelt, one of the greatest conservationist presidents in United States history, was also one of the nation's most aggressive militarists. In the late twentieth century, the organized movements for peace and for environmentalism have often gone on separate tracks. The twenty-first century will not be able to afford this separation. Arthur Westing, researcher for the Stockholm International Peace Research Institute, has written, "Today the two most immediate threats to humankind are military devastation on the one hand and environmental exhaustion on the other, both on a world-wide scale. Moreover, each of these two threats is reinforced by the other."[2]

Native American Respect for the Land

Concern for the earth has a long history in North America. Many hundreds of years before Europeans arrived, the Native Americans practiced a communal ethic of respect for nature. While that ethic took very different forms among the more than five hundred different tribes that called North America home, the original peoples shared a central belief "that the Earth is a living, conscious being that must be treated with respect and loving care."[3] Paula Gunn Allen, contemporary Laguna writer expressed how close this relationship is: "[The land] is not the ever-present 'other' which supplies us with a sense of 'I.' It is rather a part of our being, dynamic, significant real. It is ourself...."[4] Luther Standing Bear, a Lakota, confirmed the same principle of oneness: "We are all one in nature. Believing so, there was in our hearts a great peace and a welling kindness for all living, growing things."[5]

Archeologists and anthropologists have debated the extent to which Native Americans preserved a balance with nature before the European invasion. The collapse of some thriving Native American communities, such as Cahokia on the Mississippi flood plain, may have resulted in part from their overuse of natural resources. There is evidence that in some cases Native Americans altered the landscape by burning forests, by clearing woodlands for farming and fuel, and by polluting the soil with unsound irrigation practices.[6] Some Native Americans have criticized outsiders who too easily invoke Native peoples' wisdom in dealing with contemporary environmental issues. Nevertheless, Native American sensibilities remain a legitimate resource for modern environmentalists who oppose the pollution produced by technology-based industrialism. The idea of living within the limits and fruitfulness of nature can open new directions for personal living and for public policy—from recycling household trash to finding an alternative to the internal combustion engine.[7]

European Ownership

European settlers brought a new concept of individual landownership and exploitation to the New World. Land was their liberation—their path to wealth, prestige and political position. Unlike the Native Americans, the settlers bought and sold the land. They turned natural resources into money and wrought an astonishing economic success in the North American colonies. As early as 1653, Edward Johnson, a Puritan historian, saw it "as God's providence that 'a rocky, barren bushy, wild-woody wilderness' was transformed in a generation into 'a second England' for fertileness."[8] The costs of turning the land into profitable production were hardly noticed. If farm lands and plantations lost their fertility after several generations, there was always more open land in the west.

Native Americans were not the only ones who noticed the costs of the settlers' different relationship with the land. In the nineteenth century one of the best known was the eccentric naturalist, Henry David Thoreau. Most often pictured growing beans by Walden Pond, Thoreau early decried the clear-cutting logging practices of New England. In just forty years a society relying on wood for housing, fuel, and furniture decimated its original forests and was forced to import wood from nearby states. In a lecture entitled "Huckleberries," Thoreau, a careful observer of nature explained forest succession and the importance of forest management to assure that there would always be abundant wood. Thoreau proposed major preservation and prudent management of forest resources.[9]

Thoreau also opposed warfare. He saw the Mexican War (1846-48) as an iniquitous crusade to extend slavery. Rather than pay a poll tax for the war, Thoreau went to jail. He went free after just one night in jail when someone paid the tax for him, so his anti-war witness was more symbolic than costly. Nor did it affect the progress of the war against Mexico. But Thoreau went on to write a powerful and influential essay, *On Civil Disobedience*, which set forth the conditions which justified disobedience to unjust laws in view of a higher ideal. If Thoreau had connected his activist ideals to his environmentalist concerns, he might have protested more directly against the locomotive that spewed its smoke over Walden Pond or against the Billerica Dam that disrupted the migratory path of shad along the Merrimack River. In his writings he did not specifically connect his respect for nature to his war protest. Nevertheless, Thoreau's symbolic actions and his writings made him a spiritual ancestor to modern environmentalists as well as to anti-war activists who challenge the military-industrial order with civil disobedience.[10]

Warfare and Environment

The U.S. Civil War (1860-65) marked a turning point toward modern total war. One new dimension was deliberate military attack upon the countryside. "War is hell," said Union General William Tecumseh Sherman, and he proceeded to make it more hellish by unleashing a vengeful campaign of mass civilian terror through Georgia and South Carolina. Sherman terrorized the people by destroying crops, killing livestock, and burning plantation mansions. Major General Philip Sheridan used similar scorched-earth tactics in the Shenandoah Valley of Virginia to demoralize and starve the South into submission. As shocking as the new ways of warfare were, the campaigns and battles of the Civil War did not do permanent ecological damage. Nature eventually recovered, even on the shelled and burned-out landscapes of the Battles of Shiloh and the Wilderness. Nevertheless, the war's new "strategy of annihilation" was an ominous portent for the environmental effects of future wars.[11] Nature can make its recovery from fire more surely than from toxic chemicals and nuclear bombs.

The post-Civil War warfare against the Indians on the Great Plains (1854-90) did have permanent ecological effects. Led by Civil War veterans such as General Sheridan and Colonel George Armstrong Custer, the attacks on Indian villages and warriors were accompanied by destruction of the vast buffalo herds which were the Indians' main source of sustenance. The buffalo, which had numbered in the millions, were quickly driven almost to extinction. In their place came European settlers with new steel-tipped plows that destroyed the deep-rooted prairie grasses and made the great plains vulnerable to wind and water erosion. The long-term effects of the transition became evident in the drought cycle and the dust bowl of the 1930s.

Progressive Era Conservation

A great divide in the U.S. environmental movement separated those who, like Thoreau, celebrated nature for nature's sake from people who wanted to preserve and improve nature for the sake of human fulfillment. Two men who symbolized this difference were naturalist John Muir and forester Gifford Pinchot. In 1897 Muir and Pinchot together visited the Grand Canyon and came upon a tarantula. Pinchot wanted to kill the spider and Muir defended its right to live.[12] That difference led the two men down different roads of public policy. Pinchot, the scientist, believed in a careful, long-term, professionally-managed use of national forests for commercial purposes. John Muir, founder of the Sierra Club in 1892, was "the nation's archpriest of wild nature."[13] He was appalled when Pinchot and other conservationists agreed to a plan by the city of San Francisco to solve its growing need for water and electricity by damming the Tuolumne River and flooding the beautiful Hetch Hetchy valley. In Muir's eyes Hetch Hetchy was as magnificent a natural resource as the nearby Yosemite Valley, which Congress had set aside for a national park in 1872 — the first major reservation of federal land. "These temple destroyers," wrote Muir, "devotees of ravaging commercialism, seem to have a perfect contempt for Nature, and instead of lifting their eyes to the God of the mountains, lift them to the Almighty Dollar. Dam Hetch Hetchy! As well dam for water tanks the people's cathedrals and churches, for no holier temple has ever been consecrated by the heart of man."[14] Muir lost this long-running battle and died in 1914, a year after Congress approved the Hetch Hetchy project.

Theodore Roosevelt, president from 1901 to 1908, was influenced by both Muir and Pinchot, but came down on Pinchot's side in the Hetch Hetchy controversy. Roosevelt had an intense personal curiosity about the natural world, but was so obsessed in his younger years with militant manliness and mastery over nature that, in the words of one biographer, "he couldn't spot a winged or pawed creature without reaching for his gun." As president he had "learned to tame or at least cage the killer instinct in himself," and turned his energies toward mastery over Congress and over the profit-seeking cut-and-run private companies that wanted to strip federal forest lands.[15] Roosevelt expanded the use of an 1891 law to transfer 150 million acres of federally owned property into "forest reserves," to ensure they would be subjected to scientific management rather than exploitation for profit. In 1907 Congress took away the president's power to name new reserves, but before the bill took effect and in open defiance of Congress and the private exploiters, Roosevelt expanded the reserve system by another 16 million acres. Roosevelt's conservation efforts were his great legacy — to protect natural resources including coal and mineral lands, oil reserves, and power sites as well as forests, for rational human use. Under his administration the government helped to start thirty new irrigation projects, to protect eighteen national monuments (including Grand Canyon and Niagara Falls), and to establish five new national parks and fifty-one wildlife refuges.[16] Roosevelt's stunning achievements in the conservation of natural resources stand in ironic contrast to his enthusiasm for warfare which assaulted both the social and natural order.

Environmentalism

In the 1960s and 1970s a profound shift took place in U.S. attitudes toward the natural environment. Old organizations such as the Sierra Club and the National Audubon Society had had small staffs and relied on professional volunteers. Then a mass people's movement emerged with fresh energy and initiatives by ordinary people at the grass roots. The movement took a new name—"environmentalism." It produced a host of new organizations, publications, legislation, and bureaucracies. Two events marked the boundaries of the take-off period of the new movement. One was the publication in 1962 of Rachel Carson's *Silent Spring*, an exposé of how chemical insecticides, especially DDT, threatened birds, mammals, and fishes with extinction. The book was on the *New York Times* best-seller list for thirty-one weeks and became, in the words of one historian, "the *Uncle Tom's Cabin* of modern environmentalism."[17] The other symbolic event was the first national "Earth Day" on April 22, 1970, a nation-wide celebration/protest in which some ten to twenty million people participated. Between *Silent Spring* and Earth Day, the stage was set for the emergence of environmentalism as a permanent movement on the American social and political landscape.

Profound social and political changes led to the great transition. The Civil Rights Movement and the Anti-Vietnam War Movement provided new models of activist confrontation of the established order, especially by young people. The government's duplicity regarding Vietnam War policies led to a "credibility gap" and to a popular inclination to mistrust public officials and private corporations who resisted reform. Rapid economic growth after World War II created an affluent middle class which could take material basics for granted and direct their concerns to quality of life. Urban Americans turned to outdoor recreation and encountered environmental degradation in new ways. The mass media found an eager audience for new scientific information about problems such as urban smog as well as sensationalist publicity about dramatic disasters such as the 1969 California off-shore oil spill off the Santa Barbara coast.[18]

Controversies over the Vietnam War set the context for the first Earth Day in 1970. The organizers initially planned the event as an "environmental teach-in," modeled in part after the earlier anti-war "teach-ins" and "moratorium" protests. President Richard Nixon strove mightily to claim leadership on environmental issues and divert attention from the radical counter-cultural and "New Left" critics of his war policies and of the capitalist system. Nixon saw himself as a new Theodore Roosevelt, a "Republican champion of efficiency and technological improvement making peace with nature," even though he had only reluctantly signed the National Environmental Policy Act of 1969.[19] That act created the Council on Environmental Quality (CEQ) and became the foundation for the environmental reform legislation in the 1970s. With strong support from forces across the political spectrum—left wing, the middle classes, and the right wing—Earth Day 1970 broke the mold of conventional American politics. Even corporations targeted for reform, such as Dow Chemical, subsidized the event.

Less than two weeks after Earth Day the nation's college campuses exploded in response to President Richard Nixon's invasion of Cambodia and the National Guard's killing of protesting students at Kent State University. The anti-war movement faded as American troops withdrew from Vietnam in 1973, but concerns connecting warfare with the environment grew. Evidence emerged that America's chemical warfare—the dumping of 18 million gallons of toxic chemicals on the Vietnamese forests—had devastated the health of American servicemen as well as the Vietnamese people and countryside. Vietnamese health officials claimed that Agent Orange was responsible for killing or injuring 400,000 people and contributing to birth defects in 500,000 children.[20] The environmental movement kept growing to the end of the century. The pro-military and anti-environment rhetoric and policies of the Ronald Reagan and George Bush administrations (1981-1993), which severely cut back funding for the Environmental Protection Agency, only strengthened the movement.

New Organizations and Activism

The environmental movement grew through the expansion of the older
conservation groups as well as through the proliferation of local grass
roots organization. The vitality of the older groups is suggested by
membership figures:[21]

	1970 membership	1991 membership
Sierra Club (founded 1892)	113,000	650,000
National Audubon Society (1905)	120,000	600,000
Wilderness Society (1935)	54,000	350,000
National Wildlife Federation (1936)	540,000	5,600,000

Meanwhile citizens in local communities organized to address
environmental problems in their own areas. By the end of the century
more than 8,000 grassroots environmental groups had been organized
nationwide. Most of them chose to use methods of political action and
nonviolent direct action. Critics of community-based environmental
justice groups charged that their concerns did not extend beyond the
"Not in My Backyard" or NIMBY syndrome. However, sociologist
Andrew Szasz, who has studied the politics of the environmental justice
movement, acknowledged, "Many will leave [the movement] with the
same NIMBY consciousness they started with. Even so, leaders believe,
something will have happened in people's understanding of their world,
their willingness to experience solidarity with others, their willingness
to fight again another day."[22]

Several examples illustrate the range of the movement. In Kentucky
one of the largest environmental issues was the degradation caused by
coal mining companies. In the mid-1980s local people formed an
organization, Kentuckians for the Commonwealth, and brainstormed
their strategies at the Highlander Folk School in Tennessee. They chose
direct nonviolent action to place their bodies in the way of the mining
equipment. Bernadette Smith, one mining-country resident, reported,
"I sat where the loader was clearing the loose dirt. He got up to about
two feet from me before the boss finally told him to stop. They thought
I was going to move, but they were mistaken. I would have rolled right
down the hill before I would have moved!" The group also worked on

legislation, with help from the Federal Trade Commission (FTC) Environmental Rights Committee, to require coal companies to get the landowner's permission before stripping their lands. One committee member reported, "FTC approached it in an honest, non-violent way, and I believed in it. One thing I like about FTC—it's a good group of people that will stand up real quick. It's not just people wanting a fight."[23]

Local community action backed by state and federal legislation and by the support of government environmental agencies have also brought changes for people of color. African American communities, in part because of their poverty, were disproportionately victimized in hazardous waste disposal.[24] Blacks were under-represented in state and national government, and in national environmental organizations. Private and public corporations choose to locate hazardous waste landfills and other high-polluting enterprises in African American communities, in the hope of avoiding political backlash. A 1983 study of eight southern states by the U.S. General Accounting Office identified four large off-site hazardous waste landfills in black-populated areas. In 1992 the *Natural Law Journal* issued a "Special Investigation Report," that the government gave preference to white communities over minority communities in selecting sites for hazardous waste cleanup.[25]

In 1984 the residents of Carver Terrace, a small African American community in Texarkana, Texas, discovered that they were victims of widespread ground contamination from a wood treatment plant. Residents experienced a myriad of health problems, including twenty-six deaths that could be attributed to the toxins in the neighborhood. In 1985 homeowners formed Carver Terrace Community Action Group and lobbied their government officials to get the government to buy their property. Carver Terrace is now in the National Priorities Superfund List, a project created in 1980 in the last days of the Jimmy Carter administration. The Superfund (Comprehensive Environmental Response Act) was designed to identify the most dangerous toxic sites across the country and to finance their cleanup. The government failed to provide adequate funding and administrative action to achieve Superfund goals, but the program nevertheless helped to encourage and empower local communities such as Carver Terrace.

The Military Exemption

The new environmental mass movement of the 1960s onward had one blind spot—the U.S. military establishment's assault upon nature. Throughout the Cold War the U.S. armed forces were largely shielded from environmental regulations.[26] Officials at the Pentagon claimed the need for military secrecy. The environmentalist movement generally, apart from some intrepid protesters in the Friends of the Earth organization, was not inclined to challenge those who held the patriotic moral high ground. The production and testing of military weapons, and the accumulation of toxic wastes at military installations, created one of the nation's most serious environmental threats. The problem was spread widely throughout the country, because the military establishment dispersed bases and contracts to as many states as possible in order to guarantee political support for defense expenditures in the U.S. Congress. When finally forced to an accounting, the Pentagon identified more than 20,000 sites of suspected toxic contamination.

The problem was not solely one of toxic munitions. The Defense Department, one of America's largest industries, purchased nearly 200 million barrels of fuel oil per year. The U.S. armed forces had some 40,000 underground storage tanks, four times as many as Exxon Corporation, but the military lagged behind private industry in replacing the old tanks. The Air Force's Logistics Command oversaw five facilities that in 1987 generated more than a billion gallons of hazardous waste. Air Force bases were more than a quarter of the 100-plus military facilities listed on the Superfund's priority listing of worst polluted sites.[27] Pressures upon the Pentagon to clean up its polluted facilities increased with the end of the Cold War. In September 1990, the U.S. Secretary of Defense, Dick Cheney, announced a "Defense and the Environment Initiative," but the belated campaign was strongly contested within the military, and the cleanup efforts were modest in relation to the size of the problem.[28]

Nuclear weapons production, testing and storage constituted the most dramatic and dangerous form of military environmental pollution. From World War II until the 1963 Test Ban Treaty, the United States conducted a total of 183 surface tests of nuclear weapons. The deadly effects of radiation were proven not only in diseased survivors of the bombs dropped on Hiroshima and Nagasaki, but also the deaths of plant and animal life near the nuclear test site in Nevada and the effects of U.S. tests on Eniwetok Atoll and Bikini Atoll in the Marshall Islands. In 1960 the U.S. nuclear arsenal reached an absurd peak of 20,491 megatons (more than 500,000 times the combined explosive power of the Hiroshima and Nagasaki bombs). Even the harshest critics of environmentalist "doomsday alarms," such as reporter Greg Easterbrook, admitted that continued atmospheric nuclear testing at 1950s levels would have resulted in "genuine ecological catastrophe."[29] Apart from atmospheric nuclear testing, the Department of Energy had to deal with issues of production, storage and disposal of radioactive by-products at 280 nuclear weapons facilities at twenty sites across the United States. The Hanford Reservation in southeastern Washington state was the most contaminated of these sites. From its beginning as a plutonium production facility in 1943 until 1984, "over 18 million cubic feet of low-level waste, 39 million cubic feet of plutonium-contaminated waste, and 8 million cubic feet of high-level waste (were) buried at the site."[30]

Popular protests against nuclear pollution, and the threat of the arms race generally, peaked in the 1980s with a "Freeze the Arms Race" campaign—a response to the military buildup and anti-environment actions of the Reagan administration. A doomsday manifesto by Jonathan Schell, entitled *The Fate of the Earth*, galvanized people to action with graphic documentation and descriptions of the results of total nuclear war.[31] Then with the end of the Cold War and the collapse of the Soviet Union, the popular anti-nuclear movement died down. Most Americans assumed that arms reduction agreements were eliminating the nuclear threat. In fact, at the end of 1998 the U.S. still had 7,200 operational strategic nuclear weapons and a total of 1,850 megatons—sufficient firepower alone to destroy all human civilization several times over.[32] The decade of the 1990s saw no new successful arms control initiatives. In 1999 India and Pakistan acquired operational nuclear weapons. The conventional Cold War doctrines of "nuclear deterrence" became increasingly irrelevant to the prospects for proliferation of nuclear weapons to additional countries. In the absence of a widespread popular movement of concern, in October 1999 the U.S. Senate refused to ratify the Comprehensive Test Ban Treaty of 1996 which endeavored to end the world wide proliferation of nuclear weapons testing.[33]

A Maturing Movement

By the end of the twentieth century, the environmental mass movement had become an integral part of American social and political culture. A huge majority of Americans, eighty-five percent in some polls, identified themselves as "green" or environmentally aware. Federal legislation had created a huge administrative bureaucracy to monitor and regulate problems of pollution and public health. The Environmental Protection Agency had become one of the largest and most powerful of federal agencies. The major private environmental organizations counted nearly ten million members. The organizations fielded a body of sophisticated professional lobbyists that influenced policy in state and national government. Environmentalism itself became big business, using mass-marketing techniques and publishing slick multicolored magazines. The professionalization of the movement distressed some grass roots activists who preferred a movement of passion and moral zeal.

The movement had become a very broad tent, covering people of orientations diversely religious and secular, activist and intellectual, counter-cultural and scientific. In a general sense, the movement had some political impact. More than a million people signed a petition calling for the resignation of James Watt, Interior Secretary appointed by Ronald Reagan. Politicians seeking national office had to take account of the environmentalist constituency. In the presidential campaign of 2000, candidates George W. Bush and Al Gore both courted environmentalist support. But in some ways the movement remained politically weak. David E. Ortman, former staff person with the Friends of the Earth, wrote in 2000, "While corporations pour millions into 'soft money' campaign donations, the environmental community has focused more on Earth Day than Election Day. Other than the League of Conservation Voters and the Sierra Club, most major environmental organizations still do not have political action committees (PACs)."[34] What difference had the movement made for actual environmental quality? A year 2000 "30-Year Report Card" from World Watch, one of the persistently pessimistic environmental watchdog agencies, sounded continuing alarms: Escalating burning of coal and oil by a growing world population was contributing to global warming. Consumption of chemicals was exploding, with new pesticides barely staying ahead of pesticide-resistant pests. The population had increased as much in thirty years as in the 100,000 years prior to the mid-20th century, on a pace which would eventually outrun the world's base of resources. The world's population reached six billion in the fall of 1999, on course to reach ten billion by 2050.[35]

Most participants in Earth Day 2000, however, celebrated in a spirit of hope rather than despair. Jim Motavalli, editor of *E The Environmental Magazine*, offered a ten-year report card for the 1990s which had much good news (as well as dire warnings). Actions to clean up polluted air and water had taken effect. "Los Angeles had its clearest skies in fifty years." The recycling rate was up four-fold in thirty years. Major advances were afoot for harnessing wind energy, for automobiles powered by fuel cells, and for organic agriculture.[36]

Only a profound shift in American thinking could overcome the standard historical myths that natural resources were inexhaustible and that property owners, individual and corporate, had the right to do whatever they wanted in their quest for profit. Within the environmental movement, people organized and rediscovered the power of actively working to protect the land, water, air, and non-human living things. The methods used to bring about change were predominantly political, with a number of groups consciously using the tactics of nonviolence. Although problems of toxic waste fell most acutely on the poor and minorities, people involved in the movement became aware that environmental issues were connected with other issues such as race, gender, and economic and military power. In the face of the growing power of multi-national corporations, the movement needed to move toward a global consciousness — to "think globally and act globally" rather than to be limited by the slogan to "think globally and act locally."[37] The ability of the movement vigorously to connect its concerns with the problems of nuclear warfare, nuclear weapons proliferation, and the massive pollution by the military establishment would do much to determine the extent of progress toward a livable world.

Epilogue

History and Hope for a Nonviolent Future

This book is an invitation to a fresh look at United States history from the viewpoint of peace values. At the outset, we set ourselves a threefold task: to examine the roots and the legacy of violence in American history; to recover the American heritage of mutuality and independence which made for reconciliation and justice; and to re-remember the people and events in American history that worked creatively for nonviolent alternatives.

In two centuries of national life, most Americans have learned their history in terms of a master narrative of patriotic triumph and material success. If Americans occasionally resorted to violence, it was believed, the savagery was exceptional and contrary to their basic character. Richard Maxwell Brown, historian of American violence, wrote that "despite a mountain of evidence to the contrary, Americans as late as the 1940s still refused to think of themselves as essentially violent."[1] The master narrative took a major hit in the 1960s, an exceptionally violent decade of cultural transformation and exploding homicide rates. The upheavals of the 1960s also spawned a revisionist spirit among United States history scholars.

Revisionist history can appear to be demoralizing and unpatriotic. Howard Zinn, popular revisionist historian, reports that some of his readers claim to become "thoroughly alienated and depressed" by his accounts of "the massacres of Indians, the long history of racism, the persistence of poverty in the richest country in the world, the senseless wars."[2] Zinn's dilemma is typical of radical critics. Indeed, the current climate seems to trap us between the two options of triumphant nationalism and radical criticism. The theme of triumph fosters false pride while revisionist denunciations lead to despair. Nationalistic patriotism, for the most part, still owns the public square and determines the content of mass market textbooks. But revisionist books and media productions which condemn the excesses of American capitalism and militarism are abundant and flourishing.

This volume offers a perspective of constructive nonviolence as an alternative to triumphalist nationalism and destructive cultural criticism, both of which often assume that violence is redemptive. If we are to learn to speak the language of peace, we must transcend the language of violence. A healthier view of history will recover the "missing peace" in our past.

Legacy of Violence

From the time of the European discovery of North America, violence has scarred our story. Violence has pitted Whites against Indians, Whites against Blacks, farmers against landowners, vigilantes against alleged lawbreakers, labor against capital, men against women. A nation born in a violent war waged against colonial masters learned to justify all its future wars in terms of presumed advances for freedom and democracy, even when the wars were unnecessary, unprovoked, or imperialistic.

Violence in American history has often undermined the very values it is presumed to defend. The nation born in anti-colonial revolution became a great imperial power in its own right, exercising colonial political rule initially over the Philippines after the 1898 war against Spain, and economic dominance over the world economy after World War II. Moreover, successful warfare required a centralized organization that contradicted democratic procedures and principles. U.S. militarization in the Cold War led to internal spying and centralized power that were the characteristics most feared and hated in the Soviet-Communist enemy. The nuclear arms race put in place an arsenal of potential massive destruction that, if it were actually unleashed, would contradict, and indeed destroy, the humane values common to all civilizations.

Legacy of Mutuality and Interdependence

But the American story is much more than one of violence. The United States is not solely a "country made by war," as one recent military historian would have it.[3] The United States is also a country built by peacemakers. "The critical drama of our past is not violence," says peace historian Charles Chatfield, "but rather the struggle to overcome violence."[4] The elements of that drama are at hand in our historical libraries and in the minds of our elders, awaiting the honest historians, literary artists and social prophets who can craft them into a compelling narrative. If the United States is to be transformed toward peace, we must learn to tell the stories of peace.

One way to learn a more humane history is to ask more humane questions. Instead of organizing national history around the question "What makes America great?" (or around the opposite question, "Why did America fail to fulfill its promise of greatness?"), this book has asked the question, "What has moved American society towards greater peace and justice?" To understand the Native American experience, for example, we need to get beyond celebrating their violent resistance or lamenting their tragic victimization. The challenge rather is to view the Native American story from the Indian viewpoint and to investigate how they were able to adapt and survive culturally in the face of the white invasion. Contrary to the assumptions of most of the writing about Native American history, the guarantors of Indian long-range cultural survival were not their warriors but rather their prophets and peacemakers.

A perspective of constructive nonviolence remembers the peace idealism of the early republic. At the outset of our national experiment, a commitment to peace was near the core, not at the fringes, of national identity. Quaker pacifism had put a permanent stamp on the character of the middle colonies and states. A classical republican, or "Whig," political ideology saw the American experiment in democratic republicanism as an updated and more secular version of the earlier holy experiments in Pennsylvania and New England. The new republic was hostile to "standing armies," military instruments belonging to old-world monarchies and their conspiracies with ruling aristocrats.

America's early peace idealism was more than misguided romantic innocence. It led national leaders to make decisions against war in situations when warfare seemed imminent and justifiable—as in 1799 when President John Adams moved to end the "Quasi-War" with France, and in 1807 when President Thomas Jefferson avoided war with England by a strategy of economic embargo. Classical republican antipathy to "standing armies" is an authentic American ancestor of late twentieth-century concerns about the excessive power of the military industrial complex.

Hidden Heroes and Stories

Much depends upon what we define as "success." An honest portrayal of American history must distance itself from the version of pragmatism which argues that whoever or whatever wins is right. History is more than the stories of the powerful, rich and famous. We must remember those who vigorously contended for peaceable solutions to conflict, even when their faithful witness was not rewarded. Students of the United States past may well draw more inspiration from the peacemaking efforts of Joseph Galloway at the First Continental Congress than from the bare majority which rejected Galloway's plan for inter-colonial union. There may be more to learn from the Garrisonian nonviolent abolitionists in the Non-resistance Society of the 1830s than from those who made civil war more likely by insisting that only violence could solve the problem of slavery. It may be said that William Jennings Bryan "failed" as Secretary of State in his efforts to negotiate conciliation treaties with the nations of the world (1913-14) and in his advocacy of consistent U.S. neutrality after war broke out in Europe (1914-15). But in the perspective of peace values, Bryan's policies look more worthy than the world war which Americans later claimed to have won. "Success" in history, especially in victorious wars which set the stage for more warfare, is often a cruel illusion.

A constructive nonviolent perspective investigates the critical moments leading to war and asks the questions: Was this war necessary? Who was offering proposals to avoid the violence? What were the arguments for and against those proposals? What would the likely effects have been of their adoption? Too often we have blotted out the memory of peacemakers while we celebrate events of violence. Americans are remarkably well informed of the details of the Boston Tea Party of December 17, 1773, while we are quite ignorant about the success of the people in Philadelphia who at the same time were nonviolently persuading the British captain to take the East India tea back to England. Or, to choose a recent example, Americans need to reexamine the notion that President Ronald Reagan brought about the end of the nuclear arms race with his hard-line rhetoric and military buildup of 1981-85. We need to take account of the decisive influence of peace-minded anti-nuclear scientists, especially Andrei Sakharov, upon Soviet leader Michael Gorbachev to take dramatic unilateral and disproportional steps toward disarmament. If we can overcome our addiction to stories of redemptive violence, Americans will be able to credit the international peace movement properly with its decisive role in bringing about the end to the Cold War.

The breakthroughs of nonviolence in United States history have come more often from creative minorities than from established centers of power. In the vanguard of the great crusades against slavery, for women's rights, against militarism, and for civil rights, were leaders of creative minorities who knew that the ideals of peace and justice are ultimately one and inseparable. These peace prophets came upon the scene as outsiders whose alternative visions projected new possibilities for public life. They constitute a luminous honor roll: Deganawidah, Roger Williams, Henry David Thoreau, Elihu Burritt, Carrie Chapman Catt, Mark Twain, Jane Addams, Mary Harris Jones, Linus Pauling, Cezar Chavez, and many, many more.

Peacemakers have often paid a high price for their convictions. Martin Luther King, the greatest American teacher of nonviolence in the twentieth century, today is so eulogized on his national holiday that we forget how lonely his stance once was. Yet King forged the teachings of Jesus, Thoreau, and Gandhi into a movement that transformed race-relations in this country. As historian Vincent Harding argues in *Hope and History*, we must tell the story of that nonviolent movement because it carries the ideas and resources for a wider cultural transformation.[5] King was uncompromising in his commitment to the gospel of love, to the essential unity of all humankind under God. He applied the principles of nonviolence as surely to the war in Vietnam as to racial oppression at home. The civil rights movement is a fountain of hope for the future not only because it teaches us to nurture a heart of love, but also because it reminds us that nonviolent social transformation requires persistent and disciplined challenges to unjust social structures.

Abundant signs of hope lie within our history. The challenge is to seek out those signs, read them diligently, and follow their paths toward a more just and peaceable society.

Notes

Preface

[1] James A. Mercy, foreword to *Statistical Handbook on Violence in America*, ed. Adam Dobrin, Brian Wiersema, Colin Loftin and David McDowall (Phoenix, AZ: Oryx Press, 1996); Michael P. Hanagan, "American Violence in Comparative Perspective," in *Violence in America: An Encyclopedia*, ed. Ronald Gottesman (New York: Charles Scribner's Sons, 1999), 1:101; Richard Maxwell Brown, "Overview of Violence in the United States," in *Violence in America*, 1:18; Robert S. Norris and William M. Arkin, "U.S. Nuclear Forces, 2001," *The Bulletin of the Atomic Scientists*, March/April 2001, 77-79; Michael Bellesiles, introduction to *Lethal Imagination: Violence and Brutality in American History* (New York: New York University Press, 1999), 1-15.

[2] Thomas Merton, "Blessed Are the Meek: The Roots of Christian Nonviolence," *Fellowship*, May 1967, 20.

[3] Howard Zinn, *Declarations of Independence: Cross-Examining American Ideology* (New York: Harper Collins, 1990), 33-34.

[4] James Baldwin, "Unnameable Objects, Unspeakable Crimes," in *Black on Black: Commentaries by Negro Americans*, ed. Arnold Adoff (Toronto: The Macmillan Company, 1968), 95.

[5] Richard K. Leiphart, "Glad America dropped bomb," letter to editor in *The Intelligencer Journal*, Lancaster, PA, 24 August 1995, A-11.

[6] Colman McCarthy, foreword to *The Universe Bends Toward Justice: A Reader on Christian Nonviolence in the U.S.*, ed. Angie O'Gorman (Philadelphia: New Society Publishers, 1990), ix.

[7] Walter Wink, *Engaging the Powers: Discernment and Resistance in a World of Domination* (Minneapolis: Fortress Press, 1992), 13, 16.

[8] Martin Luther King, Jr., "Letter from Birmingham Jail," in *Why We Can't Wait* (New York: New American Library, 1963), 77.

[9] Merle Curti, *Peace or War: The American Struggle, 1636-1936* (Boston: J. S. Canner, 1959); Charles DeBenedetti, *The Peace Reform in American History* (Bloomington: Indiana University Press, 1980); Charles Chatfield and Robert Kleidman, *The American Peace Movement: Ideals and Activism* (New York: Twayne, 1992).

[10] Vincent Harding, *Hope and History: Why We Must Share the Story of the Movement* (Maryknoll, NY: Orbis Books, 1990), 9.

Chapter 1

[1] Sherman Alexie, *Reservation Blues* (New York: Atlantic Monthly Press, 1995), 208.

[2] On European imaginary distortions of Native American reality, see Robert F. Berkhofer, Jr., *The White Man's Indian: Images of the American Indian from Columbus to the Present* (New York: Vintage, 1978).

[3] Russell Thornton, *American Indian Holocaust and Survival: A Population History Since 1492* (Norman: University of Oklahoma Press, 1987), 32-37. The comparison with Europe does not include European Russia.

[4] Sherburne F. Cook and Woodrow Borah, "The Aboriginal Population of Hispaniola," in *Essays in Population History: Mexico and the Caribbean*, ed. Cook and Borah (Berkeley: University of California Press, 1971), 1:402-03, cited in David E. Stannard, *American Holocaust: Columbus and the Conquest of the New World* (New York: Oxford University Press, 1992), 74-75.

[5] William E. Unrau, "The Columbian Heritage: The Varieties of Violence against Native Americans in Nineteenth-Century Kansas," in *Nonviolent America: History Through the Eyes of Peace*, ed. Louise Hawkley and James C. Juhnke (North Newton, KS: Bethel College, 1993), 42.

[6] For a recent summary see Noble David Cook, *Born to Die: Disease and New World Conquest, 1492-1650* (Cambridge: Cambridge University Press, 1998).

[7] Francis Jennings, *The Founders of America: How Indians Discovered the Land; Pioneered in it; and Created Great Classical Civilizations; How They Were Plunged into a Dark Age by Invasion and Conquest; and How They are Reviving* (New York: W. W. Norton, 1994), 169.

[8] William Bradford, *Of Plymouth Plantation*, 270-71, cited in Ronald Takaki, *A Different Mirror: A History of Multicultural America* (Boston: Little, Brown, and Company, 1993), 39.

[9] See section II, "Pestilence and Genocide," in Stannard, *American Holocaust*, 57-146.

[10] Jennings, *The Founders*, 298-99.

[11] Unrau, "Columbian Heritage," 44-45.

[12] Kenneth C. Davis, "Ethnic Cleansing Didn't Start in Bosnia," *The New York Times*, 3 September 1995, sec. 4: 1, 6.

[13] Stannard, "Pestilence and Genocide," 57-146.

[14] Paul A. W. Wallace, *The White Roots of Peace* (Port Washington, NY: Kennikat Press, 1946), 13-14.

[15] John Arthur Gibson, *Concerning the League: The Iroquois League Tradition as Dictated in Onondaga* (Winnipeg: Algonquian and Iroquoian Linguistics, 1992), xxix.

[16] Matthew Dennis, *Cultivating a Landscape of Peace* (Ithaca: Cornell University Press, 1993).

[17] Dennis, *Cultivating*, 79.

[18] Daniel K. Richter, *The Ordeal of the Longhouse: The Peoples of the Iroquois League in the Era of European Colonization* (Chapel Hill: University of North Carolina Press, 1992).

[19] Donald A. Grinde, Jr., and Bruce E. Johannsen, *Exemplar of Liberty: Native America and the Evolution of Democracy* (Los Angeles: American Indian Studies Center UCLA, 1991), 246.

[20] This section follows the suggestion of James Drake, "Symbol of a Failed Strategy: The Sassamon Trial, Political Culture, and the Outbreak of King Philip's War," *American Indian Culture and Research Journal* 19 (1995): 111-41.

[21] The "War of Conquest" designation is suggested by Francis Jennings, *The Invasion of America: Indians, Colonialism, and the Cant of Conquest* (Chapel Hill: University of North Carolina Press, 1975), 298. The more Puritan-oriented account is Douglas Edward Leach, *Flintlock and Tomahawk: New England in King Philip's War* (New York: Macmillan, 1958).

[22] Neal Salisbury, "Red Puritans: the 'Praying Indians' of Massachusetts Bay and John Eliot," *William and Mary Quarterly*, 3rd ser. 31 (1974): 44.

[23] Drake, "Symbol of a Failed Strategy," 122.

[24] Francis Paul Jennings, "Miquon's Passing: Indian-European Relations in Colonial Pennsylvania, 1674 to 1775" (Ph.D. diss., University of Pennsylvania, 1965), 45-47.

[25] C. A. Weslager, *The Delaware Indians: A History* (New Brunswick: Rutgers University Press, 1972), 180-81. Anthony F. C. Wallace, "Woman, Land, and Society: Three Aspects of Aboriginal Delaware Life," *Pennsylvania Archaeologist* 17 (1947): 20-32.

[26] Paul A. W. Wallace, *Indians in Pennsylvania* (Harrisburg: The Pennsylvania Historical and Museum Commission, 1961), 46. Wallace, typical of most historical surveys of Indian tribes, has a separate chapter on Delaware warfare, but not on Delaware peacemaking.

[27] David McCutchen, translator and annotator, *The Red Record: The Wallam Olum, The Oldest Native North American History* (Garden City Park, NY: Avery Publishing Group, 1993).

[28] Herbert C. Kraft, *The Lenape: Archaeology, History, and Ethnography* (Newark: New Jersey Historical Society, 1986), 4-7.

[29] William W. Newcomb, Jr., *The Culture and Acculturation of the Delaware Indians*, University of Michigan Museum of Anthropology, Anthropological Papers, no. 10 (Ann Arbor: University of Michigan Museum of Anthropology, 1956): 5; cited in McCutchen, *The Red Record*, 13; and in Kraft, *The Lenape*, 22.

[30] David Hackett Fischer, *Albion's Seed: Four British Folkways in America* (New York: Oxford University Press, 1989), 452.

[31] Conversation of the author with Jeanne M. Oyawin Eder, Larned, Kansas, June 19, 1995.

[32] Anthony F. C. Wallace, "New Religions Among the Delaware Indians, 1600-1900," *Southwestern Journal of Anthropology* 12 (Spring 1956): 13.

[33] R. David Edmunds, *The Shawnee Prophet* (Lincoln: University of Nebraska Press, 1983), 225. See also Edmunds, *Tecumseh and the Quest for Indian Leadership* (Boston: Little, Brown and Company, 1984).

[34] Anthony F. C. Wallace, *The Death and Rebirth of the Seneca* (New York: Alfred A. Knopf, 1970).

[35] William G. McLoughlin, *Cherokee Renascence in the New Republic* (Princeton: Princeton University Press, 1968).

[36] McLoughlin, *Cherokee Renascence*, 350-51.

[37] Wilbur R. Jacobs, *Dispossessing the American Indian: Indians and Whites on the Colonial Frontier* (New York: Charles Scribner's Sons, 1971), 167.

[38] John D. Unruh, Jr., *The Plains Across: The Overland Emigrants and the Trans-Mississippi West, 1840-60* (Urbana: University of Illinois Press, 1979), 156.

[39] Jennings, *The Founders*, 368.

[40] George Bird Grinnell, *The Fighting Cheyennes* (Norman: University of Oklahoma Press, 1956), vii, ix.

[41] Quoted in Stan Hoig, *The Peace Chiefs of the Cheyennes* (Norman: University of Oklahoma Press, 1980), 7.

[42] Lawrence Hart, "Cheyenne Peace Traditions," *Mennonite Life* 36 (June 1981): 4-7.

[43] Peter Farb, *Man's Rise to Civilization: The Cultural Ascent of the Indians of North America*, rev. ed. (New York: E. P. Dutton, 1978), 110-14.

[44] James D. Drake, "Native American Wars: Warfare in Native American Societies," in *The Oxford Companion to American Military History*, ed. John Whiteclay Chambers II (New York: Oxford University Press, 1999), 478-79.

[45] Robert H. Ruby and John A. Brown, *Dreamer Prophets of the Columbian Plateau, Smohalla and Skolaskin* (Norman: University of Oklahoma Press, 1989), 127, 132, 163.

[46] From Truman Michelson, "The Narrative of a Southern Cheyenne Woman," *Smithsonian Miscellaneous Collections* 87 (1932): 2. Cited in Gretchen M. Bataille and Kathleen Mullen Sands, *American Indian Women: Telling Their Lives* (Lincoln: University of Nebraska Press, 1984), 40.

[47] Ann McMullen, "What's Wrong with This Picture? Context, Conversion, Survival, and the Development of Regional Native Cultures and Pan-Indianism in Southeastern New England," in *Enduring Traditions: The Native Peoples of New England*, ed. Laurie Weinstein (Westport, CT: Bergin and Garvey, 1994), 123.

[48] Greg Sarris, *Keeping Slug Woman Alive: A Holistic Approach to American Indian Texts* (Berkeley: University of California Press, 1993), 41.

[49] Hart, "Cheyenne Peace Traditions," 7. Conversation of the author with Lawrence Hart, Wichita, Kansas, 26 July 1995. See also Lawrence Hart, "A Gesture of Peace," in *What Would You Do?*, ed. John H. Yoder (Scottdale, PA: Herald Press, 1992), 137-41.

Chapter 2

[1] Nathan Hatch, *The Sacred Cause of Liberty: Republican Thought and the Millennium in Revolutionary New England* (New Haven: Yale University Press, 1977); Catherine L. Albanese, *Sons of the Fathers: The Civil Religion of the American Revolution* (Philadelphia: Temple University Press, 1976).

[2] Gordon S. Wood, "Disturbing the Peace," *New York Review of Books*, 8 June 1995, 19, 21, 22.

[3] Sylvester Judd, *A Moral Review of the Revolutionary War, or Some Evils of That Event Considered* (Hallowell, Maine, 1841; facsimile reprint, Jerome S. Ozer, 1972), 43.

[4] The choice of names for partisans in a civil war is controversial. Both "patriot" and "rebel" are emotion-laden terms. Formally, the Loyalists were as

"patriotic" in their loyalties as were their opponents. It is notable that "rebels" of the Civil War of 1865-60, and their supportive descendants, are more accepting of that label than are the supporters of the "rebels" of 1775-83.

⁵ Quoted in Robert Middlekauff, *The Glorious Cause: The American Revolution, 1763-1789* (New York: Oxford University Press, 1982), 342.

⁶ Lawrence Henry Gipson, *The Coming of the Revolution, 1763-1775* (New York: Harper & Brothers, 1954), 1-3. On colonial nostalgia for the mother country see David Hackett Fischer, *Albion's Seed: Four British Folkways in America* (New York: Oxford University Press, 1989), 55-57, 252-56, 468-70.

⁷ H. Trevor Colbourn, *The Lamp of Experience: Whig History and the Intellectual Origins of the American Revolution* (Chapel Hill: University of North Carolina Press, 1965), 7-9.

⁸ Gipson, *The Coming*, 10-27.

⁹ On the role of ideology in the revolution see Bernard Bailyn, *The Ideological Origins of the American Revolution* (Cambridge: Harvard University Press, 1967); and Gordon S. Wood, *The Creation of the American Republic, 1776-1787* (New York: W. W. Norton, 1969). For a cogent brief summary see George Marsden, "The American Revolution: Partisanship, 'Just Wars,' and Crusades," in *The Wars of America: Christian Views*, ed. Ronald A. Wells (Grand Rapids, MI: William B. Eerdmans, 1981), 18-21.

¹⁰ Neil B. Lehman, "The Revolution: An Unnecessary Act of Violence?" *Indiana Pennsylvania Evening Gazette*, 7 October 1976.

¹¹ Winthrop D. Jordan, "Familial Politics: Thomas Paine and the Killing of the King, 1776," *The Journal of American History* 60 (September 1973): 294-308.

¹² Barbara W. Tuchman, *The March of Folly: From Troy to Vietnam* (New York: Alfred A. Knopf, 1984), 127-231. Tuchman argues that British leaders, like many persons of power in history, did not act according to their own rational self-interest.

¹³ J. H. Plumb, "British Attitudes to the American Revolution," in *Resistance, Politics, and The American Struggle for Independence, 1765-1775*, ed. Walter H. Conser, Jr., et al. (Boulder, CO: Lynne Rienner Publishers, 1986), 462.

¹⁴ John H. Yoder, "The Burden and the Discipline of Evangelical Revisionism," in *Nonviolent America: History Through the Eyes of Peace*, ed., Louise Hawkley and James C. Juhnke (North Newton, KS: Bethel College, 1993), 23-25. Yoder wrote, "Before the fateful decisions were made, the other potential outcomes in people's minds were just as 'factual,' i.e., just as thinkable, just as doable, as what finally happened. Only after the decision does one outcome become 'fact' at the cost of the others" (29).

¹⁵ Francis Maseres, "Considerations on the Expediency of Admitting Representatives from the American Colonies into the British House of Commons," 1770.

¹⁶ Don Cook, *The Long Fuse: How England Lost the American Colonies, 1760-1785* (New York: Atlantic Monthly Press, 1995), 28. Members of Parliament did not have to reside in districts from which they were elected.

¹⁷ Bernard Bailyn, *The Ordeal of Thomas Hutchinson* (Cambridge, MA: Belknap Press of Harvard University Press, 1974), 93-98.

¹⁸ Julian P. Boyd, *Anglo-American Union: Joseph Galloway's Plans to Preserve the British Empire* (Philadelphia, 1941); John Ferling, "Compromise or Conflict:

The Rejection of the Galloway Alternative to Rebellion," *Pennsylvania History* 43 (January 1976): 5-20.

[19] Lynn Montross, *The Reluctant Rebels: The Story of the Continental Congress 1774-1789* (New York: Harper & Brothers, 1950), 50.

[20] Bernard Bailyn, "The Central Themes of the American Revolution: An Interpretation," in *Essays on the American Revolution*, ed. Stephen G. Kurtz and James H. Hutson (Chapel Hill: University of North Carolina Press, 1973), 23.

[21] The moral justification of war has been elaborated in terms of criteria which must be met if war is to be just. James Turner Johnson, in *Just War Tradition and the Restraint of War* (Princeton: Princeton University Press, 1981), suggested six criteria for the right to make war (*jus ad bellum*–just cause, right authority, right intention, proportionality, last resort, and a purpose to achieve peace) and two criteria for the law of war (*jus in bello*–discrimination and proportion).

[22] Julie M. Flavell, "Lord North's Conciliatory Proposal and the Patriots in London," *English Historical Review* 107 (April 1992): 302-03.

[23] Gene Sharp, *The Politics of Nonviolent Action* (Boston: Porter Sargent, 1973), 229.

[24] Ronald M. McCarthy, "Resistance Politics and the Growth of Parallel Government in America, 1765-1775," in *Resistance, Politics, and The American Struggle for Independence, 1765-1775*, ed. Walter H. Conser, Jr., et al. (Boulder, CO: Lynne Rienner Publishers, 1986), 472-524.

[25] Sharp, *The Politics*, 427.

[26] Paul S. Boyer et al., *The Enduring Vision: A History of the American People*, concise 3d ed. (Boston: Houghton Mifflin, 1998), 1:111.

[27] Richard Maxwell Brown, "Violence and the Revolution," in *Essays on the American Revolution*, ed. Stephen G. Kurtz and James H. Hutson (Chapel Hill: University of North Carolina Press, 1973), 84.

[28] *Ibid.*, 108

[29] Gordon S. Wood, *The Radicalism of the American Revolution* (New York: Vintage, 1992), 89, 307-08.

[30] For the argument that American colonists justified the war in essentially political terms, see Melvin B. Endy, Jr., "Just War, Holy War, and Millennialism in Revolutionary America," *William and Mary Quarterly*, 3rd ser. 42 (1985): 3-25.

[31] For an emphasis on the Holy War or millennialist justification of the war, see Nathan O. Hatch, *The Sacred Cause of Liberty: Republican Thought and the Millennium in Revolutionary New England* (New Haven: Yale University Press, 1977), 21-96; and Catherine L. Albanese, *Sons of the Fathers: The Civil Religion of the American Revolution* (Philadelphia: Temple University Press, 1976).

[32] Charles Royster, *A Revolutionary People at War: The Continental Army and American Character, 1775-1783* (New York: W. W. Norton, 1979).

[33] John W. Shy, "The Legacy of the American Revolutionary War," in *Legacies of the American Revolution*, ed. Larry R. Gerlach (Logan: Utah State University, 1978), 45-46.

[34] Charles Patrick Neimeyer, *America Goes to War: A Social History of the Continental Army* (New York: New York University Press, 1996), 8-26.

[35] Robert Middlekauff, *The Glorious Cause: The American Revolution, 1763-*

1789 (New York: Oxford University Press, 1982), 292.

[36] Robert Douthat Meade, *Patrick Henry: Practical Revolutionary* (Philadelphia: J. B. Lippincott, 1969), 2:167.

[37] Royster, *A Revolutionary People,* 33.

[38] Middlekauff, *The Glorious Cause,* 507.

[39] Neimeyer, *America Goes to War,* 164.

[40] Charles J. Stille, *Major-General Anthony Wayne and the Pennsylvania Line in the Continental Army* (1893; Port Washington, N.Y.: Kennikat Press, 1968), 238-62.

[41] Carl Van Doren, *Mutiny in January: The Story of a Crisis in the Continental Army* (New York: Viking Press, 1943), 216, 223.

[42] Don Higganbotham, *The War of American Independence: Military Attitudes, Policies, and Practice, 1763-1789* (New York: Macmillan, 1971; reprint, Boston: Northeastern University Press, 1983), 414. Royster, *A Revolutionary People,* 80.

[43] George Washington letter to William Crawford, September 21, 1767. *The Writings of George Washington from the Original Manuscript Sources 1745-1799,* ed. John C. Fitzpatrick (Washington, D.C.: Government Printing Office, 1931), 2:467-71.

[44] Arrell Morgan Gibson, *The American Indian: Prehistory to the Present* (Lexington, Mass: D. C. Heath, 1980), 254, 256.

[45] Benjamin Quarles, *The Negro in the American Revolution* (Chapel Hill: University of North Carolina Press, 1961), 19.

[46] John Hope Franklin, *From Slavery to Freedom: A History of Negro Americans,* 4th ed. (New York: Alfred A. Knopf, 1974), 92.

[47] Sylvia R. Frey, *Water From the Rock: Black Resistance in a Revolutionary Age* (Princeton: Princeton University Press, 1991), 193-99.

[48] *Ibid.,* 94-96.

[49] Bailyn, "The Central Themes," 23. For an argument that the war was not inevitable, see Ian R. Christie and Benjamin W. Labaree, *Empire or Independence 1760-1776: A British-American Dialogue on the Coming of the American Revolution* (New York: W. W. Norton, 1976), 274-81. For a contrary viewpoint—that the war was inevitable—see John W. Shy, *A People Numerous and Armed: Reflections on the Military Struggle for American Independence* (New York: Oxford University Press, 1976), 37-72.

[50] Mark A. Noll, "A History of Christianity in the United States and Canada" (Grand Rapids, MI: William B. Eerdmans, 1992), 546-47.

[51] Abraham Lincoln, "The Perpetuation of Our Political Institutions" in *The Collected Works of Abraham Lincoln,* ed. Roy P. Basler et al. (New Brunswick, NJ: Rutgers University Press, 1953), 1: 108-115; cited to in Shy, "The Legacy," 43, 59-60.

Chapter 3

[1] Reginald C. Stuart, *The Half-way Pacifist: Thomas Jefferson's View of War* (Toronto: University of Toronto Press, 1978).

[2] Quotation cited in Clifford L. Egan, *Neither Peace Nor War: Franco-American Relations, 1803-1812* (Baton Rouge: Louisiana State University Press, 1983), 75.

[3] For one sharp critique of the Quaker experiment, see Daniel Boorstin, *The Americans*, vol. 1, *The Colonial Experience* (New York: Random House, 1958), 33-69.

[4] David Hackett Fischer, *Albion's Seed: Four British Folkways in America* (New York: Oxford University Press, 1989), 3-11, 419-603.

[5] Stephen L. Longenecker, "*Wachet Auf*: Awakening, Diversity, and Tolerance among Early Pennsylvania Germans," in *Nonviolent America: History Through the Eyes of Peace*, ed. Louise Hawkley and James C. Juhnke (North Newton, KS: Bethel College, 1993), 227-43.

[6] Alan Tully, *Forming American Politics: Ideals, Interests, and Institutions in Colonial New York and Pennsylvania* (Baltimore: Johns Hopkins University Press, 1994), 429. Tully's thesis revises the dominant interpretation of American politics as the product of classical English republicanism. Tully argues that, although New England and the South took leadership in the War for Independence, the earliest formation of American party politics first developed in culturally diverse Pennsylvania and New York.

[7] Fischer, *Albion's Seed*, 584-89; Harry Elmer Barnes, *The Evolution of Penology in Pennsylvania: A Study in American Social History* (Indianapolis: Bobbs-Merrill, 1927), 28.

[8] Margaret Morris Haviland, "Beyond Women's Sphere: Young Quaker Women and the Veil of Charity in Philadelphia, 1790-1810," *William and Mary Quarterly*, 3d ser. 51 (July 1994): 419-46.

[9] Sydney V. James, *A People Among Peoples: Quaker Benevolence in Eighteenth-Century America* (Cambridge: Harvard University Press, 1963), 215.

[10] Cited by Lance Banning, *The Sacred Fire of Liberty: James Madison and the Founding of the Federal Republic* (Ithaca, NY: Cornell University Press, 1995), 397.

[11] Cited by Judith B. Markowitz, "Radical and Feminist: Mercy Otis Warren and the Historiographers," *Peace and Change* 4 (Spring 1977): 14.

[12] In recent years historians and political theorists have explored the topic of republican political thought. The following volumes are helpful, although none of them give adequate attention to issues of militarism and warfare in republican thought: Richard Vetterli and Gary Bryner, *In Search of the Republic: Public Virtue and the Roots of American Government* (Totowa, NJ: Rowman and Littlefield, 1987); Thomas L. Pangle, *The Spirit of Modern Republicanism: The Moral Vision of the American Founders and the Philosophy of Locke* (Chicago: The University of Chicago Press, 1988); Michael P. Zuckert, *Natural Rights and the New Republicanism* (Princeton: Princeton University Press, 1998); and Joyce Appleby, *Liberalism and Republicanism in the Historical Imagination* (Cambridge: Harvard University Press, 1992).

[13] Stuart, *The Half-way Pacifist*.

[14] Henry Nash Smith, *Virgin Land: The American West as Symbol and Myth* (Cambridge: Harvard University Press, 1950), 144-45.

[15] For a survey of United States history which emphasizes the use of law by powerful classes over against the dispossessed, see Howard Zinn, *A People's History of the United States* (New York: Harper Colophon, 1980).

[16] Richard Maxwell Brown, *No Duty to Retreat: Violence and Values in American History and Society* (New York: Oxford University Press, 1991), 3-8.

[17] Michael A. Bellesiles, *Arming America: The Origins of a National Gun Culture* (New York: Alfred A. Knopf, 2000), 81-82.

[18] Wynn M. Goering, "Pacifism and Heroism in American Fiction, 1770-1860" (Ph.D. diss., University of Chicago, 1984), 44-46.

[19] *Ibid.*, 46. Citation from Henry Lee, "A Funeral Oration, in honour of the memory of George Washington," quoted in *Monthly Magazine*, 2 (1800): 123.

[20] Benjamin Rush, "A Plan of a Peace-Office for the United States," in *The Selected Writings of Benjamin Rush*, ed. Dagobert D. Runes (New York: Philosophical Library, 1947), 19-22. Noted from Goering, "Pacifism and Heroism," 22.

[21] Goering, "Pacifism and Heroism," 47-48, 134-38, 174-5, *passim*.

[22] Richard Slotkin, *Regeneration Through Violence: The Mythology of the American Frontier, 1600-1860* (Middletown, CT: Wesleyan University Press, 1973).

[23] Michael True, *An Energy Field More Intense than War: The Nonviolent Tradition and American Literature* (Syracuse, NY: Syracuse University Press, 1995).

[24] Richard D. Mosier, *Making the American Mind: Social and Moral Ideas in the McGuffey Readers* (New York: Russell & Russell, 1965), 44-47.

[25] Cited in Alexander DeConde, *The Quasi-War: The Politics and Diplomacy of the Undeclared War with France, 1797-1801* (New York: Charles Scribner's Sons, 1966), 339.

[26] A recent laudatory account of Adams' behavior in this crisis is by David McCullough, *John Adams* (New York: Simon & Schuster, 2001), 515-57.

[27] See Karl-Friedrich Walling, *Republican Empire: Alexander Hamilton on War and Free Government* (Lawrence, KS: University Press of Kansas, 1999), 224-44, for a rather strained attempt to rescue Hamilton from the charge that he was a militarist.

[28] John Ferling, *John Adams: A Life* (Knoxville: University of Tennessee Press, 1992), 378.

[29] Page Smith, *John Adams, 1784-1826* (Garden City, N.Y.: Doubleday, 1962), 2:999.

[30] DeConde, *The Quasi-War*, 155-72.

[31] Ferling, *John Adams*, 355.

[32] DeConde, *The Quasi-War*, 196-98.

[33] For an argument that Jefferson should have gone to war in 1807, see Clifford L. Egan, "Thomas Jefferson's Greatest Mistake: The Decision for Peace, 1807," *Proceedings of the Citadel Conference on War and Diplomacy*, ed. David H. White and John W. Gordon (The Citadel Development Foundation, 1979), 94-97.

[34] Bradford Perkins is one of the strongest critics of Jeffersonian diplomacy and the embargo in particular. See Perkins, *Prologue to War: England and the United States, 1805-1812* (Berkeley: University of California Press, 1963), and Perkins, *The Creation of a Republican Empire, 1776-1865*, vol. 1 of *The Cambridge History of American Foreign Relations*, ed. Warren I. Cohen (Cambridge: Cambridge

University Press, 1993), 118-33. For a more peace-oriented perspective see Ralph Beebe, "The War of 1812," in *The Wars of America: Christian Views*, ed. Ronald A. Wells (Grand Rapids, MI: Eerdmans, 1981), 26-35.

[35] Page Smith, *The Shaping of America: A People's History of the Young Republic* (New York: McGraw-Hill, 1980), 594. The designation "The Strange War of 1812," also appears in Robert A. Divine et al., *America Past and Present*, 2d ed. (Glenview, IL: Scott, Foresman, and Company, 1984), 232.

[36] John William Ward, *Andrew Jackson: Symbol for an Age* (New York: Oxford University Press, 1962), 16-27.

[37] Samuel G. Goodrich, *Recollections of a Lifetime* (New York, 1857), cited in Ward, *Andrew Jackson*, 3.

[38] Robert V. Remini, *Andrew Jackson and the Course of American Freedom, 1822-1832* (New York: Harper & Row, 1981), 2:29-35. Remini emphasizes the continuity of Jacksonian Democracy with the freedom ideals of the American Revolution, but glosses over the contradiction between the peace idealism of classical republicanism and the militant violence of Jacksonianism.

[39] The label "Scotch-Irish" often used for these people is misleading, because so many of them came from the English-Scottish border and had never lived in Ireland.

[40] Quoted in Fischer, *Albion's Seed*, 765.

[41] Joe B. Frantz, "The Frontier Tradition: An Invitation to Violence," in *The History of Violence in America: Historical and Comparative Perspectives*, ed. Hugh Davis Graham and Ted Robert Gurr (New York: Praeger, 1969), 127-51; Richard Maxwell Brown, "Violence," in *The Oxford History of the American West*, ed. Clyde A. Milner II, Carol A. O'Connor and Martha A. Sandweiss (New York: Oxford University Press, 1994), 393-425.

[42] Bertram Wyatt-Brown, *Southern Honor: Ethics and Behavior in the Old South* (Oxford: Oxford University Press, 1982), 367-70.

[43] Ward, *Andrew Jackson*, 163-65.

[44] Letter from Henry Clay to Reverend Mr. Bascom, April 10, 1826, cited in Jeannette Hussey, *The Code Duello in America* (Washington, D.C.: Smithsonian Institution, 1980), 29.

[45] Richard Maxwell Brown, "Historical Patterns of Violence in America," in *The History of Violence in America: Historical and Comparative Perspectives*, ed. Hugh Davis Graham and Ted Robert Gurr (New York: Praeger, 1969), 53-55.

[46] Ulysses S. Grant, *Personal Memoirs* (New York: Charles S. Webster, 1885), 1:54.

[47] Grant, *Memoirs*, 1:56.

[48] Robert D. Richardson, Jr., *Henry Thoreau: A Life of the Mind* (Berkeley: University of California Press, 1986), 176-79.

[49] Robert Leckie, *The Wars of America*. Rev. and updated ed. (New York: Harper and Row, 1981), 328, 331.

[50] Leckie, *The Wars*, 372-73. The inscription is quoted by Howard N. Meyer, "Why Are We in Texas (and Elsewhere)?" *The Minority of One* (July-August, 1968): 17. The Leckie and Meyer accounts disagree on some details. Meyer reports that Riley's first name was John.

[51] Justin H. Smith, *The War With Mexico* (New York: Macmillan, 1919), 2:385.

[52] *Ibid.,* 322-24.

[53] Otis A. Singletary, *The Mexican War* (Chicago: University of Chicago Press, 1960), 5.

[54] Quoted in Robert W. Johannsen, *To the Halls of the Montezumas: The Mexican War in the American Imagination* (New York: Oxford University Press, 1985), 278.

[55] John A. Harper, cited in Albert K. Weinberg, *Manifest Destiny: A Study of Nationalist Expansionism in American History* (Baltimore: Johns Hopkins Press, 1935), 53.

[56] See Reginald C. Stuart, *United States Expansionism and British North America, 1775-1871* (Chapel Hill: University of North Carolina Press, 1988), 85-105.

[57] See the discussion of issues on the British side in Kenneth Bourne, *Britain and the Balance of Power in North America, 1815-1908* (Berkeley: University of California Press, 1967), 13-32.

[58] Bradford Perkins, *The Creation of a Republican Empire,* 213-17.

[59] William Stafford, *The Darkness Around Us Is Deep: Selected Poems of William Stafford,* ed. Robert Bly (New York: Harper Collins, 1993), 117.

[60] J. G. A. Pocock, "1776: The Revolution Against Parliament," in *Virtue, Commerce, and History: Essays on Political Thought and History, Chiefly in the Eighteenth Century* (Cambridge: Cambridge University Press, 1985), 87-88.

Chapter 4

[1] Winthrop D. Jordan, *White Over Black: American Attitudes Toward the Negro, 1550-1812* (Chapel Hill, NC: Published for the Institute of Early American History and Culture at Williamsburg, VA, by the University of North Carolina Press, 1968); Carl Degler, "Slavery and the Genesis of American Race Prejudice" *Comparative Studies in Society and History* 2 (Oct. 1959): 49-66.

[2] Edmund Morgan, "Slavery and Freedom: The American Paradox," *Journal of American History* 59 (June 1972): 5-29.

[3] See John Chester Miller, *The Wolf By the Ears: Thomas Jefferson and Slavery* (New York: Free Press, 1977).

[4] Barbara Fields, "Ideology and Race in American History" in *Region, Race, and Reconstruction: Essays in Honor of C. Vann Woodward,* ed. J. Morgan Kousser and James M. McPherson (New York: Oxford University Press, 1982), 147. Fields points out the ability of humans to believe things that "in strict logic are not compatible." She argues that European literary stereotypes of Africans as "docile, childlike, or primitive" were at odds with the experience of traders who knew the power and dignity of African chiefs.

[5] George Fitzhugh, *Cannibals All! or Slaves Without Masters,* ed. C. Vann Woodward (1857; Cambridge, MA: The Belknap Press of Harvard University Press, 1960), 5.

[6] Hebrew word "ebed" and Greek word "doulos." Abraham's story is in Genesis 17-25. The law of Moses made provision for "servants" or "slaves" who had been purchased. See Exodus 5 and 21. For the apostle Paul's teachings, see I Cor. 7, Ephesians 6, Titus 2. Other proslavery scriptural arguments

came from their interpretation of the curse of Ham (Hebrew=dark), the youngest son of Noah, supposedly the father of the Cushites (East Africans) who saw his father's nakedness and was condemned to be a "hewer of wood and drawer of water," which slavery supporters interpreted as slavery for Ham and all of his descendants. See Gen 9:18-10:1.

⁷ Frederick Douglass, *My Bondage and My Freedom* (New York: Miller, Orton & Mulligan, 1855; reprint, New York: Arno Press, 1968), 263.

⁸ Gerald W. Mullin, *Flight and Rebellion: Slave Resistance in 18th Century Virginia* (New York: Oxford University Press, 1972), 149. In the slave rebellion led Gabriel Prosser, more than 1000 slaves may have been organized and ready to strike against the city of Richmond, but on the night of August 30, 1800 a major storm forced the cancellation of their plans; they were betrayed by informers and the leaders were captured and executed.

⁹ Elizabeth Buffum Chace, "My Anti-Slavery Reminiscences," in *Virtuous Lives: Four Quaker Sisters Remember Family Life, Abolitionism and Women Suffrage,* ed. Lucille Salitan and Eva Lewis Perera (New York: Continuum, 1994), 94.

¹⁰ Chace, "Reminiscences," 102.

¹¹ The Methodists split in 1844 into a Methodist Church North and Methodist Church South, a division that remained until 1939 The Wesleyan Methodists had already split from the main body in 1843 in order to maintain a church reflecting more nearly the vision of their founder, John Wesley, which included the denunciation of slavery as the "sum of all villainies." African Americans formed two separate Methodist bodies in the 1790s: the African Methodist Episcopal Church and the African Methodist Episcopal Zion. The Baptist split in 1845 into the American Baptists and Southern Baptists remains to this day. The Presbyterians broke organizational unity in 1857 and reunited in 1970, but almost remained split over the issue of women's ordination.

¹² For a discussion of Garrisonian disunionism, see Aileen S. Kraditor, *Means and Ends in American Abolitionism: Garrison and His Critics on Strategy and Tactics, 1834-1850* (New York: Vintage Books, 1969), 196-216. Garrison used the quotation about the Constitution (p. 200) to begin his editorial comments, starting in 1843.

¹³ For a good collection of essays on women in the abolitionist movement, see, *The Abolitionist Sisterhood,* ed., Jean Fagan Yellin and John C. Van Horne (Ithaca: Cornell University Press, 1995).

¹⁴ Carl Degler, *The Other South: Southern Dissenters in the Nineteenth Century* (Boston: Northeastern University Press, 1982), 20.

¹⁵ *Ibid.,* 22-25. Degler quotes a speech given by Robert Breckinridge of Kentucky, who said the Colonization Society "cherished the hope and the belief also, that the successful prosecution of its objects would offer powerful motives and exert a persuasive influence in favor of emancipation. And it is with this indirect effect of the society that the largest advantage is to result in America" (24).

¹⁶ Letter from Jermain Loguen to Frederick Douglass printed in *Frederick Douglass Papers,* 25 March 1853.

[17] Benjamin Quarles, *Black Abolitionists* (New York: Oxford University Press, 1969), 3-8.

[18] Degler, *The Other South*, 29.

[19] L. Minor Blackford, *Mine Eyes Have Seen the Glory* (Cambridge, Mass., 1954), 39-42.

[20] Eugene Genovese, *The Political Economy of Slavery* (New York: Random House, 1965).

[21] An estimate found in Claudia Goldin and Frank Lewis, "The Economic Cost of the American Civil War," *The Journal of Economic History* 35 (June 1975): 299-323, puts the direct costs of the war in 1860 dollars at $3.4 billion for the North and $2.89 billion for the south, although many southern records are lost or inaccurate, making the estimate probably low. Gerald Gunderson, "The Origin of the American Civil War," *The Journal of Economic History* 34 (December 1974): 915-950, gives figures of $2.19 billion for the North and $2.02 billion for the South.

[22] Much of the primary source material on Nat Turner, including his *Confessions* to Thomas R. Gray, are collected in *The Southhampton Slave Revolt of 1831: A Compilation of Source Material*, ed. Henry Irving Tragle (Amherst, MA: University of Massachusetts Press, 1971). Eric Foner, ed., *Nat Turner* (Englewood Cliffs, N.J., Prentice-Hall, Inc., 1971) and Stephen B. Oates, *Fires of Jubilee: Nat Turner's Fierce Rebellion* (New York: Harper & Row, 1975) have written credible biographies. For those who like historical controversy see William Styron, *The Confessions of Nat Turner* (New York: Random House, 1967) and *William Styron's Nat Turner: Ten Black Writers Respond*, ed. John Henrick Clarke (Boston: Beacon Press, 1968).

[23] See Joseph Clarke Robert, *The Road from Monticello: A Study of the Virginia Slavery Debate of 1831* (Durham: Duke University Press, 1941), and Degler, *The Other South*, 14-17.

[24] *Colored American* (New York, N.Y. 9, 16, ,23, 30, 1837), speech by William Whipper, delivered at the First African Presbyterian Church, Philadelphia, Pennsylvania, 16 August 1837. Reprinted in *The Black Abolitionist Papers*, vol. 3, *The United States, 1830-1846*, ed C. Peter Ripley (Chapel Hill, NC: University of North Carolina Press, 1991), 232-51. The quote is on page 238.

[25] Samuel E. Cornish, Editorial, *Colored American* (New York, N.Y.), 4 March 1837; reprinted in *Black Abolitionist Papers*, 3: 219-20.

[26] The best general work on black abolitionists is Benjamin Quarles, *Black Abolitionists* (New York: Oxford University Press, 1969).

[27] Address by Abraham D. Shadd, William Hamilton, and William Whipper, 13 June 1832, *Minutes and Proceedings of the Second Annual Convention for the Improvement of the Free People of Colour in these United States* (Philadelphia, PA: 1832), 32-35, reprinted in *Black Abolitionist Papers* , 3: 109-115. The quote is on page 111.

[28] *Proceedings of the Antislavery Convention Assembled at Philadelphia* (New York: 1833).

[29] See Lewis Perry, *Radical Abolitionism: Anarchy and the Government of God in Antislavery Thought* (Ithaca: Cornell University Press, 1973).

[30] *The Narrative of Sojourner Truth* (Battle Creek, MI , 1878), repr. ed. Olive Gilbert (New York: Arno Presss, 1968), 114, 120; Frederick Douglass, *Life and Times of Frederick Douglass*, in *Autobiographies* (New York: The Library of America; distributed by Penguin Books, 1994), 719; Lerone Bennett, *Before The Mayflower: A History of Black America* (New York: Penguin, 1966), 157.

[31] Speech by Peter Paul Simons, delivered before the African Clarkson Association, New York, NY, 23 April 1839, printed in *Colored American* (New York, N.Y.) 1 June 1839; reprinted in *Black Abolitionist Papers*, 3: 289.

[32] *Ibid.*

[33] Harriet Jacobs, *Incidents in the Life of a Slave Girl*, ed. Jean Fagan Yellin (Cambridge, Mass: Harvard University Press, 1987), 162-63.

[34] The best discussion of free Black experience in the North is Leon F. Litwack, *North of Slavery: The Negro in the Free States, 1790-1860* (Chicago: University of Chicago Press, 1961).

[35] Abbey Kelley to Gerrit Smith, 7 August 1843, Gerrit Smith Collection, Arendts Library, Syracuse University, Syracuse, NY.

[36] "The Free Produce Question," *The Liberator*, 1 March 1850.

[37] Garrison penned this now famous statement "To the Public" for the first issue of his newspaper, *The Liberator*, 1 January 1831; reprinted in *William Lloyd Garrison and the Fight Against Slavery: Selections from "The Liberator,"* ed. William E. Cain (Boston: Bedford Books of St. Martin's Press, 1995), 72.

[38] According to the college text, Mary Beth Norton et al., *A People and a Nation* (Boston: Houghton Mifflin, 1994), 11 million pieces were sent out in a single year between 1834 and 1835 (p.377).

[39] Leonard Richards, *Gentlemen of Property and Standing: Anti-abolition Mobs in Jacksonian America* (New York: Oxford University Press, 1970). In this book Richards examines who actually made up the anti-abolitionist mobs and finds that they were often merchants and professionals—"gentlemen of property and standing."

[40] Richard Sewall, *Ballots for Freedom: Antislavery Politics in the United States* (New York: Oxford University Press, 1976), 48.

[41] *Impartial Citizen*, 11 July 1849.

[42] Proceedings of the Radical Abolitionist Convention, June 26-28, 1855. Reported in *The Radical Abolitionist*, June 1855, July 1855, and August 1855, Arendts Library, Syracuse University, Syracuse, NY.

[43] *The Liberator* , 11 October 1850. William Powell (1807-1879) was the son of a New York slave who was freed when New York abolished slavery in 1827. He settled in New Bedford, Maine, where he married and had seven children. A desire for their education led him to be among those appearing before the Massachusetts legislature to end racial discrimination in the schools in 1837. It took Massachusetts until 1855 to act, so Powell moved his family to Liverpool, England for ten years, where he continued antislavery work. A life-long Garrisonian pacifist, he continued to be active after the Civil War, acting as a delegate to the National Colored Labor Convention in 1869 and chairing the New York Civil Rights Committee in 1873.

⁴⁴ Quarles, *Black Abolitionists,* 199-201. Almost 1000 blacks left Pittsburgh for Canada; 487 of the 943 blacks living in Columbia, PA moved; and all but two members of the Colored Baptist Church of Rochester left for Canada.

⁴⁵ *Syracuse Daily Standard,* 27 September 1850.

⁴⁶ According to Stanley Campbell, *The Slave Catchers: Enforcement of the Fugitive Slave Law, 1850-1860* (New York: W.W. Norton, 1972), 166 slaves were returned to the south under the new law and only nine successful rescues occurred.

⁴⁷ Samuel J. May, *Some Recollections of Our Anti-Slavery Conflict* (Boston: Fields & Osgood, 1869; reprint, New York: Arno Press, 1968), 377.

⁴⁸ May, *Recollections,* 379.

⁴⁹ *Syracuse Standard,* 30 October 1851.

⁵⁰ Romans 13:1.

⁵¹ John 13:34; Micah 6:8. The latter was the text used by Rev. Samuel May to explain his participation in the rescue. *Rev. Samuel May to the Convention of Citizens of Onondaga County, October 14, 1851* (Syracuse: Agan and Summers Printers, 1851), 3, in the Onondaga County Historical Association, Syracuse, New York.

⁵² Larry Gara, *Liberty Line: Legend of the Underground Railroad* (Lexington: University of Kentucky Press, 1961), exposes some of the fraud while recognizing the importance of the work that actually took place. See also Charles Blockson, *The Underground Railroad* (New York: Prentice Hall, 1987), Helene Phelan, *And Why Not Every Man? An Account of Slavery, the Underground Railroad and the Road to Freedom in New York's Southern Tier* (Interlaken, NY: Heart of the Lakes Publishing, 1987); William Siebert, *Mysteries of Ohio's Underground Railroad* (Columbus, Ohio: Long's College Bookstore, 1951).

⁵³ *Reminiscences* (1878; New York: Arno Press, 1969); William Still, *The Underground Railroad* (Philadelphia: Porter and Coates, 1872; reprint, Chicago: Johnson Publishing Co., 1970).

⁵⁴ James W.C. Pennington, *The Fugitive Blacksmith* (London, 1849), 30.

⁵⁵ *North Star,* 31 August 1849, in Carleton Mabee, *Black Freedom: The Nonviolent Abolitionists from 1830 through the Civil War* (New York: Macmillan, 1970), 284.

⁵⁶ Mabee, *Black Freedom,* 268.

⁵⁷ *Madison Courier,* 15 June 1874; Elijah Anderson case file, Governor C. S. Morehead Papers, Public Records Division, Frankfort, Kentucky; Gwendolyn Crenshaw, *"Bury Me in A Free Land": The Abolitionist Movement in Indiana, 1816-1865* (Indianapolis: Indiana Historical Bureau, 1986), 31; Emma Lou Thornbrough, *The Negro in Indiana Before 1900: A Study of a Minority* (Indianapolis: Indiana Historical Bureau, 1957), 41.

⁵⁸ Lewis Harding, ed., *History of Decatur County, Indiana* (Indianapolis: B. Bowen and Co., 1915), 400-406; Gwendolyn Crenshaw, "One Ran to Freedom, Another Caught and Bonded: The Case of Caroline, A fugitive Slave, and Luther Donnell," *Black History News and Notes,* Aug./Nov. 1986, 4-8.

⁵⁹ C. Peter Ripley, ed.,"Introduction," *Black Abolitionist Papers,* 3: 50.

⁶⁰ Charles Reason (1818-1893) was the son of Haitian immigrants. He prepared for the Episcopal ministry, but was denied admission to seminary be-

cause of his race. He became a teacher, and taught in New York City's African Free Schools, New York Central College in McGrawville, and Philadelphia's Institute for Colored Youth. He taught for thirty-five years in black public schools in New York City, where he continued his struggle against racial prejudice in the post Civil War years.

Chapter 5

[1] Kenneth L. Burns, prod. *The Civil War* (New York: Public Broadcasting System, 1990), Episode 1. Geoffrey C. Ward, *The Civil War: An Illustrated History* (New York: Alfred A. Knopf, 1990), xvi.

[2] Hugh Purcell, "America's 'Civil' Wars," *History Today* 41 (May 1991): 7.

[3] Abraham Lincoln, "Gettysburg Address," November 19, 1863, in *The Heritage of America*, ed., Henry Steele Commager and Allan Nevins (Boston: Little, Brown and Company, 1951), 765.

[4] Phillip S. Paludan, "The American Civil War: Triumph Through Tragedy," *Civil War History* 20 (Sept. 1974): 239-50.

[5] For an excellent review of revisionist writing, see Kenneth M. Stampp, "The Irrepressible Conflict," in his *The Imperiled Union: Essays on the Background of the Civil War* (New York: Oxford University Press, 1980), 191-245.

[6] New York *Daily Tribune*, 16 Nov. 1860. Cited in Jeter Allen Isely, *Horace Greeley and the Republican Party, 1853-1861* (Princeton: Princeton University Press, 1947), 308.

[7] Daniel W. Crofts, *Reluctant Confederates: Upper South Unionists in the Secession Crisis* (Chapel Hill: University of North Carolina Press, 1989), xvi-xvii, 214, 256.

[8] Glyndon G. Van Deusen, *Horace Greeley: Nineteenth-Century Crusader* (Philadelphia: University of Pennsylvania Press, 1953), 261-68.

[9] Winston Churchill, "If Lee Had Not Won the Battle of Gettysburg," *Wisconsin Magazine of History*, Summer 1961, 243-51.

[10] John S. Rosenberg, "Toward a New Civil War Revisionism," *American Scholar* 38 (Spring 1969): 267.

[11] Peter Kolchin, *Unfree Labor: American Slavery and Russian Serfdom* (Cambridge: The Belknap Press of Harvard University Press, 1987).

[12] William Pfaff, *The Wrath of Nations: Civilization and the Furies of Nationalism* (New York: Simon & Schuster, 1993), 172.

[13] Robert W. Fogel and Stanley L. Engerman, *Time on the Cross*, vol. 1, *The Economics of American Negro Slavery* (Boston: Little, Brown and Company, 1974), 5. For a critique see Kenneth M. Stampp, "*Time on the Cross*: A Humanistic Perspective," in *The Imperiled Union*, 72-102.

[14] Robert William Fogel, *Without Consent or Contract: The Rise and Fall of American Slavery* (New York: W. W. Norton, 1989), 413-17.

[15] Quoted in Alan T. Nolan, *Lee Considered: General Robert E. Lee and Civil War History* (Chapel Hill: University of North Carolina Press, 1991), 27-28.

[16] Quoted in David Herbert Donald, *Lincoln* (New York: Simon & Schuster, 1995), 209.

[17] William W. Freehling, *The Reintegration of American History: Slavery and the Civil War* (New York: Oxford University Press, 1994), 212.

[18] Donald, *Lincoln*, 15.

[19] David M. Potter, *The Impending Crisis 1848-1861* (New York: Harper & Row, 1976), 496-97.

[20] Cited in Charles P. Roland, *The Confederacy* (Chicago: University of Chicago Press, 1960), 52.

[21] Crofts, *Reluctant Confederates*, 247, 254.

[22] *Ibid.*, 272-73.

[23] *Ibid.*, 353-60.

[24] Allan Nevins, *The Emergence of Lincoln*, vol. 2, *Prologue to Civil War 1859-1861* (New York: Charles Scribner's Sons, 1950), 394.

[25] Martin B. Duberman, *Charles Francis Adams, 1807-1886* (Boston: Houghton Mifflin, 1960), 248.

[26] *Journals of Ralph Waldo Emerson with Annotations*, ed. Edward Waldo Emerson and Waldo Emerson Forbes (Boston: Houghton Mifflin and Company, 1913), 461-62 Quoted in James G. Randall, *Lincoln, the Liberal Statesman* (New York: Dodd, Mead, 1947), 55-56.

[27] J. G. Randall and David Donald, *The Civil War and Reconstruction*, 2d ed. (Lexington, MA: D. C. Heath, 1969), 531-32.

[28] Donald, *Lincoln*, 269, 529.

[29] Quoted in Donald, *Lincoln*, 523.

[30] Emory M. Thomas, *The Confederate Nation 1861-1865* (New York: Harper & Row, 1979), 301. A recent laudatory biography insists that Davis did not consider a guerilla campaign. See William J. Cooper, Jr., *Jefferson Davis: American* (New York: Alfred A. Knopf, 2000), 527.

[31] See Richard E. Beringer, Herman Hattaway, Archer Jones, and William N. Still, Jr., *Why the South Lost the Civil War* (Athens, GA: University of Georgia Press, 1986) for an argument that the "weakness of southern nationalism" was the "proximate cause of Confederate defeat," and that "a creditable nationalism" would have enabled Confederates to respond positively to Davis' call for guerilla warfare, 3, 421-22, *passim*.

[32] Burns, *The Civil War*, Episode 5, "The Universe of Battle."

[33] Nolan, *Lee Considered*, 112-33.

[34] One attempt at the subject for twentieth-century warfare is by Joanna Bourke, *Face-to-Face Killing in Twentieth-Century Warfare* (New York: Basic Books, 1999).

[35] See, for example, the camaraderie of soldiers after the Seven Days Battle when Yanks and Rebs "gathered berries together and talked over the fight, traded tobacco and coffee and exchanged newspapers as peacefully and kindly as if they had not been engaged for the last seven days in butchering one another." Shelby Foote, *The Civil War: A Narrative*, vol. 1, *Fort Sumter to Perryville* (New York: Random House, 1958), 519.

[36] Gerald F. Linderman, *Embattled Courage: The Experience of Combat in the American Civil War* (New York: The Free Press, 1987), 72.

[37] Samuel Horst, *Mennonites In the Confederacy: A Study in Civil War Pacifism* (Scottdale, PA: Herald Press, 1967), 23-27; James O. Lehman, "Conscientious Objectors during the Civil War," in *Nonviolent America: History Through the Eyes of Peace*, ed. Louise Hawkley and James C. Juhnke (North Newton, KS: Bethel College, 1993), 81.

[38] Dave Grossman, *On Killing: The Psychological Cost of Learning to Kill in War and Society* (Boston: Little, Brown and Company, 1995), 24-25.

[39] S. L. A. Marshall, *Men Against Fire: The Problem of Battle Command in Future War* (Gloucester, MA: Peter Smith, 1978), 56-57. See also Gwynne Dyer, *War* (New York: Crown Publishers, 1985), 118-20.

[40] Francis A. Lord, *Civil War Collector's Encyclopedia: Arms, Uniforms, and Equipment of the Union and Confederacy* (Harrisburg, PA: The Stackpole Company, 1963), 242; Grossman, *On Killing*, 21-22.

[41] Grossman, *On Killing*, 249-61.

[42] The Public Broadcasting Service series by Ken Burns, *The Civil War*, gave little attention to religion. See Walter Unger, "Telling the Whole Story—The Role of Religion in the Civil War," *Mennonite Brethren Herald*, 15 May 1992, 12-13.

[43] C. C. Goen, *Broken Churches, Broken Nation: Denominational Schisms and the Coming of the American Civil War* (Macon, GA: Mercer University Press, 1985), 12-13; Sydney E. Ahlstrom, *A Religious History of the American People* (Garden City, NY: Doubleday, 1975), 2:105-11.

[44] Julia Ward Howe, *Reminiscences, 1819-1899* (Boston: Houghton, Mifflin and Company, 1899), 273-80. Mary H. Grant, *Private Woman, Public Person: An Account of the Life of Julia Ward Howe from 1819 to 1868* (Brooklyn: Carlson Publishing, 1994), 136-39.

[45] Rev. William Gaylord, 5 October 1862, at Fitzwilliam, NH, quoted in James H. Moorhead, *American Apocalypse: Yankee Protestants and the Civil War, 1860-1869* (New Haven: Yale University Press, 1978), ix.

[46] Abraham Lincoln message to Congress, December 1862, in *Abraham Lincoln: Speeches and Writings, 1859-1865* (New York: The Library of America, 1989), 415.

[47] B. T. Lacy, Episcopal rector, quoted by Charles Reagan Wilson, *Baptized in Blood: The Religion of the Lost Cause, 1865-1920* (Athens: The University of George Press, 1980), 5.

[48] Linderman, *Embattled Courage*, 19-20.

[49] Drew Gilpin Faust, "Christian Soldiers: The Meaning of Revivalism in the Confederate Army," *Journal of Southern History*, 53 (February 1987), 63.

[50] *The Presbyterian*, 23 April 1864, 66, quoted in Moorhead, *American Apocalypse*, 70.

[51] George Ide, *Battle Echoes, or, Lessons from the War* (Boston: Gould and Lincoln, 1866), 30, quoted in Moorhead, *American Apocalypse*, 147.

[52] Michael A. Bellesiles, *Arming America: The Origins of a National Gun Culture* (New York: Alfred A. Knopf, 2000), 265.

[53] Sheldon M. Novick, *Honorable Justice: The Life of Oliver Wendell Holmes* (Boston: Little, Brown and Company, 1989), 85.

[54] Cited in George M. Fredrickson, *The Inner Civil War: Northern Intellectuals and the Crisis of Union* (New York: Harper Torchbooks, 1965), 219.

[55] Oliver Wendell Holmes, Jr., "Harvard College in the War," 25 June, 1884, in *The Mind and Faith of Justice Holmes: His Speeches, Essays, Letters and Judicial Opinions*, ed. Max Lerner (New York: The Modern Library, 1943), 23.

[56] Novick, *Honorable Justice*, 257-59, 458-59.

[57] Richard Maxwell Brown, *No Duty to Retreat: Violence and Values in American History and Society* (New York: Oxford University Press, 1991), 34-35.

[58] Shelby Foote quoted in *U. S. News and World Report* 24 September 1990, 75.

[59] Beringer, et. al., *Why the South*, 398-417.

Chapter 6

[1] Eric Foner, *The Story of American Freedom* (New York: W. W. Norton, 1998), 100.

[2] For a critique of the final segment in the Burns documentary see Eric Foner, "Ken Burns and the Romance of Reunion," in *Ken Burns' The Civil War: Historians Respond*, ed. Robert Brent Toplin (New York: Oxford University Press, 1996), 103-18.

[3] Eric Foner, *Reconstruction: America's Unfinished Revolution, 1863-1877* (New York: Harper & Row, 1988); Leon F. Litwack, *Been in the Storm So Long: The Aftermath of Slavery* (New York: Alfred A. Knopf, 1979); Vincent Harding, *There is a River: The Black Struggle for Freedom in America* (New York: Harcourt Brace Jovanovich, 1981).

[4] Russel B. Nye, *William Lloyd Garrison and the Humanitarian Reformers* (Boston: Little, Brown and Company, 1955), 179-88. John L. Thomas, *The Liberator: William Lloyd Garrison, A Biography* (Boston: Little, Brown and Co., 1963), 437-47.

[5] One recent summary of the literature is by Alex Lichtenstein, "Was the Emancipated Slave a Proletarian?" *Reviews in American History* 26 (March 1998): 124-45.

[6] Edward Magdol, *A Right to the Land: Essays on the Freedmen's Community* (Westport CN: Greenwood Press, 1977), 13.

[7] Anthony F. C. Wallace, *The Death and Rebirth of the Seneca* (New York: Alfred A. Knopf, 1970).

[8] Leon F. Litwack, *Been in the Storm So Long: The Aftermath of Slavery* (New York: Alfred A. Knopf, 1979), 97, 75-76.

[9] W. E. Burghardt Du Bois, *Black Reconstruction: An Essay Toward a History of the Part which Black Folk Played in the Attempt to Reconstruct Democracy in America, 1860-1880* (New York: S. A. Russell Company, 1935), 110.

[10] Foner, *Reconstruction*, 436.

[11] Quoted in Litwack, *Been in the Storm So Long*, 176.

[12] Magdol, *Right to the Land*, 41.

[13] Foner, *Reconstruction*, 59.

[14] For one version of the Davis Bend story, see James T. Currie, *Enclave: Vicksburg and Her Plantations, 1863-1870* (Jackson: University Press of Mississippi, 1980).

[15] Whitelaw Reid, *After the War: A Tour of the Southern States, 1865-1866*, ed. C. Vann Woodward (New York: Harper & Row, 1965), 59.

[16] Harding, *There is a River*, 316.

[17] Willie Lee Rose, *Rehearsal for Reconstruction: The Port Royal Experiment* (New York: Oxford University Press, 1964), 378-408.

[18] Reid, *After the War*, 219.

[19] David Hackett Fischer, *Albion's Seed: Four British Folkways in America* (New York: Oxford University Press, 1989); Richard Slotkin, *Regeneration Through Violence: The Mythology of the American Frontier, 1600-1860* (Middletown,CN: Wesleyan University Press, 1973).

[20] Richard Maxwell Brown, "Historical Patterns of Violence in America," in *Violence in America, Historical and Comparative Perspectives*, ed. Hugh Davis Graham and Ted Robert Gurr (Washington, D.C.: National Commission on the Causes and Prevention of Violence, 1969), 47.

[21] George C. Rable, *But There Was No Peace: The Role of Violence in the Politics of Reconstruction* (Athens: The University of Georgia Press, 1984), 1-15.

[22] Daniel E. Sutherland, ed., *Guerillas, Unionists, and Violence on the Confederate Home Front* (Fayetteville: The University of Arkansas Press, 1999).

[23] Dan T. Carter, *When the War Was Over: The Failure of Self-Reconstruction in the South, 1865-1867* (Baton Rouge: Louisiana State University Press, 1985), 14.

[24] Foner, *Reconstruction*, 426.

[25] *Ibid.*, 342.

[26] *Ibid.*, 437.

[27] Bernard Weisberger, "The Dark and Bloody Ground of Reconstruction Historiography," *Journal of Southern History*, 25 (November 1959): 427-47.

[28] Michael Perman, "Counter Reconstruction: The Role of Violence in Southern Redemption," in *The Facts of Reconstruction: Essays in Honor of John Hope Franklin*, ed. Eric Anderson and Alfred A. Moss, Jr. (Baton Rouge: Louisiana State University Press, 1991), 132.

[29] Martin Meredith and Tina Rosenberg, *Coming to Terms: South Africa's Search for Truth* (New York: Public Affairs, 1999).

[30] Andrea Schultze, "The Challenge of Jubilee to the Situation of Church Land in South Africa Today," *International Review of Mission* 88 (July 1999): 255.

Chapter 7

[1] Robert J. Samuelson, "Century of Freedom," *Washington Post*, 22 December 1999: <wysiwyg://156/http://washingtonpost.com/wp-dyn/articles/A22883-1999Dec22html>

[2] Eric Foner, *The Story of American Freedom* (New York: W. W. Norton, 1998), 116.

[3] George Fitzhugh, *The Sociology of Slavery*, 1851.

[4] Paul Buhle and Alan Dawley, *Working for Democracy: American Workers from the Revolution to the Present* (Urbana: University of Illinois Press, 1985), 9.

[5] Theda Skocpol, *Protecting Soldiers and Mothers: The Political Origins of Social Policy in the United States* (Cambridge: Belknap Press of Harvard University Press, 1991).

⁶ Leon Fink, *Workingmen's Democracy*.

⁷ Melvyn Dubofsky, *We Shall Be All: A History of the Industrial Workers of the World* (Quadrangle Books, 1969); Donald E. Winters, Jr., *The Soul of the Wobblies: The I.W.W., Religion, and the American Culture in the Progressive Era, 1905-1917* (Westport, CT: Greenwood Press, 1985).

⁸ Mary Jones, *The Autobiography of Mother Jones* (Chicago: Charles Kerr, 1925).

⁹ Lawrence Goodwyn, *The Populist Moment: A Short History of the Agrarian Revolt in America* (New York: Oxford University Press, 1978), 22.

¹⁰ Goodwyn, *The Populist Moment*, 26.

¹¹ Joshua Freeman, et al., *Who Built America? Working People & the Nation's Economy, Politics, Culture & Society* (New York: Pantheon Books, 1992), 2:147.

¹² Washington Gladden, *Working People and Their Employers* (New York: Lockwood, Brooks and Co., 1876).

¹³ Marnie Jones, "Writing Great-Grandfather's Biography," *American Scholar* 56 (Autumn 1987): 525.

¹⁴ Robert M. Smith, "Beyond Progressivism: The Careers of Samuel "Golden Rule" Jones and Nelson O. Nelson, *The Midwest Review* 10 (1988): 43-54.

¹⁵ Nick Salvatore, *Eugene Debs: Citizen and Socialist* (Urbana: University of Illinois, 1982), 270-75.

¹⁶ Salvatore, *Eugene Debs*, 295.

¹⁷ Quoted in Martin Ridge, *Ignatius Donnelley: The Portrait of a Politician* (Chicago: University of Chicago Press, 1962), 315.

¹⁸ William Serrin, *Homestead: The Glory and Tragedy of an American Steel Town* (New York: Times Books, 1991); Paul Krause, "Labor Republicanism and 'Za Chlebom'; Anglo-Americans and Slavic Solidarity in Homestead," *Struggle a Hard Battle* (DeKalb, Illinois: Northern Illinois University Press, 1986), 143-69.

¹⁹ "State Income Inequality Continued to Grow . . . ." Joint report of the Economic Policy Institute and the Center on Budget and Policy Priorities," Washington, DC, 18 January 2000 <www.cbpp.org/1-18-00sfp.htm>

²⁰ United for a Fair Economy Research Library, <http://www.ufenet.org/research/CEO_Pay_charts.html>; "Executive Pay," *Business Week*, 16 April 2001, 77-78.

²¹ Robert B. Reich, *The Work of Nations: Preparing Ourselves for 21ˢᵗ Century Capitalism* (New York: Alfred A.Knopf, 1991). Reich, Secretary of Labor in the administration of President Bill Clinton, wrote that the recent growing disparities of wealth are due to the rapid rise of an elite class of "symbolic analysts" whose skills are more marketable in the global economy than are those of "routine producers" and of "in person servers."

Chapter 8

[1] Abigail Adams to John Adams, 31 March 1776, in *The Feminist Papers,* ed. Alice Ross (New York: Bantam Books, 1981), 10, 11.

[2] *Ibid.,* John Adams to Abigail Adams, 14 April 1776.

[3] Peggy Reeves Sanday, *Female Power and Male Dominance: On the Origins of Sexual Inequality* (Cambridge: Cambridge University Press, 1981), 4.

[4] Riane Eisler, *The Chalice and the Blade: Our History, Our Future* (San Francisco: Harper and Row, 1988), xvii and chapter 4.

[5] *Ibid.,* xix.

[6] Sam Keen, *Face of the Enemy: Reflections of the Hostile Imagination* (San Francisco: Harper and Row, 1991) uses provocative posters collected from around the world to show images of "the other" as a threat to women, thus providing a justification for war.

[7] Beryl Lieff Benderly, "Rape-Free or Rape-Prone," in *Cultural Mosaic: Readings in Cultural Anthropology* ed. Karin Li Simpkins and Nicholas Freidin (Dubuque, IA: Kendall/Hunt, 1998), says the United States ranked somewhere in the middle of rape-prone societies: "There are extremely violent societies where women are three times more likely to be attacked than they are in the United States" (137). Sanday, *Female Power and Male Dominance,* asserts that danger (whether from external attackers or scarce resources) "brings soldiers and fighters to the front line and encourages the development of male-dominated social structures." But even this generalization does not always hold true, since cultures with a prior commitment to peace, like the Hopi, withstand pressures from scarce resources.

[8] Thelma Goodrich, *Women and Power: Perspectives for Family Therapy* (New York: W.W. Norton, 1991), 11.

[9] National Victim Center, 2111 Wilson Boulevard, Suite 300 Arlington VA 22201.

[10] American Medical Association, "Violence Against Women: Relevance for Medical Practitioners," *Journal of the American Medical Association,* 267 (June, 1991): 3184-89.

[11] Family Violence Prevention Fund, at http://www.endabuse.org/index2.php3. According to the National Victim Center, the number is one woman every 15 seconds, which still puts the figure at over 6700 women being battered daily. See also United Health-Care's OPTUM Medical and Human Risk Management Services.

[12] Department of Justice, Bureau of Justice Statistics (Washington D.C.: GPO, 1994), 2.

[13] Isabelle Horon and Diana Cheng, "Enhanced Surveillance for Pregnancy-Associated Mortality—Maryland, 1993-1998," *Journal of the American Medical Association* 285, no. 11 (21 March 2001): 1455. These findings were reported in *Women's Health Weekly* 5 Apr. 2001, under the title "Pregnant Or Recently Pregnant Women More Likely To Die From Homicide Than Any Other Cause."

[14] Ron Acierno, "Prevalence Estimates: Intimate Partner and Domestic Violence," from the National Violence Against Women website: http://www.nvaw.org/research/dvprevalence.shtml May 30,2001.

[15]*Domestic Violence for Healthcare Providers*, 3d ed. (Colorado Domestic Violence Coalition, 1991).

[16] Andrea Dworkin, *Life and Death: Unapologetic Writings on the Continuing War Against Women*. (New York: Free Press, 1997), 65, 66.

[17] Christine Courtois, *Healing the Incest Wound: Adult Survivors in Therapy* (New York: Norton, 1988).

[18] Elizabeth Pleck and Joseph Pleck, eds., *The American Man* (Englewood Cliffs, NJ: Prentice-Hall 1980), 12.

[19] George Fox, *A Collection of Many Select and Christian Epistles* (T. Sowle, 1698), 2:323, quoted by Mary Mapes Dunn, "Latest Light on Women of Light" in *Witnesses for Change: Quaker Women over Three Centuries*, ed. Elisabeth Potts Brown (New Brunswick: Rutgers University Press, 1989), 72-73.

[20] Rosemary Radford Ruether, *Women and Redemption: A Theological History* (Minneapolis: Fortress Press, 1998), 144.

[21] See Margaret Hope Bacon, *Mothers of Feminism* (San Francisco: Harper and Row, 1986). Mary Mapes Dunn (note 19) recognizes the importance of broadening the research on Quaker women from their public life to examine the "purely female experience of life" and to examine the ways in which they were similar to the women of their times, as well as different. A fascinating collection of primary source documents on early Quaker women, both English and American is found in Mary Garman, Judith Applegate, Dortha Meredith and Margaret Benefield, *Hidden in Plain Sight: Quaker Women's Writings, 1650-1700* (Wallingford, PA: Pendle Hill Publications, 1995). A general history is Hugh Barbour, *The Quakers* (New York: Greenwood Press, 1988).

[22] The Great Binding Law http://www.kahonwes.com/constitution.html

[23] Alice Rossi,ed., *The Feminist Papers* (New York: Bantam Books, 1987), 413-420. Three of the women at the convention, Elizabeth Cady Stanton, Susan B. Anthony and Matilda J. Gage, in later life compiled a meticulous six-volume history of the suffrage movement which is widely available: *History of Women Suffrage* (Rochester, N.Y.: Charles Mann, 1888).

[24] See Matthew Frye Jacobson, *Whiteness of a Different Color: European Immigrants and the Alchemy of Race* (Cambridge, Mass: Harvard University Press, 1998), for a clear presentation of the many factors influencing racial perceptions, especially during the late nineteenth century.

[25] Gail Bederman, *Manliness and Civilization* (Chicago: University of Chicago Press, 1995), 11, 15ff, 239.

[26] Michael Welch, "Violence Against Women by Professional Football Players," *Journal of Sport and Social Issues* 21 (Nov. 1997): 392.

[27] Michael Messner and Donald Sabo, *Sex, Violence and Power in Sports: Rethinking Masculinity* (Freedom, CA: The Crossing Press, 1994), 29.

[28] Anne Longley, "Out of Bounds," *People* 2 Oct. 1995, 91.

[29] Jon M. Kingsdale, "'The Poor Man's Club': Social Functions of the Urban Working Class Saloon," *American Quarterly* 25 (Dec. 1973): 472-89.

[30] Francis Willard, *Woman and Temperance* (Hartford, Conn.: Park Publishing Co., 1883), 451. Quoted in Nancy A. Hardesty, *Your Daughters Shall Prophesy: Revivalism and Feminism in the Age of Finney* (Brooklyn: Carlson Publishing, 1991), 139-40.

[31] Nancy Wooloch, *Women and the American Experience* (New York: Alfred Knopf, 1984), 337, 338.

[32] *Ibid.*, 341.

[33] Charlote Perkins Gilman, *The Home: Its Work and Influence* (New York: 1903), 165, 335.

[34] Charlotte Perkins Gilman, *With Her in Our Land*, ed. Mary Jo Deegan and Michael Hill, (1916; Westpoint, CN: Praeger, 1987), 70, 80.

[35] Carol Tavris, *The Mismeasure of Women* (New York: Simon and Schuster, 1992), 20-21, 24.

[36] Sara Evans, *Born for Liberty: A History of Women in America*, (New York: The Free Press, 1989), 222. See also *Rosie the Riveter*, an excellent film about women on the domestic front.

[37] Alan Brinkley, *The Unfinished Nation* (New York: McGraw Hill, 2000), 890

[38] Jane Tompkins, *West of Everything: The Inner Life of Westerns* (New York: Oxford University Press, 1992), 127, 128.

[39] Betty Friedan, *The Feminine Mystique* (Norton: New York, 1963). Friedan interviewed doctors, professors, marriage counselors, clinicians, psychiatrists and ministers as well as suburban women. She found evidence that the "problem with no name" had to do with the tensions between cultural standards and expectations by which most women were trying to live and the "voice inside herself" that "denies the conventional accepted truths by which she had been living."

[40] In 1964, the year of the Gulf of Tonkin resolution, there were fifteen women in Congress. Congress was 97% male.

[41] Marc Fasteau, "Vietnam and the Cult of Toughness in Foreign Policy," in *The American Man*, ed. Elizabeth Pleck and Joseph Pleck (Englewood Cliffs, NJ: Prentice Hall, 1980), 377-415. Quotations from 379, 382, 384.

[42] *Ibid.*, 398.

[43] Alice Walker, *Anything We Love Can Be Saved* (New York: Random House, 1997), 42.

[44] See Elizabeth Pleck, *Domestic Tyranny: The Making of American Social Policy against Family Violence from Colonial Times to the Present* (New York: Oxford University Press, 1987).

[45] Patrick Tracey, "Christy's Crusade," *Ms.*, April/May 2000, 53-61.

[46] Joan Biskupic, "Justices Reject Lawsuits for Rape," *The Washington Post*, 16 May 2000, A1.

[47] Fox Butterfield, "Ashcroft Supports Broad View of Gun Rights," *New York Times*, 24 May 2001, A1.

[48] Gordon Mott, "Following A Wife's Move," in *Against the Tide: Pro-Feminist Men in the United States, 1776-1990*, ed. Michael Kimmel and Thomas Mosmiller (Boston: Beacon Press, 1992), 464.

Chapter 9

[1] Richard Slotkin, "Buffalo Bill's 'Wild West' and the Mythologization of the American Empire," in *Cultures of United States Imperialism*, ed. Amy Kaplan and Donald E. Pease (Durham: Duke University Press, 1993), 168, 172-76.

[2] For a general post-Cold War survey of this phenomenon see Gabriel Kolko, *Century of War: Politics, Conflicts, and Society Since 1914* (New York: The New Press, 1994).

[3] Theodore Roosevelt, quoted in Arthur A. Ekirch, Jr., *The Civilian and the Military* (New York: Oxford University Press, 1956), 132.

[4] John Hay, London, to Theodore Roosevelt, 17 July 1898; reprinted in William Roscoe Thayer, *The Life and Letters of John Hay* (Boston and New York: Houghton Mifflin, 1915), 337.

[5] Michael Walzer, *Just and Unjust Wars: A Moral Argument with Historical Illustrations* (New York: Basic Books, 1977), 101-04.

[6] Brian McAllister Linn, *The U.S. Army and Counterinsurgency in the Philippine War, 1899-1902* (Chapel Hill: University of North Carolina Press, 1989), 155

[7] Stanley Karnow, *In Our Image: America's Empire in the Philippines* (New York: Ballantine Books, 1989), 194.

[8] Karnow, *In Our Image*, 191-94.

[9] Theodore Roosevelt, "The Strenuous Life," a speech before the Hamilton Club, Chicago, 10 April 1899, in *The Strenuous Life: Essays and Addresses* (New York: The Century Company, 1902; reprint, St. Clair Shores, MI: Scholarly Press, 1970), 15.

[10] Michael C. Robinson and Frank N. Schubert, "David Fagen: An Afro-American Rebel in the Philippines, 1899-1901," *Pacific Historical Review* (February 1975), 68-83; William B. Gatewood, *Black Americans and the White Man's Burden, 1898-1903* (Urbana: University of Illinois Press, 1975), 288-90. These two accounts of Fagen's story differ in some details.

[11] Quoted in Robert W. Rydell, *All the World's a Fair: Visions of Empire at International Expositions 1876-1916* (Chicago: University of Chicago Press, 1984), 161.

[12] Robert A. Divine et al., *America Past and Present*, 2d ed. (Glenview, IL: Scott, Foresman and Company, 1987), 628.

[13] A good overview of the voluminous literature on the Progressive Era is Arthur S. Link and Richard L. McCormick, *Progressivism* (Arlington Heights, IL: Harlan Davidson, 1983).

[14] Quoted in Michael True, *An Energy Field More Intense Than War: The Nonviolent Tradition and American Literature* (Syracuse: Syracuse University Press, 1995), 44. Twain's satirical verse, written in 1901, was not published until later.

[15] Richard E. Welch, Jr., *Response to Imperialism: The United States and the Philippine-American War, 1899-1902* (Chapel Hill: University of North Carolina Press, 1979), 43-44, 52, 70-71, 89.

[16] Merle Curti, *Peace or War: The American Struggle 1636-1936* (New York: W. W. Norton, 1936; reprint, Boston: J. S. Canner & Company, 1959), 207.

[17] William James, "The Moral Equivalent of War," in *Nonviolence in America:*

A *Documentary History,* ed. Staughton Lynd and Alice Lynd (Maryknoll, NY: Orbis Books, 1995), 65-75.

[18] Jane Addams, *Newer Ideals of Peace* (New York: The MacMillan Co., 1907; repr. Jerome S. Ozer, 1972), 236, 237.

[19] John C. Farrell, *Beloved Lady: A History of Jane Addams' Ideas on Reform and Peace* (Baltimore: Johns Hopkins, 1967), 144-45.

[20] Curti, *Peace or War*, 197.

[21] "A Pacifist in Charge of our Foreign Relations," *The Literary Digest,* May 1913, 1, cited in John Whiteclay Chambers II, *The Eagle and the Dove: The American Peace Movement and United States Foreign Policy, 1900-1922,* 2d ed. (Syracuse: Syracuse University Press, 1991), 27.

[22] Chambers, *The Eagle and the Dove,* xlii. See also Merle Eugene Curti, *Bryan and World Peace* (1931; New York: Octagon Books, 1969).

[23] For a broad summary of the issues for diplomatic history, friendly to the revisionists, see Walter LaFeber, "Liberty and Power: U.S. Diplomatic History, 1750-1945," in *The New American History,* ed. Eric Foner (Philadelphia: Temple University Press, 1990), 271-89; William Appleman Williams, *The Tragedy of American Diplomacy* (Cleveland: World Publishing Co., 1959); *The Contours of American History* (Cleveland: World Publishing Co., 1961); *The Roots of the Modern American Empire* (New York: Random House, 1969).

[24] For examples of the "organizational" or "corporatist" interpretation see Robert Wiebe, *The Search for Order* (New York: Hill and Wang, 1967); Thomas J. McCormick, "Drift or Mastery: A Corporatist Synthesis for American Diplomatic History," *Reviews in American History* 10 (December 1982): 318-29; Martin J. Sklar, *The Corporate Reconstruction of American Capitalism, 1890-1916: The Market, The Law, and Politics* (New York: Cambridge University Press, 1988).

[25] Samuel P. Huntington, "The Making of the American Military," excerpt from *The Soldier and the State: The Theory and Politics of Civil-Military Relations* (Cambridge: Belknap Press of Harvard University Press, 1957), in *The American Military: Readings in the History of the Military in American Society,* ed. Russel F. Weigley (Reading, MA: Addison-Wesley Publishing Company, 1969), 119-20, 125.

[26] See the essay by Peter Karsten, "Militarization and Rationalization in the United States, 1870-1914," in *The Militarization of the Western World,* ed. John R. Gillis (New Brunswick: Rutgers University Press, 1989), 30.

[27] Theodore Roosevelt, *The Strenuous Life,* 2, 7.

[28] Marshall Murdock editorials in *The Wichita Eagle,* May 1, and July 22, 1898

[29] Charles Chatfield, *The American Peace Movement: Ideals and Activism* (New York: Twayne Publishers, 1992), 25. On the Progressive Era peace movements see also David S. Patterson, "An Interpretation of the American Peace Movement, 1898-1914," in *Peace Movements in America,* ed. Charles Chatfield (New York: Schocken Books, 1973), 20-38; Chambers, *The Eagle and the Dove,* xxxi-lxxxvii; and Charles DeBenedetti, *The Peace Reform in American History* (Bloomington: Indiana University Press, 1980), 59-107.

[30] Melvin Small, *Was War Necessary? National Security and U.S. Entry Into War* (Beverly Hills, CA: Sage Publications, 1980), 153-214.

[31] Small, *Was War Necessary*, 210-14.

[32] LeRoy Ashby, *William Jennings Bryan: Champion of Democracy* (Boston: Twayne Publishers, 1987), 145-48.

[33] Ellis W. Hawley, *The Great War and the Search for a Modern Order: A History of the American People and Their Institutions 1917-1933* , 2d ed., (New York: St. Martin's Press, 1992), 16-30.

[34] Woodrow Wilson, "An Address to a Joint Session of Congress," 2 April 1917, in *The Papers of Woodrow Wilson*, ed. Arthur S. Link (Princeton: Princeton University Press, 1983),41: 519-27.

[35] Allen F. Davis, "Welfare, Reform and World War I," *American Quarterly* (Fall 1967): 516-33.

[36] Randolph Bourne, "Twilight of Idols," *The Seven Arts*, 2 (October 1917): 688-702, in *War and the Intellectuals: Essays by Randolph S. Bourne, 1915-1919*, ed. Carl Resek (New York: Harper & Row, 1964), 59.

[37] David M. Kennedy, *Over Here: The First World War and American Society* (New York: Oxford University Press, 1980), 52.

[38] Bourne, "Twilight of Idols," in *War*, 54.

[39] Randolph Bourne, "War and the Intellectuals," *The Seven Arts*, 2 (June 1917), 133-46, in *War and the Intellectuals*, ed. Resek, 314.

[40] Bourne, "War and the Intellectuals," 12.

[41] Charles F. Howlett, *Troubled Philosopher: John Dewey and the Struggle for World Peace* (Port Washington, NY: Kennikat Press, 1977), x, 5-7, 37.

[42] John Dewey, "What America Will Fight For," *New Republic* 18 Aug. 1917, 68-69.

[43] H. C. Peterson and Gilbert C. Fite, *Opponents of War 1917-1918* (Seattle: University of Washington Press, 1968). On the German-American wartime experience see Frederick Luebke, *Bonds of Loyalty: German-Americans and World War I* (DeKalb, IL: Northern Illinois University Press, 1974).

[44] James C. Juhnke, *Vision, Doctrine, War: Mennonite Identity and Organization in America, 1890-1930* (Scottdale, PA: Herald Press, 1989), 236-37, 238, 240; Daniel R. Beaver, *Newton D. Baker and the American War Effort 1917-1919* (Lincoln: University of Nebraska Press, 1969), 231-39.

[45] James C. Juhnke, "Mob Violence and Kansas Mennonites in 1918," *Kansas Historical Quarterly* 43 (1977): 334-50.

[46] Ray H. Abrams, *Preachers Present Arms* (New York: Round Table Press, 1933). For a positive view of organized church agency work during the war, see John Piper, Jr., *The American Churches in World War I* (Athens, OH: Ohio University Press, 1985).

[47] Lyman Abbott, "To Love is to Hate," *The Outlook* 15 May 1918, 99, quoted in Abrams, *Preachers Present Arms*, 110.

[48] Kennedy, *Over Here*, 59-88.

[49] William Gibbs McAdoo, *Crowded Years: The Reminiscences of William G. McAdoo* (Boston: Houghton Mifflin, 1931), 378-79, quoted in Kennedy, *Over Here*, 105.

[50] Cited in John Whiteclay Chambers II, *To Raise an Army: The Draft Comes to Modern America* (New York: The Free Press, 1987), 165, 266-67.

[51] David D. Lee, *Sergeant York: An American Hero* (Lexington: University Press of Kentucky, 1985), 47; Nat Brandt, "Sergeant York," *American Heritage* 33 (Aug./Sept. 1981): 56-64.

[52] Quoted in Kennedy, *Over Here*, 212.

[53] Jane Addams, "Patriotism and Pacifists in War Time," *The City Club Bulletin* 10 (16 June 1917); reprinted together with *Peace and Bread in Time of War*, intro. by Blanche Wiesen Cook (New York: Garland Publishing, 1972), 21.

[54] *The Papers of Woodrow Wilson*, ed. Arthur S. Link (Princeton: Princeton University Press, 1982), 40:533-39.

[55] Carl von Clausewitz, *On War* , ed. and trans. Michael Howard and Peter Paret (Princeton: Princeton University Press, 1976), 69.

[56] Thomas J. Knock, *To End All Wars: Woodrow Wilson and the Quest for a New World Order* (New York: Oxford University Press, 1992), viii-x.

[57] John Dewey, "The Future of Pacifism," *New Republic*, 28 July 1917, 358. On Dewey's pacifist impulses see Alan Ryan, *John Dewey and the High Tide of American Liberalism* (New York: W. W. Norton, 1995), 29, 157.

[58] George F. Kennan, *American Diplomacy, 1900-1950* (Chicago: University of Chicago Press, 1951), 66.

Chapter 10

[1] Studs Terkel, *"The Good War": An Oral History of World War Two* (New York: Pantheon Books, 1984), vi. Terkel's ironic label provided an image for many interpretive essays which contrasted the positive and negative results of the war. See, for example, Richard Polenberg, "The Good War? A Reappraisal of How World War II Affected American Society," *The Virginia Magazine of History and Biography* 100 (July 1992): 295-322; Ken Brown, "Was the 'Good War' a Just War?" in *Nonviolent America: History Through the Eyes of Peace*, ed. Louise Hawkley and James C. Juhnke (North Newton, KS: Bethel College, 1993), 88-103; and Roger Daniels, "Bad News from the Good War: Democracy at Home During World War II," in *The Home-Front War: World War II and American Society*, ed. Kenneth Paul O'Brien and Lynn Hudson Parsons (Westport, CN: Greenwood Press, 1995), 157-72. On the other hand are many books which celebrate the experience of war without irony, such as Tom Brokaw, *The Greatest Generation* (New York: Random House, 1998).

[2] www.washingtonpost.com/ac2/wp-dyn/a5988-2000

[3] Paul Fussell has suggested that the *Why We Fight* series did not answer the question of its title so much as foster emotional hatred of the enemy. Paul Fussell, *Wartime: Understanding and Behavior in the Second World War* (New York: Oxford University Press, 1989), 138.

[4] David S. Wyman, *The Abandonment of the Jews: America and the Holocaust, 1941-1945* (New York: Pantheon Books, 1984), 311-30.

⁵ Clayton R. Koppes and Gregory D. Black, *Hollywood Goes to War: How Politics, Profits and Propaganda Shaped World War II Movies* (New York: Free Press, 1987).

⁶ Daniels, "Bad News from the Good War," 163; Robert C. Mikesh, *Japan's World War II Balloon Bomb Attacks on North America* (Washington D.C.: Smithsonian Institution Press, 1973).

⁷ William L. O'Neill, *A Democracy at War: America's Fight at Home and Abroad in World War II* (New York: The Free Press, 1993), 433-34.

⁸ See the final chapter, "The Cost and Impact of War," in Gerhard L. Weinberg, *A World At Arms: A Global History of World War II* (Cambridge, England: Cambridge University Press, 1994), 894-920.

⁹ Eric Markusen and David Kopf, *The Holocaust and Strategic Bombing: Genocide and Total War in the Twentieth Century* (Boulder, CO: Westview Press, 1995), 1-2.

¹⁰ Bartholomew H. Sparrow, *From the Outside In: World War II and the American State* (Princeton: Princeton University Press, 1996), 3-6.

¹¹ Ivan J. Kaufman, "Democracy, Nonviolence and the American Experience," in *Nonviolent America*, 223-26.

¹² On the tensions between American democratic ideals and centralized state sovereignty in wartime, see Bruce D. Porter, *War and the Rise of the State: The Military Foundations of Modern Politics* (New York: The Free Press, 1994), 243-96.

¹³ See the Schowalter Oral History collection on Conscientious Objectors in World War II at Bethel College, North Newton, Kansas; Al Keim, *The CPS Story: An Illustrated History of Civilian Public Service* (Intercourse, PA: Good Books, 1990). Some leaders of the historic peace churches and the Fellowship of Reconciliation approved the nonpayment of alternative service workers to ensure the independence of the CPS programs from the government's war effort and to require an appropriate sacrifice and self-denial in wartime. See A. J. Muste, *The World Task of Pacifism* (Pendle Hill Pamphlet, 1941), in *The Essays of A. J. Muste*, ed. Nat Hentoff (Indianapolis: Bobbs-Merrill, 1967), 232.

¹⁴ Quoted in Page Smith, *Democracy on Trial: The Japanese American Evacuation and Relocation in World War II* (New York: Simon & Schuster: 1995), 117.

¹⁵ Quoted in Jacobus tenBroek et al., *Prejudice, War and the Constitution* (Berkeley: University of California Press, 1968), 83-84.

¹⁶ Roger Daniels, *Concentration Camps USA: Japanese Americans and World War II* (New York: Holt, Rinehart and Winston, 1972), xi, 70, 72-73, 95, 130.

¹⁷ Peter Ota, oral interview by Studs Terkel, in Terkel, *"The Good War ,"* 30.

¹⁸ Daniels, *Concentration Camps*, 114.

¹⁹ *Ibid.*, 75.

²⁰ E. B. Sledge, *With the Old Breed at Peleliu and Okinawa* (Novato, CA: Presidio Press, 1981), 34; Terkel, *"The Good War,"* 61-62.

²¹ S. L. A. Marshall, *Men Against Fire: The Problem of Battle Command in Future War* (Gloucester, MA: Peter Smith, 1978).

²² Porter, *War*, xiii-xiv.

²³ Franklin D. Roosevelt, "The President Appeals to Great Britain, France, Italy, Germany, and Poland to Refrain from Air Bombing of Civilians," 1 September 1939, in *The Public Papers and Addresses of Franklin D. Roosevelt*, vol. 8,

War and Neutrality, 1939 (1941; New York: Russell & Russell, 1969), 454.

[24] Michael Walzer, *Just and Unjust Wars: A Moral Argument with Historical Illustrations* (New York: Basic Books, 1977), 42.

[25] For description and analysis of American strategic bombing in World War II, see Ronald Schaffer, *Wings of Judgement: American Bombing in World War II* (New York: Oxford University Press, 1985); and Conrad C. Crane, *Bombs, Cities, and Civilians: American Airpower Strategy in World War II* (Lawrence, KS: University Press of Kansas, 1993).

[26] Lee Kennett, *A History of Strategic Bombing* (New York: Charles Scribner's Sons, 1982), 129, 142-62, 185.

[27] Markusen and Kopf, *The Holocaust and Strategic Bombing*, 161-62.

[28] Jeffery S. Underwood, review of *America's Pursuit of Precision Bombing, 1910-1945*, by Stephen L. McFarland, *Journal of American History* 82 (March 1996), 1610.

[29] Markusen and Kopf, *The Holocaust and Strategic Bombing*, 180.

[30] Michael Walzer, *Just and Unjust Wars*, 251-68, developed a moral argument to justify mass bombing of civilians in urban areas in cases of "extreme emergency," which, for Walzer, did not include the bombings of Dresden or Hiroshima. For a critique of Walzer, see Brown, "'The Good War'," 96-103.

[31] The continuing relevance of the "principle of discrimination" between combatants and noncombatants was observed in the 1991 Persian Gulf War when the United States committed itself to a strategy of precision bombing, so the killing of many Iraqi civilians in the Amiriya bunker became highly controversial. See Crane, *Bombs, Cities, and Civilians*, 154-59.

[32] Richard H. Minear, "Atomic Holocaust, Nazi Holocaust: Some Reflections," *Diplomatic History* 19 (Spring 1995): 347-65.

[33] On the question of the uniqueness of the Holocaust, see Alan Rosenberg and Evelyn Silverman, "The Issue of the Holocaust as a Unique Event," in *Genocide in Our Time: An Annotated Bibliography with Analytical Introductions*, ed. Michael N. Dobkowski and Isidor Wallimann (Ann Arbor, MI: Pierian Press, 1992), 47-65.

[34] The literature on the use of atomic weapons is extensive. In 1995 two major studies reviewed the evidence and issues from opposing viewpoints. Against the use of the bombs was Gar Alperovitz, *The Decision to Use the Atomic Bomb and the Architecture of an American Myth* (New York: Alfred A. Knopf, 1995). Justifying the bombs was Robert James Maddox, *Weapons for Victory: The Hiroshima Decision Fifty Years Later* (Columbia: University of Missouri Press, 1995).

[35] The U. S. government's postwar "Strategic Bombing Survey" concluded that Japan would have surrendered before 1 November 1945, "even if the atomic bombs had not been dropped, even if Russia had not entered the war, and even if no invasion had been planned." See The United States Strategic Bombing Survey, *Japan's Struggle to End the War* (Washington D.C.: 1946), 13. For a brief summary of the issues see William E. Juhnke, Jr., "Teaching the Atomic Bomb: The Greatest Thing in History," in *Nonviolent America*, 108-12.

[36] Quoted in Alperovitz, *The Decision*, 233, 238.

[37] Gar Alperovitz in two books, *Atomic Diplomacy: Hiroshima and Potsdam;*

The Use of the Atomic Bomb and the American Confrontation with Soviet Power (New York: Simon and Schuster, 1965), and *The Decision* (1995), has argued that a primary American motive for dropping the bombs was to gain relative advantage against the Soviet Union in postwar diplomatic relations. The view that use of the bombs was not much of a decision is stated by Barton J. Bernstein, "Understanding the Atomic Bomb and the Japanese Surrender," *Diplomatic History* 19 (Spring 1995): 227-74.

[38] Robert E. Conot, *Justice at Nuremberg* (New York: Harper & Row, 1983).

[39] For a brief summary of the question of Hirohito's guilt, see the introduction by Sir William Flood Webb, leader of the Tokyo International Military Tribunal, in David Bergamini, *Japan's Imperial Conspiracy* (New York: William Morrow and Company, 1971), ix-xiv. Bergamini argues that Hirohito was deeply involved in Japanese politics and war decisions. See also Phillip R. Piccagallo, *The Japanese on Trial: Allied War Crimes Operations in the East, 1945-1951* (Austin: University of Texas Press, 1979); and Richard H. Minear, *Victors' Justice: The Tokyo War Crimes Trial* (Princeton: Princeton University Press, 1971), 110-17. Brigadier General Telford Taylor, a key figure at the Nuremburg trial, has written that the air attacks were not regarded as war crimes because "there were no recognized laws of war pertaining to aerial bombardments during World War II," in Taylor, *The Anatomy of the Nuremberg Trials: A Personal Memoir* (New York: Alfred A. Knopf, 1992), 640.

[40] Haruko Taya Cook and Theodore F. Cook, *Japan at War: An Oral History* (New York: The New Press, 1992), 15.

[41] Saburo Ienaga, *The Pacific War: World War II and the Japanese, 1931-1945: A Critical Perspective on Japan's Role in World War II* (New York: Pantheon Books, 1978), 256.

[42] Cook and Cook, *Japan at War*, 16n. In 1994, at age 81 and after a 31-year-court battle, Ienaga was vindicated by a Tokyo High Court ruling. See "Scholar Wins Ruling on Nanjing Massacre," *New York Times*, 13 May 1994, A3.

[43] Charles Smith, "Sort of Sorry: War-Apology Resolution Falls Short, Upsets Many," *Far Eastern Economic Review*, 22 June 1995, 21; Ustinia Dolgopol, "Women's Voices, Women's Pain," *Human Rights Quarterly* 17 (1995): 127-54.

[44] T. R. Reid, "Regrets and Resistance: In Japan, Some Lessons of World War II Are Still Hard to Learn," *The Washington Post*, 28 August 1994, C2.

[45] For characterizations of the scholarly consensus that use of the atomic bombs was not warranted by military necessity, see J. Samuel Walker, "The Decision to Use the Bomb: A Historiographical Update," *Diplomatic History* 14 (Winter 1990): 110; and Minear, "Atomic Holocaust, Nazi Holocaust," 360. This viewpoint, and an analysis of the roots of the rationale for the bombings are covered most extensively in Gar Alperovitz, *The Decision to Use the Atomic Bomb*. Among the general or popular histories which do justify the bombs are the following: David McCullough, *Truman* (New York: Simon & Schuster, 1992); O'Neill, *A Democracy at War*, 416-422; and Weinberg, *A World At Arms*, 888-91.

[46] John R. Dichtl, "A Chronology of the Smithsonian's 'Last Act'," *OAH Newsletter* November 1994, 9; "Enola Gay Controversy Continues," *OAH Newsletter*, February 1995, 3.

[47] *Enola Gay: The First Atomic Mission,* produced and directed by Jonathan S. Felt, 16:34 min., The Greenwich Workshop, Inc., 1995, videocasette.

[48] David Awbrey, "Thank God for the Bomb," in *Nonviolent America,* 124-26.

[49] On the differences between isolationists and pacifists see Lawrence S. Wittner, *Rebels Against War: The American Peace Movement, 1941-1960* (New York: Columbia University Press, 1969), 24-30; and Justus D. Doenecke, *Storm on the Horizon: The Challenge to American Intervention, 1939-1941* (Lanham: Rowman & Littlefield, 2000).

[50] Manfred Jonas, *Isolationism in America, 1935-1941* (Ithaca, NY: Cornell University Press, 1966).

[51] Melvin Small, *Was War Necessary? National Security and U.S. Entry Into War* (Beverly Hills: Sage Publications, 1980), 215-67.

[52] A. J. Muste, *Nonviolence in an Aggressive World* (New York: Harper & Brothers, 1940), 157-61; Muste, "Where are We Going?" (1941) in *The Essays of A. J. Muste,* 252.

[53] Dorothy Day, "Our Stand," *The Catholic Worker,* June 1940, 1, 4. Quoted by Eileen Egan, "Dorothy Day: Pilgrim of Peace," in *A Revolution of the Heart: Essays on* The Catholic Worker, ed. Patrick G. Coy (Philadelphia: Temple University Press, 1988), 80.

[54] Milton S. Mayer, "I Think I'll Sit This One Out," *The Saturday Evening Post,* October 1939, cited in *Instead of Violence: Writings by the Great Advocates of Peace and Nonviolence Throughout History,* ed. Arthur and Lila Weinberg (New York: Grossman Publishers, 1963), 163.

[55] Doenecke, *Storm on the Horizon,* 212.

Chapter 11

[1] Vincent Harding, *Hope and History: Why we Must Share the Story of the Movement* (Maryknoll, NY: Orbis Books, 1990), 106-07.

[2] Ellen Levine, *Freedom's Children: Young Civil Rights Activists Tell Their Own Stories* (New York: Avon Books, 1993), 59.

[3] John M. Glen, *Highlander: No Ordinary School, 1932-1962* (Lexington: University of Kentucky, 1988).

[4] Aldon D. Morris, *The Origins of the Civil Rights Movement: Black Communities Organizing for Change* (New York: Free Press, 1984) 41; Thomas R. West and James W. Mooney, *To Redeem a Nation: A History and Anthology of the Civil Rights Movement* (St. James, NY: Brandywine Press, 1993), 149.

[5] Howell Raines, *My Soul is Rested: Movement Days in the Deep South Remembered* (New York: G.P. Putnam's Sons, 1977), 60-66.

[6] Raines, *My Soul is Rested,* 65.

[7] Ella Baker, "Developing Community Leadership," *Black Women in White America: A Documentary History,* ed. Gerald Lerner (New York: Pantheon, 1972), 351.

[8] West and Mooney, *To Redeem a Nation,* 92.

[9] Eric Burner, *And Gently He Shall Lead Them: Robert Parris Moses and Civil Rights in Mississippi* (New York: New York University, 1994). 114.

[10] Seth Cagin and Philip Dray, *We Are Not Afraid* (New York: Macmillan, 1998), 353.

[11] Cagin and Dray, 30.

[12] Richard Kluger, *Simple Justice: History of Brown Versus Board of Education* (New York: Knopf, 1976).

[13] Morris, *The Origins*, 31; Charles Kellogg Flint, *A History of the National Association for the Advancement of Colored People* (Baltimore: Johns Hopkins Press, 1967).

[14] James Washington, ed., *Testament of Hope: Essential Writings of Martin Luther King* (San Francisco: Harper and Row, 1986), 43-53; West and Mooney, *To Redeem a Nation*, 111-15.

[15] Lewis W. Jones, "Fred L. Shuttlesworth: Indigenous Leader," in *Birmingham, Alabama, 1956-1963*, vol. 8 of *Martin Luther King, Jr., and the Civil Rights Movement*, ed. David J. Garrow (Brooklyn NY: Carlson, 1989), 138.

[16] Glenn T. Eskew, "The Alabama Christian Movement for Human Rights and the Birmingham Struggle for Human Rights, 1956-1963," in *Birmingham*, 75.

[17] Martin Luther King, Jr., *Why We Can't Wait* (New York: New American Library, 1963), 100.

[18] Howard Zinn, *SNCC: The New Abolitionists* (Boston: Beacon Press, 1965), 34

[19] Morris, *The Origins*, 131.

[20] James Farmer, *Lay Bare the Heart: An Autobiography of the Civil Rights Movement* (New York: Arbor House, 1986), 194.

[21] Raines, *My Soul is Rested*, 121.

[22] Levine, *Freedom's Children*, 54.

[23] King, *Why We Can't Wait*, 85.

[24] Morris, *The Origins*, 268

[25] Levine, *Freedom's Children*, 107.

[26] King, *Why We Can't Wait*, 101.

[27] Farmer, *Lay Bare the Heart*, 247.

[28] *Ibid.*, 246-54.

[29] Anne Moody, *Coming of Age in Missippi* (New York: Dial Press, 1968), 254.

[30] "Letter to King," *New Leader*, 24/6 (1963): 5.

[31] King, *Why We Can't Wait*, 84.

[32] Raines, *My Soul is Rested*, 285.

[33] Stephan Lesher, *George Wallace: American Populist* (New York: Addison-Wesley, 1994), 174.

[34] *Ibid.*, 182.

[35] *Ibid.*, 174.

[36] Raines, *My Soul is Rested*, 285.

[37] *Report of the National Advisory Commission on Civil Disorders* (New York: E. P. Dutton, 1968), 10.

[38] *Report of the National Advisory Commission*, 10.

[39] Morris, *The Origins*, 287.

[40] Nathan Rutstein, *Healing Racism* (Springfield, MA: Whitcomb Publishing, 1993), 163.

[41] June Cross and Henry Louis Gates, "The Two Nations of Black America," PBS *Frontline* program, 1998.

[42] King, *Why We Can't Wait*, 77.

[43] Pam McAllister, *You Can't Kill the Spirit* (Philadelphia, PA: New Society Publishers, 1988), 5.

Chapter 12

[1] George F. Kennan, *American Diplomacy, 1900-1950* (New York: New American Library Mentor Book, 1951), 66. David Halberstam has called Kennan's book "one of the most influential books of an entire generation," in *The Best and the Brightest* (Greenwich, CN: Fawcett Crest Book, 1972), 134.

[2] Kennan, *American Diplomacy*, 77.

[3] George F. Kennan, "America's Far-Eastern Policy at the Height of the Cold War," in his *At a Century's Ending: Reflections, 1982-1995* (New York: W. W. Norton, 1996), 110-15.

[4] Robert H. Johnson, *Improbable Dangers: U.S. Conceptions of Threat in the Cold War and After* (New York: St. Martin's Press, 1994), 3.

[5] Vladislav Zubok and Constantine Pleshakov, *Inside the Kremlin's Cold War: From Stalin to Khrushchev* (Cambridge: Harvard University Press, 1966), 2-7.

[6] U. S. Bureau of the Census, *Historical Statistics of the United States: Colonial Times to 1957* (Washington, D.C.: U.S. Government Printing Office, 1960), 736.

[7] Michael S. Sherry, *In the Shadow of War: The United States Since the 1930s* (New Haven: Yale University Press, 1995), 130.

[8] Frank Kofsky, *Harry S. Truman and the War Scare of 1948: A Successful Campaign to Deceive the Nation* (New York: St. Martin's, 1993).

[9] Eric F. Goldman, *The Crucial Decade and After: America, 1945-1960* (New York: Vintage Books, 1960), 91-112.

[10] Johnson, *Improbable Dangers*, 1.

[11] Stephen E. Ambrose, *Rise to Globalism: American Foreign Policy Since 1938*, 4th ed., (New York: Penguin Books, 1985), 131.

[12] Zubok and Pleshakov, *Inside the Kremlin's Cold War*, 39-40.

[13] Graham White and John Maze, *Henry A. Wallace: His Search for a New World Order* (Chapel Hill: University of North Carolina Press, 1995), ix. See also J. Samuel Walker, *Henry A. Wallace and American Foreign Policy* (Westport, CN: Greenwood Press, 1976).

[14] Robert A. Garson, *The Democratic Party and the Politics of Sectionalism, 1941-1948* (Baton Rouge, LA: Louisiana State University Press, 1974), 106.

[15] Henry Wallace published some wartime speeches and essays in *The Century of the Common Man*, ed. Russell Lord (New York: Reynal & Hitchcock, 1943). See *Prefaces to Peace: A Symposium* (New York: Simon and Schuster, 1943), 390, 400, 407.

[16] Kennan, *At a Century's Ending*, 110-15, 129-33.

[17] Norman D. Markowitz, *The Rise and Fall of the People's Century: Henry A. Wallace and American Liberalism, 1941-1948* (New York: Free Press, 1973), 327-28.

[18] Peter W. Rodman, *More Precious Than Peace: The Cold War and the Struggle for the Third World* (New York: Charles Scribner's Sons, 1994), 3.

[19] George McT. Kahin, *Intervention: How America Became Involved in Vietnam* (New York: Alfred A. Knopf, 1986), 92.

[20] William J. Duiker, *Vietnam: Revolution in Transition*, 2d ed. (Boulder: Westview Press, 1995), 205-10.

[21] Rodman, *More Precious*, 8.

[22] Sherry, *In the Shadow of War*, ix-xii.

[23] For contrasting views of Eisenhower's military and peace contributions, see Blanche Wiesen Cook, "Dwight David Eisenhower: Antimilitarist in the White House," *Forums in History* (St. Charles, MO: Forum Press, 1974); and H. W. Brands, "The Age of Vulnerability: Eisenhower and the National Insecurity State," *American Historical Review* 94 (1989): 963-89

[24] Fred J. Cook, *The Warfare State* (New York: Macmillan, 1962).

[25] Paul Boyer, *By the Bomb's Early Light: American Thought and Culture at the Dawn of the Atomic Age*, 2d ed. (Chapel Hill: University of North Carolina Press, 1985).

[26] Robert Jay Lifton and Greg Mitchell, *Hiroshima in America: Fifty Years of Denial* (New York: G. P. Putnam's Sons, 1995), 337-39.

[27] *The Bulletin of the Atomic Scientists* (June 1947), cover.

[28] Mike Moore, "Midnight Never Came," *The Bulletin of the Atomic Scientists*, Nov./Dec. 1995, 16-27; Mike Moore, "14 Minutes to Nuclear Midnight," *The Chronicle of Higher Education*, 5 April 1996, A52; "Doomsday Clock moves up," *The Wichita Eagle*, 12 June 1998, 3A.

[29] Charles DeBenedetti, *The Peace Reform in American History* (Bloomington: Indiana University Press, 1980), 138.

[30] Alice Kimball Smith, *A Peril and a Hope: The Scientists' Movement in America, 1945-47* (Chicago: The University of Chicago Press, 1965).

[31] "The Franck Committee: Report on the Atomic Bomb," in *Peace/Mir: An Anthology of Historic Alternatives to War*, ed. Charles Chatfield and Ruzanna Ilukhina (Syracuse, NY: Syracuse University Press, 1994), 304-06.

[32] Thomas Hager, *Force of Nature: The Life of Linus Pauling* (New York: Simon and Schuster, 1995).

[33] Bradford Lyttle, *You Come With Naked Hands: The Story of the San Francisco to Moscow March for Peace* (Raymond, NH: Greenleaf Books, 1966), 52-54.

[34] See the excellent overview and analysis of the peace movement in Charles Chatfield, *The American Peace Movement: Ideals and Activism* (New York: Twayne Publishers, 1992), 165-85.

[35] Amy Swerdlow, *Women Strike for Peace, Traditional Motherhood and Radical Politics in the 1960s* (Chicago: University of Chicago Press, 1993), 111

[36] Harriet Hyman Alonso, *Peace as a Women's Issue: A History of the U.S. Movement for World Peace and Women's Rights* (Syracuse, NY: Syracuse University Press, 1993), 204-07.

[37] Melvin Small, *Johnson, Nixon, and the Doves* (New Brunswick, NJ: Rutgers University Press, 1988), 225-34. See also Charles DeBenedetti and Charles Chatfield, *An American Ordeal: The Antiwar Movement of the Vietnam Era* (Syracuse, NY: Syracuse University Press, 1990), 399-400, 406-408.

[38] Lawrence S. Wittner, "The Reagan Administration and Nuclear Disarmament: New Light on a Contested Issue," paper presented at the American Historical Association, Chicago, 8 January 2000.

[39] The fullest account is Raymond L. Garthoff, *The Great Transition: American-Soviet Relations and the End of the Cold War* (Washington, D.C.: The Brookings Institution, 1994).

[40] Frances Fitzgerald, *Way Out There in the Blue: Reagan, Star Wars and the End of the Cold War* (New York: Simon & Schuster, 2000), 314-69.

[41] John Lewis Gaddis, *The United States and the End of the Cold War: Implications, Reconsiderations, Provocations* (New York: Oxford University Press, 1992), 155-67.

[42] Peter Schweizer, *Victory: The Reagan Administration's Secret Strategy that Hastened the Collapse of the Soviet Union* (New York: Atlantic Monthly Press, 1994); Jay Winik, *On the Brink: The Dramatic, Behind-the-Scenes Saga of the Reagan Era and the Men and Women Who Won the Cold War* (New York: Simon & Schuster, 1996).

[43] Garthoff, *The Great Transition*, 505.

[44] Fitzgerald, *Way Out There*, 474.

[45] This thesis is developed at length by Matthew Evangelista, *Unarmed Forces: The Transnational Movement to End the Cold War* (Ithaca, NY: Cornell University Press, 1999).

[46] David Cortright, *Peace Works: The Citizen's Role in Ending the Cold War* (Boulder, CO: Westview Press, 1993), 199.

[47] *The Christian Science Monitor*, 20 April 2000, 24.

[48] The Korea statistic is from Lloyd Gardner, "Korea's Martyrdom: The Unlimited 'Limited War'," *Reviews in American History* 24 (June 1996), 322. The Vietnam statistic is from Gloria Emerson, *Winners & Losers: Battles, Retreats, Gains, Losses, and Ruins from the Vietnam War* (New York: W. W. Norton, 1992), inside front cover.

[49] Data from Center for Defense Information.

[50] Edward Pessen, *Losing Our Souls: The American Experience in the Cold War* (Chicago: Ivan R. Dee, 1993), 11.

[51] Kennan, *American Diplomacy*, 77.

Chapter 13

[1] William Thomas, *Scorched Earth: the Military's Assault on the Environment* (Philadelphia: New Society Publishers, 1995), 31.

[2] Arthur Westing, *Cultural Norms, War and the Environment* (Oxford: Oxford University Press, 1988), 1.

[3] Annie Booth and Harvey Jacobs, "Ties That Bind: Native American Beliefs as a Foundation for Environmental Consciousness," *Environmental Ethics* 12 (Spring 1990): 32.

[4] Booth and Jacobs, "Ties that Bind," 34.

[5] *Ibid.*, 27.

[6] Shepard Krech III, *The Ecological Indian, Myth and History* (New York: W. W. Norton & Company, 1999), 76-77, 122, 133.

[7] Bill Devall and George Sessions, *Deep Ecology: Living As If Nature Mattered* (Salt Lake City: Peregrine Smith Books, 1985); Kirkpatrick Sale, "Deep Ecology and its Critics," *The Nation*, 14 May 1988, 670-75.

⁸ Cited in Benjamin Kline, *First Along the River: A Brief History of the U.S. Environmental Movement*, 2d ed. (San Francisco: Acada Books, 2000), 20.

⁹ Donald Worster, *Nature's Economy*, 2d ed. (New York: Cambridge University Press, 1994), 59-76.

¹⁰ Philip Shabecoff, *A Fierce Green Fire: The American Environmental Movement* (New York: Hill and Wang, 1993), 53.

¹¹ Russell F. Weigley, *The American Way of War: A History of United States Military Strategy and Policy* (Bloomington: Indiana University Press, 1977).

¹² Gifford Pinchot, *Breaking New Ground* (New York: Harcourt, Brace, 1947), 103; cited in Patricia Nelson Limerick, *The Legacy of Conquest: The Unbroken Past of the American West* (New York: W. W. Norton & Company, 1987), 293-94.

¹³ Shabecoff, *Fierce Green Fire*, 71.

¹⁴ Cited in Stephen Fox, *John Muir and His Legacy* (Boston: Little, Brown and Company, 1981), 144.

¹⁵ H. W. Brands, *T. R.: The Last Romantic* (New York: Basic Books, 1997), 621-25.

¹⁶ Nathan Miller, *Theodore Roosevelt: A Life* (New York: William Morrow and Company, 1992), 472.

¹⁷ Stephen Fox, cited in Shabecoff, *Fierce Green Fire*, 4.

¹⁸ Riley E. Dunlap and Angela G. Mertig, "The Evolution of the U.S. Environmental Movement from 1970 to 1990: An Overview," in *American Environmentalism: The U.S. Environmental Movement, 1970-1990*, ed. Dunlap and Mertig (Philadelphia: Taylor & Francis, 1992), 1-10.

¹⁹ Robert Gottlieb, *Forcing the Spring: The Transformation of the American Environmental Movement* (Washington, D.C.: Island Press, 1993), 109; Kirkpatrick Sale, *The Green Revolution* (New York: Hill and Wang, 1993), 26.

²⁰ James William Gibson, "Revising Vietnam, Again," *Harpers Magazine*, April 2000, 83.

²¹ Sale, *The Green Revolution*, 33,80. The figures for the National Wildlife Federation may have been inflated by including periodical subscribers.

²² Andrew Szasz, *Ecopopulism: Toxic Waste and the Movement for Environmental Justice* (Minneapolis: University of Minnesota Press, 1994), 160-61.

²³ *Environment and Development in the USA: A Grassroots Report for UNCED*, compiled by the Community and Environmental Health Program of the Highlander Research and Education Center. (Washburn, TN: Highlander Research and Education Center, n.d.).

²⁴ Robert D. Bullard and Beverly H. Wright, "The Quest for Environmental Equity: Mobilizing the African American Community for Social Change," in *American Environmentalism*, ed. Dunlap and Mertig, 39-49

²⁵ Kathlyn Gay, *Pollution and the Powerless* (New York: Franklin Watts, 1994), 25.

²⁶ Seth Shulman, *The Threat at Home: Confronting the Toxic Legacy of the U.S. Military* (Boston: Beacon Press, 1992), 7; Susan D. Lanier-Graham, *The Ecology of War: Environmental Impacts of Weaponry and Warfare* (New York: Walker and Company, 1993).

²⁷ Shulman, *The Threat*, 24-25.

²⁸ *Ibid.*, 115-25.

²⁹ Gregg Easterbrook, *A Moment on the Earth: The Coming Age of Environ-*

mental Optimism (New York: Viking, 1995), 526.
    [30] Lanier-Graham, *The Ecology of War*, 104.
    [31] Jonathan Schell, *The Fate of the Earth* (New York: Knopf, 1982).
    [32] Robert S. Norris and William M. Arkin, "U.S. Nuclear Forces, 2001," *The Bulletin of the Atomic Scientists*, March/April 2001, 78.
    [33] Stephen I. Schwartz, "Outmaneuvered, Outgunned, and Out of View," *The Bulletin of the Atomic Scientists* 55 (January/February 1999): 24-31.
    [34] David E. Ortman, e-mail message to the author, 29 April 2000.
    [35] "Major Global Trends, 1970 to 2000," *World Watch Earth Day 2000*, March/April 2000, 10-13.
    [36] Jim Motavelli, "Flying High, Swooping Low: Assessing the Environmental Movement at the Close of the 'E Decade,'" *E Magazine*, January/February 2000, 32.
    [37] David E. Ortman, e-mail message to the author, 28 April 2000.

Epilogue

    [1] Richard Maxwell Brown, "Overview of Violence in the United States," *Violence in America: an Encyclopedia*, ed. Ronald Gottesman (New York: Charles Scribner's Sons, 1999), 1.
    [2] Howard Zinn, "Unsung Heroes," *The Progressive*, 1 June 2000, 16.
    [3] Geoffrey Perret, *A Country Made by War: From the Revolution to Vietnam, The Story of America's Rise to Power* (New York: Random House, 1989).
    [4] Charles Chatfield, "Nonviolence and United States History: Insofar As," in *Nonviolent America: History through the Eyes of Peace*, ed. Louise Hawkley and James C. Junke (North Newton, KS: Bethel College, 1993), 259.
    [5] Vincent Harding, *Hope and History: Why we Must Share the Story of the Movement* (Maryknoll, NY: Orbis Books, 1990). See especially chapter five, "'God's Appeal to This Age': The Search for Alternatives to Violence," 91-104.

Index

A

Abbott, Lyman 191
Adams, Abigail 155-156
Adams, Charles Francis 112
Adams, John 62-64, 155-156
Adams, John Quincy 93
Addams, Jane 150, 167, 182, 193-194
Aguinaldo, Emilio 177
Alexie, Sherman 15
American Colonization Society 82
American Federation of Labor 145-146
American Peace Society 181
Anderson, Elijah 99-100
Andros, Gov. Edmund 24
Anti-Imperialist League 181
Anti-slavery 78-102
Atomic bombs 207-209, 246, 264-265
Augustus, Caesar 11

B

Baker, Ella 218
Baker, Newton D. 190-191
Baldwin, James 10

Ballou, Adin 11, 89
Barton, Clara 120
Billups, Charles 227-228
Birney, James 93
Black Codes 130
Black Kettle 30, 33
Blackford, Mary Berkeley Minor 83-84
Boston Tea Party 38, 43, 112
Bourne, Randolph 189-190
Bradford, Gov. William 17
Breckinridge, Robert J. 82
Brent, Linda 91
Brown, Charles Brockden 60
Bryan, William Jennings 181, 183-184, 187-188, 272
Buffum, Elizabeth 79
Burke, Edmund 38-39
Butler, Benjamin F. 129

C

Canada 26, 36, 50, 67, 74, 86, 96, 100
Capitalism 139-154
Capper, Arthur 191

Capra, Frank 198
Carnegie, Andrew 181-182
"Caroline," escaped slave 100
Carson, Rachel 260
Carter, Jimmy 263
Catt, Carrie Chapman 180
Central Intelligence Agency 243-244
Chosen People 35, 44
Church of the Brethren 250
Churchill, Winston 106-107
Civil Rights Movement 215-234
Classical Republicanism 56-58
Clay, Henry 67, 70, 82, 93-94
Cody, William 175
Cold War 235-254
Coffin, Levi 98
Colonization (of blacks) 82-84
Communitarianism 88-91
Condolence ceremony 20
Congress of Racial Equality 219, 226-227
Connor, Eugene "Bull" 227-228
Conscientious objectors 116, 190-191, 203, 250
Conscription 192
Continental Congress 40-41, 42
Cooper, James Fenimore 60-61
Cornish, Samuel E. 86, 92
Counterfactual history 41, 73-74, 106-108, 111, 135, 240-241
Crazy Horse 15
Crittenden, John J. 111-112
Cuba 176-177
Cultural survival 32
Custer, George Armstrong 30

D
Davis, Caleb 96
Davis, Jefferson 114

Day, Dorothy 11, 212-213
Debs, Eugene 151
Declaration of Independence 35, 142, 163
Deganawidah 18-21, 161
Democracy 50, 55, 203-205, 219-221
Dennis, Matthew 20
Denominations 55
Dewey, John 180, 189-190, 196
Direct action 91-94
Dix, Dorothea 120
Doddridge, Joseph 82
Donnelly, Ignatius 152
Douglass, Frederick 78, 85, 92, 98
Dream Dance cult 32
DuBois, W. E. B. 126
Dueling 70
Dunmore, Earl of 48
Duty to retreat 58-59, 121

E
Edwards, Jonathan 44
Einstein, Albert 10
Eisenhower, Dwight D. 11, 244-245
Emancipation, gradual 84-85
Emancipation Proclamation (1775) 48
Embargo (1807-1809) 65
Emerson, Ralph Waldo 73, 113
Environmentalism 260-267
Evangelical religion 87-88, 117-119, 162, 180

F
Fagen, David 178
Family violence 157-159
Federalist Party 63, 67
Finney, Charles 87-88

Fischer, David Hackett 25-26
Fitzhugh, George 140-141
Fogel, Robert W. 107-108
Forrest, Nathan Bedford 132
Fourteenth Amendment 130, 152
Franklin, Benjamin 21, 37, 39, 54
Freedmen's Bureau 129-130
Freud, Sigmund 10
Friedan, Betty 170
Fries, John 64
Fugitive Slave Law 94-97

G

Galloway, Joseph 40, 272
Garrrett, Thomas 99
Garrison, William Lloyd 80-81, 92,124
Gault, Eric 33
Gender constructions 156-173
Genocide 17-18
George III 37, 38, 41
Geronimo 15
Gideonites 128
Gilman, Charlotte Perkins 167
Gompers, Samuel 146
Good, Christian 116
Gorbachev, Mikhail 251-253
Grant, Ulysses S. 11, 71-72
Greeley, Horace 105-106, 112
Gun culture 59, 120

H

Hamer, Fannie Lou 219
Hamilton, Alexander 63
Hancock, John 35
Handsome Lake 27
Harding, Vincent 14, 215
Harrison, William Henry 26

Hart, Lawrence 33
Helper, Hinton Rowan 84
Henry, Patrick 40, 45
Henry, William "Jerry" 96-97
Hiawatha 19
Hicks, Edward 23
Holmes, Oliver Wendell 59, 120-121
Holocaust 199, 201, 207
Hopedale community 89
Howe, Julia Ward 117-118
Hutchinson, Thomas 39-40, 43

I

Imperialism 184
Industrial Workers of the World 146
Industrial Revolution 139-154
Inequality 142-144, 153-154

J

Jackson, Andrew 28, 69-71
Jacobs, Wilbur 28
James, William 182
Janney, Samuel 83
Japanese Americans 203-204
Jefferson, Thomas 35, 48, 49, 54, 57, 65-66, 77, 139-140
Jennings, Francis 29
Jigonhsasee 19
Johnson, Andrew 129-131
Jones, Mary Harris 146-147
Jones, John Paul 35
Jones, Samuel M. 149-150
Just war 41, 45, 205, 282, 306

K

Kelley, Abbey 92
Kelley, Florence 180
Kennan, George F. 196, 235

Kerner Commission 231-232

Killing in war, 46,113, 115-117

King, Martin Luther 12, 217, 222-227, 229-230, 273

King Philip's War 22-23

Knights of Labor 144-145

Komotalakia (Sanpoil Chief) 31

Ku Klux Klan 132-134

L

Land Reform 127, 129

League of Peace 18-23, 161

Lean Bear 30

Lease, Mary Elizabeth 148

Lee, Robert E. 11, 104, 113, 115

Liberty Party 81, 93-94

Lincoln, Abraham 51, 104, 109-113, 114, 118

Logan, George 63

Loguen, Jermain 83, 98

Louisiana Purchase 64

Lovejoy, Elijah 93

Lundy, Benjamin 82

M

Madison, James 56, 66-67, 139

Mahan, Alfred Thayer 185

Malcolm X 233

Mandela, Nelson 135

Manhood 24, 164-165, 170

Manifest Destiny 74

Marshall, John 68

Maseres, Francis 39

Massachusetts 44

Massasoit 22

Mayer, Milton 213

McCarthy, Colman 11

McCarthy, Joseph 242

McGuffey's Readers 61

McKinley, William 181

Melville, Herman 61

Mennonites 116, 191, 250

Merton, Thomas 10

Metacom 22-23

Militarism 185-186, 244-246

Military and the environment 264-266

Military industrial complex 76, 244-245

Millennialism 44, 117-118, 121

Mississippi Freedom Democratic Party 221

Mixon, Eliza 126

Mob violence 43-44, 70, 119

Montgomery, Benjamin 127

Moses, Robert 219-220

Mott, Lucretia 80, 163

Muir, John 258-259

Muste, Abraham J. 11, 212-213

Mutiny (1781) 46

Myth of redemptive violence 11

N

National Association for the Advancement of Colored People 222

Native American tribes

Cherokee 27-28

Cheyenne 29-30, 32, 33-34

Iroquois 18-23, 27,161

Lenni Lenape 23-26, 48

Narragansett 22

Pequot 22

Pomo tribes 32-33

Powhatan tribe 26

Sanpoil 31

Native Americans
Diseases 16
Massacres
  Gnadenhutten (1782) 48
  Sand Creek (1866) 30
  Washita (1868) 30
Prophets 26-27
Revitalization 26-27
in War for Independence 47-48

N
Nixon, Richard 261
Noll, Mark 50
Nonresistance Society 80-81
Nonviolent Resistance 42-44
North, Lord Frederick 41
Northhampton Association 89
Nuclear weapons 9, 255
Nuclear Freeze campaign 250-251

P
Paine, Thomas 38
Parks, Rosa 217
Patriarchy 159-160
Pauling, Linus 248
Peace Chiefs 29
Peace movement 53, 68-69, 80-81,
  181-184, 212-214, 247-251, 265
Pearl Harbor 198
Penn, William 23, 25,54
Pennington, J. W. 99
Pequot War 22
Perry, Oliver Hazard 65
Philadelphia Tea Party 43
Pinchot, Gifford 258-259
Plains Indians 28-30
Polk, James K. 71, 93-94
Pontiac 15

Populist movement 147-149
Posner, Blanche
Potlatch ceremony 31
Powell, William 95
Powderly, Terrence 145
Praying Indians 22-23
Proclamation of 1763 47
Prosser, Martin and Gabriel 78
Providential interpretation 117-119
Puritans, Puritanism 17, 22, 23, 44,
  117, 257

Q
Quakers 25, 43, 54-56, 79-80, 160-162

R
Radical Abolitionist Party 94
Reagan, Ronald 251-253, 261
Reason, Charles 101
Red Record (Wallam Olum) 24
Republican Party 134
Revere, Paul 35
Revitalization movements 26-27,
  124-127
Revivalism 87-88
Rhett, Robert Barnwell 110, 128
Riley, Thomas 72-73
Rinowehan 23-24
Roosevelt, Franklin Delano 202, 204,
  212, 239-240
Roosevelt, Theodore 147, 153, 175,
  181, 185-186, 255, 259-260
Rush, Benjamin 60
Rush-Bagot agreement 74
Russia 107

S
Sand Creek Massacre 30
Sarris, Greg 32

Scientists 247-249, 253

Scotch-Irish 69, 286

Scott, Winfield 72

Segregationists 230-232

Seneca Falls Convention (1848) 163

Sequoyah 28

Serfdom 107

Seward, William H. 111

Sharp, Gene 42

Sherman, William Tecumseh 114, 129

Shuttlesworth, Fred 223-224, 226-227

Simons, Peter Paul 90-91

Sitting Bull 15

Skolaskin (Sanpoil) 31

Slavery 48, 77-78

Sledge, E. B. 204-205

Smith, Jacob W. 178

Smith, Justin H. 73

Socialist movement 151

South Africa 36, 135-137

Southern Christian Leadership Conference 222-226

Stafford, William 75

Stalin, Joseph 236-237

Stamp Act 42

Standing armies 44, 56-57, 64

Stanton, Elizabeth Cady 163

Stephens, Alexander 108, 110

Stephens, Uriah 144

Stills, William 98

Stowe, Harriet Beecher 162-163

Strategic bombing 205-209

Student Nonviolent Coordinating Committee 218-220, 225-226

Sunday, Billy 191

Sweet Medicine 29

Szilard, Leo 247-248

T

Tappan, Arthur and Lewis 81

Taylor, Zachary 72

Tecumseh 15, 26-27

Tenskatawa 26-27

Thoreau, Henry David 72, 257-258

Tolstoy, Leo 13, 89

Torrey, Charles T. 99

Tragic interpretation 103-104, 121-122

Trail of Tears 28

Truman, Harry 209, 237-241

Truth, Sojourner 11, 90

Truth and Reconciliation 135-137

Tubman, Harriet 99

Turner, Nat 85

Twain, Mark 181

U

Underground Railroad 79, 97-100

Unruh, John D, Jr. 28

V

Violence 9

W

Wald, Lillian 150

Walker, Alice 171

Wallace, George 230-231

Wallace, Henry 240-241, 247

Wallam Olum (Red Record) 24

Waller, Littleton 177-178

Wampanoag tribe 22-23

Warren, Mercy Otis 56-57

Wars

    Pequot war (1637) 22

King Philip's War (1675-76) 22-23

French and Indian War (1754-63) 37

War for Independence (1775-83) 35-51

Quasi-War with France (1797-1800) 62-64

Barbary War (1801) 54

War of 1812 26, 66-68

Mexican War (1846-1848) 71-74, 90

Civil War (1861-1865) 103-122, 258

Spanish-American (1898)176-177

Philippines (1899-1902) 177-178

World War I (1917-1918) 187-194

World War II (1941-1945) 197-214

Korean War (1950-1953) 238-239, 253

Vietnam (1950-1973) 242-243, 253-254, 261

Persian Gulf (1990-1991) 103

Washington, George 35, 46, 47, 59-60, 63

Washita Massacre 30, 33

Welfare 143-144

West, Benjamin (front cover), 23

Whipper, William 86, 87

White Antelope 30

Willard, Frances 166

Wilson, Woodrow 153, 187-188, 194-196

Wink, Walter 12

Woolman, John 11

Women Strike for Peace 249-250

Women's Christian Temperance Union 166

Women's International League for Peace and Freedom 249

Workingman's Party 144

X

XYZ Affair 62-63

Y

York, Alvin C. 192-193

Z

Zinn, Howard 10, 269-270